MEMORY WARS

MEMORY WARS

SETTLERS
AND NATIVES
REMEMBER
WASHINGTON'S
SULLIVAN
EXPEDITION
OF 1779

A. LYNN SMITH

University of Nebraska Press
LINCOLN

The University of Nebraska Press is part of a land-grant institution with campuses and programs on the past, present, and future homelands of the Pawnee, Ponca, Otoe-Missouria, Omaha, Dakota, Lakota, Kaw, Cheyenne, and Arapaho Peoples, as well as those of the relocated Ho-Chunk, Sac and Fox, and Iowa Peoples.

Publication of this volume was assisted by a grant from the Academic Research Committee at Lafayette College.

All royalties for this book donated to the American Indian Law Alliance.

Library of Congress Cataloging-in-Publication Data
Names: Smith, Andrea L., author.
Title: Memory war: settlers and natives remember Washington's Sullivan Expedition of 1779 / A. Lynn Smith.
Other titles: Settlers and natives remember Washington's Sullivan Expedition of 1779
Description: Lincoln: University of Nebraska Press, 2023 | Includes bibliographical references and index.
Identifiers: LCCN 2022049629
ISBN 9781496206961 (hardcover)
ISBN 9781496235305 (epub)
ISBN 9781496235312 (pdf)
Subjects: LCSH: Sullivan's Indian Campaign, 1779. | Sullivan, John, 1740–1795—Monuments. | Memorials—Social aspects—New York (State) | Memorials—Social aspects—Pennsylvania. | Memory—Social aspects—New York (State) | Memory—Social aspects—Pennsylvania. | Iroquois Indians—Wars—New York (State) | New York (State)—History—Revolution, 1775–1783. | Pennsylvania—History—Revolution, 1775–1783. | BISAC: HISTORY / United States / Revolutionary Period (1775–1800) | SOCIAL SCIENCE / Ethnic Studies / American / Native American Studies
Classification: LCC E235 .S64 2023 |
DDC 973.3/35—dc23/eng/20230127
LC record available at https://lccn.loc.gov/2022049629

Set in Scala OT.

To Richard and Nathaniel

CONTENTS

ILLUSTRATIONS

Maps

ACKNOWLEDGMENTS

This book had its start over a decade ago with a puzzling monument close to my college campus, what I came to see as one element of a sprawling commemorative complex. Like all books, this was a collaborative effort throughout that was made possible by the goodwill and generosity of so many people along the way.

Several people welcomed me in the earliest stages by inviting me to their homes, writing clubs, and hikes, by introducing me to their family members and friends, by taking my family on special museum tours, and by including me in heritage celebrations and overnight canoe sojourns. They include Dick Cowles, Jack Andrus, David Buck, Amy and Bill Abruzzi, Joseph Fischer, Ken Layou, and Joan O'Dell. Penelope Kelsey, Larry Hauptman, Alyssa Mt. Pleasant, Terry Abrams, Randy John, Doug George-Kanentiio, Jack Rossen, Kurt Jordan, Deb Twigg, and Nina Versaggi all directed me to important resources and people. The beautiful maps were drawn by Erin Grebs.

It was when I began visiting local Haudenosaunee cultural centers that I developed a full sense of this project. I cannot thank center representatives enough for taking the time to meet with me. In particular, Kandice Watson at Shako:wi Cultural Center, Oneida Indian Nation; Jake Edwards, Phil Arnold, and Sandy Bigtree at Skä•noñh–Great Law of Peace Center; G. Peter Jemison and Michael Galban at Ganondagan Seneca Art and Culture Center; and Jaré Cardinal, Randy John, David George-Shongo, and Joe Stahlman at Onöhsagwë:dé Cultural Center, Seneca Nation of Indians—all have offered their precious time and insights. This project would have taken a very different shape without your honesty, your kindness, and your generosity. Thank you, thank you, many times over.

Members of the Neighbors of the Onondaga Nation have taken time out to meet with me on several occasions, and I especially thank Sue Eizholer, Gail Bundy, and Andy Mager. Andrew Zellers-Frederick and other members of the Lehigh Valley Revolutionary War RoundTable offered their support, as did women of several chapters of the Daughters of the American Revolution, who provided time and documents, always impressing me with their attention to detail; I'd like to single out Meg Venn and Amy Ellsworth in particular.

I want to thank all the people whom I interviewed. As well as the people mentioned above, there were many more, including Mike Gipson, Kae and Arthur Smith, Bob Veleker, Anne Armezzani, Mollie Elliott, Dan Rhodes, Annette Schultz, Lucille Sturmer, Ed McMullan, Pam DeWitt, Richard Sala, Bob Ensinger, Jean Dendler, Dave Sechrist, Steve Chisarik, Earl Robinson, Deb Twiggs, Keith Brown, Fred Robets, Bertha and Eleanor Sturman, and several people who asked to remain anonymous.

Throughout this project, I have been amazed at the wide range of archives this project required. Archivists working in all manner of facilities assisted me, including the professional staff at Pennsylvania State Archives, Cornell University's Kroch rare books library, and the special collections at the University of Rochester and Syracuse University. I never would have found my way to the extensive sesquicentennial materials at the New York State Archives had it not been for the assistance of Jim Folts and Larry Hauptman. I gained a real appreciation for the local archivists working with shoestring budgets in repurposed buildings—I consulted collections housed in former jails, schools, train stations, museums, and department stores, buildings that sometimes closed in the winter months due to a lack of heat, and the summer due to its superabundance. For their exacting help, I especially want to recognize Paula Radwanski and Ken Layaou of the Wyoming County Historical Society; Matt Carl and Denise Golden of Bradford County Historical Society; Amanda Fontenova, Luzerne County

Historical Society; Rachel Dworkin, Chemung County Historical Society; Eileen McHugh, Cayuga Museum of History and Art; Rebecca McClain, Oneida County History Center; Sarah Kozma, Pamela Priest, and Maria Lore, Onondaga Historical Association; and Brad Davis, Northampton County Historical and Genealogical Society. They provided many of the images in this book. Joy O'Donnell, archivist, the National Society for the Daughters of the American Revolution, offered vital early support. My colleagues at Skillman Library provided the very foundation on which this project was built; I thank especially Ester Barias-Wolf, Karen Haduck, and John Clark. Joan O'Dell, Leonard Ziegler, Randy John, and Dick Cowles all brought my attention to materials from their personal archives, and I am grateful for their generosity.

This project was carried out in collaborative conversation with so many people across the years that it is difficult to fully capture. The problem-based interdisciplinary research of mentors Tad Park and Jane Hill continue to provide inspirational models. At various moments, its scope seemed preposterous, and I was propelled forward by my energizing conversations with Tony and Simon Connor, Kristín Loftsdóttir, Susan Carol Rogers, Allison Alexy, Aomar Boum, and Hsain Ilahiane. I presented early versions of this material at academic venues and public meetings. These included the meetings of the American Anthropological Association; the Society for Applied Anthropology; the Canadian Anthropological Society Annual Conference; the Conference on Iroquois Studies; the symposium "Revisiting George Washington's assault on the Haudenosaunee 240 Years Later," organized by Syracuse University and Skä•noñh–Great Law of Peace Center in Syracuse, New York; and the New York History Conference in 2018. I also presented material at talks sponsored by the Seneca-Iroquois National Museum, Salamanca, New York; the Horseheads Historical Society, Horseheads, New York; and the Dietrich Theater of Tunkhannock, Pennsylvania. An early version of chapter 1 appeared as "Savagism, Silencing, and American Settlerism: Commemorating the Wyoming Battle of the American Revolutionary War" in *Settler Colonial Studies*; a version of chapter 6, coauthored with Nëhdöwes (Randy A. John), appeared in

New York History as "Monuments, Legitimization Ceremonies, and Haudenosaunee Rejection of Sullivan-Clinton Markers"; and chapter 7 had its start as "Settler Colonialism and the Revolutionary War: New York's 1929 'Pageant of Decision,'" *The Public Historian*. Editors and anonymous reviewers of these journals deserve special recognition for helping me improve and further reflect.

Funding for ethnographic research was provided by the Wenner-Gren Foundation for Anthropological Research, a Richard King Mellon Research Fellowship, and a grant from the Academic Research Committee, Lafayette College. I am grateful for the research leave that allowed me to complete the manuscript. Some of the writing was carried out at a Highlights Foundation Writing Retreat led by Kate Brandes and funded by the Lehigh Valley Engaged Humanities Consortium; I thank Kate Pitts and Charlotte Nunes for their enthusiastic support. This project has continued through rotations of provosts, presidents, deans of research, and department heads at Lafayette College; I'd like to single out Dave Shulman, Jamila Bookwala, John Meier, Bill Bissell, Alison Byerly, and Caroline Lee. Conversations with my colleagues in the Department of Anthropology and Sociology across the years have energized and engaged me, and I also thank Monica Salas Landa, Neha Vora, Howard Schneiderman, Rebecca Kissane, Carlos Tavares, and Michaela Kelly for their wit and verve. Conversations with Wendy Wilson-Fall, Mary Armstrong, Paul Barclay, and Angelika Von Wahl are always enriching. I thank students in my courses who have listened with patience to various renditions of some of this material, offering their own reflections and critiques, as have students in Angelika Von Wahl's courses. I am grateful to work in such a supportive environment.

Many colleagues have provided comments on early drafts. I especially thank Laurence Hauptman, Edward Countryman, Jessica Dolan, Randy John, Marian Leech, Becca Scott, Ilana Abramovitch, and two anonymous readers for the University of Nebraska Press for their care and thoughtful suggestions. Randy John has provided innumerable resources, including several images found within, and we cowrote a portion of what became chapter 5. I was blessed to have connected with senior editor Matt Bokovoy, who understood the gist of the project well before anyone else. I appreciate his guidance and patience throughout. Of course, I take responsibility for any errors found within.

With no small irony, this project was interrupted by a house fire that displaced me and my family for well over a year, a period that stretched into the pandemic. I thank Judy Faber for providing emergency housing and Penny, Speed, Tears, Nancy, and Wesley for their good humor and levity throughout this time. This project would have ended then and there had not the good women at a local firm been able to salvage my soot-covered notes, documents, and books.

Finally, my family and friends have helped me in more ways than I can capture here. At different times Beth Epstein, Alex Shapiro, Heather Baker, Mary Freeman, Julianna Acheson, Ilana Abramovitch, Alice Apley, Kate Brandes, Pat Janssen, Reeve Kelly, Brandi Janssen, and Lilly Nolan have been sources of moral support and intellectual inspiration. My sisters and stepmother, Joan, have patiently waited for this work to be done, always pushing me forward with love. My uncle, Civil War historian Richard W. Smith, has offered his unwavering and hearty enthusiasm from the start, while my son, Nathaniel, who has lived with this project most of his life, has offered irresistible distraction, and this combination has made this journey possible. I dedicate this book to them.

NOTE ON TERMINOLOGY

Writing for multiple audiences poses many challenges, not the least of which is terminology. This book covers vast historical ground across which the names people used for themselves and the names others used for them shifted. I use "Haudenosaunee," "Iroquois," "Five Nations," and "Six Nations" interchangeably, depending on time period. "Haudenosaunee" has various spellings in English; here I use the spelling I have found most often in English-language texts. Although the French-origin "Iroquois" was the standard ethnonym in English-language texts in previous centuries and Haudenosaunee has entered common parlance more recently, I may employ Haudenosaunee anachronistically at times, knowing that some historians will wince. In the text, I use English-language names for Haudenosaunee nations but want to identify their names in their own languages here. The original five nations are Kanyen'kehaka (Mohawk), Onyota'a:ka (Oneida), Onöñda'gega' (Onondaga), Gayogohono (Cayuga), and Onöndowa'ga:' (Seneca).[1] Deciding on any one spelling is also a great simplification; Randy John identifies 250 different recorded names for the Onöndowa'ga:' (Senecas).[2]

I use Lenape and Delaware interchangeably. Labels like Delaware, Munsee, and Lenape emerged over time, and the use of an encompassing term is not intended to imply homogeneity or political unity across such an extensive region in early contact times. The ethnonym Lenape was not used in early published sources but is often preferred in the present day; both appellations are used by contemporary descendants.[3]

I use "Native American," "Indigenous," and "Native" inter-changeably, recognizing that all these global categories are prob-lematic as they lump together so many distinct populations and are very much a creation of the settler-colonial situation that I am critiquing.

If the settler-colonial studies literature has a problem, it starts with the word "settler."[4] Far too often scholars employ this term without modifier, which only furthers the fiction that only Euro-peans were able to establish settlements and settle.[5] While clunky, whenever possible I refer to non-Natives as "settler-colonists," "white settlers," "Euro-Americans," or "non-Natives." I recognize that lumping together so many different people into these aca-demic categories simplifies, and renders the migration histories and cultural, national, religious, and status distinctions subordinate to the position they occupy in the settler-colonial power structure.

Place-names are another issue altogether and part of what I am critiquing. "North America" to Haudenosaunee and Lenape is "Turtle Island" in English. Almost all place-names used in this book are new terms or garbled renditions of Indigenous ones.[6] "Sullivan Trail" is a case in point; as I am often calling into ques-tion the appropriateness of this label, it sometimes appears in quotation marks. Non-Native renditions of Native place-names are further distorted by cultural biases, such as the common use of "Castle" for important Haudenosaunee settlements. When there are multiple names for towns, I include the different ren-ditions in the footnotes.

The Susquehanna River and the Susquehannah Company are two spellings of the same word. Similarly, readers will encounter Allegany Territory of the Seneca Nation of Indians, which is along the Allegheny River. These are not misspellings. I should note that in the Seneca language, the Allegheny River is the Ohi:yo' (beautiful river).[7]

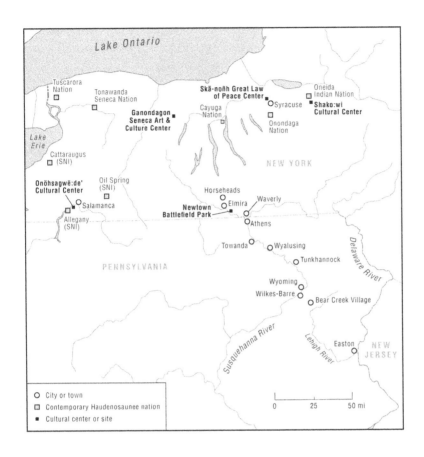

MAP 1. Field sites. Erin Greb Cartography.

Introduction

The Stories We Tell

I n an essay on settler constructions of the past, anthropologist Deborah Bird Rose asks how it is that settler-colonial peoples come to imagine a sense of belonging to their beloved homelands. "We cannot help but know that we are here through dispossession and death," she writes, asking, "What are some of the stories we tell to help us inscribe a moral presence in places we have come to through violence?"[1] This book can be viewed as an extended meditation on this question. It explores the "stories we tell" in one part of the United States and considers how these stories both reflect and shape the nation's settler-colonial character. Part history, part ethnography, this book explores stories from the start of the nation and considers their continued reverberations. I start this journey with a commemorative marker outside my office window.

> This stone marks the road over which General John Sullivan marched June 18, 1779, to quell the Indian insurrection and avenge the Wyoming massacre.
>
> Erected by the George Taylor Chapter, Daughters of the American Revolution June 18, 1900

Right over There

A boulder behind a sorority parking lot, along a back road to my college campus in Easton, Pennsylvania, recognizes an expedition of the Revolutionary War. Established in 1900 by the Daughters of the American Revolution (DAR), it highlights the Sullivan Expedition, which left Easton in June 1779 for what is now central New

FIG. 1. George Taylor Chapter DAR Sullivan Marker, 1900, Sullivan Road, Easton PA. Photo courtesy of the author.

York. British and Indian attacks on frontier towns were having dramatic success, as at the Battle of Wyoming (July 3, 1778), referenced in the marker as the "Wyoming Massacre." (The U.S. state of Wyoming memorializes the same Pennsylvania battle.) Sullivan "quelled" the "Indian insurrection" by destroying Indian villages, crops, and stored foods; it took his men nearly four months to carry out their assignment. Even if the Easton marker is easily missed today, it is one of several dozen commemorative stones, monuments, and street names spanning a vast territory, indicating the route Sullivan's troops took and identifying the names of the Indian villages they destroyed. They comprise what I refer to as the "Sullivan commemorative complex."

The placement of this marker and the words of Suzan Shown Harjo (Cheyenne and Muscogee), an activist and poet, were early inspirations for this project. In a discussion of Native American history and sacred sites in Jed Riffe's film *Who Owns the Past?*, Harjo states, "We *know* who we are, and we *know* where we came from. Most of our sacred places are called 'Here,' 'Right over there.' 'Two hours away.' 'The place where we originated.' 'The place where we were born.'" As I learned more about this series of plaques to a military campaign that crosses the landscape, Harjo's words spoke to me. I was researching settler-colonial historical consciousness—how dominant people in a settler-colonial society understand their past—working with French settlers from Algeria and Mormon settlers of Arizona.[2] I too should look "here." Since Native American sacred sites are "here," "right over there," so too are sites of dispossession and violence. We need not go far to find evidence of settler-colonial exploits and the "stories we tell," because these locations, too, are "right over there" or at most "two hours away."

Commemorative markers, place-names, statues, and monuments tell Americans which pasts to remember and why. They are so pervasive that they can serve as an unseen backdrop for daily life. Once noticed, however, they can become focal points for activism. These instruments of public memory contain a political potency—a potency especially evident in the contemporary era, which has been punctuated by conflicts over how difficult pasts such as slavery and the Civil War have been narrated in public spaces. This book raises similar questions about the public memory of the Revolutionary War.

The events of the American Revolutionary War are rarely considered points of contention. Instead, they are called on to bring about national unity. Since the start of the nation, this foundational conflict and its protagonists have been celebrated by national leaders and the public alike. Historian Michael Kammen has described the war as "the single most important source for our national sense of tradition."[3] Over time, some of its actors have been elevated in popular culture to serve as sources of inspiration and insight.[4] These "Founding Fathers," our Revolutionary "demigods," are heroes of the national origin story, central figures in a conflict that serves as the starting point and source of the nation's values and moral codes.[5] Americans regularly draw on episodes from the Revolutionary War to rebuild consensus during times of national strife, as they did in the aftermath of the Civil War.[6] The Revolutionary War was also a time of horror, betrayal, trickery, and despair, however, leading some scholars to refer to it as the "first American civil war."[7] While perspectives of enslaved Africans, pacifists, and Loyalists now receive increased attention in scholarly works, often neglected is the war's complex meanings for Native Americans.[8] In many regions, the war removed Native peoples from the land or set the stage for land grabs of unimaginable scale with unforgettable consequences.[9]

The Sullivan Expedition of 1779 is a notable example of such wartime horror. Gen. George Washington commanded Sullivan to cause the "total destruction and devastation" of Iroquois settlements and to destroy both crops in the ground and stored foods.[10] From the perspective of Sullivan and his men, the operation was a remarkable success. Because Native leaders evacuated villages in advance of the massive army to preserve civilian life, Sullivan's troops engaged in only one major battle and suffered few casualties; their time was spent attacking dwellings, crops, and orchards. From the vantage point of the Native inhabitants of the obliterated settlements, it was a disaster. Much of their known world was destroyed, and hundreds of displaced Indigenous people perished from disease, starvation, and exposure while seeking shelter at Fort Niagara and points farther north that winter.[11]

Despite the devastating effects of this scorched-earth campaign, Euro-Americans in Pennsylvania and New York have honored it with monument dedications, reenactments, place-names, and historical markers (see figure 2). These individual elements of the Sullivan commemorative complex were never coordinated by an overarching authority but instead emerged independently over the years. The first markers were temporary ones designating the burial places of fallen soldiers. Private benefactors and mem-

FIG. 2. Dedication of New York Sullivan-Clinton Campaign memorial in Elmira NY, September 1929. Photographs of Observances of the 150th Anniversary of the American Revolution, Series B0567–85, Folder 26, Elmira Scenes, New York State Archives.

bers of patriotic societies developed additional stone memorials in the nineteenth century. The states of New York and Pennsylvania became involved at the centennial and sesquicentennial anniversaries in 1879 and 1929, placing dozens of stone monoliths with bronze plaques along roadsides, followed by countless metal signs. Although state involvement slowed by the mid–twentieth century, individuals and social clubs took the initiative to develop new markers and restore damaged ones. The most recent of these new markers was dedicated in 2017 in Bear Creek Township, Pennsylvania (see figure 3), and more are planned as I write.[12]

This book asks how we should interpret the enshrining of this expedition in place-names and monuments. What does this practice tell us about how Euro-Americans have understood their role in the Revolution and the Revolution's role in their lives? Who were the Sullivan advocates and why did they decide to fix his story to the land in the way that they did? For many people, honoring

FIG. 3. Admiring a new Sullivan Memorial, June 2017, Bear Creek PA.
Photo courtesy of the author.

this military operation appears tasteless at best, especially since descendants of Sullivan's foes were living nearby when the markers went up. These commemorative projects could be interpreted as examples of victors living to tell the tale, post-conflict gloating, pointed reminders of colonial domination, or worse.[13] Considering how and when this story was recognized and by whom tells us much about how the violent start of the nation has been explained, or explained away.

The Sullivan commemorative complex represents more than a recognition of the American Revolution. It can also be seen as an unapologetic celebration of settler-style colonialism, for Sullivan's immediate goal was to remove Native people from their homelands. At Sullivan commemorative events, the story of the Revolutionary War and the story of the conquest and colonization of North America intersect in discomforting ways, often resulting in a contradictory and ambivalent message. Even while speakers at marker dedications express their gratitude to Revolutionary War veterans or their reverence for mission "mastermind" George

Washington, when they recount what soldiers actually did, as members of Sullivan's forces in 1779, they also expose the "annihilating drive" scholars find characteristic of settler-colonialism and the early American experience.[14]

In some respects, the individual elements of the Sullivan complex are ordinary features of the American landscape. As a Seneca consultant I met in Salamanca, New York, explained to me, "Military commemorations are nothing new in this country; you have them all over." In his view, war is about winning, and it is normal to try to mark where the victories happened. He added, "You always celebrate when you win, and the dominant culture will continue to show that it's the dominant culture. The thing they sometimes forget is that the people you are occupying never forget, never. Even if it comes down to only three people left, they will never forget."[15] I discuss his views further in this book, but for now I want to emphasize this consultant's precise use of pronouns. "The people *you* are occupying" is how he put it, parsimoniously underscoring the power relations between us and situating me as a member of an occupying force. My positionality as a white Euro-American matters, as we will see. And he is right to note that markers, statues, and other reminders of wartime achievements can be found across the United States. Many of these memorials celebrate victories in Indian wars and, in doing so, construct an exclusive "we," an imagined national community formed in opposition to a Native other.

Public celebrations of colonial conquest are not limited to the United States, of course. At the height of European imperialism, invading forces marked colonial landscapes with memorials to European heroes of their colonial wars. In French colonial Algeria, the French "made Algeria French" with extensive renaming programs and by installing heroic monuments.[16] In his revolutionary treatise *The Wretched of the Earth*, Frantz Fanon describes the colonial world as "a world of statues," reminders of the colonizers' might. As he put it, "Every statue, all these conquistadors perched on colonial soil, do not cease from proclaiming one and the same thing: 'We are here by the force of bayonets.'"[17] Algerian revolutionaries understood this message and made the obliteration of these symbols of French rule one of their first acts at independence in 1962.[18] In the United States, in contrast, statues and place-names glorifying victors of Indian wars persist on the landscape, where they continue to assert a dominant story. What does their persistence reveal about the tenacity of colonial mentalities here? Who notices these memorials as celebrations of colonial conquest and for whom do they remain invisible or unremarkable? Part of a wider movement underway to revisit American history through a settler-colonial lens, this book underscores both the symbolic value of the past and the dilemmas posed to contemporary Americans by the inertia generated by the very materiality of the national commemorative landscape.[19] Residents of the United States live among remnants of battlefields, destroyed villages, sacred places, land grabs, and massacres, even as the evidence of this dispossession and violence may be screened from view, or reframed and revered. To emphasize the ubiquity of monuments that glorify U.S. colonialism, this book starts "right over here" with memorials to General Sullivan's expedition in the town where I now work, with the goal of prompting readers into similar discoveries wherever they may be based.

Revolution and Native Lands

The land now dotted with Sullivan memorials is the ancestral territory of several Indigenous communities, most notably Haudenosaunee nations, principal targets of Sullivan's maelstrom, and Lenapes, also known as the Delaware Indians. By the time the Revolutionary War began, Native people along the eastern portion of what is now known as North America had navigated almost two centuries of conflict and social upheaval as a succession of European powers competed for command of the continent and its rich resources. As historian Colin Calloway has written, scholars who have tried to view the Revolution from an Indian standpoint have found it difficult to divorce the years 1775–83 from the changes affecting Indian America throughout the eighteenth century, a century that led to so much death, migration, disruption, and "cultural cacophony."[20]

Algonquian-speaking peoples lived in a vast region of the mid-

Atlantic, with Unami or Lenape speakers along the Lenapewihit-tuck (Delaware River) watershed—in what is now portions of New Jersey, eastern Pennsylvania, Maryland, and Delaware. By the mid–eighteenth century, European colonists referred to them as Delaware Indians.[21] When Charles II granted Quaker William Penn a vast charter in 1681 and Quaker immigration to Penn's "holy experiment" increased dramatically, Lenape communities were pressured into selling prime agricultural lands along the Delaware River, moving ever north and west.[22] The Walking Purchase of 1737 dispossessed Delawares of their remaining agricultural and hunting land in the Delaware Valley, and many of its residents moved to the Susquehanna and Ohio Valleys, establishing such villages as Wyoming, mentioned in the plaque at the start of this chapter, and Chemung, which was destroyed by Sullivan's troops.[23] Some fifteen years later, an area within this tract was plotted out and became the town of Easton, which later served as the staging ground for Sullivan's 1779 campaign.

The Iroquois, or Haudenosaunees ("people building a long-house"), had a different early experience with European colonists and remained a formidable force, rooted in their vast ancestral homeland, at the time of the Revolution (see map 2).[24] People's relationship to a land where they have lived for millennia will be profound, and land and territory are central features of Haudenosaunee identity.[25] Mohawk historian Susan M. Hill observes that when asking in the Mohawk language what clan one is in, the question literally means, "What clay are you made of?"[26] The co-constructed nature of people and place is perhaps best illustrated by the names Haudenosaunee nations call themselves in their own languages which, as Hill observes, all relate characteristics of their original national territories. The five nations are: Kanyen'kehaka (Mohawk), People of the flint; Onyota'a:ka (Oneida), People of the standing stone; Onöñda'gega' (Onondaga), People of the hills; Gayogohono (Cayuga), People of the marshy area; and Onöndowa'ga:' (Seneca), People of the great hills.[27] Well before European contact, these five nations were brought together by Peacemaker and joined in a confederacy (or the League of the Iroquois), which became the Six Nations with the incorporation

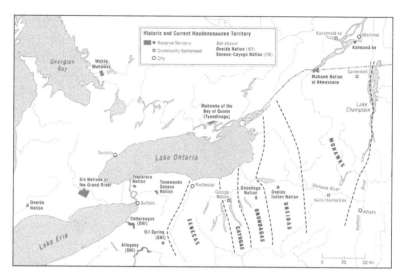

MAP 2. Historic and current Haudenosaunee territory. Erin Greb Cartography.

of the Tuscaroras in the early eighteenth century.[28] Matrilineal kin groups lived in distinctive bark-covered longhouses, sixty to a hundred feet long or more, which were found in all early Haudenosaunee settlements, and their diverse diet centered on the cultivation of the three sisters: corn, beans, and squash.[29] Their land was imagined as a symbolic longhouse.[30]

At the time of European contact, Haudenosaunee nations lived along strategic north–south and east–west communication and trading routes, and their survival depended on their leaders' skill in alliance-building and diplomacy. They so expertly navigated Dutch, English, and French rivalries that the early eighteenth century ushered in a "golden era of Iroquois diplomacy" that lasted over fifty years.[31] A seventeenth-century alliance made with the English, known metaphorically as the Covenant Chain, was regularly renewed and played a role in determining Haudenosaunee responses to the Revolutionary conflict.[32]

It is difficult to overstate the turmoil and disruption that the brewing conflict now known as the Revolutionary War created for Native peoples. Even as some Indians tried to stay out of this civil war, knowing which way to turn was challenging, and maintaining inter–Indian nation alliances was even harder. As Calloway elucidates, the three-part division of colonial society into rebel, loyalist, and neutral was "replicated with numerous variations in countless Indian communities in North America." The rebel/British conflict "revealed existing fissures as well as creating new ones," and neutrality was often impossible to maintain, especially for people relying on either or both sides for their livelihood.[33] The Confederacy tried to remain neutral as tensions grew between its British allies and the rebellious "patriots." After the Royal Proclamation of 1763 failed to stem the tide of colonists encroaching on Haudenosaunee lands, the Confederacy agreed to the Treaty of Fort Stanwix of 1768, yet whites continued to flood onto its lands.[34] Growing violence and threats to their way of life made it increasingly difficult for Confederacy members to stay out of the conflict, with geography influencing destinies.[35] After influential British Indian commissioner Sir William Johnson died in mid-1774, links to the British became more tenuous.[36] Making matters worse, a horrible epidemic struck the Onondaga in 1777.[37] When Seneca, Mohawk, and Cayuga warriors agreed to aid the British side in the Battle of Oriskany (near present-day Utica) in 1777, they found themselves fighting against fellow Confederacy members, from the Tuscarora and Oneida nations, who were assisting the American side. This was one of the bloodiest battles of the Revolution, and its horror and the sundering of the Confederacy took lasting tolls.[38] After the bloodshed at Oriskany, British commanders and Indian allies alike realized that a shift in strategy was in order, and they turned to guerrilla attacks on frontier towns. As Graymont writes, if the Tories and Indians couldn't conquer and hold the Mohawk Valley, "at least they could make the valley a no man's land."[39] As this new strategy was achieving some remarkable successes, Congress ordered General Washington to address this threat, and he responded with his "Indian Expedition."

Washington's "Indian Expedition"

Washington's Indian Expedition has been described as "one of the most carefully planned campaigns of the entire war."[40] This multimovement operation involved at least 4,500 men, over a quarter of the Continental Army, and because Maj. Gen. John

Sullivan was head of its primary operation, it became commonly known as the Sullivan Expedition.[41] It was composed of four forays into Indian territories, with the largest component led by Sullivan (see map 3).

Washington's orders to Sullivan on May 31, 1779, were blunt: "The expedition you are appointed to command is to be directed against the hostile tribes of the six nations of Indians, with their associates and adherents. The immediate objects are the total destruction and devastation of their settlements and the capture of as many prisoners of every age and sex as possible. It will be essential to ruin their crops now in the ground and prevent their planting more." After outlining troop composition and recommended tactical movements, Washington instructed him on how the Iroquois should be treated, writing, "the country may not be merely *overrun* but *destroyed*" (emphasis in the original). He added, "You will not by [any] means, listen to any overture of peace before the total ruin of their settlements is effected . . . Our future security will be in their inability to injure us . . . and in the terror with which the severity of the chastisement they receive will inspire [them]."[42] Although Sullivan did not succeed in capturing many prisoners, he followed the rest of these instructions to the letter.

An initial assault, launched in April 1779 by Colonel Van Schaick, devastated the Onondaga Nation. Troops burned two villages and the longhouse that held the League's symbolic council fire.[43] That summer, three coordinated troop movements took place: Sullivan, with three brigades, traveled from Easton and Wyoming north along the Susquehanna River; Gen. James Clinton of New York traveled south from the Mohawk Valley to meet Sullivan's forces at Tioga (now Athens, Pennsylvania); and Daniel Brodhead marched north from Fort Pitt to attack Indian settlements along the Allegheny River (see map 3). The original plan was for these three branches to join forces to seize the major British installation of Fort Niagara; this Niagara component was abandoned in the end, and the destruction of Indian settlements became the troops' main occupation. Most of this destruction was carried out by Sullivan's three brigades in the summer of 1779 and directed to the heart of the Haudenosaunee homelands. According to Sullivan's

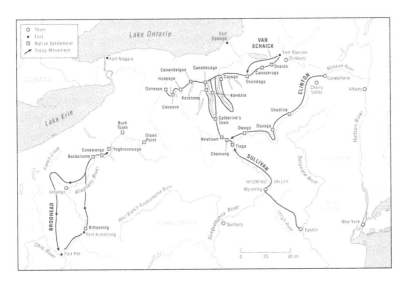

MAP 3. Washington's Indian Expedition troop movements.
Erin Greb Cartography.

accounting, they burned forty settlements and hundreds of acres of crops, orchards, and stored foodstuffs, including an estimated 160,000 bushels of corn.[44] Gen. James Clinton brought similar destruction along the Mohawk River. Gen. Daniel Brodhead destroyed 165 houses in eleven Delaware and Seneca settlements and over five hundred acres of crops along the Allegheny River.[45]

The Sullivan Campaign did not end the war. The brigades that served under Sullivan left for other staging grounds, and the war raged on until British capitulation at the Battle of Yorktown (Virginia) in October 1781. Although a chorus of non-Native writers and speakers at historic and contemporary events commemorating Sullivan have claimed that the operation shifted the wartime balance of power, contemporary historians are mixed in their assessment of its strategic effects.[46] Joseph Fischer called it a "well-executed failure," as Sullivan never made it to the British base at Fort Niagara and never obtained the prisoners Washington had hoped could be used in future bargaining.[47] Upon returning to Fort Pitt, Gen. Daniel Brodhead continued to face threats from Shawnee, Wyandot, and Haudenosaunee forces, indicating that his raids "had not completely accomplished their purpose of permanently silencing these Indians."[48] Barbara Graymont points out that the expedition was designed to break the power of the Iroquois and make the border regions safe, but it did not achieve either and, in fact, rallied the Iroquois to increase attacks against white settlements for the next several years.[49] As Calloway notes, even while seeking refuge in Niagara, Iroquois vowed to take revenge. After delineating the results of their raids on frontier communities that ravaged New York and Pennsylvania, he concludes, "Washington's war on Iroquoian homes and food generated more, not fewer, raids on American settlers."[50]

In white scholarship on the Iroquois, the Sullivan Expedition—or the Revolutionary War more generally—often serves as a turning point, a dividing line in a narrative of the rise and fall of the Iroquois Empire, with the alleged "fall" characterized by defeat, despair, dependency, and alcoholism.[51] This narrative of decline emerged early and can be found in such works as DeWitt Clinton's essay on the Iroquois that he read to the New York Historical Society in 1811, and anthropologist Lewis Henry Morgan's seminal *The League of the Iroquois* (1851). This trope was fixed on the 1929 stone memorials in New York State that we consider in chapter 5.[52] We should be vigilant whenever settler-colonists announce Native decline. Aside from a few thousand Haudenosaunees and their allies who moved to Canada, most people displaced by Sullivan's raids returned and, on paper, held vast amounts of land, including all of western New York, most of central New York, and much of northern and western Pennsylvania.[53] This was still Indian Country, and land cessions did not commence until after the war's end. Recent works by Alyssa Mt. Pleasant and Beth Ryan demonstrate the continued presence of Haudenosaunee people in central New York even decades after the Revolutionary War.[54] Sullivan's raids allowed thousands of patriot soldiers to become intimately familiar with the rich bounty of established Haudenosaunee agricultural communities as they destroyed them, however, and when veterans returned home, they brought with them tales of a veritable Garden of Eden. The subsequent mass migration of Euro-Americans over the century became another invasion that culminated in the seizure of vast amounts of land by squatters, speculators, and state authorities through treaties of varying degrees of legality.[55]

Washington's Indian Expedition received ample criticism by Native leaders in its immediate aftermath and by historians more recently. Seneca leader Cornplanter traveled to Philadelphia in 1790 with leaders Half Town, Big Tree, New Arrow, and Guyasuta, and they gave a series of speeches addressed to George Washington in which they condemned the raids (see part 3).[56] A few years later, Cornplanter reprimanded surveyor John Adlum for making false accusations of Seneca wartime behavior, reminding him how Sullivan's men had behaved fifteen years earlier:

> You in your books charge us with many things we never were guilty of—But if we were to or could write books we could tell you of things, that an Indian never practices and would be ashamed to be charged with. Whenever we treated with you at the end of a war, there was always an article that all prisoners on both sides should be delivered up.—-Did you ever deliver up any? Did you ever deliver up one? *I answer for you* NO . . .
>
> Does your books tell you of Indian legs being skin[n]ed and tanned? Do your books tell you of parts of Indians being skinned, and those skins being dressed and made razor strops of? I know that all these things were done by the whites and I heard them boast of it. Does your books tell you, then an Indian ever did such a thing [?][57]

Scholars also note that Van Schaick's men attacked Onondagas, who were mostly "neutral or friendly to the patriots," leading them to "overwhelmingly" side with the British.[58] Sullivan's troops indiscriminately targeted patriot Oneida and Tuscarora allies and the peaceful Mohawks living in Lower Mohawk Castle as well as foes, and Sullivan refused to heed Oneida allies' pleas to spare Cayuga settlements.[59] There is clear evidence of atrocities, as Cornplanter described. Troops murdered some noncombatants rather than take them prisoners.[60]

Possibly reflecting some uneasiness about these aspects of the mission, major white settler commemorations of the Sullivan Expedition would not develop for nearly a century; it was "the forgotten campaign."[61] In an address published in *New York History*, Lyman Butterfield observed that the expedition "assumed little importance in the early histories of the American Revolution and has done little better in later ones or in general American histories and textbooks," in part due to General Sullivan's "poor press"; as a result, the campaign "never entered our national folklore."[62] The operation did enter local folklore, however. Euro-Americans found in this expedition an inspirational and serviceable tale, and the story of the expedition and the story of their settlements became enmeshed in their public commemorative projects. Understanding how and why this occurred is the focus of this book.

Studying the Sullivan Commemorative Complex

A project of this scope required an interdisciplinary methodology at the intersection of cultural anthropology, geography, museology, and history. My first task was reconnaissance. There is no one agency overseeing these historical sites and no guidebook to follow, so I had to piece together the Sullivan commemorative complex myself, from an array of sources. Over and over, since 2011, I have roughly followed the path taken by Sullivan's troops from Easton, Pennsylvania, into central New York to locate memorials, spending weeks at a time in the small towns along them (see map 1). The military expedition is also commemorated by street names and by public celebrations, reenactments, Boy Scout canoe trips, special newspaper series, and museum exhibits all along the way.

Since most markers in the complex are approximately a century old, they are not easy to find. It took me and a colleague five hours to locate each marker in Pennsylvania, while listening to *Warrior Road*, a CD driving tour put out by the Luzerne County Historical Society of Wilkes-Barre, Pennsylvania.[63] A scant mile north of the Tri-Delt parking lot at Lafayette College, we encountered the second of the Easton markers—a large granite monolith, installed by state officials in 1929, with a dingy bronze plaque—located on a tiny triangular park in a leafy suburb.[64] We were traveling on "Sullivan Trail," a two-lane road that continued north through former dairy farms, now being carved into housing developments for commuters who work in New York City. Reaching the town of Wind

FIG. 4. Pennsylvania Learned Tavern campsite memorial, 1929, Tannersville PA. Photo courtesy of Nathaniel Janssen.

Gap, we had trouble locating the next monument, which was in a busy parking lot across the street from a bright red CVS. The memorials continued northward into the heart of the old Pocono Mountain tourist area. We crossed a chaotic maze of highways—north–south running 611, 209, and 33 and east–west 80, which today is a parking lot of tractor-trailers. Roadside bars, sporting goods stores, and bait-and-tackle shops belied the region's tourist past. The traffic was atrocious. "I'm having a hard time imagining the past here," my companion commented, looking around at the Burger Kings, a car wash, gas stations, and a Dunkin' Donuts, bright red, orange, and yellow signage blasting out in all directions. I was distracted by oversized pickup trucks passing my car with bumper stickers featuring silhouettes of pinup women and rifles. The next monolith was also in a CVS parking lot, and across from a PNC bank, next to a newer roadside sign at a busy intersection and practically falling into a creek (figure 4). This monument looked a bit forlorn, and the Revolutionary War seemed to be the last thing on anyone's mind.

A few additional monuments are hidden in the woods in a

FIG. 5. Susquehanna River, facing north. Tunkhannock PA is visible to the right of the river. Photo courtesy of the author.

remote part of the Pocono Mountains. After passing the village of Bear Creek, we descended the mountains overlooking the vast Wyoming Valley, where a key episode of violence occurred. We crossed the working-class neighborhoods of the Wilkes-Barre conglomeration, where we met the grand Susquehanna River, and the road now followed great river bends as I drove northwest (see figure 5). Along the river was the most beautiful farmland I had ever seen. The monuments competed for my attention; they punctuated the journey to Tunkhannock, Towanda, and then the Athens/Sayre centers near the New York State border, placed right next to the highway or in scenic overlooks with vistas of dairy farms scattered on the rich river floodplains.

It is along this part of the journey that evidence of the Pennsylvania fracking boom starts to show: speeding mud-splattered work trucks carrying all manner of pipes, tubing, and curious-looking machinery zoom past. The road is now newly paved and widens at the hills. On the ascents, I sometimes pass convoys of enormous water tanker trucks. This stretch is often white-knuckle

FIG. 6. New York State roadside sign designating Dean's Cove. Photo courtesy of Michaela Kelly.

driving, and as I near the small town of Wysox, a giant orange sign proclaims, strangely precise: *Aggressive Driver High Crash Area Next 7¼ Miles*. I finally pull over, having reached a peaceful spot near the confluence of the Susquehanna and Chemung Rivers, in what is now Athens, Pennsylvania. A plaque explains that it was also the site of the former Fort Sullivan, where Sullivan and his troops waited for General Clinton and his men before heading north into Iroquois Territory.

Over the New York State border, stone monoliths continue to be visible from roadways that pass through verdant farms and the luxuriant landscape of Finger Lakes towns nestled along the elongated hillsides of glacial moraine. This is the homeland of the Haudenosaunee. Thirty-five stone Sullivan-Clinton memorials were established in 1929, followed by dozens of blue-and-gold roadside signs that herald the former locations of Native villages and orchards that were destroyed by the troops (see figure 6).

This project brought me into the deep past and hurtling forward into a troubling present: that of mass consumption, mainstream tourism, deindustrialization, failing dairy farms, and the boom towns created by hydraulic fracking. History is fixed in text on plaques, emerges in conversation, and is reproduced through a variety of media and local events: the "that was then" sections of local newspapers, the celebration of significant "birthdays" of prominent buildings and bridges, at local historical talks, walking tours, and museum exhibits. I visited tourism centers, attended pow-wows, went on multiday river sojourns, and spent time at Native American cultural centers.

Because this commemorative complex has deep roots, I also followed archival methods, digging into libraries and local and state archives across New York and Pennsylvania to put some order to the story of so many memorials, the labor of so many. Because these archives were often based in towns that hosted markers, I conducted ethnographic fieldwork during the same research trips. Local archives were sources of insights into commemorative events and sites, and places where I met a decidedly historically minded set. I set up interviews with people of interest, met reenactors who held unrelated "day jobs," and interviewed people's friends and their friends, meeting eighty-year-old women in their homes for tea and uproarious interviews about a whole host of topics. Heritage "pilgrims" follow "Sullivan's Trail," and I had chance encounters in parking lots, and at museums and historical society talks. I taped as many of these interviews as was feasible and include large excerpts of the tape transcripts as illustrations. I visited Haudenosaunee cultural centers as a tourist and had guided tours. I interviewed current and former directors and attended public events they held. I presented preliminary findings at public lectures, historical society meetings, meetings of local chapters of the Daughters of the American Revolution, academic conferences, an event at the Allegany Territory of the Seneca Nation of Indians, and another cosponsored by the Onondaga Nation's cultural center: Skä•ñonh–Great Law of Peace Center.

Through this fieldwork, I learned that people living near these memorials of the Sullivan Campaign are unevenly engaged by the monuments and the past they fix onto the land. For some people, the markers are completely unseen. Others find them offensive.

FIG. 7. Reenacting the Newtown Battle. Photo courtesy of the author.

A white man I met at the Wyoming County Historical Society in Tunkhannock, Pennsylvania, practically spits whenever he mentions Sullivan's name and even dislikes repeating the road name "Sullivan Trail." "Guess what he was doing! He was *following* the *Indian trails*." He was frustrated that people attributed all early roads to Sullivan's troops. "Why does Sullivan get all the credit?" he asked. Yet the same memorials serve his neighbors as important sites for social interaction. People get together to fundraise and repair them; they navigate by them when metal detecting. Sullivan memorials serve as sites for alternate ways of engaging with the past when people unite around them in period dress to fight mock battles (see figure 7). As I became more familiar to community members, I also encountered people who challenge the dominant narrative and carry out self-directed interventions. Many people are in conversation with the long-gone early monument creators, and the dialogue is sometimes contentious.

Ethnographies often commence with a rich descriptive representation, bringing the reader along on a journey "to the field." In this case, the journey *is* the field, as I am analyzing commemorative projects that roughly follow a lengthy scorched-earth military operation. This is a study of the commemoration of that operation, and of the building of certain kinds of communities and societies through its celebration—and its recollection. I interrogate public memorials to the Sullivan Expedition as windows into settler-colonial historical consciousness, sites that reflect and shape how settler-colonists understand their past and their relationship to the land. Enshrined in place-names and historical markers, and recognized at grand monument dedication events, reenactments, and massive historical pageants, the military campaign has played no small role in how people in Pennsylvania and New York—Native and non-Native—relate to their past. These activities have spanned hundreds of years, and some are ongoing into the present era. They have been carried out by different actors at different times. What types of commemorative events did they plan, and what lessons did these performances communicate to participants at the time? How do these stories reverberate today? This commemorative complex develops a particular kind of history: while overtly about the Revolutionary War, it also celebrates colonialism. It is time to turn to what is meant by describing Sullivan's expedition as a settler-colonial project and the United States as a "settler-colonial society."

Settler-Colonial Cultural Formations

There is growing consensus in colonial studies that settler-colonialism should be viewed as a distinct colonial form.[65] In contrast to economic colonies designed to extract resources with Indigenous labor, in settler colonies, settlers intend to stay, and the societies they build are predicated on their "replacing natives on their land," as Australian historian Patrick Wolfe expressed.[66] Settler-colonialism is characterized by an internal logic, the "logic of elimination," the elimination of the Native and population *replacement*.[67] This logic persists even after initial wars of conquest. In Wolfe's view, it is a logic "impervious to regime change," a structural feature shaping evolving settler-colonial societies.[68] Scholarship demonstrating that settler-colonial countries as distant from each other as Australia, Canada, and the United States developed remarkably similar practices has energized settler-colonial studies.[69] What may appear to be unrelated approaches to Native peoples— the breaking up of communal title, territorial removal, sequestration on reserves, the imposition of private property regimes, and assimilation programs (boarding schools, the prohibition of Native languages and religious practices, promoting the adoption of Native children, and Native citizenship laws)—are, in fact, variations on a common theme. All these practices and institutions can be seen as efforts to address the "threat posed by the continued survival of Indigenous peoplehood," a peoplehood considered a direct challenge to settler society.[70]

Insights from settler-colonial studies are revolutionizing the very historiography of many settler societies.[71] Influenced by theoretical developments in Native American and Indigenous studies, a similar paradigm shift is reaching scholarship on the United States as historians and social scientists increasingly revisit U.S. history as a story of settler-style colonization that is ongoing into the present day.[72] Anthropology has been slow to adapt. A main point of Audra Simpson's tour de force, *Mohawk Interruptus*, is to demonstrate how foundational texts on Haudenosaunee nations were integrally tied to the settler-colonial project, and she challenges anthropologists studying Native Americans to ground their research within a clear understanding of the wider colonial context within which they and their work are situated.[73] I want to extend Simpson's critique to argue that anthropologists of *non-Native* North America must also take into account the role of settler-colonialism on their focus of study and their practice. In this book, I turn the ethnographic gaze to settler-colonists and their cultural formations.

If the logic of elimination has shaped the social and political institutions of distinct settler-colonial societies, what have been its lasting *cultural* consequences? In *Culture and Imperialism*, Edward Said highlights the need to explore the cultural forms that "nurtured the sentiment, rationale, and above all the imagination of empire."[74] New works in American studies, political science, and Native American studies are following a similar agenda for the cultural projects of settler-colonialism. Can we identify a settler-colonial "common sense," as Mark Rifkin puts it, dominant yet often unseen patterns of thought and taken-for-granted ways of seeing?[75] A focus on hegemonic cultural forms can be an elusive exercise as we must work to bring into focus that which is often taken for granted or hiding in plain sight. In her discussion of settler-colonial aesthetics in contemporary Hawai'i, artist Karen Kosasa discusses a "settler imaginary," concepts and images that help settlers direct their lives and encourage them to "misrecognize the colony as a democratic space of opportunity."[76] She identifies an aesthetic of "blankness" generated through "acts of erasure" that remove references to colonialism and allow settlers to remain naive to the colonial situation and their place in it. She asks, "How are settlers educated not to see the colony and its colonial practices? How does their 'failure of vision' prevent them from seeing the political difference between themselves as colonizers and indigenous people as colonized?"[77] The "failures of vision" I consider here are rooted in commonplace understandings of the past. I believe that it is here that we must start to elucidate how settler-colonists misrecognize the colony and their place in it.

History, Memory, and Narration

This book explores a set of commemorative projects as a means of elucidating settler-colonial historical consciousness, ways of understanding and relating to the past. Because I am concerned with the politics of the past in both the past and the present, this work takes inspiration from Stephan Palmié and Charles Stewart's call for an "anthropology of history," a project that turns "history itself" into an object of anthropological study.[78] *History* in English refers to a time past and a story of what happened, as well as a prominent academic discipline with a well-established methodology.[79] Although many people reading this book follow the tenets of this methodology, as do I, not all the people I discuss in it are or were equally invested in or trained in historical methods. The many sites discussed here that were the work of nonprofessionals demonstrate that a national historical consciousness is forged from multiple sources, with academic history-making one approach to the past among many. As British social historian

Raphael Samuel writes, "History is not the prerogative of the historian, nor even . . . a historian's 'invention'. It is, rather, a social form of knowledge; the work, in any given instance, of a thousand different hands."[80] While I may not be able to consider thousands of perspectives, I will certainly consider more than one.

The memory studies literature is especially helpful for a project that moves beyond academic history-writing. As the British Popular Memory Group writes, "We must include *all* the ways in which a sense of the past is constructed in our society."[81] French sociologist Maurice Halbwachs is credited with developing the concept of "collective memory" in his landmark works, *Les cadres sociaux de la mémoire* and *La mémoire collective.*[82] In *Les cadres,* Halbwachs insisted on a *social* source of memory, proposing the existence of social frameworks within which individual memories and thoughts are situated and made meaningful. While he admitted that individuals have unique memories due to different life circumstances, he believed that even these individual memories are social at their core. They leave a lasting impression to the extent that they are linked or interrelated to the thoughts "that come to us from the social milieu." We can never escape or think outside this milieu.[83] Considering such social groups as families, religious communities, and social classes, he argued that people in these communities are bound together by shared understandings of the past. Even though individuals in communities of memory do not all have identical life experiences, their individual memories are shaped by, connected to, and integrated into a wider, shared orientation to the past.

Halbwachs's insights have inspired a burgeoning interdisciplinary memory studies literature as scholars explore how social memories are learned, transmitted, and changed.[84] People learn what to remember and what to forget through "mnemonic socialization," lessons transmitted both explicitly and implicitly, whether through public ceremonies, at school, or in the family.[85] Societies will experience time and record, transmit, and understand "pastness" in diverse, culturally specific ways; this is the subject of a vast literature in anthropology and related fields.[86] Stabilized in song, story, texts, images, and rituals, representations of the past can be maintained and reproduced not only for generations but for eons.[87]

Since any given society will necessarily be composed of multiple coexisting communities and competing cultural traditions, temporalities, and historical epistemologies, they will interact on what the Popular Memory Group has described as a society's "public 'theatre' of history."[88] Political leaders have long been aware that the past is a vital political resource that can help defend or justify a particular social order, and they may strive to place a historical vision that best reflects their worldview front and center on this national stage in hope that it may become pervasive or even hegemonic.[89] As Linda Tuhiwai Smith observes, "History is mostly about power."[90] Yet officially promoted versions of the past enter onto a public stage that is already crowded with many voices. In the cacophony that follows, certain versions of the past become central while "others are marginalized or excluded or reworked."[91]

We can conceptualize the resulting understandings of and approaches to the past within a given community or society as its wider "historical consciousness," a concept I use, in its broadest sense, to mean an awareness of and relationship to the past. I prefer this expansive concept to "collective memory" or "national memory," as it can encompass the diverse memory practices and media considered here, practices that range from the works of professional historians and academic historiography to public memorial development, public performance, community storytelling, smaller non-Native and Native communities of memory, and everyday talk.[92] Multiple historical consciousnesses can coexist in any one society, as the anthropological literature makes clear. Finally, unlike some models of historical consciousness, I intend no underlying evolutionary framework; I do not imagine societies without "historical consciousness," and I apply this concept to Native and non-Native communities alike.[93] This concept allows me to avoid terminology that sometimes implies radical breaks in awareness of, approaches to, or representations of pastness according to some purported level of psychic or technological development.[94] That said, we will encounter great contrasts in how the Sullivan story appears in Native and non-Native projects, contrasts rooted in lived experiences of the raids and respective positions in a colonial field of power.

Settler-Colonial Historical Consciousness

The national histories of settler-colonial states such as Australia, Canada, and the United States are founded on similar "foundational fictions," myths and tropes that help justify dispossession.[95] As Australian historian Bain Attwood has argued, people living in societies founded on the seizure of another people's land will find it difficult to establish a national identity as a moral society without engaging in processes of deflection, rationalization, or outright denial of their ancestors' actions.[96] Frontier violence is rationalized, justified, or even glorified in popular culture, it is presented as "exceptional," or its instigation is attributed to the victim.[97] Scholars in Native American studies and historiography have long noted blind spots in American historical consciousness, with Native Americans written out of the narrative arc of nineteenth-century progressive historiography, becoming "history's shadow," or being relegated to "colonial time"; contemporary historians continue to confront this systematic erasure.[98] Scholars diagnosing these trends identify an array of deficiencies in settler memory work, deploying such metaphors as erasure, aporia, aphasia, repression, screen memories, disavowal, and denial.[99]

These "warpings" in settler-colonial historical consciousness can be traced to the social form's eliminatory logic. While settler-colonial cultural formations resemble those of other colonial situations in their dehumanization of the Indigenous population, the division of the social world into binary oppositions (such as "civilized" versus "savages"), and their associated racializing ideologies and practices, the logic of elimination shapes settler-colonial historical consciousness in unique ways.[100] Since the underlying logic is rooted in the assumption that settler-colonists will ultimately replace Indigenous people (rather than living alongside them and exploiting their labor), settlers keep trying to tell a story of such a transition of populations. The past is imagined as occurring in two phases: the time of the Natives (prehistory) followed by the time of the settler-colonists (history), with these periods segre-

gated conceptually. This partition in settler historical consciousness helps prevent acknowledgement of the inevitable period of
contact (read "conflict") between the two groups. Instead, Native
people are represented as living some distance away in time or
space, or both.[101] We know, of course, that this settler imaginary
is a fantasy, that settler-colonists essentially landed into a Native
American storyline and haven't left, as the careful work by many
historians cited in this book makes abundantly clear. However,
in the popular imaginary, this is not always certain. Settlers must
work hard to develop plausible origin stories that accommodate
the partitions in their historical consciousness and appease the
elimination fantasy. The deployment of the Sullivan story in such
endeavors is the focus of this book.

A landmark work advancing our understanding of settler-
colonial historical consciousness is Anishinaabe historian Jean
O'Brien's masterpiece, *Firsting and Lasting*. Through an analysis
of nineteenth-century local history texts, she identifies "replacement narratives," constructs through which settler-colonists explain
to themselves how they came to "replace" the territory's Indigenous inhabitants.[102] These "origin myths" assign "primacy to non-
Indians who 'settled' the region in a benign process involving
righteous relations with Indians and just property transactions
that led to an inevitable and . . . lamentable Indian extinction."[103]
In the New Englander projects she studied, replacement narratives were developed with rhetorical strategies she identifies as
"firsting" and "lasting." Local histories obsessively documented
"firsts": the first white baby born, the first settlement, the first
house, asserting that non-Indians were the first people worth recognition and, in this way, claiming indigeneity for themselves.[104]
They also engaged in "lasting," establishing monuments and texts
about the last or vanishing Indian whom they were replacing, and
New Englanders lamented the loss of the "last remnant" of this
or that Indian nation.[105] The Sullivan memorials we consider here
help construct additional replacement narratives that offer plausible origin stories for the residents of Pennsylvania and New York.

Where should we turn to examine settler-colonial historical
consciousness? Some scholars are exploring literature, film, pop-

ular culture, and historiography.[106] Narratives about the national past are also inscribed in stone or engraved in metal and found on roadside plaques, my focus here.

Settler Sites of Memory

To commemorate, according to the *Oxford English Dictionary*, is to "call to remembrance . . . by some solemnity or celebration" and "to mention as worthy of remembrance." Commemorative projects are, almost by definition, valorizing projects that honor the people or events in question. The public monuments, place-names, and other memorials settler-colonists established to recognize the Sullivan Expedition are no different, and they follow a commemorative form common in contemporary nation-states.[107] When memories are fused to place, they become "sites of memory," places where people express shared knowledge about the past.[108] Because these historical markers and place-names are commemorating events from the past, we can also call them "memorials," sites that remind us of particular histories and ask us to remember.[109] This commemorative form is in the spotlight as the fates of memorials to Confederate heroes and Christopher Columbus are up for debate in the United States. What is the import of items of public history-making from yesteryear? Do historical markers continue to shape the imaginations of the next generation?

While research shows that local historical sites and museums greatly influence Americans' views of the national past, they remain relatively under-theorized and often have a poorly known history.[110] People often assume that the very existence of a marker or monument reflects public consensus on the subject or the heavy hand of the state. Their authoritative appearance masks their origins and can leave the impression of popular or official approval. The full story of a memorial's establishment is often far more complicated, and usually far more interesting.

U.S. commemorative trends follow a long-standing practice; certainly, monumental art is as old as humanity.[111] In the nineteenth century, European nation-states like France commissioned so much monumental art that observers wrote of their "statumania."[112] U.S. commemorative practices largely followed European aesthetic trends, and statues and historic sites proliferated across the country, especially after the Civil War. Although "memorial manias" and aesthetic trends may have traveled to the United States from Europe, European financing strategies did not.[113] State officials played a central role in commissioning public memorials in nineteenth- and early twentieth-century Europe, while in the United States, most early marker developers did so on their own. The early U.S. republic had an aversion to celebrations of pastness and what was considered "old-world" ancestor worship, and instead manifested an "obsession" with newness, as historian Michael Kammen documents.[114] The new nation's indifference to historic sites would be shocking by contemporary standards. What we would now view as national treasures, such as Benjamin Franklin's home, were demolished in prior centuries without incident.[115] The prevailing assumption for much of early U.S. history was that "governments bore no responsibility for matters of collective memory," an attitude that persisted well into the 1930s.[116] As Kammen puts it, "If people wanted to commemorate an anniversary, or save a site, they would have to take the initiative . . . the time, energy, and above all the money must come from them."[117]

This early orientation has had a tremendous influence on the U.S. monumental landscape. In the absence of federal direction and resources, most U.S. monuments and historical markers were developed by wealthy benefactors, local organizations, or civic and patriotic societies. As a result, local elites have been able to dominate the public face of the national past to a degree difficult to measure.[118] In *Lies across America: What our Historic Sites Get Wrong*, sociologist James Loewen examined all roadside historical markers in thirty-four states and came to a discouraging conclusion: because the people who put up markers and monuments were "usually pillars of the white community," the overall narrative that emerges from the sum of their labors is greatly skewed.[119] "Americans still live and work in a landscape of white supremacy," he bluntly concluded decades ago.[120] Local initiative, moreover, almost necessarily leads to an evasion of uncomfortable pasts.[121] As Loewen pointed out, local control means "the site will tell a story favorable to the local community, and particularly to that part of the community that erected or restored it," quipping that the story told is that "everything that happened here was good."[122] Any study of U.S. historical markers will be as much about this local context as it is about the story the markers purportedly broadcast, and the Sullivan markers are a case in point.

Because most markers are developed long after the event being commemorated, historical sites are always a "tale of two eras," the "manifest narrative: the events or person heralded in its text or artwork," and the story of the monument's establishment.[123] We will be interested in the Sullivan Expedition, already the subject of a substantial historiography.[124] The story of the *commemoration* of Sullivan, on the other hand, is almost untold, and piecing together this story required considerable original research. I add a third era for our consideration, that of the present day. The meanings and uses of commemorative memorials will change over time, and the fullest discussions of public history take the longitudinal and ethnographic approach followed here.[125]

These eras help establish the structure of this book. In part 1, "Origins," I explore the inception of many of the Sullivan markers, organized by era and by state. I turn to the contemporary relevance of these commemorative labors in part 2, "Reverberations." Over the course of this project, while seeking out people who are actively "celebrating Sullivan," I have encountered others who are not, and a subset of this group have carried out projects that counter the dominant Sullivan story (chapter 12). Finally, in part 3 I consider how Haudenosaunee cultural centers treat the same era, disrupting the dominant settler-colonial Sullivan narrative in fundamental ways.

Memory Entrepreneurs and Commemorative Performance

The women and men who first fixed the Sullivan story to the land were mostly elite white Euro-Americans who found in this event of the Revolutionary War lessons they felt were urgently needed. I consider them "memory entrepreneurs," a concept loosely based on sociologist Howard Becker's classic concept of the "moral entrepreneur."[126] In Becker's model, moral entrepreneurs are people who, in attempting to mark out appropriate rules of behavior, are also constructing deviance. Becker outlines a prototype, the "crusading reformer," someone who feels that prevailing rules are not enough, someone who is "fervent and righteous, often self-righteous," who truly believes that their agenda will benefit others or minimize exploitation and suffering. The memory entrepreneurs in this book were similar. They found in the events of American history vital lessons to share with a wider public. At different moments, new memory entrepreneurs take the lead, developing markers for personal and professional reasons, often responding to quite local concerns.

The fact that multiple distinct Sullivan commemorative projects were carried out independently across two states offers us a unique opportunity to observe the effects of local contexts on how the national past is understood. I examine multiple instantiations of the Sullivan story, including individually designed projects and large state-sponsored programs. The detailed microhistorical approach I follow in part 1 has several goals. Elites played a dominant role in shaping the memorial landscape, certainly, but lumping them together into an "undifferentiated" bloc can unwittingly grant them greater mystique and power.[127] A closer look helps deconstruct this mystique and reveals that their projects were far less coordinated than one might think; they often competed or worked at cross-purposes, and always responded first to very local political and social contexts.[128] When we consider an array of such projects, we find that even though they narrate a common military operation, the Sullivan memorials carry different meanings in Pennsylvania and New York.[129] It is for this reason that I follow a state-by-state rather than a chronological structure in part 1. The campaign was not well known when memory entrepreneurs planned their programs, and thus their locally developed Sullivan projects did not simply add texture to a preexisting and well-consolidated national story, but helped determine how that national story was told. When we cross from Pennsylvania to New York, the markers contribute to narrations that develop different protagonists, construct different kinds of Native enemies, and offer different moral lessons. The expedition is even given different names. It becomes different events.

I move beyond marker texts to include in this analysis the commemorations in which they feature. Critics of historical monuments often focus on texts and aesthetics to the neglect of commemorative practice. Like the markers themselves, these practices can appear unremarkable at first glance—standing, sitting, singing, saluting flags. There is real power in these actions, however. Mass "mnemonic synchronization" occurs at marker dedications as participants learn, in a group, not only content about the past but also general attitudes about it.[130] I have found anthropologist Paul Connerton's insights in *How Societies Remember* particularly helpful in this regard. Public commemorative ceremonies are rituals, he argues, repetitive and rule-bound practices that deliberately comment on and help elicit sentiments and attitudes toward a version of the past.[131] At Sullivan commemorative events, speeches identify which historical figures and behaviors to emulate, and the spoken words and embodied actions of people, carried out in unison, guide participants toward appropriate attitudes toward these actors: they "pledge allegiance," bow their heads in supplication, and vow their love for the nation in song. These commemorative events often follow a "rhetoric of reenactment."[132] Participants are encouraged to not only contemplate a past era, but also to temporarily return to it, reenact it. By observing an event on the same day on the calendar, a common practice for Sullivan campaign celebrations, it is as if participants are returning to that time.[133] Commemorators may repeat the language of past historical actors, a form of "temporal heteroglossia" that involves mixing the language of the past with that of the present and, in doing so, even contemporary speakers may find themselves talking about "savages" and "gallant men."[134] I add to Connerton's model a genealogical dimension, as memory entrepreneurs have often sought descendants of historical figures to play privileged roles in their ceremonies.

How do these memorials and their commemorative performances relate to settler-colonialism and the creation of "settler-colonists?" I argue here that seemingly innocuous rituals of this sort have been vitally important in helping forge what Benedict Anderson termed an "imagined community," in this case, an imagined settler-colonial community, one that is united by a common historical consciousness. Settler-colonial societies are, by definition, new societies, new nations in the making, and by performing commemorative rituals as a group, participants help bring that group into being. Connerton emphasizes the performative function of ritual language, noting that the use of words such as "us" or "we" at a public event can help create community.[135] Because Sullivan's soldiers were fighting a Native foe, in repeating the Sullivan story, the "we" deployed at marker unveilings is almost necessarily a non-Native one, and through these ceremonies, a group of white settler-colonists of disparate backgrounds is consolidated, recreated, and consecrated. The actions carried out at marker dedications, the texts inscribed in stone, and statements made at annual contemporary rituals construct an exclusive settler community that excludes the Native.

Telling War Stories

The elements of the Sullivan commemorative complex offer a rich set of examples through which to explore what I have described as warpings in settler-colonial historical consciousness. What are the rhetorical devices used by memory entrepreneurs in developing their Sullivan stories? Texts on roadside markers distill complex narratives into concise expressions with haiku-like simplicity, making them an especially efficient mode of communication and excellent site for an analysis of settler-colonial ways of framing the past. Speeches at marker dedications develop this meaning in greater detail, and newspaper articles, speeches, and conversations with people at dedication events add further insights. Together these cultural projects develop what I call here "Sullivan stories," narrations of the Sullivan Expedition that have been "stabilized culturally" through repeated tellings and inscriptions.[136] I am less concerned with the truth-value of these Sullivan stories than with their salience over time, examining how different Sullivan stories emerged in different local contexts.

Historical representations are never straight reflections of what

happened in the past. Storytellers and historians alike will emphasize some elements over others, abbreviate in response to their
audience, and relegate some characters or incidents to oblivion. As
anthropologist Michel-Rolph Trouillot brilliantly argues in *Silencing the Past*, because historical narratives cannot possibly include
every single detail of a historical event and remain intelligible,
silencing is a necessary component of historical production.[137] He
identifies several key moments when silencing can occur: at the
moment of fact creation, during the making of archives, at the
moment of fact retrieval, and during the making of histories.[138]
At these moments, some elements of "what happened" are left
out, and this is not always intentional. Witnesses die before they
tell their stories or evidence is lost at sea; only some documents
survive or are incorporated in an archive; and historians are limited to certain sources due to personal or professional biases, lack
of funding, or lack of time. As a result, any historical narrative,
whether written or spoken, can be viewed as a "particular bun-
dle of silences."[139]

The structuring of an account can also shape its ultimate meaning, as Hayden White demonstrates in his 1973 masterpiece, *Metahistory*. Historians face the problem of creating coherence, and
certain emplotments and forms of argumentation may shape the
kind of story they relate.[140] Periodicity offers an almost invisible
means of forcing certain plotlines and foreclosing other narrations. In *Time Maps* sociologist Eviatar Zerubavel reminds us that
there are no natural breaks in the unbroken stream of time, and
he discusses the politics and consequences of "lumping together"
stretches of time, and creating artificial breaks ("splitting").[141] Lumping and splitting have helped shape whole fields of study, structure
the subfields of the discipline of history, and determine journal
foci, as when the Americas before 1492 is identified as "prehistory."[142] Conventional periodicities can force storylines and cause
historians to remove content that doesn't fit.[143] Splitting off and
rendering inconsequential whole stretches of time, what Zerubavel
terms "mnemonic decapitation," is a powerful tool common to
settler-colonial societies that we will see deployed by the marker
developers and their narrations.[144]

The effects of this kind of "periodization play" may be especially powerful when narrating wartime conflict. Isolating a chunk of time and calling it a "war" is already a strategic move, and deciding when to start a story of "a war" is a political choice with powerful consequences.[145] When and why did the war begin? Who started it? How these questions are answered will set into play a cascade of explanations and insinuations of responsibility. The consequences of this manipulation of war stories are powerfully illustrated by Abenaki historian Lisa Brooks's award-winning book, *Our Beloved Kin*. Brooks identifies what she terms "modes of containment" that have been deployed in narrations of King Philip's War in the seventeenth century. She demonstrates how even naming a war can contain it.[146] The war's standard appellation suggests that it was all about one man (the Wampanoag leader Metacom, or "King Philip") rather than part of a complex and much longer lasting movement.[147] Ending a narrative at a conventional date, such as the summer of 1676, also "contains" the war by preventing the development of a longer narrative arc that includes the Indigenous resistance that continued well after Metacom's death. Isolating specific periods of strife in this way and labeling them as discrete "wars" prevents recognition of what might be similar across a series of conflicts and inhibits the telling of a fuller story.[148]

Narrating the story of the Sullivan Expedition carries many challenges, as the preceding discussion makes clear. First off, recounting elements of the Revolutionary War for an audience that includes Americans is burdened by the weight of this foundational event, with heroes enshrined in national holidays, place-names, the nation's capital, and lore centuries deep. To look critically at any part of this war is, to many, to challenge the war itself, to interrogate its actors, and to call into question the moral standing of the nation that was one of its consequences. Moreover, any account I write about this military operation will silence or "contain" some elements and engage in mnemonic decapitation of whole swaths of time, and it may strategically or inadvertently lay blame or imply ulterior motives.

Consider, to start, its name, "Sullivan Expedition," a name that already redirects our attention. Washington identified his mission as the Indian Expedition, which in many ways is a more accurate descriptor. It was later associated almost exclusively with its leading military officer (Maj. Gen. John Sullivan) and is conventionally known as the Sullivan Expedition, a usage I also deploy while aware that it silences the focus of the missions (against "Indians") and its master planner, Washington. As Calloway maintains, "The expedition was Washington's from start to finish."[149] This usage further "contains" in that its sub-missions are often neglected in historical summaries. Even the descriptor "expedition" is problematic, for it is a neutral term associated with such activities as a mountain-climbing adventure. Calling the invasion of Indian territory and the burning of households and crops an "expedition" can be read as callous, and this euphemistic language can set narrators along a narrow track, one that emphasizes troop strengths or difficult geographies. This would never be how people subjected to this mission would describe it. In Haudenosaunee oral testimony, it is often summed up as "the invasion," "the burning," or the "whirlwind."[150]

When should accounts of Washington's Indian Expedition begin? In this book, we will encounter many different beginnings that set narratives down different tracks.[151] In Pennsylvania projects, the Sullivan Expedition is usually presented as a retaliation for a battle that occurred the year before, the Battle of Wyoming, which took place near present-day Wilkes-Barre, Pennsylvania. It is difficult to overstate the degree to which that battle, known even today as the "Wyoming Massacre," shapes how Euro-Americans in northeastern Pennsylvania understand the Revolutionary era (the focus of chapter 1). Early Pennsylvania markers to Sullivan were established by women whose ancestors were killed not during the Sullivan Campaign but at the Battle of Wyoming. Their markers to Sullivan directly or indirectly recognize Wyoming (as we see with the Easton plaque, discussed at the start of this chapter). By celebrating Sullivan, these women were recognizing their kin lost at the Wyoming battle and, in doing so, positioning their families as victims of alleged Indian savagery (the focus of chapter 2). In this framing, the Sullivan Expedition becomes a mission of righteous vengeance, and the loss of "the Native" is celebrated.

In New York, in contrast, officials of a state that was deeply implicated in the lengthy dispossession of the Haudenosaunee nations found in the Sullivan story a useful way to obscure that past. By developing a "noble savage" whose tragic flaw was unwavering loyalty to the British, their Sullivan story attributes the taking of Haudenosaunee lands to that loyalty, a fateful decision that "caused" Sullivan's necessary and inevitable response.[152] Swept from view are decades of land swindles carried out at the highest level that occurred well after the expedition. The state's involvement in this rendition of the Sullivan story when a major Haudenosaunee claims case was in play is the focus of chapters 5–7.

Native American accounts are rooted in a different epistemology and periodicity. They start far earlier and represent an unbroken memory of horror that is not the subject of celebratory projects. One published account we consider commences with the foundation of the League of the Iroquois, well before the arrival of Europeans on the continent, a periodicity that changes everything.[153]

Settler-Colonial and Native Memoryscapes

The multiple monuments, street names, and historical markers commemorating the Sullivan story help to construct a culturally infused "sense of place."[154] They contribute to a settler-colonial memoryscape—a landscape full of historical reminders. In the brilliant *Memory Lands*, Christine DeLucia discusses the memoryscape associated with King Philip's War, exploring practices of placemaking three centuries deep, and demonstrates how land itself can be a "potent vector of memory production."[155] The memoryscape created by the Sullivan commemorative complex is a recent construction that overlays a memoryscape millennia deep. Despite extensive disruption, the preexisting Haudenosaunee memoryscape has not been lost.[156] One might imagine a country's landscape of memory composed of layers that add to the historical richness of a place and create a kind of multicultural historical capital. This is misleading, and it can be dangerous to consider Euro-American settler and Native memoryscapes in the same frame. First and foremost, settler-colonial placemaking is inherently destructive. Settler-colonial memorials often assert a vantage point diametrically opposed to a Native one, and in the battle for dominance on a "public theatre of memory," memory entrepreneurs may dismiss, attempt to obliterate, or even incorporate and "cannibalize" previously hegemonic historical traditions, resulting in a settler-colonial memoryscape that comments on or is at war with its Indigenous counterparts.[157]

This ambivalent and oppositional relationship between Euro-American and Native memoryscapes is exemplified by the Sullivan memorials. Many settler-colonists who feature in this book were very much preoccupied with the land's original inhabitants, and their memorials often mention the role of Indigenous actors or respond to prior naming traditions. Since Sullivan's troops were removing a Native people from their homeland, the Sullivan commemorative complex marks out key sites of a Native memoryscape while honoring the agents of its eradication. In doing so, the memorials can be seen as efforts to create a Euro-American settler space out of a Native one. They are monuments to replacement. In claiming that such a population transition has occurred, right at this spot, at a specific date, Sullivan memorials can be seen as attempts to make that transition a reality. However, the markers and their initiators were naive or engaging in wishful thinking, for descendants of those displaced by Sullivan's troops persist and their former village sites remain important elements in a rich and much deeper Native memoryscape that lives on into the present day. This Native memoryscape has not been erased or removed, but is strong, and Haudenosaunee actors may even use the Sullivan markers to tell an oppositional story.[158]

It is important to comment a bit more on how local Native Americans relay their own accounts of the Sullivan story, how they relate to the settler Sullivan commemorative complex, and what this book does and does not tackle. In the many published works on the Sullivan Expedition, there is little effort to delve into published or existing Native oral testimonies, so the story is usually told from a white perspective, and almost exclusively a "patriot" one at that, although a recent project has made real progress in this regard.[159] A different kind of book would explore this "interpretive silence" by plumbing oral historical accounts and conducting interviews with Haudenosaunee to enrich our understanding of this military operation and its effects.[160] Stories of the expedition and the chaos it wrought still live within contemporary Haudenosaunee communities, and I include some of them here. The politics of fully delving into such stories to tell a more complete narration of the Sullivan Campaign are fraught for me, a white settler. As Emilie Cameron argues in her work on a white settler story in Nunavut, seeking "counter-stories," Native stories "from the margins," can easily lead to a reproduction of colonial relations. Native interlocutors may be asked to "resist, talk back, or renarrate in direct response to Qablunaaq [non-Native] stories," a process that can leave the structure of the dominant narrative in place.[161] As Mark Rifkin so clearly demonstrates in *Beyond Settler Time*, bringing settler and Native stories into a common narrative arc can deny Indigenous temporal sovereignty, a tack I try to avoid here.[162] I am sensitive to the need to practice "decolonizing methodologies" and to allow for "rhetorical sovereignty."[163] I want to avoid fitting Native narrations into dominant constructions that use dominant terms, framing, or periodicity. I am not interested in advancing standard historiography on Washington's Indian Expedition using Native accounts to tell a "fuller" history; rather, I want to step back and compare Native and non-Native accounts. I interrogate *public* memorials, for it is not my place to expose personal or sensitive Haudenosaunee or other Native stories and their associated places of memory. This is the subject of an important and wholly different work that Haudenosaunee historians are already conducting.[164] At the same time, there are several important public-facing Haudenosaunee cultural centers in the vicinity of the Sullivan markers. After a close study of the deployment of the Sullivan story by white settlers in part 1, Origins, and contemporary reactions to them by Native and non-Native people in part 2, Reverberations, in part 3, Interventions, I explore how the military operation is treated at these cultural centers. These centers are engaged in a very different kind of place-making and means of fixing history on the land, and thus merit a distinct treatment unencumbered by dominant terminology, historical figures, and periodicities. In part 3, we turn to very different framings grounded in a radically different historical epistemology. Some readers may find this rendition disorienting. It is not merely that Native concepts and terms in Indigenous languages are used, as are other ways of conveying information. As Cameron found in contrasting Inuit and Canadian settler narratives of a common historical event, the cultural centers may not tell a story that non-Native peoples will expect.[165]

For a people living in their homeland since time immemorial, whose stories start at the beginning of time, Sullivan was not the start or end of any story. The military operation, while horrific, is one of many attempts by white invaders to seize Haudenosaunee property and sovereignty. This much longer story has an earlier start date, and it is a story that is ongoing. Long after the Revolutionary War, attacks on Native sovereignty have included deceptive land deals, threats of allotment, military conscription, mandated U.S. citizenship (in 1924), hunting and fishing regulations, boarding school incarceration, the seizure of land by the state of New York for highway construction, the seizure of land by the federal government to build the St. Lawrence seaway and the Kinzua Dam, and the associated flooding of huge portions of the Allegany Territory of the Seneca Nation of Indians. Outlining how the Sullivan story is recounted at Haudenosaunee cultural centers reveals in striking clarity the "mnemonic myopia" that limits settler-colonial historical consciousness.[166] Gone, in some cases, is Sullivan's name or a period of time called "the Revolutionary War." I am in no way arguing that the horror of Sullivan is diminished or forgotten. Rather, in these centers we find the expedition reduced, reframed, and rendered as one of many troubling acts by white people. For non-Native observers, these stories can be unsettling, not only because they upend standard periodization— they commence in an era that most non–Native Americans know vaguely, starting well before the seventeenth century—but also because they continue into the contemporary era, involving such seemingly unrelated topics as cigarette taxes and road construction. Non-Native readers may find themselves implicated.

I have constructed the book in this way, ending with the Haudenosaunee voices so that the Haudenosaunee leaders of these cultural centers have the last word. These cultural centers intervene in the relentlessly bombastic celebrations of colonial conquest exemplified by the Sullivan place-names, markers, and ceremonies. They intervene not by challenging small details in the dominant Sullivan story, but by offering a wholly different narrative structure, focus, and perspective. In the process, even Sullivan is cut down to size and becomes one of a series of rapacious outsiders trying to thwart an invincible foe, an annoying, mosquito-like presence, one of many such annoyances to brush off, to overcome, to survive. Some people reading this book may be considering ways to revise the public history landscape. The Haudenosaunee cultural centers should be a starting point. They offer rich models of memory work that reach outward and beyond.

PART ONE

Origins

Settler-Colonial Public Memory

Pennsylvania: In the Shadow of Wyoming

ONE

Yankee Insurgency and the Battle of Wyoming

O n June 16, 1900, a group of Easton's "most distinguished
citizens" met to inaugurate a marker to the Sullivan Expedition on the road behind the home of Francis A. March
Sr., English professor at Lafayette College.[1] Mrs. Margaret Mildred Stone Conway March and other members of the local chapter of the Daughters of the American Revolution (DAR) stood
in a circle, dressed in white, as they presented their memorial
to the city.[2] This historical marker was one of several Sullivan
memorials developed in Pennsylvania at the turn of the century.
Other markers were unveiled in the mountains outside Wilkes-
Barre in 1896 and 1898, followed by memorials in Athens (1902),
Towanda (1908), and Wyalusing (1914). These projects were the
work of individual actors or patriotic societies working without
official direction. Why were so many Pennsylvanians establishing memorials to Sullivan at this time?

We start this book in Pennsylvania, with this turn-of-the-century
spotlight on the Sullivan Expedition. Most Sullivan memorials in
New York appeared much later, in 1929. Pennsylvania's precocity
is noteworthy given the colony's resistance to the mission when it
was underway; local hesitation to supply the troops delayed Sullivan for months, causing General Washington to reprimand the
Pennsylvania Executive Council.[3] These markers are of further
significance because they were the work of elite white women,
operating alone or as members of patriotic societies, long before
women had full citizenship rights. Most significantly, for our pur-
poses, they articulate a particular framing of the Sullivan Expedi-

tion, a framing that persists in the state to this day. In northern Pennsylvania, the Sullivan Expedition is understood in relation to, and as a consequence of, the Battle of Wyoming (July 3, 1778), a Revolutionary War battle that occurred the previous year. The Wyoming battle, famous for the imbalanced casualty rates and the fact that British troops included a large number of Indian allies, became known as the "Wyoming Massacre." At marker dedications, Sullivan and Wyoming are presented as linked military operations, as "two parts of one drama," with the Sullivan Expedition presented as the "retributive sequel of the massacre of Wyoming."[4] This Wyoming-centric framing of the Sullivan Expedition is evident in the text of the 1900 Easton DAR marker, which claims that Sullivan's goal was to "avenge the Wyoming Massacre." In mentioning the Wyoming bloodbath, the marker text redirects attention from the horrors of Sullivan's scorched-earth tactics to alleged acts of Indian savagery. Starting the Sullivan story with the Wyoming battle does more than develop a clear plotline or justify Sullivan's tactics, however. In this region of Pennsylvania, bringing up the Wyoming battle also means taking a political stance, for the majority of the Wyoming dead were settlers from the Connecticut colony, settlers already in direct conflict with Pennsylvanian authorities. Mentioning Wyoming here means taking a side in the Connecticut-Pennsylvania intra-settler war. Because the Sullivan markers in Pennsylvania were established in the shadow of Wyoming, it is with that battle and the intrasettler conflict that we must start.

Conflicting Claims

Well before the Revolutionary War, European immigrants of the colonies of Pennsylvania and Connecticut fought over the lush bottomlands of the Susquehanna River. Each side appealed to the British Crown and later the Continental Congress for help in resolving the intractable feud, which lasted from the 1750s to the early nineteenth century. In this chapter, we consider this dispute in some detail because so many of its important details are obscured in later commemorations. The dispute originated when the English king Charles II granted the Connecticut colony a strip of land from the Narragansett Bay to "the South Sea" (the Pacific Ocean) in 1662, then granted part of the same strip (between 41 and 42 degrees latitude) to William Penn in 1681. While any territory along these latitudinal lines could have been at stake, what was fought over was principally the northern Susquehanna River Valley.[5]

The Susquehanna River descends into the Chesapeake Bay, and its northern branches stretch across resource-rich mountains.[6] Native peoples had been living there for thousands of years in settlements that prospered from the abundant river and forest resources.[7] When the Susquehannocks moved south, the region became a sanctuary for Native people fleeing conflict with Europeans, including Conoys, Nanticokes, Tutelos, Shawnees, Munsees, Tuscaroras, and Lenapes (Delawares).[8] Multinational Native settlements grew abundant crops of corn, beans, and squash in the fertile river soils.[9] The wide Wyoming Valley of the Susquehanna River, claimed by the Iroquois since 1675, was inhabited by Munsees, Delawares, Mahicans, and Nanticokes by the 1750s.[10] "Wyoming" is likely derived from the Munsee word *xwé:wamənk*, "at the big river flat."[11]

Tensions arose in the 1750s, when Connecticut colonists created the Susquehannah Company, with the express purpose of colonizing Susquehanna Valley lands.[12] Pennsylvania officials were alarmed and feared that such a move might upset the British-Iroquois alliance.[13] A congress held at Albany in 1754 was partly designed to address these concerns and to renew relationships between the British and northeastern Indians.[14] At this meeting, delegates of both Connecticut and Pennsylvania made private deals with different Iroquois representatives for Wyoming Valley lands, and the Susquehannah Company's envoy obtained title to millions of acres illegally.[15]

While the Susquehannah Company's plans were on hold during the Seven Years' War (1756–63), Iroquois leaders and Pennsylvania authorities were encouraging Indigenous people to settle in the valley.[16] Lenape leader Teedyuscung moved there from the Forks of the Delaware in 1754, and Philadelphia Quakers helped him build homes at Wyoming.[17] Teedyuscung and his allies repelled the first waves of Susquehannah Company settlers, but he was burned to death in his home in the spring of 1763 by a mysterious fire that destroyed his town and caused survivors to flee.[18] Many scholars now suggest that Connecticut settlers likely started the fire, and note that ten to twelve Connecticut families moved onto Teedyuscung's village site less than two weeks after it was destroyed.[19]

Tensions between European settlers and Indians were igniting into violence across the wider northeast. In 1763 and 1768, British colonial authorities set boundaries that European settlers were not to cross.[20] The 1768 Stanwix Treaty involved huge land cessions to Pennsylvania and New York and moved the boundary of white settlement west, with Native leaders agreeing only as long as existing Native settlements, such as Wyoming, remained the property of their inhabitants, and their hunting, travel, and trade rights were protected.[21] The treaty was interpreted by many European Americans as a green light for settlement in lands to the east of the treaty line, however, precisely where Susquehannah Company members intended to colonize, and Company immigration picked up almost immediately. Pennsylvania authorities were prepared. Arriving Connecticut immigrants encountered Governor Penn's representatives, who ordered them to leave and marched their leaders to a Northampton County jail.[22]

The next several years repeated this pattern, with Connecticut settlers moving onto Wyoming Valley lands to be expelled by Penn representatives, and vice versa, with the valley changing hands several times. When Susquehannah Company members (or "Yankees") began arriving in large groups, they drove from "their" lands people whose titles were backed by Pennsylvania law, whom they referred to as "Pennamites." There was jurisdictional chaos: surveyors representing both Governor Penn and the Susquehannah Company often operated in the same region at the same time.[23] The conflict periodically erupted into total war. Since each side recognized that occupying the land was the first step in controlling it, Pennamites and Yankees carried out vicious scorched-earth raids that destroyed each other's farmsteads and livestock.[24] The Yankee-Pennamite War had begun.

This animosity between Pennamites and Yankees is sometimes

attributed to cultural differences: many of the "Pennamites" had German or Dutch ancestry, while the Connecticut settlers were almost all of British descent (and certainly New Englanders).[25] Differences in colonial settlement policies were also key. Pennsylvania's methods of distributing land have been described as "feudal" and "routinely disliked."[26] Only the Penn family (the proprietors) could purchase land from its Indigenous inhabitants. They chose the best lands for themselves and opened up others for sale through a quit-rent system that encumbered buyers for perpetuity.[27] Speculation was rampant. Individuals bought land from the Penn family or from speculators, while others squatted, hoping to gain title that way.[28] Lands weren't put on the market regularly but disposed of "to whom, on what terms, in such quantities and locations as the proprietor or his agent thought best."[29] The practices of the Susquehannah Company contrasted greatly. As a private company of land speculators, it offered land at a flat fee. It also followed a highly centralized system that planned out whole townships before settlers even left Connecticut. Identical townships, governed through democratic procedures, were five square miles and divided into fifty-three lots, with fifty reserved for settlers, one for schools, one for the church, and one for the minister.[30]

In many ways, the split between the Connecticut Yankees and the Pennamites was a miniature version of the larger conflict between patriots and the British that culminated in the settler revolt that we call the American Revolution.[31] Pennamite settlement practices resembled practices of prior feudal social orders, while the Susquehannah Company epitomized the new American settlerism ideology as elucidated by political scientist Aziz Rana.[32] According to Yankee leaders, only people willing to commit to the Susquehannah Company–Connecticut Colony settlement vision were considered worthy participants.[33] Their planned "utopias" were culturally homogeneous and difficult for non-Yankee Europeans to join (and required Indian land). Company settlers were often interrelated or knew each other before leaving Connecticut, and they selected the best lots for themselves or their fellow New Englanders.[34]

The balance of power shifted to the Yankees in 1770, when Susquehannah Company representatives made a deal with Lazarus Stewart and the Paxton Boys. They were known vigilantes—originally from the Lancaster, Pennsylvania, area—who were wanted by the Pennsylvania colony for their brutal massacre of their peaceful Susquehannock neighbors, in Conestoga, in December 1763.[35] In exchange for their help in expelling the Pennamites, the Company offered Stewart and his fifty-person gang a six-square-mile township. Violence increased with the Paxton Boys' arrival, and by the spring of 1771, Company settlers were moving in by the hundreds.[36] By 1772 the last of the Delawares left their homes in the upriver settlement of Wyalusing.[37] Connecticut establishments multiplied so quickly that the Connecticut Assembly created the "town" of Westmoreland in 1774, a town that spanned a vast area ranging from the Delaware River to fifteen miles west of Wilkes-Barre. The assembly made it part of Litchfield County, Connecticut.[38] Westmoreland included parts of the Pennsylvania counties of Northampton and Northumberland, which were established by that colony in 1752 and 1772 (see map 4).[39]

After a failed Pennsylvania attempt to remove the Yankees, in December 1775, Congress gave the Connecticut settlers temporary jurisdiction, which led to eight years of de facto Connecticut rule.[40] Yankee harassment of Pennamites was continual at this time. Company settlement leaders wielded considerable power and could remove inhabitants' settling rights and even confiscate their property. They perceived holding land through Pennsylvania title as "unfaithfulness" punishable by expulsion.[41] As historian Anne Ousterhout observes, Company partisans were determined to prevent "any more people that they called Pennamites from moving into the area, to expel those already there, and, in general, to enforce Connecticut's laws."[42]

Impending war with Britain only intensified the conflict. A military association the Connecticut settlers created in March 1776 was designed with the Pennamites foremost in mind, not the British.[43] Westmoreland County's Committee of Inspection provided further means to harass Pennamites. It required all inhab-

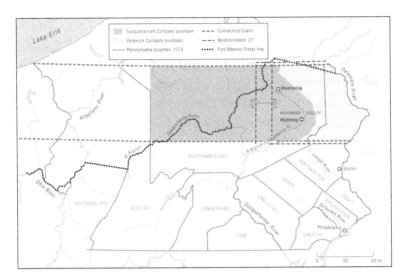

MAP 4. Competing claims: Susquehannah Company and Pennsylvania boundaries. Erin Greb Cartography.

itants to sign an oath promising to follow Connecticut colony laws; anyone who did not was considered a counterrevolutionary.[44] Over time, the Yankee-Pennamite binary became conflated with Revolutionary-era social categories, and Connecticut settlers of the Wyoming Valley began to equate "Yankee" with "Patriot," while "Pennamite," "Loyalist," and "Tory" became synonymous terms. People who held land under Pennsylvania title were censored, called "Tories," and even expelled, sometimes to less developed areas upriver.[45]

Why were so many of Pennsylvania's disaffected (or "Loyalists") from parts of the colony with border conflicts, such as the Wyoming Valley?[46] Ousterhout reasons that this was due less to their "loyalty" to the Crown than to their dissatisfaction with their treatment by their neighbors before the war.[47] In the Wyoming Valley, some disaffected Pennamites felt so harassed that they decided their only recourse was to join the British. A measure of the level of desperation they experienced is indicated by the fact that many families made the risky journey north to join British forces at Fort Niagara during the treacherous winter months of 1778.[48]

The Battle of Wyoming

The Battle of Wyoming erupted during the unfinished Yankee-Pennamite conflict.[49] This was one of the more successful attacks developed by British and Indian forces after the Battle of Oriskany. The Wyoming Valley was an obvious target for the British and their Indian allies: Lenapes (Delawares) and Iroquois had long complained about white encroachment on these lands, and the heavily fortified valley posed a real threat to the Iroquois as it was along water routes into Cayuga and Seneca territories.[50] In late June, hundreds of troops led by British colonel John Butler traveled from Fort Niagara for the assault. Attacking forces included some 464 members of nearly a half dozen Indian nations, including Senecas, Cayugas, Onondagas, Tuscarora leader Sagwarithra, and Delawares, directed by Seneca leaders Sayenqueraghta (Old Smoke) and Cornplanter. Also attacking were 110 of Butler's Rangers, mostly Loyalists, and a Loyalist detachment of the "Royal Greens," the King's Royal Regiment of New York.[51] Defending the valley were 60 Continentals of the Third Connecticut Regiment, under Lt. Col. Zebulon Butler, a Continental officer on furlough, (no relation to John Butler), and 390 members of the Twenty-Fourth Connecticut Militia, led by Col. Nathan Denison.[52]

As the British forces approached, two Wyoming Valley forts, Wintermoot and Jenkins, quickly surrendered. Colonels Zebulon Butler and Nathan Denison were in a third fort, Forty Fort, along with most of the rebel troops and many civilians seeking refuge. They refused an order of surrender, however, hoping to hold out for reinforcements. Had they remained there, the outcome would likely have been quite different. However, British leader John Butler ordered the Wintermoot and Jenkins forts burned, anticipating this would lead the rebels into thinking that British forces were departing, and lure them out of Forty Fort's safety. The plan worked, and the rebels exited the fort into an ambush. After a rebel command was misinterpreted as a call for a retreat, the militiamen fled in all directions, and mass chaos and carnage followed. Col. Zebulon Butler managed to escape. Nathan Denison met with John Butler the next day to organize a capitulation.[53]

Col. John Butler's articles of capitulation mandated the surrender of rebel troops and the dismantling of their forts and promised that civilians and their property would be protected; in return, combatants pledged future neutrality.[54] Civilians did not wait to see if the promised protections would be respected and fled the valley in all directions in what was later termed the "Great Runaway." The victors did not protect property as promised, burning over a thousand dwellings and making off with livestock. Battle casualties were extremely uneven in the end: there were over three hundred patriot losses, and three dead on the British side.[55]

From Battle to Massacre

In its immediate aftermath, the Battle of Wyoming became a tale of sacrifice and valor that was widely recounted in the colonies. Early newspapers published graphic "eye-witness" accounts that strayed wildly from British commander Butler's assertion that the only people killed were men in arms.[56] Solomon Avery, a man from Connecticut who was not at the battle, "testified" that the entire settlement was set ablaze, incinerating two thousand people, including half of the valley residents. An account published in the *New-York Journal* on July 20, 1778, reported false stories of women and children burned alive in their homes and was republished in nearly every American paper, living on "for decades in the American imagination."[57] Papers recounted horrific tales of Indian barbarism, including an incredible story of an Indian woman, "Queen Esther," who was alleged to have brained nearly a dozen prisoners on a rock. Esther Montour is a historical figure who was married to Munsee leader Eghohowin, and who established a village of Munsee Delawares near Athens, Pennsylvania, in 1772. This story of Esther's alleged actions after the Wyoming battle appears in many white settler accounts and was repeated and republished in many classic secondary sources, although recent works challenge its veracity.[58] Here, I am less interested in its factuality than its persistence in stories settler-colonists tell.

These gruesome accounts followed foundational motifs in American literature rooted in captivity narratives, and that evolved into an early American rhetorical formula that historian Peter Silver calls the "anti-Indian sublime."[59] This formula developed in the Middle Atlantic British colonies in the mid-1750s at the start of the Seven Years' War, when French-allied Indians carried out violent attacks on farmsteads, attacks designed to "induce the greatest fright possible." These acts often prompted the—probably intentional—mass "unsettling" of the countryside as settlers fled in terror.[60] Early publishers filled midcentury newspapers with accounts of these attacks in such "rich, hallucinatory detail that they could themselves become mildly traumatic to read."[61] These accounts settled into what Silver notes was a limited set of images, with scalping as the standard icon of Indian forms of warfare.[62] As Silver describes, articles repeated references to scalpings and detailed descriptions of "bashed-in skulls and cut-out tongues," fixing in readers' imaginations the idea of Indian violence as "peculiarly vicious, able to be told at a glance by its injuries."[63]

Silver argues that these accounts were engaged in the aesthetics of the sublime, an aesthetics characterized by a fascination with strong feelings, "the feeling of being awed, struck with wonder—or horror—at something outside oneself."[64] The American variant, the "anti-Indian sublime," included "an insistence on making the audience look at distinctively 'Indian' injuries such as scalpings" and, in this way, commanded the readers' sympathetic sorrow and anger.[65] This kind of writing was so effective that it quickly spread, and writers deployed it to make arguments against other populations such as Quaker politicians or the French.[66] They deployed it during the Revolutionary War, with accounts of the Wyoming battle constituting a prime example. We shouldn't underestimate the role these accounts played in the patriots' war effort, as historian Robert Parkinson demonstrates in his book *The Common Cause*.[67] As the rift grew, many colonists were unwilling to commit to either side. To confront this ambivalence, patriot political leaders used the press as a tool to destroy "as much of the public's affection for their ancestors as they could."[68] When Britain's plans to recruit Indians and African Americans in the war effort became known, patriot publicists exploited this fact and conflated these "alien" groups with the British to drive European settlers from their cause. As Parkinson explains, desperate to boost their side, patriot leaders embraced anti-Indian and anti-African prejudices, which proved "the most powerful weapons in the colonial cultural arsenal."[69] Anti-Indian savagism and prejudice, inflamed by gruesome narratives told with horrific detail, helped unite uncommitted and dissimilar immigrant families around a common fear, thus bolstering the patriot ranks.[70]

The Battle of Wyoming was not the only Revolutionary War battle with hundreds of patriot losses. According to some calculations, it was the fourteenth deadliest battle of the war, and in Pennsylvania, it was surpassed in patriot dead by the Battles of Germantown and Brandywine.[71] Certainly for relatives of the victims, the loss of life was unimaginable. We also should consider the special meaning the battle acquires when viewed within the context of the Yankee-Pennamite War, however. Most of the men killed at Wyoming in 1778 were on the patriot side, surely, but more than that, they were mostly Connecticut Yankees who had settled with or were members of the Susquehannah Company. There were few Pennamites killed because early residents with Pennsylvania titles had been expelled or harassed, fled, or moved away voluntarily, some to join the side of the British. The "Pennsylvanians" serving with the patriots, such as wanted Indian killers like Lazarus Stewart and his Paxton gang, had already demonstrated their fealty to the Yankee side.[72] Accounts of the battle are often told from a Connecticut, and not a Pennamite, vantage point, and sometimes further anti-Pennamite rhetoric by emphasizing the purported barbarity of "Tory" participants in particular.[73] Many of the "Tories" who joined John Butler's forces were, in fact, local Pennamites who had suffered losses at the hands of Yankees.[74] The fact that one of the articles of capitulation included the promise that "properties taken from the people called Tories, up the River be made good, and they to remain in peaceable possession of their farms" suggests that some of the Pennamites who joined Butler's forces did so in the hope of reclaiming lands they had lost to the Yankees.[75] Yankee-sympathizing chroniclers also criticize Pennsylvania authorities for failing to help those besieged, stating that when Zebulon Butler called for reinforcements from neighboring Northumberland County in Pennsylvania, help was not forthcoming.[76] Given the long-standing conflict Wyoming Valley Yankees had waged with Pennsylvania authorities, however, it is understandable that these same authorities would not rush to the defense of their adversaries. Another grievance of battle survivors was the fact that, in the terms of capitulation, the victors had promised to respect Yankee property, but then plundered it, burning houses and destroying crops.[77] However, plundering practices of this sort had been practically the norm in prior conflicts between Yankees and Pennamites.

Post-Wyoming: The Settler Feud Continues

The Yankee-Pennamite conflict persisted well after the Battle of Wyoming. Many Yankee settlers fled back to Connecticut, never to return, while those who stayed behind were so impoverished that they petitioned the Connecticut General Assembly for assistance in 1780.[78] Conflict with the Pennamites remained the primary concern of the Pennsylvania-based Yankees. In 1779 Pennsylvania officials submitted a complaint to the national government. Lawyers met at a national court in Trenton and determined, with the Trenton Decree of December 30, 1782, that the land was indeed under Pennsylvania jurisdiction.[79] By this time, the Susquehannah Company had developed seventeen townships that were spread out to include as much of the fertile river valleys as possible. As local historian Louise Welles Murray writes, "If Connecticut, *as a State*, acquiesced, the settlers under the Susquehanna [*sic*] Company *did not*" (emphasis in the original).[80]

The last phase of the war commenced after the 1782 Trenton Decree as Connecticut settlers aimed, at all costs, to hold onto their lands. Some settlers mobilized through written appeal, sending petition after petition to Connecticut, Pennsylvania, and Congress, and found it expedient to reiterate well-known Wyoming battle horrors in these pleas. Others chose outright violence. Backcountry residents, who became known as "Wild Yankees," mounted a twenty-year resistance movement as they fought not only other settlers but eventually the state of Pennsylvania.[81] Historian Paul Moyer outlines a litany of events: a Pennamite gang led by Henry Shoemaker entered Connecticut claimant Dorcas Stewart's home, threw her effects outside, and tore the house down; Connecticut man Waterman Baldwin allegedly accosted Pennamite William Lantarman while he was harvesting grain, and said that he would scalp him; Yankee Daniel Gore allegedly confronted Pennamite Nicodemus Travis over a wagon of oats. When Catherine Bowerlane's family fled due to "Yankee violence," her husband returned to harvest their grain, only to be killed.[82] By January 1785 an estimated six hundred Pennamites had been forced off their property by Yankees.[83]

In the final phase of the conflict, Company officials dramatically accelerated their colonization program and even began moves toward the creation of a separate state. Ethan Allen was offered land and a prominent position in the Susquehannah Company, and he was asked to recruit "hardy Vermonters" to the cause in return.[84] The Company changed its internal structure in 1785 and began to offer 300 acres free to anyone able to move there quickly, stay three years, and defend their claims.[85] New town creation accelerated dramatically. While only a few towns were created between 1786 and 1793, sixteen were formed in 1794, and a remarkable 218 new towns were established in 1795.[86]

When rumors of a separatist movement reached Pennsylvania authorities, they passed an act, in March 1787, designed to divide Yankee interests.[87] The Confirming Act recognized the tenures of people with Connecticut claims who were on these lands before the 1782 Trenton decree, but not the claims of nonresident landowners and people who arrived after 1782. This clever tack "reshaped the geography of resistance": the Wyoming Valley, where Yankees had first settled, became the domain of a more established, moderate faction hoping to work with the state, while the newer settlements, north of the Tunkhannock Creek, that were established after 1782 became the domain of the "Wild Yankees."[88] Pennsylvania also divided Northumberland County to create a new county, Luzerne County, which encompassed the area where most of the Connecticut claimants lived. As Moyer notes, "Yankee hardliners opposed the move, fearing that it would bring state authority closer to their doorsteps."[89] "Wild Yankee" leader John Franklin attempted to disrupt the formation of the Luzerne County militia in 1787 with a group of armed followers. When he was arrested for treason and brought to jail, his followers kidnapped Luzerne County clerk Timothy Pickering from his Wilkes-Barre home, in June 1788, and held him hostage for a month in an unsuccessful attempt to force Pennsylvania authorities to free Franklin.[90]

The dispute dragged on until the early 1800s.[91] The state of Pennsylvania passed a series of acts that were aggressive and conciliatory in turn, while Connecticut families turned to the Pennsylvania political system to secure power by electing pro-Yankee leaders. They filled juries in the county courts with Yankee partisans, which led to the dismissal of cases against Yankee insurgents. Even "Wild Yankee" John Franklin of the Pickering kidnapping fame was elected sheriff of Luzerne County after being released from jail.[92]

Yankee settlers living in Susquehannah Company–sponsored towns prospered through trade in agricultural products and lumber. By the early nineteenth century, the "Yankee notable" had emerged, elites with special prestige granted to men who had extensive kin networks and were Yankee settlements' founding fathers, or "pioneers."[93] The center of Yankee Pennsylvania remained the Wyoming Valley, with the city of Wilkes-Barre the community's heart and soul. Yankee descendants soon inscribed their version of the past in public memorials and local histories.[94]

Commemorating Wyoming

The Wyoming Valley experienced dramatic economic growth in the nineteenth century. Fueled by the discovery of great seams of anthracite coal, Yankee notables and their descendants began turning their lush farms into industrial staging grounds and shifting trade from agricultural products to coal. Wilkes-Barre became a thriving center of industry, extraction, and banking, and the home of a new "anthracite aristocracy," with the Connecticut Yankee families its founding members.[95] Rapid industrialization required labor, and the city and its surrounding communities expanded dramatically as immigrants from England, Wales, Ireland, and later Italy and Eastern Europe settled in the city and patch towns surrounding the mines.[96]

Although Pennsylvania's Yankees eventually accepted Pennsylvania jurisdiction, they did not forget the Battle of Wyoming. From 1779 on, the battle played a key role in local social life and in consolidating and maintaining a Yankee identity amid so much social change. The mass grave was a site of solemn annual recognition, and news articles as early as 1809 appealed to locals to raise money for a marker.[97] Speeches given at the battle's fifty-fourth anniversary, in 1832, provide a window into how local understandings of the battle had evolved. Speakers minimized links to the Revolutionary War and instead emphasized local heroism in the face of alleged Indian savagery. As Rev. James May explained, "The battle fought in this valley on the 3rd of July, 1778, was *not* one of great political moment in the controversy then pending between the United States and Great Britain." Instead, he continued, "It was the struggle of *fathers, and husbands, and brothers,* for the protection of their property and of their families, and for their own lives, against *savages* who were descending upon their homes, coveting the price of scalps and thirsting for plunder (emphasis added)."[98] This conflict became known locally as "the Indian battle."[99] May so downplayed the intrasettler struggle that, in his rendition, Pennamites and even the British vanished from the story. What mattered in this telling was the fact that so many of the dead were *scalped*.

Rev. Nicholas Murray spoke next, calling on his fellow citizens to help raise funds for a monument "over the bones of the patriots murdered at the battle of Wyoming."[100] His speech was dramatic: Why should they contribute to this fund? "Let this scalped skull answer," he exclaimed, holding up a skull exhumed at the site. It was the message found on the marks on the deceased men's bones that communicated most loudly. Although bodily mutilation was an early English practice in North America, scalping had become the symbol of Indian barbarism in the nineteenth-century American mind, a barbarism that brought into relief the contrasting "civilized" humanity of the victims' descendants gathered that day.[101]

Monument construction, begun in the 1830s, was completed in 1862, when a Ladies' Wyoming Monumental Association took over the job.[102] They developed a 62-foot obelisk, reflecting the Egyptian revival vogue for memorials to the Revolutionary War (see figure 8).[103] When the commemorative exercises for a centennial celebration were placed in the hands of a committee of seventeen men, they developed a commemorative form that persists into the present day.

A Centennial Affair

The Battle of Wyoming's hundredth anniversary, in July 1878, put the story of the battle into the national spotlight. As in other communities across the country, patriotic fervor surrounding the centennial of the nation's beginnings was partly fueled by a desire for national unity after the Civil War.[104] Along with throngs of other people, U.S. president Rutherford B. Hayes, several members of his cabinet, and several governors attended.[105] The centennial celebration blended public with private historical tradition and national with local concerns. It was also this year that the "massacre" moniker became part of the event's official label. The centennial ceremonies were developed and designed by a close-knit group of "massacre" victim descendants who fostered a decidedly pro-Yankee vantage point. These men first met at the ninety-ninth anniversary to start their planning. With Judge Steuben Jenkins at the helm, they decided to form a committee of seventeen, "all lineal descendants of the participators [sic] in that disastrous massacre," offering in the *Scranton Daily Times* details about each man to provide their credentials.[106] Steuben Jenkins, for instance, was a descendant of John Jenkins Jr., Susquehannah Company surveyor and one-time "Wild Yankee." Why seventeen members? To commemorate the Susquehannah Company's original seventeen townships.[107]

Jenkins's committee placed a Yankee reading of the event onto the national stage. The emphasis on the number seventeen, which was sacred in Susquehannah Company lore, was such that when they decided to add a "committee of ladies" to work with the decoration committee, they asked the chair to add exactly seventeen women.[108] This focus on symbolic names and numbers connected to the region's Yankee heritage is evident in other local naming

FIG. 8. Wyoming Monument, Wyoming PA. Image courtesy of Luzerne County
Historical Society Archives.

practices. "Forty Fort" was named after the first forty Susquehan-nah Company settlers; local towns, creeks, and streets bear the surnames of founding Susquehannah Company men; and the Westmoreland Club, an exclusive private club in downtown Wilkes-Barre, was named after the old Connecticut town and county.

One of the first decisions the committee of seventeen made was regarding the naming of the event. Although one of Sulli-van's soldiers had derided it as "the Battle of the Two Butlers" in his journal, locals invariably referred to it as a massacre or as the "Indian battle," as we have seen.[109] The committee of seventeen voted to add the words "and massacre" to its official title. Commit-tee members noted "it is true that there was a battle," but added that after the battle, "there was a terrible massacre of the unre-sisting prisoners, of whom none escaped that day of blood upon the plain. All perished who fell into the hands of the blood thirsty savages on the evening of that fatal day. It was not only a nobly fought battle, but the night of that terrible day witnessed such horrid scenes of rapine and murder and outrage upon the con-quered, that the story of our wrong was heard around the world."[110]

"Bloodthirsty savages." "Horrid scenes of rapine and murder." In these discussions, committee members emphasized the actions of the *Indian* (but not the *British*) foe, as had May several decades earlier, in language reminiscent of the "anti-Indian sublime." When put to the vote, it was unanimous: it will "now be '100th anniversary of the battle and massacre of Wyoming.'"[111]

The two-day centennial event was enormous, with an estimated sixty thousand people in attendance.[112] The day was sweltering and the crowds "immense," with trains "pouring their thousands from north and south with astounding rapidity," and Wyoming village and its vicinity "one living mass of hurrying and perspir-ing humanity."[113] The *Daily Times* reported that the "sun poured down his hottest rays from an early hour. Blinding clouds of dust on all the approaches to the grounds filled eyes, ears and mouths, while every hour added to the immense throng that gathered at the Lexington tent."[114] The heat was so extreme and "the crowd so utterly unmanageable" that they cut the original program by a third. The crowd perked up with the arrival of "eighteen Onondaga Indians in full war paint and feathers," described in the local press as "being the direct descendants of the redskins who perpetrated the massacre."[115] Speeches emphasized the sacrifice of the patriot victims and the brutality of their victors. Key positions in the program were given to people descended from men killed at the battle, and many speeches and poems described the violence in grotesque detail.[116] Even the opening prayer, given by Rev. D. J. Waller, "a descendant of a family that suffered severely in the massacre," was grisly. He proclaimed, "Help us, O Lord today as the revolving year and rounded century recall the scenes of carnage and sounds of wailing."[117]

President Hayes's speech was brief. He pointed out that similar centennial ceremonies were being carried out across the country, adding that "the celebration of to-day is peculiar. It is not the celebration of great military achievements or wonderful statesmanship."[118] The president summed up the battle much in the same way May had done decades before: "It is a pioneer celebration, in honor of the men and women who settled this valley, reclaimed the wilderness and made it fitted for civilization."[119] He discussed how "almost every part of the United States has its similar celebration in honor of the pioneers." He concluded with what may have seemed a startling aside to local residents used to viewing "Indian wars" as located in a distant past when he "paid an eloquent tribute en passant to the gallant Custer, and said in case war with the Indians could not well be avoided it should be short, sharp and decisive." He ended his speech by "recommending that the Indian be dealt with fairly as a neighbor, and at the same time that the military forces be kept on a good war footing."[120] Clearly ongoing wars in the West were on his mind that day.

Homes in town were elegantly decorated, and families displayed their connections to early valley history in creative ways that often highlighted conflicts with Indians. One man displayed a portrait of his relation, Frances Slocum, a famous white captive, while another displayed the painting "The Last Scalp," depicting the killing of his ancestor, Lt. John Jameson, on August 8, 1782, "he being the last man killed in Wyoming by the Indians."[121]

Two days after the centennial festivities, the executive committee decided to keep the Wyoming Centennial Association, composed of Connecticut Yankee battle victim descendants, as a permanent organization. This organization was later renamed the Wyoming Commemorative Association (WCA), and it helps direct the annual event to this day.[122]

Removing Context, Removing Complicity

Savagism has played a long-standing role in settler disavowal of the violence of settler colonialism.[123] What is the specific work achieved by the savage trope in narrations of the Wyoming battle, and how does this work relate to local understandings of the Sullivan Expedition? Eighteenth-century accounts of Indian savagery and Indian-style warfare, presented in exceptionally graphic language, were remarkably successful in garnering readers' sympathy; what can be overlooked is just how much these accounts helped to erase. In his study of conspiracies of silence, cognitive sociologist Eviatar Zerubavel has shown how changing the subject can be an effective social silencing strategy, writing "almost paradoxically, a silence is often covered up with sound."[124] The anti-Indian sublime was "noise" that successfully blocked out other possible interpretations of the past. Forcing the focus so intently on a graphic, horror-filled foreground ensured that the background, with all its complexities, remained unseen. The anti-Indian sublime removed context, as Silver observes: "Long chains of cause and effect had led to the scenes that provincial writers kept describing. But with one sight—a mutilated corpse—forever swimming into view, the back stories faded. The high emotion of this kind of writing was, on its own terms, unanswerable."[125] With readers' attention focused on peoples' suffering, the same sufferers' *prior* acts became irrelevant.

The Wyoming battle was further memorialized in poetry, literature, and artwork and inspired the naming of the U.S. territory (and state) of Wyoming.[126] In these renditions of the battle, the marks of the tomahawk, the scalping of the dead, visions of burning children and gruesome tortures are conjured up again and again, epitomized by the image of "Queen Esther" dashing men's heads with a rock in a maniacal frenzy.[127] The wider context, which includes painstaking Iroquois-British alliances, treaties promising to retain the Wyoming Valley for Iroquois and their allies, and decades of intracolonist warfare, is overshadowed if not completely erased. Not only does the Yankee-Pennamite conflict drop out of the typical narrative, but so too do clear links with the Revolutionary War. In 1832 commemorators heard that the battle was "not one of great political moment in the controversy then pending between the United States and Great Britain," but instead was known locally as the "Indian battle." In 1878 the president of the United States explained that the battle was "not the celebration of great military achievements," and instead described it as a "pioneer celebration." In each case, both the intrasettler war and the battle's relationship to the Revolutionary War are minimized and the many-sided struggle is distorted into a simple binary between brave pioneers and marauding Indians. Pennamites, if they appear at all, are dehumanized as faceless Tories. In the process, the figure of the Connecticut Yankee shifts from early aggressor toward other settlers (and perhaps murderers of Teedyuscung, burned alive in his sleep) to exalted and martyred victim. Not only that, in clearing the story of their conflict with Pennamites, Connecticut Yankees discursively secure the place of "firstness" for themselves.

Graphic renditions of savagism helped erase sociocultural difference. Certainly depicting diverse Indigenous communities as a monolithic "savage" bloc is an important step in their racialization. What is sometimes overlooked is how the same trope has also facilitated the erasure of intrasettler distinctions, a significant move needed to develop a unified American settler identity that transcended distinct ethnic or other groups. Historian James Paxton finds a similar practice in local histories describing Mohawk Valley wartime violence. He points out that ethnic and racial diversity in this region was greatly reduced after the war, with the departure of Loyalists and Mohawks, and asserts that the Othering of former Native neighbors "became a necessary stage in healing internal divisions and redrawing community boundaries after the Revolutionary War," boundaries redrawn along racial lines.[128] Accounts of wartime violence helped solidify a settler-Indian binary in the postwar era in a regional setting that had been more culturally heterogeneous before the war, and helped consolidate a white American settler political identity. Similarly, in their analysis of the use of the Jane McCrea murder story, Jeremy Engels and Greg Goodale argue that "learning to desire revenge against the nation's enemies was one of the ways that people in the U.S. came to see themselves as Americans."[129]

The ideology of savagism has served different functions for Euro-Americans since the fifteenth century. As historian Jean O'Brien points out, representation of Indians as "premodern" served New Englanders in their attempts to relegate Native populations to the deep past and present themselves as the "first" people worthy of note.[130] In the case of Wyoming narrations, that brutal savages murdered women and children is about the one "true" thing residents know, even though that is not what happened. Emphasizing Yankee suffering may have allowed participants to deflect attention from their ancestors' actions when they forcibly established themselves in the valley and helped turn men that Pennsylvania authorities had considered dangerous renegades into heroes of the new settlerism ideology and of the new nation this ideology helped create. Focusing on savagism allowed Yankee tellers to downplay their cessionist past and prove their belonging to their new state through their martyrdom. In contrast to the New Englanders O'Brien studied, whose replacement narratives developed a "noble"—yet vanishing—Indian, in the Wyoming replacement narrative, there is no romantic nostalgia for the Indigene, but rather a celebration of their departure.

Finally, "savagist" tellings of the Battle of Wyoming set up the Sullivan Expedition as inevitable revenge. In northeastern Pennsylvania, Wyoming and Sullivan are understood as two halves of one drama, linked as cause and effect, with the Sullivan Expedition understood as a justifiable or even necessary response to barbaric horrors. The George Taylor chapter in Easton, Pennsylvania, perpetuated this vision in its marker to the Sullivan Expedition, which positioned the mission as just retribution for Wyoming. We find this framing, complete with the savage trope and valorization of Yankee forebearers, in the markers to the Sullivan Expedition that were established by women like Mrs. March in late nineteenth-century Pennsylvania, the subject of the next chapter.

TWO

Patriotic Women Celebrate Sullivan

A few years before the women of the George Taylor chapter of the DAR presented their Sullivan marker to the city of Easton, Mrs. Martha Bennett Phelps dedicated a Sullivan memorial in the mountains overlooking the Wyoming Valley. On Saturday, September 12, 1896, hundreds of people boarded a train in downtown Wilkes-Barre as her guests. Mrs. Phelps originally intended for the exercises to take place at the site of her new monument, but a sudden downpour caused a last-minute change in plans, and the group congregated at Wyndcliffe, her summer "cottage" at the mountain summit. The Wyndcliffe mansion was decorated for the festive affair. "The mantels, doorways and windows were beautiful with a profusion of bright colored autumn leaves," reported the *Wilkes-Barre Semi-Weekly Record*. Guests enjoyed ice cream in the shape of soldiers while taking in the dramatic view. The journalist noted that Wyndcliffe's "generous interior" and "spacious porches" were large enough to accommodate the entire gathering, who enjoyed "glimpses of the Wyoming Valley through the shifting clouds."[1] A band stationed at the porch led the group in singing patriotic songs; the main event after the marker dedication was an address prepared by Mrs. Phelps.

Martha Phelps established this marker with her own funds and placed it in the care of the Wyoming Valley Chapter of DAR, an organization she joined a few years later and in which her daughter, Anna Phelps, was a charter member. This stone memorial as well as the Pennsylvania markers developed in 1898, 1900, 1902, 1908, and 1914 were all the products of women operating alone or organized into hereditary social clubs, either chapters of the DAR or the Colonial Dames. These women's clubs and their public history projects emerged in a rapidly industrializing region of Pennsylvania with an economy that by then revolved around the exploitation of anthracite coal. Dueling headlines on page one of the *Wilkes-Barre News* on October 13, 1900, capture this context. On the right: "A Monument Dedicated. Marks the Site of Jenkins Fort, a Revolutionary Defense," an article relating the neighboring Dial Rock DAR chapter's commemoration of a fort that featured in the Battle of Wyoming (1778). On the left, in larger lettering, reads: "The Miners' Strike Far From Settlement. The Scranton Convention Likely to Reject the Offer of the Operators. Delegates Nearly All Opposed to It." Coal from the Scranton–Wilkes-Barre region was enriching the capitalist classes while cities like Wilkes-Barre and the surrounding patch towns were burgeoning with immigrants and alive with labor disputes. It is at this moment that elite white women were taking part in historical preservation activities and commemorating episodes of the distant Revolutionary War.

This conjuncture of rapid social change unleashed by industrialization and the emergence of patriotic societies is worth further comment. The women taking part in these public memory projects were among the new elite of the Gilded Age. Mrs. Phelps's involvement indicates her comfortable economic standing and connection to wider national trends. The story here is further complicated by the local emphasis on the Battle of Wyoming, however. Sullivan commemorative activities in this part of the country often read the expedition as a necessary consequence of the bloodshed at Wyoming the year before. Many of the memory entrepreneurs organizing the events were dedicated members of a Yankee faction, moreover, and their public history projects served as reminders of the special antiquity of their ancestors' immigration to the region.

Patriotic Women and the National Past

In the aftermath of the Civil War, ceremonies honoring Civil War dead and organizations uniting veterans increased dramatically along with public expressions of patriotic sentiment.[2] Centennial celebrations—like that of the Wyoming battle, discussed in the previous chapter—furthered interest in the Revolutionary War.[3] Patriotic clubs proliferated dramatically at this time, and women's societies were an important component. Many of these clubs were hereditary societies open to people of the "requisite pedigree."[4] While it was in the interest of the contemporaneous veterans' organizations to be as inclusive as possible in order to secure the greatest political influence for their members, hereditary societies followed the opposite tack. As historian Wallace Evan Davies observed, they had "no desire to attract hordes of people, for that would render impossible any pretensions to the exclusiveness which was often their strongest appeal."[5]

Foremost among women's hereditary patriotic clubs were the National Society of the Colonial Dames of America and DAR, organizations that both had their start in 1890. Women could apply to join the DAR if they could demonstrate direct lineal descent from a soldier, sailor, or other individual who assisted the patriot cause during the Revolutionary War.[6] The Colonial Dames was a more exclusive organization. Colonial Dames members were required to show proof of descent from an ancestor who arrived in an American colony before 1750; membership was offered by invitation only.[7] DAR members often viewed the Dames as "too snobbish and far less constructive," although some women joined both organizations.[8] The DAR grew quickly to thirty thousand members by 1900, and is currently the largest hereditary patriotic organization in the country.[9]

Women's patriotic organizations became dominant actors in educating the populace in patriotic practices such as singing the new national anthem or pledging allegiance to the flag (with a brand-new verse penned in 1892).[10] They also became involved in historic preservation.[11] Local press coverage indicates the novelty of these activities. When Easton's George Taylor DAR chapter dedicated its Sullivan marker in 1900, DAR members were accompanied by a male contingent that included members of the Grand Army of the Republic, Sons of Veterans, Sons of the American Revolution, the City Guard, and Easton Cadets, and Dr. E.

D. Warfield, the president of Lafayette College.[12] The mayor of Easton emphasized not the historical event being recognized that day, but the fact that women had organized it. He proclaimed that it was one of the "most pleasant" civic engagements that he had been called upon to participate in, "because it was the work of the women of Easton, of whom we all as citizens are justly proud." He seemed particularly impressed by the fact that the George Taylor chapter had "no male advisory board connected with it," and that the "great work was done by women alone."[13]

At a time when women did not yet enjoy the right to vote and had limited political and professional options, some elite white women were becoming involved in shaping national culture by joining voluntary organizations and carrying out public history projects. Members of the DAR and the Colonial Dames were especially avid memory entrepreneurs, who viewed the national past and Revolutionary War as sources of "moral uplift, social cohesion, and national unity."[14] They lobbied state and federal governments for funds to preserve buildings and develop archives, and erected thousands of monuments and plaques across the country.[15] These amateur groups were often working in a vacuum. From the 1870s until World War I, the federal government refused to participate in historic preservation[16] Middle- and upper-class white Anglo-American women filled the void, as historian Francesca Morgan observes, sometimes standing "between many historical artifacts and oblivion."[17] Both the Colonial Dames and the DAR engaged in national heritage preservation during their earliest years. The DAR established monuments to leading national figures such as Martha Washington, marked graves of Revolutionary War soldiers, labeled historic sites, and preserved landmarks.[18] They also promoted the study of American history by offering essay contests at schools, sponsoring lectures, and urging the establishment of positions in American history at colleges.[19] An early mission of the National Society of the Colonial Dames of America was to preserve the history of the thirteen colonies and "teach the lessons of patriotism to the citizens of the future."[20] Accordingly, the organization published colonial-era manuscripts and recorded and preserved colonial structures. Women played prominent roles in these activities until the

1930s, when state and federal agencies began to take over these tasks (and placed trained professionals, usually men, in charge).[21]

These patriotic organizations carried out their historic preservation activities with a real sense of urgency. The unprecedented social and economic change fostered by capitalist expansion—increased immigration, rapid urbanization, social inequality, and dramatic population growth—challenged the local and national social and physical fabric.[22] Scholars often attribute the development of hereditary organizations attracting a mostly wealthy, white, "old stock" Anglo-American membership at a time of rapid immigration to related status anxieties of the upper classes.[23] The women who joined the DAR were overwhelmingly white, middle and upper class, and Anglo-Saxon, although some Roman Catholics and small numbers of Jews joined before World War II.[24] They were educated beyond high school, married later than the norm, and had fewer children than the national average.[25] In the first decades of the organization, members' political orientations were more diverse than we might imagine, however, and ranged from "progressive to centrist to apathetic to reactionary."[26]

The women of northeastern Pennsylvania who developed Sullivan markers in the late nineteenth and early twentieth centuries were aligned with these national trends. Whether in urbanizing industrial cities, such as Wilkes-Barre, Easton, and Athens/Sayre, or in the more rural Susquehanna Valley towns of Wyalusing or Towanda (see map 1), DAR members were among the wealthiest women in their communities, often interrelated and from early Connecticut families, and married to prominent entrepreneurs and lawyers. Local DAR chapters engaged in Americanization projects, such as offering prizes to children of foreigners for "proficiency in American institutions" to "combat anarchism."[27] Rather than merely reflecting status anxiety or asserting Anglo-supremacy, however, these organizations may have been engaging in intra-"Anglo" rivalry as well, as women of means used their personal pedigrees and private clubs to elevate some white families, Connecticut Yankee ones in particular, over others. We start our discussion with the Sullivan markers established in the mountains of Wilkes-Barre, including Martha Phelps's marker. By the late nineteenth century,

Wilkes-Barre was one of the wealthiest cities in the country, and Wilkes-Barre women were at the vanguard of the vanguard.

Wilkes-Barre Discovers Sullivan

Twenty years after the massive centennial for the Battle of Wyoming, Wilkes-Barre women established the first DAR chapter in the state of Pennsylvania, a mere six months after the formation of the national organization.[28] Founding regent Katherine Searle McCartney was a descendant of several Connecticut families, including the famed "Wild Yankee" John Jenkins Jr., who served in the Sullivan Campaign as a scout and the Susquehannah Company as land surveyor; and Constant Searle Sr., a Connecticut man who lost his life at the Battle of Wyoming.[29] Her husband was a leading member of the Luzerne County Bar.[30] Soon after forming the chapter, McCartney sought historic sites to preserve, posting a query in the *Wilkes-Barre Record* soliciting "any information they may have of points and matters of local history, and thus aid us in the work for which our society was formed, namely 'the preservation of local history, the marking of historic spots'."[31] Early chapter activities centered on the Wyoming battle. In 1892, a chapter member presented a paper at the first Continental Congress of the National DAR Society, titled "The Wyoming Massacre," and Regent McCartney gave an address at the Wyoming Commemoration on July 3, 1895, in which she read an essay, written by a Connecticut DAR member, about the ordeals of Yankee Katharine Gaylord, who fled with her children after her husband was killed at Wyoming.[32] The chapter's first local public monument recognized Wyoming as well. It featured the notorious "Queen Esther," the Native woman attributed with bludgeoning rebel soldiers on a rock in the immediate aftermath of the Battle of Wyoming (see chapter 1). "Queen Esther's Rock," or the "Bloody Rock," as it was sometimes known, was so famous that by the end of the nineteenth century, it was being chipped down to nothing by relic hunters. The DAR stepped in to save it. It purchased the plot of land surrounding the rock and prepared a cage to preserve it for perpetuity (see figure 9), commissioning a tablet stating the following:[33]

"Queen Esther's Rock" near the battlefield of Wyoming. The fence and grating surrounding and covering it were erected by Wyoming Valley Chapter, D. A. R. in 1895.

FIG. 9. Cage protecting Queen Esther's Rock. RG 13. 112, Records of the Pennsylvania Historical and Museum Commission, courtesy of Pennsylvania State Archives, Harrisburg PA.

Upon This Rock,
The Indian Queen Esther
Slaughtered the brave patriots
Taken in the Battle of July 3d, 1778.
Presented by the Wyoming Valley Chapter
of the
Daughters of the American Revolution
1895.[34]

The Wyoming Valley chapter continues to maintain the site to this day, where it holds an annual ceremony coinciding with the Wyoming battle commemoration. The marker conjures up the graphic settler legend of Indian savagery exemplified by the anti-Indian sublime, and contemporary dedication exercises repeat this rhetorical strategy when DAR representatives read statements written in this style by early Yankee war heroes.[35]

Martha Phelps's Marker

Martha Phelps unveiled her marker to Sullivan's men in the mountains overlooking the Wyoming Valley a year after the Queen Esther marker dedication (see figure 10). Martha's marker, described as a column of "mountain red stone" as "high as a man's head," bore a decidedly gruesome text that again engaged in savagism:

> Near this spot April 23, 1779, Captain Davis, Lieutenant Jones, Corporal Butler, and two privates belonging to the advance guard of the expedition under Major General John Sullivan, were scalped, tomahawked and speared by the Indians. Their bodies were buried here. Those of the two officers were re-interred and buried in Wilkes-Barre, July 29, 1779. 1779–1896

Why recognize these men here, now? The bodies of Captain Davis and Lieutenant Jones were long gone. Hastily buried where they died in April 1779, their remains were exhumed in July 1779 by Sullivan's men, who carried them down to the Wyoming Valley and reburied them, with Masonic rites, in a burial ground near the Wilkes-Barre fort.[36] They were removed yet again to the Hollenback burial ground in 1867, in response to the city's rapid growth, where their remains lay when Phelps established her marker in the mountains above.[37] While we never learned why Phelps believed the men were killed in the vicinity of her marker, we do know that the marker location was on the road to her grand summer home.

Martha Bennett Phelps was a descendant of the Slocums, a Quaker family from Rhode Island that moved to the Wyoming Valley in 1777.[38] Her father, Ziba Bennett, became phenomenally wealthy in coal, railroad, and financial interests, and the family was so well positioned that they hosted President Hayes when he came to the Wyoming centennial commemoration in 1878.[39] Like other women of her status, she attended private school (in Flushing, New York), where she met her future husband, John Case Phelps, a man of Connecticut ancestry and Yale graduate who by

Monument erected by Mrs. John Case Phelps at Laurel
Run, Luzerne county, Pennsylvania, September 12, 1896.

FIG. 10. Martha Phelps's 1896 Laurel Run Memorial. RG 13. 112, Records of the
Pennsylvania Historical and Museum Commission, courtesy of Pennsylvania
State Archives, Harrisburg PA.

then was a prominent New York merchant.[40] When they moved to Wilkes-Barre, he became involved in managing railroads and part owner of his father-in-law's bank.[41] The family lived in the exclusive Wilkes-Barre riverside neighborhood and appeared regularly in society pages. After raising four children, Martha became actively involved in local philanthropy. By the time of the marker unveiling, she was a widow (John Phelps died in 1892), four of her five children were married, and they all attended the dedication with their families.[42]

Following the standard invocations and patriotic singing, Martha's son Francis read her speech. The bulk of her address was composed of lengthy excerpts from journal entries of Sullivan's soldiers, describing their travels through the region as they descended into the Wyoming Valley, including excerpts she claimed were from Lt. John Jenkins Jr.:

> The troops prepared themselves for Wyoming, from which we were now distant only seven miles. This day we marched with regularity, and at a distance of three miles came to the place where Capt. Davis and Lieut. Jones, with a corporal and four privates, were *scalped, tomahawked and speared by the savages,* fifteen or twenty in number; two boards are fixed at the spot where Davis and Jones fell, with their names on each, Jones's being besmeared with his own blood. In passing this melancholy vale an universal gloom appeared on the countenances of both officers and men without distinctions, and from the eyes of many, as by a sudden impulse, dropped the sympathizing tear (emphasis added).

Jenkins's journal entry was the source of the phrase inscribed on Martha's marker: *scalped, tomahawked, and speared by the savages.* These terms would reappear, in varying arrangements, throughout her speech and can be seen as the ceremony's recurring motif.

Martha turned from the Sullivan Expedition to a discussion of the Wyoming battle, continuing to cite from Jenkins's journal, including passages about the notorious Queen Esther, announcing, "At the battle before spoken of about 220 men were massacred within the space of an hour and a half, more than a hundred of whom were married men; their widows, afterward, had all their property taken from them, and several of them with their children were made prisoners. It is said Queen Esther of the Six Nations, who was with the enemy, *scalped and tomahawked with her own hands, in cold blood,* eight or ten persons."[43] Martha couldn't resist including a statement about the alleged barbarism of Indian women in particular, again citing Jenkins, who reported, "The Indian women in general, were guilty of the greatest barbarities. Since this dreadful stroke they have visited the settlement several times, each time killing, or rather torturing to death."

At the start of her speech, Phelps preempted questions by suggesting that guests might wonder if she had indeed found the burial site: "Perhaps some of you will ask—are you sure any bones of Revolutionary soldiers lie near this place. Is this the spring near the Laurel Run where the savages waited in ambush near the gallant little band?"[44] She responded, "In order to prove our right to erect the memorial on this spot we must bring the testimony of many witnesses." In the discourse that followed, none of the "witnesses" she cited offered more than a vague understanding that the men were killed somewhere near the extensive Laurel Run watershed. They could have met their demise anywhere in a vast region.

Martha also wove into her narrative the story of her great-aunt, the famed Frances Slocum, the girl "stolen four months after the battle of Wyoming" who was discovered by her brother in the 1860s but refused to leave her Indian family.[45] She made a point of reporting how the Slocums were members of the Society of Friends, and for that reason had been "unmolested" by Indians during their early years in the valley, until the fateful day of July 3, 1778, when one of Frances's brothers decided to join the rebels. This act, she suggests, made the family a "shining mark for Indian vengeance." Frances, age six and a half, was abducted and, soon after, her father Jonathan and grandfather (Isaac Tripp) were *"speared, tomahawked and scalped by the savages,"* she explained.[46] This aside positioned her family as a Wyoming battle participant (through Jonathan), and later victims of similar foes.

Speared, tomahawked, scalped. Scalped, tomahawked, speared. Martha's speech continuously repeated these terms. One wonders how she knew these facts (and how a person could be scalped before being speared!).The point seemed not to be the accuracy of descriptions, but to transmit emotionally charged descriptors of a specific form of warfare attributed to "Indians." Throughout her discourse, the Indians were presented as "savages," and their foes were "massacred" or described as "gallant," terms that helped Phelps construct the "civilization-barbarism" binary so pervasive at that time.

Martha also name-dropped the famed Yankee historian Charles Miner, "whom I remember well as an honored guest at my father's house, where he was almost sure to come in June" bringing his blind daughter, who brought roses for her mother, calling them the "Lady Bennett." These digressions seemed motivated to provide "good" Wyoming Valley Yankee credentials despite her possibly discrediting outsider status and connection to pacifist Rhode Island Quakers.[47] She also seemed motivated to elevate her family members by asking each of her sons to play an official role in the afternoon's events.[48]

The Colonial Dames' Response

Wilkes-Barre also hosted a chapter of the Colonial Dames. The development in the same city of both DAR and Colonial Dames chapters sometimes led to gentle mockery in the press. In 1894 the *Wilkes-Barre Semi-Weekly Record* announced, there is "no antagonism between them," they are just managed "on different lines," explaining, "The Dames try to keep their ranks very exclusive, while the Daughters eagerly welcome any woman with a just claim to membership."[49]

Competition between these organizations may have motivated the establishment of the second local Sullivan marker. Only two years after Phelps's Laurel Run dedication, the Wilkes-Barre branch of Colonial Dames hosted a celebration quite similar to Martha's in location, structure, and framing. This ceremony was also held in the mountains overlooking the valley, and also held in the early fall, in Bear Creek Township at the grand home of lumber and ice magnate Albert Lewis.[50] The focus again was on Sullivan's journey; this time, the women chose to mark the site of a bridge over Bear Creek allegedly built by Sullivan's troops. The text read, "This stone marks the site of a bridge built by Sullivan's Army on its march against the Six Nations in 1779. It was presented by Mr. Albert Lewis to the Wilkes-Barre Branch of the Colonial Dames, and by them inscribed—1898."[51]

The Colonial Dames had to involve Mr. Lewis in their festivities because he owned all the land in the vicinity and they needed his permission to erect their marker on his property. It is likely that Albert Lewis was also an attraction as he was one of the wealthiest men around. He started his career as a railroad clerk living at a company boarding house in Carbon County, but soon became a favorite employee of Asa Packer, millionaire owner of the Lehigh Valley Railroad.[52] After crushing a finger in 1865, Lewis left train conducting and began trading in lumber. By the late 1870s, he owned vast tracts of upper Lehigh River timberlands.[53] He purchased the Bear Creek lands in 1883, and by the mid-1880s, he owned almost all the property in the township.[54]

At this time, the mountains surrounding the Wyoming Valley were being developed into summer resorts for families who had made their fortunes in mining and banking. Bear Creek was one of the most exclusive of such communities due to Lewis's careful direction.[55] After damming the creek to form a lake, he created the village and maintained control over how many house sites were sold. He ensured that it would remain a dry community by purchasing and then closing all nearby establishments that sold liquor.[56] After his first wife died of tuberculosis, he remarried and extravagantly outfitted his surroundings.[57] By the time of the marker dedication, he had built not only a massive Tudor-style mansion, the Mokawa Inn, but also a boathouse and bowling alley, and he had established a Lehigh Valley Railroad station in the village center.[58] He treated the entire Colonial Dames gathering to a meal at his home, which was decorated with "autumn foliage and ferns and wild flowers."[59]

The Colonial Dames dedication offered club members a way to demonstrate their historical research skills, clearly an important form of cultural capital for women in this social realm. The dedication speech included an extensive recounting of the Indian war elements of the Sullivan Expedition. Like Phelps, the Dames offered no definitive proof that Sullivan's troops had built the bridge in question. As Miss James explained, "It is true that nothing appears in all the journals of the Sullivan march identifying this bridge . . . [for] the last bridge mentioned being the Brandy bridge thirty-seven miles from Wyoming." But it was possibly built by Sullivan's men, for they had built bridges at other locations: "We see by the diaries that bridges were frequently necessary for the passage of artillery, and they would naturally have been such as this, of huge trees felled and placed as stringers, crossed by other great trees which grew about so thickly about them."[60]

Social Climbing with Public History

Scholars of women's nineteenth-century engagement in public history-making activities often stress the desire of wealthy women to instruct the masses into a proper reading of American history through their patriotic ceremonies. Such an educational function seems almost entirely lacking in these mountaintop tributes to Sullivan, which were held so far from the city center. If their primary mission had been a pedagogical one, surely the women would have carried out their programs in full view of more people. The choice of the mountains for a Sullivan marker is all the more surprising since it was in the Wyoming Valley, not the mountains, where Sullivan and his men spent most of their time. Moreover, any trace of their travels through the wooded mountains had likely been obliterated long before by local lumbering operations; Lewis had so clear-cut the trees on his lands that he was shifting his entrepreneurial energies to ice manufacturing.[61] Instead, the two mountaintop Sullivan marker dedications appear to be as much about social positioning as public history outreach. The late–nineteenth century Wilkes-Barre "anthracite aristocracy" was a close-knit group of interrelated families with core membership drawn from original Susquehannah Company settlers.[62] The men worked in the same banks and railroads, attended the same prestigious social clubs, and built mansions on their grand riverside lots. Outsiders drawn to the area by the "intense demand for entrepreneurial talent and capital" were also mostly of British stock and were integrated socially through intermarriage with the founding families and through work ties and common institutions such as churches, private clubs, debating societies, and educational facilities.[63] Their children attended the same private schools and Ivy-League colleges and married and forged business partnerships with the same original Connecticut families.

For women living in such a rarefied social stratum, creating social distinction was likely difficult. At a time when elites in other cities were jockeying for position by moving to even larger homes in leafy suburbs, Wilkes-Barre's upper classes could not. The city they had built was still an active industrial site, with trains moving massive amounts of coal to enormous collieries. Mine tunnels burrowed under town streets, and railroads and boat traffic transported millions of tons of coal in all directions. Elite households were constrained to a few large streets that fronted the river.[64] The mountains offered some relief from the noise and dust of the city and became sites for ever-grander displays of wealth. Society pages are full of reports about the privileged Wilkes-Barre residents migrating to their summer "cottages" for the season, and the Wyoming Valley DAR held some of its early functions there.[65] In this competitive setting, highly educated elite women with no occupation after marrying off their children may have embraced genealogical diversions with special enthusiasm, for genealogical research had the added potential benefit of revealing family ties to Revolutionary War heroes, the original Susquehannah Company settlers or, best of all, to Wyoming battle victims.

Adding to our sense that the first two Pennsylvania Sullivan markers were established in a spirit of competition is the fact that the 1896 and 1898 marker dedication events had almost completely distinct guest lists. Out of 178 total people who attended the dedications, only thirteen people (including Martha Phelps) attended both events. The ceremonies were so similar: women taking the lead, commemorating Sullivan, holding events in late summer at wealthy coal/lumber baron homes, special train service to the site, lengthy historical addresses read and penned by women, and extensive coverage by the same local paper. And yet so few people attended both functions, suggesting factions within the Wilkes-Barre upper class. This context may explain the hint of status anxiety we see in Phelps's address. Unlike their Connecticut neighbors, the Slocums had been Quaker pacifists from Rhode Island.[66] It may be for this reason that Phelps continued to touch on her family's connections to hallowed local Yankees, whether by citing John Jenkins Jr. in the marker text, discussing her family link to the Wyoming battle through the Frances Slocum capture story, or by claiming the highly venerated Connecticut Yankee historian Charles Miner as family friend.

Yankee Daughters

Following the 1896 and 1898 mountain marker dedications, women living in communities near the route taken by Sullivan's troops also formed DAR chapters. Early chapter activities included hosting colonial teas, sponsoring historical essay competitions, marking Revolutionary War graves, and contributing to the financial support of indigent "real daughters" (i.e., the first-generation daughters of Revolutionary War veterans). They also established Sullivan markers. The George Taylor chapter established its Easton, Pennsylvania, marker in 1900; the Tioga chapter set up one in Athens in 1902; the George Clymer chapter established a marker in Towanda in 1908; the Mach-wi-hi-lusing chapter established one in Wyalusing in 1914; and all local chapters including the Dial Rock, Asa Stevens, and Tunkhannock chapters partnered with the state in its 1929 marker program.[67]

In contrast to the two marker dedications held at mountain summer homes, the ceremonies held in the Susquehanna River towns of Tunkhannock, Athens, Towanda, and Wyalusing were less exclusive, and women from other chapters attended and even spoke at each other's events.[68] The monuments themselves followed similar aesthetics. Most involved rough-hewn granite blocks with a metal tablet affixed. Ceremonies varied only slightly with each location and reflected the organization's goal of shaping the patriotic sentiments of the next generation. They incorporated children in significant roles such as unveiling the marker while dressed in colonial-era attire. These commemorations included singing such songs as "America" and "The Star-Spangled Banner," and lyrics were often included in their printed programs. We should consider the performative functions of these activities. As Paul Connerton points out, words stated in unison can presuppose or bring into existence sentiments such as respect, veneration, or gratitude.[69] In these commemorations, a love of the nation was fostered through collective recitation of patriotic songs stating as much. DAR events excelled in the gestural and genealogical dimensions of reenactment rhetorics, as organizers included descendants of the historical actors being celebrated, attired in clothing from a former time, staging a kind of reincarnation of early settler-colonists at their ceremonies.

These were Yankee-dominated affairs. Women wishing to join a DAR chapter needed to document their lineal descent from a man or woman who assisted or served in the Revolutionary War, an individual known in DAR parlance as their "patriot."[70] Women could record additional war-serving ancestors, and higher status was (and is) awarded women with more than one patriot.[71]After constructing a database of the patriots identified by the charter members of local DAR chapters, I found some striking patterns. Given the constant migration in early American history, we might expect that people in these towns at the turn of the twentieth century would have ancestors with Revolutionary War records from across the eastern portion of the country. Yet the vast majority of the local chapter members identified ancestors who served in Connecticut units: 80 percent of the Wyoming Valley DAR charter members' patriots, and 87 percent of the Dial Rock chapter.[72] This could simply reflect the fact that these towns were settled under the Susquehannah Company and the women were descendants of early Company partisans. Since Connecticut Yankees persisted regionally as an interrelated and elite faction, it is also possible that more women of this background had the leisure time and resources necessary to participate in these clubs. However, it is also possible that they found, in forming a DAR organization, a means of asserting Connecticut Yankee supremacy. A related pattern is the number of men claimed as patriots who served—or died—at the Wyoming battle. Many women had ancestors who had served with Sullivan, but far more prevalent on these lists are Wyoming "martyr" ancestors. It appears that women in the Sullivan-marker-establishing chapters preferred to identify Connecticut war veterans as their patriots, especially men killed at the Wyoming battle.

Tunkhannock is a case in point. A full 74 percent of the women of the Tunkhannock chapter identified Connecticut "patriots." Five women claimed Anderson Dana, two identified Constant Searle Sr., and eight claimed Asa Stevens as their patriot, all men killed at Wyoming. Connecticut ancestry was even more concentrated in the Mach-wi-hi-lusing chapter, formed in Wyalusing, Pennsylvania, in July 1911.[73] Ancestors of these women are a veritable who's who in early Connecticut Yankee history, including several men killed at Wyoming (Thomas Brown, Perrin Ross, Asa Stevens, and Aholiab Buck); Joseph Elliott, who served at Wyoming and allegedly narrowly escaped Queen Esther's wrath; and Justus Gaylord Jr., son of a man killed at Wyoming who, in turn, signed up with Sullivan. Some women in this chapter traced themselves back to not one or two people who served in the Revolutionary War, but a half dozen, such as Susie Dodge Hallock, who listed nine Connecticut men as patriots and collaterals.[74]

When women identified identical ancestors, they were related. These chapters were clearly family affairs: many consisted of sisters, mothers, and daughters. This filial dimension is perhaps best demonstrated by the Lieutenant Asa Stevens Chapter of Standing Stone. These women chose to name their chapter after Wyoming battle victim Asa Stevens, and every charter member was one of his descendants, or 100 percent Wyoming martyr ancestry.

Analysis of charter membership lists suggests that the strong interfamily linkages that Edward Davis found in his study of Wilkes-Barre's anthracite aristocracy extended into the northern river towns. In such a close-knit social realm, it is worth noting that two DAR chapters (Tioga and George Clymer) had in-marrying women at the helm, suggesting that elite newcomers may have found, in forming a DAR chapter, an effective way to integrate themselves and their daughters into a tight-knit Yankee-dominant milieu. Consider the case of Charlotte Maurice, who formed the Tioga chapter in Athens in 1900. Maurice moved to the area in 1869, from Massachusetts, following her marriage to a local bridgeworks entrepreneur, Charles Stewart Maurice.[75] She belonged to several patriotic hereditary societies, including the Colonial Dames of America (through twenty-six ancestors), the Mayflower Society, and the Society of Founders and Patriots.[76] The Maurice family was so wealthy that they were original shareholders in the exclusive Jekyll Island resort in Georgia, and they spent part of each year there with the Vanderbilts and other Gilded Age millionaires. Yet it is in Athens that Charlotte Maurice raised her nine children and focused most of her philanthropy. Described as "My Lady Bountiful" by the families of her husbands' employees, she served the Packer Hospital as the first president of the Athens Auxiliary and was the first president of the Ladies' Library Club.[77]

Even though the Tioga chapter of the DAR that Charlotte formed had a high proportion of chapter patriots from Massachusetts units, chapter activities continued to reflect the local Connecticut Yankee influence. Because Athens was created after the Trenton Decree and had been a hotbed of "Wild Yankee" activity, patriots of the Tioga chapter's charter members included such "Wild Yankees" as Thomas Kinney, Elisha Satterlee, and Simon Spalding, and early chapter activities lauded the Battle of Wyoming. When the chapter marked the graves of Revolutionary War soldiers in November 1901, Miss Madege Rogers of Sheshequin read a poem about the Wyoming Massacre, "narrating the facts of that awful scene of carnage." The minister, Reverend Shugar of Chemung, began his address "by telling that his great grandfather was murdered at the Wyoming Massacre." Shugar was also a veteran of the Civil War and was accompanied by comrades in the Grand Union of the Republic (GAR), a fraternal organization for Union veterans. His reflections on one war seemed to have led him to consider rather graphically his own recent service.[78]

Maurice's Tioga chapter developed one of the most elaborate (and wordy) of the DAR Sullivan plaques in 1902 (see figure 11). It marked the location of Sullivan's fort in Athens with the following inscription:

FIG. 11. Fort Sullivan memorial, Tioga Chapter of the DAR (1902), Athens PA. Photo courtesy of the author.

In Sullivan's Expedition, the march that destroyed savagery and opened the Keystone and Empire States to civilization, four brigades furnished by the states of Pennsylvania, New York, New Jersey and New Hampshire, with Proctor's Artillery and Parr's Riflemen, took part. At this Tioga Point, long the southern door of the Iroquois Confederacy, 5000 troops encamped. Named by the Continentals and garrisoned by 250 soldiers of the 2nd New Jersey regiment under Colonel Israel Shrieve, here stood FORT SULLIVAN, with four block houses, curtains and abatis, from August 11th to October 3rd, 1779.

This tablet is erected by the Tioga Chapter, Daughters of the American Revolution, 1902.

Their marker dedication on October 3, 1902, was a grand event. William Elliot Griffis, a prolific writer who authored books on

Japan as well as a 1900 fictional account of the Sullivan Expedition, *Pathfinders of the Revolution,* gave the main address.[79] In his speech, he noted his interest in marking "every point possible" of the Sullivan Expedition with "appropriate and enduring monuments" (a task the state would take up a generation later; see chapter 3).[80] The marker unveiling drew members of patriot societies from the surrounding area.[81] Local Connecticut Yankee families played a prominent role, as did Maurice's next-door neighbors, the Perkins family. The expenses of the bronze tablet and of moving the boulder were borne by regent Mrs. Maurice and her two immediate neighbors.[82] Like the Phelps marker, the new monument that they funded was placed in front of their homes, adding unique symbolic value to their residence and neighborhood.[83]

Patriotic Placemaking: Linking Family and Land

In her study of the memorial to the Battle of Saratoga (1777), Carolyn Strange describes the 1877 centennial address as an "exuberant, all-male, all-white" event, noting the absence of women, who were excluded from such ceremonies well into the 1880s.[84] In many regards, the women in this chapter were breaking new ground, and their entry into the public sphere must have been exhilarating for some and alarming for others. These women were well off for the most part; the men in their families were involved in extractive industries and related services, profiting from the immigrants drawn to the region to work in foundries, railroads, and coal-related industries. A standard interpretation would find these women motivated to join the DAR as a means of elevating their families above those of the Italian, Irish, and other immigrants in their communities and, through their sense of their superior ancestry, claiming responsibility for educating the less fortunate into basic patriotic values and love of country by mounting public ceremonies.[85] While this assessment may apply to these female memory entrepreneurs, there seems to be more than national pride or even Anglo-supremacy at work here. In the case of the two plaques established in the mountains of Wilkes-Barre in 1896 and 1898, competition seems to be less with new immigrant families than with other elite women. These markers suggest the use of history by wealthy socialites to foster not so much public edification as their own place within a competitive local class hierarchy at a time of great socioeconomic flux. Participation in hereditary organizations also provided an entry for women whose marriages brought them to Pennsylvania. One way to integrate into the social cliques of the very elite was through patriotic social clubs, using their forebears as an entry card, a form of symbolic capital that could be parlayed for greater social capital.

The commemorative projects the northeastern Pennsylvania DAR chapters engaged in focused primarily on the Battle of Wyoming. Celebrating Sullivan was secondary in some ways as it was imagined as the necessary conclusion to Wyoming.[86] Wyoming-related activities continued to reproduce images of savagism, with a focus on alleged Indian forms of warfare (see chapter 1). Since the actors were often women from early "pioneer" families, they were elevating themselves by valorizing their ancestors' heroism, offering these actions as instructive morality tales to serve the wider community. Charter membership lists and DAR activities demonstrate that northeastern Pennsylvania communities were still in the shadow of Wyoming in the early twentieth century. In this part of the state, it was not enough to demonstrate descent from a Revolutionary War hero. Ideally, one would claim a connection to the early Connecticut colony, the Susquehannah Company or, better yet, someone who served and died at the Battle of Wyoming.

The Sullivan dedication ceremonies of hereditary patriotic groups closely followed the rhetorics of reenactment, especially along genealogical, gestural, and linguistic dimensions. They sought out descendants of historic figures to play key roles in the unveiling and often recited early texts verbatim. Place and timing were less important. The mountaintop dedications were held when convenient to the participants. Marker placement was often approximated, as we have seen. Morgan writes that DAR members were "proudly amateur public historians" who "aimed their histories at schoolchildren and popular audiences instead of at academic ones," and on "history's usefulness in moral uplift, social cohesion, and national unity," valuing "reverence over objectivity."[87] By bringing young children to unveilings in colonial dress, by narrating hand-to-hand combat, DAR members attempted to draw the spectators into the story, making moments of the national past more emotionally accessible for the audience.[88] Whether or not Sullivan actually built the bridge later labeled as such by the Colonial Dames, and whether or not soldiers Davis and Jones were, in fact, killed in the manner described or at the place marked, was beside the point. The goal was not accuracy but to engage in patriotic placemaking, to arouse peoples' sentiments about the grand times of yesteryear, and to bring them together into a common community.

There is a clear settler-colonial dimension to all this activity. These commemorative events established a particular "we" that sympathizes with the Yankee side of the intrasettler conflict, with Wyoming "martyrs" in particular, one that is constructed in opposition to Indian "savagery." In fixing Sullivan's journey (and the Wyoming story) to the land with their historical markers, women were fixing their family stories there as well. Reflecting on DAR-sponsored markers in California, historian David Glassberg comments that the name of the organization on the plaques is the most important part.[89] We see that here as well. By securing their organization's name in metal on an immovable and natural-cut boulder, they were locating their own families in "time and space," and engaging in an elaborate kind of "firsting" that erases the first people on the land.[90] No matter how early the Connecticut settlers arrived in the area, however, they would never be first. Local women were responding to this settler-colonial predicament by placing elements of their fused family and national stories to specific spots on the land, right where they lived. They could use these historical markers and their family histories connected to them to secure their belonging to a place in which they had only just arrived.

Public commemorative practices shifted—but only marginally—when the state of Pennsylvania began to oversee the development and care of historical markers and developed a series of memorials to the Sullivan Expedition in 1929, the focus of the next chapter.

THREE

"Bootleg" Monuments and the Pennsylvania Historical Commission

T he state of Pennsylvania established twenty-two stone monoliths marking Sullivan's route from Easton to the New York border for the expedition's 150th anniversary in 1929.[1] Today these stones are hard to locate and appear overwhelmed by competing signage. When they were inaugurated in 1929, however, they represented the height of commemorative fashion. They were developed by a new agency charged with bringing Pennsylvania's public history-making into the modern era. This agency faced no small challenges at first, particularly that of the "bootleg" marker.

During a July 1928 meeting of the Pennsylvania Historical Commission (PHC), chairman Henry Shoemaker called attention to what he referred to as "bootleg" monuments found across the state and asked if it would be advisable to establish legislation "to prevent the erection of markers and monuments without the authority of the Commission."[2] The problem the commission was facing was not unique to Pennsylvania but stemmed from the inevitable tension that would arise when state administrations began to wrest control of public history-making activities from nongovernmental organizations. Before the creation of the PHC in 1913, most historical markers in the state were these so-called bootleg memorials that local historical societies and patriotic organizations developed without state oversight. The Sullivan markers discussed in the previous chapter represent prime examples. Shoemaker felt that his new commission should have some say over which past was commemorated and how. Members of

Pennsylvania's newly formed state commission were in an awkward position, however. The commission was formed to add to the state's commemorative landscape and set the direction of future memorial activities yet, due to a desperate lack of resources, they would have to rely on funding from the same private organizations whose bootleg markers they deplored. How would this conflict be resolved, and what would be the consequences when the commission marked the 150th anniversary of the Sullivan Expedition in 1929? In this chapter, we follow the shift to state-sponsored public history-making to better understand Pennsylvania officials' decision to celebrate Sullivan with memorials along the route of the campaign. Because the PHC continued to work with the same local patriotic societies we encountered in the previous chapter, there were more continuities in the work of the new state agency than one might expect.

The Pennsylvania Historical Commission

Pennsylvania statehood dates to December 12, 1787; it was over a century later that the state established a commission to oversee the development and management of historical landmarks. When formed in 1913, the Pennsylvania Historical Commission (PHC) was composed of five members, appointed by the governor, who served on a voluntary basis.[3] These unpaid volunteers had their hands full. They were charged with "the duty of marking and preserving the antiquities and historical landmarks of Pennsylvania" as well as with preservation or restoration of "ancient or historic public buildings, military works, or monuments connected with the history of Pennsylvania," and with receiving "bequest of relics or other articles of historical interest."[4] The commission was directed to carry out these activities "upon its own initiative or upon the petition of municipalities or historical societies."[5]

Given the daunting nature of their task and the fact that their budget was immediately reduced from $40,000 to $10,000 due to insufficient state revenue, inaugural members "unanimously concluded" at their first meeting that they would start by engaging in "inquiry, report and recommendation."[6] They conducted a multiyear survey to identify just which historical monuments had been established in the state thus far, sending out queries and conducting site visits. What they found was an astounding diversity of monumental types and forms. Along with the memorials the Pennsylvania state legislature had funded to mark the Civil War dead, countless privately sponsored monuments had been established over the past century. The commission's first compilation of state markers included the disclaimer, "This does not pretend to be a complete list. It has been impossible to secure such within the limits of the compiler's employment."[7] Shoemaker's "bootleg" monuments recognized the birthplaces of prominent people ("Birthplace of Thomas Buchanan Read," bronze tablet, Chester County Historical Society, 1912); sites important to local industry (site of building of John Fitch's steamboat, granite column erected by Bucks County Historical Society in 1902); and locations of Revolutionary War fame ("Point where Lafayette received his first wound," Brandywine Battlefield, a column of terra-cotta erected by the "citizens and school children of Chester County" on September 11, 1895).[8] Multiple markers commemorated encounters or conflicts with Indigenous people, including the locations of Moravian settlements and so-called massacre sites. DAR chapters had developed dozens of markers.[9] Private organizations had been busy.

When commission members began to articulate an agenda for the state's public historical landscape, they seemed more influenced by the commemorative activities of other states than any consensus regarding Pennsylvania's contributions to the nation's past. The prominent role of New England and Virginia in narrations of the national past irked committee members, and they wrote, "New England has occupied a prominent part in the development of American history, as it is written by New Englanders, and Pennsylvania has been placed too far in the background. It is time for Pennsylvania to have its history told by those who study it from a nearer viewpoint than the hills of New England."[10] Pennsylvanians, they claimed, specifically "the Quaker, the Scotch-Irish and the Pennsylvania German influences" were "as dominant" in shaping American institutions as "Puritans of New England" or "Cavaliers of Virginia."[11] Commission members decided to start by commemorating the early Indian period and that of the French and Indian (or Seven Years') War, eras that had been relatively neglected.[12] Yet even the emphasis on the state's Indigenous past was influenced by competition with other states. Commission members lamented the fact that "other states, with *far less Indian history* of national importance, have made much of what history they do have" (emphasis added).[13]

Hampered by inadequate funding in its first decades, the PHC found itself relying almost entirely on the efforts of private organizations. It lauded cities like Lancaster for developing historical monuments "under the patronage of the local county historical Society, without State aid."[14] The PHC's first foray into public history-making, the Fort McCord Memorial, offers an example of such thrift that would raise eyebrows today. The PHC assisted the Enoch Brown Association in completing its monument to an event from the Seven Years' War. The marker was in the form of a Celtic cross and commemorated a 1756 "massacre," with an inscription that reproduced the savagism of the era: "The site of Fort McCord, where twenty-seven pioneer settlers, men, women and children, were massacred by Indian savages or carried into captivity, April 1, 1756."[15] In their annual report, the PHC wrote that the monument should be "an inspiration to other communities."[16] This praise was not due to the marker's religious motif, message, or even its historical significance, but rather its cost. As the PHC explained, "The land was donated, as was also much of the work."[17] The commission added that it provided $500 to demonstrate its willingness to "help those who help themselves."[18]

By 1918 the PHC was encouraging stylistic uniformity.[19] Embracing the ethos of the Progressive Era, commission members saw their role as democratic and educational, to "arouse the interest of the people."[20] Marker dedications often had several hundred people in attendance. In northeastern Pennsylvania, where the PHC collaborated with descendants of early Susquehannah Company pioneers, continuity with past practices is evident. In Bradford County, Pennsylvania, the PHC cosponsored two markers related to the Sullivan Expedition before establishing its Sullivan series six months later.

Marking "Indian Hill" and "Lime Hill"

In November 1928 the PHC assisted the Bradford County Historical Society in dedicating markers to battles at "Indian Hill" and
"Lime Hill" along what is now Route 6 near Wyalusing, Pennsylvania. Today, these stone monoliths are interspersed with the
Sullivan memorials the state established six months later. The
November dedications reflected both local popular understandings of the past and the influence of PHC chairman Henry Wharton Shoemaker. He was appointed chairman in 1923 by fellow
conservationist and Progressive, Governor Pinchot of Pennsylvania. Shoemaker was raised in an elite milieu in New York City.
His family's fortune began with Schuylkill County coal, and he
often returned to visit his Pennsylvania grandparents.[21]After grad-
uating from Columbia University, he created a Wall Street bro-
kerage firm with his brother; after his brother's accidental death
and his own scandalous divorce, he left the New York scene and
moved to central Pennsylvania and began running newspapers.[22]A
staunch supporter of Teddy Roosevelt, Shoemaker promoted Progressive positions in his newspapers such as governmental control of coal and other natural resources (an irony given the source
of his inherited wealth), and better treatment of Native Americans.[23]As chairman of the PHC, and later as state archivist and
director of the state museum, he devoted much of his life's energies to promoting Pennsylvania's cultural and natural resources.[24]
As biographer Simon J. Bronner observes, Shoemaker hoped to
communicate Pennsylvania's "special mystique," which was no
easy task since the state, at the time, was the country's "industrial giant."[25] He worked hard to create "a popular bucolic image
to preserve the legendary spirit of Pennsylvania and to assimilate
the state's new residents."[26]

During the first three years of his chairmanship (1924–26), the
PHC developed twenty-seven markers, with much of the expense
met by private contributions, including Shoemaker's personal
funds.[27] These markers fostered a romantic vision of Pennsylvania that emphasized positive relationships with Native Americans.
Many markers also engaged in "lasting," noting the birthplaces of

the "last" Indians and former Indian towns.[28] Staging was a primary focus, and dedications often featured "Chief Strong Wolf in native costume" who, the Commission reported, added "much of picturesque interest to the meetings."[29] That Chief Strong Wolf was a hallmark of these early dedications can be seen in the PHC's decision to use his image shaking hands with Pennsylvania governor John S. Fisher at the Kittanning Indian Town Marker as the frontispiece of the lavishly illustrated fourth PHC annual report.[30] The November Bradford County marker dedications continued this trend.

The two markers were dedicated on November 9, 1928, and Wyalusing students were given a half day off to promote student attendance.[31] The Indian Hill marker commemorates a 1778 skirmish between patriot troops, under Col. Thomas Hartley, and unidentified Indian opponents. Soon after the Battle of Wyoming, Colonel Hartley of the Additional Continental Regiment was sent to Fort Augusta, downriver from Wyoming, to protect the frontier.[32] He decided to take troops on the offensive and attack the village of Tioga, one of the staging areas for the Indian-British attack of Wyoming, with an ultimate goal of destroying the even larger multinational Munsee stronghold of Chemung, where they felt much of the Wyoming plunder had been brought.[33] Hartley left Fort Muncy with approximately two hundred men, including Col. Nathan Denison of Wyoming battle fame, who had promised his own future neutrality as part of the terms of the surrender that he had helped orchestrate a few months earlier.[34] Hartley's troops traveled along the Sheshequin path and destroyed the Indian villages of Sheshecunnunk and Tioga, taking multiple prisoners and scalps.[35] When he learned that British allies under Walter Butler had gathered a large force at Chemung, Hartley returned toward Wyoming, traveling along the Susquehanna River this time and again destroying every Indian settlement they could find along the way, including "Queen Esther's Town," across the Chemung River from Tioga. Unidentified assailants pursued them most of the way back to Wyoming.[36] The "Indian Hill" stone ostensibly marks the site where Hartley faced the largest resistance. His forces lost four men and had ten wounded in the skirmish, and their Indian attackers lost at least ten men before retreating.[37] Hartley and his troops returned to Wyoming on October 1 with scalps, prisoners, and plunder that included almost fifty cattle and twenty-eight canoes.[38] Despite the pleas of Connecticut partisans for the property, it was auctioned off and distributed according to rank, as dictated by military law.[39]

Local historian David Craft identifies the Hartley expedition as a "precursor to Sullivan," and this perspective appears in the marker text, which reads as follows:[40]

INDIAN HILL BATTLEFIELD

On September 29th, 1778 on the hill one mile southeast of this marker in the most desperate engagement between Indians and white men in Bradford County Colonel Thomas Hartley defeated the Indians. He left Fort Muncy September 21st, on the 27th, burned Tioga Queen Esther's town and reached Wyalusing at eleven o'clock on the night of September 28th. This campaign ended Indian incursions in Bradford County and prepared the way for the Sullivan Expedition. Hard by on the east of this marker led the Old Warrior Path and the Sullivan Trail.

Marked by the Pennsylvania Historical Commission and the Bradford County Historical Society 1928.

What seemed notable to the people who wrote the marker text is that Hartley attacked "Queen Esther's town," suggesting the lasting power of the Queen Esther story in the white settler imagination (see chapter 1).[41] We do not know where the "Indian Hill" moniker came from, but it helped shift the meaning of the marker away from the Revolutionary War to anti-Indian warfare. It is also unclear how the PHC or the local historical society was able to identify the roadside location of the skirmish site, but it seems likely that a local family donation and influence played a role. After outlining what he could glean from the sources, Craft reported that the skirmish probably occurred near a place owned by the late Hamilton Brown on top of Browntown Mountain.[42] The marker also celebrates a kind of "lasting" in that it asserts that the "campaign ended Indian incursions in Bradford County."

The "Lime Hill" marker was dedicated the same day and marks a similar event. According to white settler lore, after Lieutenant Franklin killed an "Indian" in the Wyoming Valley in June 1781, Indians who were presumed relatives of the murdered man came to his house, in the village of Hanover in the Wyoming Valley, in September 1781 and captured two of his sons, returning in April 1782 to take his wife and four remaining children. At that time, a group of men, including Thomas Baldwin, formed a party to pursue them and caught up with the group at Wyalusing, where there was a skirmish. Settler-colonial reports state that six unidentified Indians were killed and two wounded and three of the Franklin children were saved, but the unidentified Indians made off with the baby and killed Mrs. Franklin, and two of Baldwin's men were wounded. The marker dedication featured descendants of Baldwin and Joseph Elliott, who was second in command.[43]

The Lime Hill marker reads much like the Indian Hill one:

LIME HILL BATTLEFIELD

April 14 1782 In attempting to rescue Mrs. Roswell Franklin and her four children who had been captured by Indians, Sergeant Thomas Baldwin and his party met the enemy near this spot. After four hours of fighting, three of the children were rescued but Mrs. Franklin was killed. Sergeant Baldwin's breastworks were located seventy rods northwest of this marker.

Marked by the Pennsylvania Historical Commission and the Bradford County Historical Society, 1928

The two marker dedications held that cold November day featured a Native American participant, like many PHC public history exercises under Shoemaker's direction (see figure 12). This time, Oklahoma Delaware "Chief War Eagle" was recruited to play the part, commencing the marker dedications with a prayer (described in the PHC program as an "invocation to the Great Spirit").[44] "Chief War Eagle" was also known as Witapanóx'we (and James Carlos Webber on the Dawes rolls). That year he also worked with Frank Speck of the University of Pennsylvania recording traditions in the Delaware language, research funded by the

PHC.[45] He was born in the Cooweescoowee district of the Cherokee Nation (Indian Territory) around 1880 to a father who was a member of the Cherokee Nation of the West and a mother of Munsee descent, and by the 1920s was elected secretary of the Delaware executive council.[46] Soon after the November 1928 marker dedications, Witapanóx'we traveled to the state of Delaware to participate in a large pan-Indian pow-wow hosted by Nanticoke Indians.[47] His visage that day in November seems to sport a smirk, and one wonders what he was thinking, and how the well-traveled man was received, particularly since the participants in these Bradford County gatherings were a close-knit group of white Connecticut Yankee descendants who were celebrating the "last Indian battles" of the region. What is more, the marker texts contradict each other: the Indian Hill marker explains that the 1778 episode "ended Indian incursions in Bradford County," while the Lime Hill marker recognizes a so-called Indian incursion that happened four years later.

The DAR women who unveiled the Indian Hill marker, Clara Walker Bonfoey and Adelaide Kenney, were descendants of Col. John Franklin and Gen. Simon Spalding, respectively, two men who had led units with Hartley on his raids (see figure 13). Nobody represented Hartley that day.[48] Why feature Franklin and Spalding? They were not the only men with Hartley and, in his reports after returning to Wyoming, Hartley singled out not these men, but a Captain Stoddard and Mr. Carbery. (Captain Spalding was even offered a backhanded compliment: "He exerted himself as much as possible."[49]) It may be that only descendants of Spalding and Franklin remained in the area.[50] Their inclusion could also be interpreted as a nod to the Sullivan Expedition, which occurred the following year, for both men participated in that mission.[51] However, it is also worth noting that both men were heroes of the Yankee position in the Yankee-Pennamite war and staunch supporters of the Connecticut claim. It is they who invited Ethan Allen and his Green Mountain Boys to the area to create a breakaway state, and when Franklin was arrested for treason for these actions and brought to Philadelphia, Spalding and other local Wild Yankees were the ones who kidnapped the federal official

<small>FIG. 12.</small> Delaware chief War Eagle at Lime Hill monument unveiling, November 1928. Courtesy of Bradford County Historical Society, Towanda PA.

and held him as ransom to secure Franklin's release (see chapter 1). Historian Charles Miner describes Franklin as "for thirty years the prime and popular leader of the Yankee interests in northeastern Pennsylvania."[52]

Historian and Athens resident Louise Welles Murray, descendant of both Pennamite and Yankee ancestors, was well positioned to reflect on such Yankee biases in local society. In her 1908 history of Tioga Point, she discusses how Yankee partisanship continued to animate residents into the twentieth century.

FIG. 13. Unveiling Lime Hill monument, November 1928. Courtesy of Bradford County Historical Society, Towanda PA.

Regarding the likes of John Franklin, Simon Spalding, Elisha Satterlee, and other Wild Yankees, she writes, "They resisted Pennsylvania unto death, and even then their bitterness long pervaded the thoughts and actions of their families. In the local controversy three names stand out in letters of fire, FRANKLIN, SATTERLEE, MATTHEWSON . . . Seek to-day these descendants, and they are ready still to rehearse the wrongs of their ancestors, the stories all wrapped up in family tales and traditions of a hundred years" (emphasis in the original).[53]

It appears that "stories all wrapped up in family tales" persisted into the late 1920s and were sanctified in Bradford County, by the state of Pennsylvania, in the form of these two cosponsored markers. In its Indian Hill and Lime Hill markers, the PHC fostered white settler tales of heroic pioneers and attacking Indians, stories linked to the Wyoming battle, and which connected that battle to the Sullivan Expedition. Although Hartley was from Berks County and was leading a Pennsylvania unit, it was not Pennsylvania men who were honored at the Hartley monument inauguration ceremony, but two Wild Yankees who worked hard to fight Pennsylvania jurisdiction. Even while battling "bootleg" markers, the state of Pennsylvania sponsored historic markers that celebrated the state's former foes.

Six months later, PHC representatives returned to Bradford County to dedicate Sullivan markers for the 150th anniversary of the Sullivan Expedition. These markers offered a more neutral telling of the Sullivan story.

The State Commemorates Sullivan in 1929

Both Pennsylvania and New York developed programs to commemorate the sesquicentennial of the Sullivan Expedition in 1929. In contrast to Pennsylvania, New York's memory entrepreneurs had a sizable budget and planned a year-long extravaganza that wove the Sullivan story into the story of the "Empire State" (see chapters 5–7). The Pennsylvania celebrations were more muted, suggesting either less local interest or diminished political purchase in narrating the expedition there. The PHC formed a subcommittee led by commission secretary and Wyoming Valley resident Dr. Frances Dorrance.[54] Dorrance was a remarkable woman. Descendant of famed Wyoming battle victim George Dorrance, she was a graduate of Vassar, held a doctorate in archaeology, served as director of the prestigious Wyoming Historical and Geological Society, one of the early institutions established by Connecticut Yankee elite in Wilkes-Barre, and helped found the Society for Pennsylvania Archaeology.[55] For decades, her sister Anne was the director of the Wyoming Commemorative Association and in charge of the annual "Wyoming Massacre" celebration. Frances

FIG. 14. Dedication of Pennsylvania Historical Commission Sullivan monument at Standing Stone PA, 1929. Courtesy of Bradford County Historical Society, Towanda PA.

Dorrance likely heard Dr. Griffis speak at the Tioga DAR event in Athens in 1902 or the Wyoming commemoration the next year; it is his words that are engraved in the Tioga DAR chapter's marker (chapter 2). In his 1903 speech, Griffis proposed that the Sullivan Expedition be commemorated with a series of markers denoting the company's campsites. This became the PHC plan under Dorrance's direction. The Sullivan program became one of the state's five "markers-in-a-series" that reflected the growing influence of automobile tourism.[56] With twenty-two markers altogether, the Sullivan project was the most ambitious of the five.

Under Dorrance's direction, the PHC developed materials on the expedition, including a map for dissemination in schools and a volume of source material, and spent "untold time" writing letters, traveling to locales, interviewing locals, and meeting with highway officials to plan out where markers should be placed.[57] The group also communicated with the historical and patriotic organizations in charge of local celebrations.[58] It is interesting that it is under the leadership of one of the revered Connecticut families that the state's markers became more neutral in their wording. Under Dorrance's leadership, the PHC commissioned twenty-two rough-hewn granite blocks, approximately seven feet high, affixed with bronze tablets that bore the Pennsylvania coat of arms, the name of the expedition ("The Sullivan Expedition against the Iroquois Indians, 1779"), a map of the route, a brief text, and names of the PHC and any other cooperating organization (see figure 14).[59] A few markers designated forts, including Fort Augusta, departing base for some of Sullivan's troops, but eighteen designated campsites.[60] The markers were identical; it is in the dedications that we find more variation. A comparison of the 1929 Sullivan marker unveilings in Easton and Athens exposes both the influence of local communities and an evolution in views of the expedition.

"A Hair-Raising Indian Rout"

The Athens, Pennsylvania, unveiling was cosponsored with New York State's sesquicentennial programming, and coordinated by the Tioga chapter of the DAR, renamed the Tioga Point chapter.[61] Program planning was in the hands of chapter historian Louise Welles Murray, who communicated regularly with the New York state historian, Alexander C. Flick, responsible for that state's programming. In this correspondence, Murray is less interested in promoting a "Yankee" vantage on the Sullivan Campaign and more concerned with finding ways to reach local children.[62] She decided to dramatize the meeting of Clinton's and Sullivan's units at Athens.[63] While she may have minimized Yankee partisanship, her speech still employed the language of savagism.

Some 2,500 people attended the Sullivan marker dedications that took place on August 24, 1929, and to "hear three stirring addresses by noted historians."[64] After Boy Scouts unveiled the marker (see figure 15), the program started with DAR regent Mrs. C. C. West, accompanied by PHC representative Shenk, who stood in for Shoemaker that day. There were no Native participants to offer initial blessings. Instead, the program commenced with "a hair-raising Indian rout" staged by the Athens Boy Scouts. A speech by Shenk and the singing of "America" was followed by an address by Louise Welles Murray "on the actual expedition as far as Athens, the camp at Athens and the joining of Sullivan's and Clinton's troops here preparatory to starting the offensive against the savages." The Lehigh Valley Shop Band played music. A local man, described in the printed program as a descendant (George West), gave "an impressive impersonation of Captain Simon Spalding," followed by a reenactment of the meeting of Sullivan and Clinton, put on by members of the Athens American Legion.[65]

From the point of view of the local DAR chapter and historical societies, the final program was a tremendous success, and masses of people—including the sought-after children—attended. One wonders what images of Native Americans they picked up from the experience. Indian savagery was discussed in the historical address and enacted by Boy Scouts. Also prominent on the program, published by the Tioga Point Historical Society, were the names of local heroes. The DAR regent was positioned within the pantheon of Wyoming martyrs by the inclusion of her maiden name (Satterlee) in the printed program; both Simon Spalding and Elisha Satterlee were Mrs. Satterlee West's ancestors and prominent men of Wild Yankee fame. Even while the marker text offered the more neutral state-sponsored language, participants engaged in a public performance that elevated certain (Yankee) families over others.

"Several Soldiers Were Executed"

The city of Easton dedicated its new marker to the Sullivan Expedition in October 1929. At first glance, the dedication appears to repeat the exercises of the 1900 DAR dedication of the plaque that referenced the "Wyoming Massacre" (see chapter 1). Patriotic societies and schoolchildren attended, and the marker was cosponsored by the Valley Forge Chapter of the Sons of the American Revolution. However, in contrast with the 1900 DAR marker dedication, this time a PHC member (Rev. John Stoudt of Allentown) proposed the marker, and final approval was tended by an Easton City Council vote.[66] The historical address, offered by Dr. William Mather Lewis, president of Lafayette College, also indicates a shift in interpretation. Lewis directed much of his discourse to the

FIG. 15. Boy Scouts unveiling Fort Sullivan marker, Athens PA, August 1929. RG 13.100, box 1. Records of the Pennsylvania Historical and Museum Commission, courtesy of Pennsylvania State Archives, Harrisburg PA.

youth present, emphasizing the "unselfish devotion" of people of the past. He developed a picture of Easton at the time of the Revolution ("a village of not more than 150 houses") and noted that "twenty years before the Indians had assembled here for important treaties with the English," suggesting a civil interaction with Native peoples that contrasted sharply with the approach taken by Sullivan's troops. He indirectly critiqued Sullivan's scorched-earth tactics, stating that the expedition was a response to "Indian activity," which he blamed partly on the behavior of European "frontiersmen." (It "probably could have been avoided with proper management on the part of the frontiersmen. Instead of gaining their friendship, they encouraged enmity.") He also underscored the difficulties the expedition posed for the residents of Easton, offering a more nuanced assessment: "The gathering of such a large number of troops in Easton was not without its unpleasant features. Because of poor supply service, the troops lacked clothing, food and pay, and as a result there was much insubordination and incipient mutiny. A large number of troops filled with discontent in a small town during the hot summer days created a situation that was decidedly unpleasant for the townspeople. Several soldiers were executed, some for the murder of an Easton resident."[67]

Previous marker dedications had not referenced troop mutinies or soldier criminality and execution. After outlining the troops' activities in Indian country, Lewis dismissed the very event he was supposed to laud by adding that this military expedition "does not have a great place in many histories of the Revolution." His overall takeaway was less on celebrating Sullivan and more on teaching youth the value of self-sacrifice to the national community.[68]

This chapter has shown that as Pennsylvania shifted from an era of "bootleg" historical markers to increased state involvement, there were more continuities than one might expect. The Indian Hill and Lime Hill projects represent a hybrid or transitional type: they were initiated by communities, with the PHC playing a supportive role. These successive lasting ceremonies rehearsed worn tales of savagism reanimated each year by Wyoming commemorations, and connected local heroes to Wyoming, and that battle to Sullivan. The dedication ceremonies featured descendants of the white historical actors they were celebrating. Lineal connection to historical figures became less important in the 1929 state-sponsored dedications. The PHC's reenactment strategy emphasized place and time: they intended to dedicate markers at Sullivan's actual campsites on the same calendrical date, creating a kind of rolling dedication ceremony. Because these ceremonies were in the hands of local communities, they varied widely, however, from critical reassessment to patriotic partisanship, as we have seen. Sometimes PHC members did not even attend the dedications.[69]

"Neutral Words Like 'Killed'"

Following the completion of its Sullivan series, the PHC faced the onset of the Great Depression, staff rotations, and shifting budgets. The many historical markers it cosponsored during its initial years proved difficult to oversee. Copper and bronze plaques often "vanished" from their stones. When Mrs. Coon, regent of the Wyoming Valley DAR chapter, wrote to the PHMC in 1939 to inform it of a plaque missing from Martha Phelps's Lauren Run marker and loose screws on the 1929 PHC Shades Creek Sullivan memorial, the new director of the PHC, Dr. Stevens, expressed frustration with his inability to manage so many historic sites scattered across such a vast territory. He explained to Mrs. Coon that he had no resources to replace the lost marker, and he hoped he would have funds in the next budget "to make a survey of all of the markers and make whatever repairs and additions are necessary." He added, "It is unfortunate that some two hundred of these markers have been erected throughout the State and it has never been possible to keep track of them and adequately service them."[70]

As road conditions improved and traffic speeds increased, it became difficult for motorists to read the plaque texts, and the huge stones on which they were affixed were becoming dangerous roadside hazards. The state began to install gold-and-blue metal markers that were easier to read from a car, known derisively as "history on a stick."[71] Chaos sometimes ensued when the old stone boulders were moved for road construction. The Lime Hill stone was hauled away during the rebuilding of Route 6 in 1972 and never returned.[72] When Mrs. Isabelle Welles Tiffany, secretary of the Mach-wi-hi-lusing chapter of the DAR, contacted the PHMC to inquire about it, Mr. A. Henry Haas of the Historical Marker Program suggested that its replacement was problematic, explaining, "The plaque you mention is of an obsolete type erected by the old Historical Commission in conjunction with a local society." Haas did not get into the backstory, but a bureaucratic overhaul led to the creation of a new administration in 1945, the Pennsylvania Historical and Museum Commission, which coincided with Henry Shoemaker's retirement. Stevens became the commission's first professionally trained historian who was not a volunteer.[73] Haas explained that the new organization "inaugurated a program to mark historic sites with attractive, and more legible blue and gold historical markers in 1945," which Haas noted could be found "in every county of the state."[74] He added, "No provision has been made for the replacement of these plaques once they have been damaged or removed. Usually, if enough local interest is elicited, the responsibility of relocating them is assumed by some local patriotic, fraternal, civic or service organization."[75]

For the Bradford County descendants of the original marker developers, the new metal signs would not do. They continued to press the matter, eventually leading Haas to make a site visit to meet Mayor Keeler of Wyalusing.[76] After this visit, and several additional years of difficulty, the stone monument was finally moved to a new piece of land donated by a DAR chapter member and affixed with bronze plaques in October 1976.[77] But a dozen years later, the new bronze plaques were reported missing again. This time the PHMC sought insurance moneys for the missing Lime Hill plaque, and staffer Marilyn Levin recommended that they consider switching to aluminum, which was cheaper.[78] A 1929 PHC-sponsored Sullivan plaque erected in Bear Creek Township went missing in the 1980s, and it took the community almost forty years to replace it.[79]

Even the new blue-and-gold signs were not foolproof. In 2004

Henry Farley, director of the Bradford County Historical Society, wrote an article in the *Rocket-Courier* stating that after the PHMC came up with the "modern style" of historic marker, it removed and repainted several plaques in 1994, only to return them to the wrong posts! By that time, out of twenty-nine metal markers in the county, thirteen were missing or misplaced, including several Sullivan signs. A large 1929 PHC stone memorial in Tunkhannock vanished altogether.[80]

Although PHMC directors lauded their new professional standards and new marker format in self-promoting articles, the new markers continued to broadcast the same old framing of the past.[81] While we saw a somewhat more neutral presentation of the Sullivan Expedition in the state's 1929 markers, when the "Queen Esther" American Legion Post (ALP 670) of Wyoming, Pennsylvania, requested a new marker to assist visitors in locating "Queen Esther's Rock," the state complied. The blue-and-gold sign, dedicated in July 1962, reads as follows:

THE BLOODY ROCK

On the night of July 3,
1778, after the Battle
of Wyoming, fourteen or
more captive American
soldiers were murdered
here by a maul wielded
by a revengeful Indian
woman, traditionally but
not certainly identified
as "Queen Esther."

PENNSYLVANIA HISTORICAL AND MUSEUM COMMISSION

The marker text did not go unnoticed even at the time. Louise Welles Murray's daughter, Elsie, wrote to Stevens on September 12, 1962, complaining about the text, which she felt was offensive to Native Americans. The reply, by bureau director Kent, gives us some indication of her complaint (as her original letter is missing). He explained that since it was a short marker it was "exceptionally difficult to compose." "For example, we couldn't get neutral words like 'killed' or 'dispatched' to fit in place of 'murdered.' There was no space to explain all the background, that Esther or Catherine were partly white, that in Indian terms the action was not murder, and that it may have actually been merciful in sparing the captives death by torture." He added, "I would hope that the numerous historical markers making friendly reference to the Indians would counteract any ill effects which might arise from the wording in one particular marker." He informed her in conclusion that "there was a strong demand from people in Wyoming, and something had to be provided."[82]

Conclusion to Pennsylvania Chapters

I have argued in this section of the book that early understandings of the Sullivan Expedition in the state of Pennsylvania were shaped by the Yankee-Pennamite war and the Battle of Wyoming. News accounts in the aftermath of the Battle of Wyoming spread such wild rumors that Wyoming became a potent symbol of the horrors of purported Indian-style warfare. Accounts told in the rhetorical frame of the "anti-Indian sublime" made their way into texts inscribed in stone and bronze by Yankee-dominated DAR chapters, memorials that persist on the landscape today. The Sullivan Expedition, linked to and in the shadow of Wyoming, was regularly presented as a concluding chapter and mission of vengeance, a direct and inevitable response to Wyoming.[83]

Change was slow when the state of Pennsylvania developed a historical commission and charged that commission with creating some order in the commemorative landscape. The difficulty of this transition was not unique to Pennsylvania. In the 1930s there was a "dramatic breakthrough" in the federal government's sense of responsibility for the country's historical inheritance.[84] As Kammen observes, "If it weren't for the Great Depression, it would have taken much longer for government at any level to be concerned with American history."[85] In Pennsylvania, continuities in how the past was told persisted after the shift to public marker development in part because the newly formed PHC had few resources at its disposal and had to work with voluntary patriotic societies that cosponsored its programming. Early appointees like Shoemaker were given great latitude in directing programming according to their personal inclinations, and Shoemaker promoted a nostalgic, folksy image of the state, perhaps to draw tourism, claiming to have penned some four thousand signs himself.[86] While a shift to less sensational language, exemplified by uniform stylistic features, was apparent in the 1929 Sullivan markers, even the revamped, more "professional" commission, the PHMC, continued to establish markers that reference Indian "massacres," as we saw in the 1962 Queen Esther sign.

Today in this part of Pennsylvania, it is not the Sullivan Expedition that draws the largest crowds, but the popular patriotic ceremony held at the site of the Wyoming Monument to commemorate the "Battle of Wyoming and Massacre" each year on July Fourth, which is described in part two of this book. We first turn to the commemorative complex in New York State, where elements of the Sullivan commemorative complex offer a very different treatment of the same military operation.

New York: Replacement through Just Warfare

FOUR

Ambivalent Festivities and the Newtown Centennial of 1879

L ike Pennsylvania, the State of New York held a centennial celebration in 1879 and a historical marker program in time for the 1929 Sullivan sesquicentennial. The tenor and message of the Sullivan commemorative complex differs greatly in this state, however. This is partly because it is here where most of the devastation of Native villages occurred. Put differently, much of the state was Haudenosaunee country before the Revolutionary War. The rise of the "Empire State" was only possible with the seizure of vast amounts of Haudenosaunee land and the dispossession and displacement of established Native communities.[1] After the war was over, it seemed that everyone wanted this land, and much of it was obtained through threats, deception, graft, and greed, with relentless pressure put on Haudenosaunee nations by speculators, capitalists, politicians, and state officials at the highest levels.

The Sullivan story entered settler-colonial historical consciousness relatively late in New York. Aside from a localized focus on two soldiers' demise, the expedition was "rediscovered" in time for a centennial commemoration.[2] Although local patriotic societies, like the Daughters of the American Revolution, emerged in late–nineteenth century New York as in Pennsylvania, their commemorative activities were less focused on this component of the Revolutionary War.[3] It was only when a state agency was created in the 1920s in preparation for the sesquicentennial of the Revolutionary War that interest in the 1779 Sullivan operation became widespread.

This chapter explores the 1879 centennial commemoration of the Battle of Newtown and emphasizes the ambivalence expressed during the fanfare. Speeches given that day were starting to weave a new replacement narrative, however, one suggesting that the land of New York was obtained by Sullivan through a fair fight. The state historian would consolidate this "replacement through just warfare" argument and fix it on bronze plaques in the 1920s, during a time of unprecedented land claims action and activism, the subject of chapters 5–7.

Inventing a Tradition

Just days after the centennial celebration of the Battle of Wyoming in July 1878, lawyer and amateur historian William Fiske Warner of Waverly, New York, began promoting a similar commemoration of the Battle of Newtown, the sole pitched battle of the months-long Sullivan Expedition. It took place on August 29, 1779, near present-day Elmira, New York, along the Chemung River, at the multinational Native settlement of "New Town."[4] After the Continental Army detected an ambush set up by Mohawk leader Joseph Brant, Seneca leader Sayenqueraghta, Maj. John Butler, and some eight hundred to one thousand troops, Sullivan's men repositioned and opened fire. Realizing they were nearly surrounded, British troops and their Indian allies made a hasty retreat. Thirteen people were killed.[5]

Warner began publishing articles in Waverly and Elmira presses, reminding readers about the Newtown battle's upcoming anniversary. He had authored a newspaper serial, the "Centennial History of Tioga County," and attributed his "discovery" of the Sullivan Expedition to his research for that publication.[6] Born in Hardwich, Vermont, he moved to Owego, New York, in 1834, where he practiced law, founded the Owego Gas Light Company, and became actively involved in Owego public life, serving as clerk (1848–54) and many terms as village president. After he moved to Waverly in 1871, he pursued the same legal and entrepreneurial pursuits.[7] We know that the success of the Wyoming centennial was on Warner's mind. In a July 1878 letter to the *Elmira Daily Advertiser*, he said his goal was "not to give an account of the late commemoration at Wyoming, but to draw attention once more to the project of ceelbrating [*sic*] the centennial of the [Newtown] battle next year," explaining, "The contest which settled so speedily the question of occupation of this vast territory took place at Chemung, on the 29th day of August, 1779."[8] He believed that the "importance of this battle has escaped the observation of historians" and hoped that it could receive the credit it was due. In his view, the battle's significance was not in the numbers killed, "but by the results accomplished and the consequences which follow." Given such an accounting, he estimated that this battle would "hold rank" with that of Saratoga, and far above many "given prominence in the history of the Revolution."[9]

In contrast to the Battle of Wyoming, there was no extensive white settler tradition commemorating the Newtown battle. While several members of the many-thousand-strong army eventually returned to the region and made their homes there, it remains unclear whether or not they communicated information about the battle locations to their descendants, for the route of Sullivan's troops was "re-discovered" by Euro-American settlers again and again.[10] This lack of unbroken settler tradition allowed Warner the freedom to propose his new hometown of Waverly, New York, as the ideal location for the centennial celebration, for it was "between Camp Sullivan at Tioga Point and the battle ground, and in full view of each."[11] Waverly had the added benefit of being "of easy access to all who might desire to attend." Although nothing in particular had happened in Waverly that day, "the stirring scenes which preceded and the final conflict occurred *within view*" (emphasis added).[12]

Warner's bold proposal to hold a battle commemoration in Waverly, New York (Tioga County), may have sparked interest in his plans, but probably not the kind he had hoped, for subsequent meetings led to his overthrow by Chemung County residents who claimed the event as their own. After Warner chaired an initial organizational meeting at his Waverly law offices on August 1, 1878 (with local historian David Craft, of Wyalusing, Pennsylvania; Charles Fairman, the editor of the *Elmira Daily Advertiser*; and Elmira postmaster Daniel Pickering), they called for a second meeting to be held at the end of the month at the Fishler House in Wellsburg, the village closest to the battlefield. That meeting served as both centennial planning meeting and celebration of the ninety-ninth anniversary of the battle.[13] No doubt intending to drum up interest, Fairman published a five-column historical account of the "Battle of New Town" in the *Elmira Daily Advertiser* two weeks before the meeting.[14]

The August 29 meeting in Wellsburg was well attended and set the course for later events. An increased interest in historical commemoration during this era is often attributed to efforts to cope with the devastating Civil War losses, and it is of interest that many of the men planning the Elmira celebration were veterans of that war.[15] The meeting chair was now Elmira Civil War hero Gen. A. S. Diven, and gone was the proposed Waverly setting. When Warner opened the discussion with "an interesting resume" of General Sullivan's expedition and read letters he had received from prominent people who had expressed interest in participating, local lawyer Ariel Thurston returned the discussion to "the object of this meeting," which he thought was to "settle upon ways and plans for the celebration," suggesting some impatience. Thurston got right to the point, recommending that "what should be done was to lay the foundation for a monument on that day . . . of course an historical address is contemplated, and perhaps a poem. Who is to do all this, and how is it to be done?" He suggested a committee and a large one at that.[16]

First came the problem of the *name* of the event. Were they commemorating the "battle of *Chemung*," or that of "*New Town*"? Warner proposed "Chemung," as it was "an Indian name, and New Town was not. Chemung embraced the whole region." (The "Battle of Chemung" was also the title of one of his letters to the local paper; I should note that there was indeed a raid on the village of Chemung a few weeks before the Newtown battle.)[17] However, General Diven countered that "New Town" was the name given in the administrative report of the battle and argued that even if this identification had been in error, it must be preserved.[18] His view carried.[19] They also debated whether to dedicate a finished monument that day or simply lay the foundation. Mr. Pickering suggested that they have the monument built during the year, "to be ready at the celebration," arguing that, "if it was left to be done afterwards, it would probably not be done at all," an observation that suggests lukewarm public interest in the project.[20]

Having settled on the question of a monument, its placement, and the name of the battle to be celebrated, the committee set to work to create the administrative apparatus needed to carry out its grand plans. They formed committees and subcommittees composed of hundreds of vice presidents, from twelve counties, and set meeting dates. To help generate public interest, the men resolved that "the newspapers of the several counties in New York and Pennsylvania" in the areas traversed by Sullivan "are respectfully requested to lend their influence in arousing an interest in the centennial celebration, by publishing during the coming year such historical matter relating to the same as their space will permit, thus rendering a service which will be thankfully appreciated by the executive committee and the public."[21] Fairman, as editor of the *Elmira Advertiser*, followed his own advice to the letter.

Local residents were slow to understand what was afoot. An August 1879 editorial in the *Waverly Advocate* stated, "People are many times confused and misled in reading of the battle of New Town and the battle of Chemung," and clarified the matter:

> The old Indian town was at the latter place, and was a large and flourishing village. A New Town had been built at the mouth of Newtown creek, now Elmira. Finding the valley of Chemung very desirable for raising corn, beans, etc., for supplying the British army, another town was commenced on the battle ground opposite Wellsburg. This was called Lower New Town, and contained about forty log huts, which were torn down and the logs used in their fortifications. Hence, some in speaking of the battle called it the "battle of New Town," but which should more properly have been called the battle of Lower New Town.[22]

As the boosters put together their grand event, they fanned jealousies in other communities that were also planning Sullivan centennials. A Geneseo newspaper expressed concern that Elmira was stealing Geneseo's thunder, writing, "The battle of New Town should be commemorated, but we do not think it should supersede the centennial which ought to be observed in this county on the 15th of September, 1779." The editors of the Elmira paper responded that they "certainly have no desire to supersede any celebration which may be contemplated in the 'Genesee country,'" adding, "but our friends in that region should remember that it was the Battle of New Town which opened their beautiful country to the white man. That battle destroyed the supremacy of the six nations, and drove them back to the protection of their British allies at Fort Niagara." We can see in this statement the beginnings of a replacement narrative that would build (see chapter 5). The article ended with rhetorical flourish: "The Battle of New Town was the great and decisive event of the march. If any notice is to be taken of the expedition in its centennial return, the commemoration of that Battle should be the central point of all proceedings."[23]

The men who gathered in Wellsburg in August 1878 became the executive committee that organized the centennial celebration. Many of these trustees were relative newcomers to the area and held overlapping political and career connections. By the time of the centennial, the role of president was occupied by Judge Hiram Gray of Elmira. Gray was elected as Democrat to the twenty-fifth Congress (1837–39) and served as justice of the Supreme Court of New York in the 1840s through 1860s. It is in his law office that Alexander S. Diven started his legal career.[24] Diven had moved to Elmira in 1845, where he developed a law firm. He became involved in local railroads, playing leadership roles in multiple railroads, including the New York and Erie Railroad, the Chemung Railroad, and the Canandaigua and Corning Railroad Company.[25] Opposed to slavery, he became an early member of the Republican Party, was elected to the New York Senate and, in 1860, to Congress, where he was one of the first members to introduce a resolution to enlist African Americans in the army. Soon after the start of the Civil War, he asked for a leave of absence to "go home and raise a regiment of troops," and he formed the 107th New York Volunteers.[26] After serving (at Antietam and Chancellorsville), he was appointed commander of the Elmira post and remained in Elmira after the war, where he continued to run his railroad operations and helped establish the Elmira College for women.[27] Another trustee, Capt. Uriah S. Lowe, had served on Diven's staff in Elmira while Diven was in charge of the Western Division of the State of New York.[28] Diven was credited with bringing Trustee Ariel Standish Thurston to the region from New Hampshire.[29] A local history described Thurston as an antislavery Democrat and trustee Francis Hall as an abolitionist.[30] Daniel Pickering originated in Smithfield, Pennsylvania, and served Chemung County as constable, collector, school commissioner, supervisor, and sheriff; and as postmaster of Elmira from 1861–67 and 1877–81.[31] Several other trustees were in local government as well.[32] While Warner stayed on the committee, he was one of its few members not residing in Chemung County.

Many of these men were from opposing political parties, and we should briefly consider the local political context. The economic collapse of 1873 had brought about a five-year recession, which may explain the fanfare surrounding national centennial festivities. The Philadelphia Centennial Exposition (1876) emphasized technological marvels, which Richard Slotkin finds ironic, for these marvels "also represented new forms of human misery and social danger," and communicated both the "growth of Big Business" and the related "bankruptcy and ruin of many small businesses."[33] Two years later, a railroad strike swept the country. This was a time of foment during which the independent Greenback party emerged, which established an anti-monopoly platform and challenged the selling of public land to corporations like railroads.[34] The Greenback movement gained real traction in Elmira and nearby towns and garnered more than 25 percent of the vote in Chemung County in 1878, the year these men were organizing their gala event.[35] While overcoming the horrors of the Civil War may have been foremost on their minds, we should note the prominence of railroad men and their allies on the planning committees.

As the year proceeded, the "Committee on Celebration" identified a site for the monument and ceremony.[36] They proposed to erect a monument on the hill overlooking the actual battleground, a site that seemed of special interest due to its proximity to new railroad lines. As Warner explained, a hilltop monument would "be easily seen by a spectator standing upon any one of the three bridges at Elmira . . . from Spanish Hill at Waverly, eleven miles distant," and "from the cars on the Erie Railway it will be a conspicuous object for the distance of ten miles."[37] Selecting this site would serve as a form of advertising of the event. As one article explained, "If a traveler who is going west on the New York, Lake Erie and Western Railroad" looks toward Elmira, "he will observe a conspicuous hill, bare of trees on the top, and standing at least 1,200 feet above the general level of the valley. On its summit he will see a tall staff from which is floating a flag. It marks the spot on which is to be erected a monument commemorating Sullivan's fight around the base of the hill. The hill itself has been named Sullivan Hill."[38]

As the date neared, executive committee member Charles Fairman made good his promise to promote the event, and announcements in the *Elmira Daily Advertiser* increased in number:

> August 8th: "It is a settled fact that the Centennial Fire works in this city will be the grandest display ever known in the Southern Tier."
>
> August 13th: "Two weeks from next Friday will occur the Centennial Celebration of the Battle of Newtown, to the eternal glorification of General Sullivan and his army of noble followers. The event will be second in importance to no other that ever happened in this valley with the exception of that which the celebration commemorates."
>
> August 16th: "It is settled, and may be depended on, that the Centennial Celebration of the Battle of Newtown is to be not only a rouser, but elegant in all respects."

Descendants of Sullivan, Clinton, and other prominent campaign participants were invited and their acceptance letters published in the paper, as were those of prominent civic societies. The Masonic Lodge planned a complimentary reception Friday night at their new temple, bringing an orchestra from Buffalo.[39] The *Hornellsville Tribune* mocked the event, reporting, "Unless Elmira takes proper precautions there will be more people killed at the celebration than there was at the battle of New Town one hundred years ago."[40]

A Centennial Spectacle

On a Saturday morning in August 1879, the town of Elmira, New York, became a busy transit hub as travelers streamed into town to head out on the journey to a small nearby hill where a monument had been built to mark the hundredth anniversary of the Sullivan Campaign (see figure 16). One eyewitness described the scene as follows: "There were more people in Elmira at 9 o'clock than the city could comfortably hold and so they began their exodus towards Wellsburg . . . Over that long five-mile stretch the teams moved, making one long procession in every road and by-road, while in, among, over, upon and about every load settled several inches of dust, which, kicked up from the feet of every slowly stepping animal, rose in vast clouds from the finely powdered soil."[41] At the monument site, beer and other refreshments were on offer, as were a host of sideshows such as wheels of fortune, soapbox tricksters, and "other devices for securing the rural dollar," creating a carnival-like atmosphere. People who avoided these distractions sat on the ground, with their "heavy lunch baskets," under umbrellas they brought as shade from the hot sun.[42] Twenty to fifty thousand people gathered in this way to participate in the much-awaited commemoration of the Battle of Newtown.[43] Because the state later published a tome reproducing the day's speeches and related celebrations, we have a detailed window into the day's events and the worldview of that time.[44]

The 1879 celebration was remarkably well attended and occurred without major mishap. It was a grand event that contained all the standard elements of commemorative events of that era: a lengthy procession involving bands, members of the military, civic organizations, and political dignitaries; a monument unveiling; addresses; poetry; and fireworks. It commenced Thursday night with a speech presented at the First Presbyterian Church.[45] On Friday morning, special trains left Elmira, starting at 9:00 a.m.,

FIG. 16. Sullivan Monument, ca. 1879. The monument collapsed and was replaced with a stone obelisk in 1912. In VF 500–110: War-American Revolution (1775–1783), Sullivan-Clinton Expedition (1779)–Centennial (1879), Subject Files, Chemung County Historical Society, Elmira NY.

and official participants gathered at the Elmira Courthouse to take carriages to the monument site.[46] The monument was hollow, with stairs leading up to a viewing area at the top, surrounded by an iron railing, where a "magnificent view" of the city of Elmira and the countryside could be obtained.[47] Public exercises started after midday, with speeches, poems, and shorter addresses given by over a dozen people. The day was hot, and participants listened to hours of orations held on multiple stages. These activities were followed by a "brilliant illumination" of Elmira at night, a reception at the new Masonic Temple, and fireworks.[48] The festivities were attended not only by thousands from Pennsylvania and New York, but also by the governors of New York, Pennsylvania, and New Hampshire. The most prominent political figure and the individual who was the greatest attraction was Gen. William Sherman of Civil War fame.

What was the overall takeaway? The day's oral presentations were remarkably diverse, and reading them in succession leaves a sense of ambivalence rather than a clear, singular message. While the meaning of the Sullivan Expedition in New York would be streamlined in the tightly managed 150th anniversary commemorations of 1929, the erudite and rambling speeches that hot summer day of August 1879 offered a full array of perspectives and revealed deep ambiguities surrounding the campaign. Members of New York's educated elite would have been familiar with the "myth of the Iroquois empire" promulgated by New York writers.[49] Speakers cited the address on the Iroquois given to the New York Historical Society by DeWitt Clinton in 1811, in which he described the Iroquois as the "Romans of the Western world," a phrase repeated in many addresses. Lewis Henry Morgan's *League of the Iroquois* (1851) was widely read by this time. The Sullivan Expedition, in contrast, seemed a relatively unknown topic for many in the audience. Some speakers outlined the campaign's motives, tactics, and results in great detail and in language that suggested that they were deeply troubled by the information. It is also evident that some of the speakers were learning of the details of the expedition for the very first time that day.

"Malice Enough in Our Hearts"

Newspaper editor and New York senator (1854–57) and assemblyman (1878–79, 1881–83), Hon. Erastus Brooks of Richmond County, New York, expressed ambivalence throughout the lengthy speech that he gave at the First Presbyterian Church. He had intended to present it during the main celebration, but as it grew in length, he asked the organizers if he might present it in its entirety the night before rather than drastically reducing it. He first reminded listeners what was happening in 1779, which he claimed was perhaps the most remarkable year of the century. At home, "unmixed gloom pervaded the land." He described the loss of Charleston, the failure to drive the British from Castine, Maine, and the hopeless nature of the colonies' financial situation. He then turned from the Battle of Wyoming to that of Newtown, stating that "the first witnessed, perhaps, the most bloody massacre of the century, and the second hinged upon the first in the abandonment of all that had been peaceful and hopeful between the white settlers and the natives."[50]

Brooks then launched into Sullivan's actions in detail, making indirect and sometimes veiled criticisms of Sullivan, Americans more generally, and even George Washington. He explained that he would not stop to ask "why the Indians all through the war of the Revolution, and long before, with rare exceptions were more loyal to the English than to Americans."[51] In raising this point, he seemed to be calling into question the wisdom of the latter camp. The failure of the Americans to see the Indians for who they were was nearly fatal:

> During the greater part of the war, the Indians were most effective allies of the invading enemy. They knew every by-path, clearing, and water-course of the wilderness. They were brave, crafty, enduring, generally faithful to each other, patient and revengeful; and while no one will question the good intentions of those who in Congress pressed the order of retaliation for what had been done at Wyoming, I must think that the greatest enemies of all, were the white men who first fired the hearts of the Indians to take the lives of their American brethren. If I am not wrong, also,

the work of vengeance in 1779 [Sullivan's campaign] was greatly overdone. . . . After the battle of Newtown, the axe and the torch destroyed the now as then, beautiful Genesee Valley. Not a blade of corn in all the extended orchards, not a dwelling in all the habitations of the Six Nations were spared. Everywhere on the line of march, there was waste and devastation in the worst forms of war.[52]

The greatest enemies were the "white men"? Sullivan's vengeance was "overdone"? As if this weren't enough, he turned to the question of just retaliation for alleged Indian savagery. Are only Indians capable of cruelty? He explained that he had thought so before, but he had since realized that every race is capable of every cruelty: "Men of war when the blood is hot and the passions revengeful, are capable of any cruelty, and especially is this true if there is the *excuse of retaliation*."[53] "Excuse of retaliation," in this case, was a not-so-subtle critique of the revenge justification for the campaign. Again and again he delineated for the listener the destruction: "The forty Indian towns destroyed one hundred years ago in the Genesee Valley, and the one hundred and twenty-eight houses burned in these towns, most of them as we read, 'large and elegant,'" adding, "we can well believe, with old Nathan Davis, that it was an awful spectacle to see every dwelling, cabin, blade of corn and tree bearing fruit on fire, and the black smoke ascending, like the torments of hell."[54]

Later in the speech, he further humanized the enemy by providing the names of said villages, stating, "Burning villages and destroying crops was the one great purpose of the campaign of 1779, and General Sullivan must have done his work thoroughly when forty villages were destroyed, five of them very large, known as Catharinestown, Kanadesaga (the present Geneva), Canandaigua, Honeoye, and Geneseo, the last being the capital of the western tribe of the confederacy."[55] The public might have thought, "Yet certainly these Indians were uncivilized, despite living in dwellings like ours." Not according to Brooks, and he described the towns of the Confederacy as follows: "Of the tribes known as 'The Six Nations,' Big Tree was the capital. The grand council-house was built of peeled logs, two stories high, with gable ends painted red; the dwellings giving the appearance of both thrift and comfort. One hundred and twenty-two of these cabins, all well provisioned, were in an hour swept off by the torch."[56]

As to the people, he said they were "in great advance of their contemporaries anywhere in the land." He cited DeWitt Clinton's 1811 speech, in which he stated, "They were a peculiar and extraordinary people, contra-distinguished from the mass of Indian nations by great attainments in polity, by negotiations, in eloquence, and in war."[57] We find here a speaker praising the oratory, political, and military skill of Sullivan's enemy.

Furthermore, Brooks called into question over and over the *justice* of the campaign. He questioned the decision to attack the entire Confederacy when some tribes by then were allies of the revolutionaries, stating that "the expedition of General Sullivan was practically against the whole confederacy of Senecas, Mohawks, Oneidas, Cayugas, Tuscaroras, and Onondagas, though the Oneidas and Onondagas took no part in the campaign of Brandt and the Johnsons, and some sixty of the Onondagas were in the field on the American side."[58] After discussing Sullivan's puzzling decision to turn back before attempting to reach Niagara, he added the following critique, "Equally mysterious was General Sullivan's order to destroy the homes and make prisoners of the Mohawks at Johnson Castle. They were, and had been, neutral in war, peaceable as neighbors, and had openly refused all appeal to follow the warriors of their own tribe into Canada. General Sullivan, however, held that they were giving information to the enemy, but it was assertion without proof."[59]

In Brooks's account, when General Gates received Washington's orders, he declined them not due to his old age, as is usually reported, but because he saw them as problematic. "General Gates, to whom these orders were given, declining to accept the command, for reasons not stated, but probably because the service was not congenial to him."[60] Not only were these orders "not congenial," but Brooks compared them with "the continued oppressions of King George," adding that "the Indians never forgave, and have never forgotten, the act of Congress of 1779, or the effect of that act upon the bravest and wisest of all the North American Indians."[61]

In his concluding remarks, Brooks reminded the listener yet again of the paradise lost, in detail that is difficult to revisit, and offered Sullivan's own words by way of conclusion:

> General Sullivan found, as I have said, a paradise of beauty all through the September days of 1779, and changed the abounding harvest, and the richly-laden fruit trees of the waiting orchards, into a wilderness. In fields of plenty he sowed dragons' teeth, which literally sprung forth armed men. "The Indians shall see," said General Sullivan in his report to Congress, "That there is malice enough in our hearts to destroy everything that contributes to their support." And this, in one sentence, tells the whole story of the campaign.[62]

Romans of the Western World

A similar ambivalence—if not admonishment—is found in the statement read at the opening of the main festivities by the Honorable Ellis Roberts of Utica. Roberts was a Republican representative from New York (1871–75). He framed the battle as a matter of vengeance for the victims of both Cherry Valley and Wyoming.[63] He went further than Brooks in that he repeated verbatim Sullivan's orders and reminded the audience that the man who penned them was no less than General Washington himself: "No mistake can exist as to the plan of the campaign. General Washington wrote to General Gates: 'It is proposed to carry the war into the heart of the country of the Six Nations, to cut off their settlements, destroy their next year's crops, and do them every other mischief which time and circumstances will permit.'" Roberts then repeated General Sullivan's orders, including how he was directed "to lay waste all the settlements around, so that the country may not only be overrun but destroyed."[64] Recognizing the dire straits the patriots were in, Washington wrote to the president of Congress that if the expedition were to fail, "we should perhaps lose an army, and our frontiers would be deluged in blood."[65] After delineating in excruciating detail the destruction of Indian towns, Roberts again linked Washington to the violence, telling his audience that Washington himself approved the thoroughness with which he did his work, writing to the president of Congress, "I congratulate Congress on his (General Sullivan's) having completed so effectually the destruction of the whole of the towns and settlements of the hostile Indians in so short a time, and with so inconsiderable a loss of men."[66]

Roberts, like Brooks, seemed troubled. He turned to the question of the savagery of Sullivan's foe: "We speak of these tribes as savages and barbarians. They were without the graces of civilization, and they fought to kill." Is this how they should be viewed? Not at all. Instead, he described Sullivan's foe as a kind of New World Greco-Roman superman, asserting, "When the earliest white man visited them, they lived in cabins, they cultivated grain, they raised a species of wild potato, they practiced skillful fortification, they were the arbitrators and negotiators for other tribes, they often matched the skilled diplomatists of France and England in making treaties. As warriors, their exploits do not suffer in grandeur and heroism by any comparison. They ran in conquest farther than Greek arms were ever carried and to distances which Rome surpassed only in the days of its culminating glory."[67] He called the Iroquois "more than the 'Romans of this Western World,' as DeWitt Clinton styled them," describing them as "the proudest representatives of natural manhood ever discovered."[68] He also discussed their oratory skills and didn't stop there, for he brought up the question of citizenship rights.[69] Not only did the Iroquois live in the area far longer and more peaceably than had his own nation ("for more than three hundred years, for more than thrice the period of our national existence, united and maintaining their political organization"[70]). Adding insult to injury, we extended citizenship rights to our recent Civil War foes, but not to the Iroquois, as he observed: "We make haste to introduce into the body of citizens and of legislators, those who defied the national authority, and it is well. Why should not the original lords of the continent, the first champions of union and independence, the pristine apostles of personal liberty, now in the rounded centuries, receive the decoration of citizens?"[71]

"We Are All At War"

Up until this point in the speeches, the editor compiling them offered no evidence of audience members' responses. What must they have thought, at this point, of General Sullivan and his orders? Farmers whose life work involved tilling the land may have found stories of its blighting difficult indeed. Many people were likely confused: the so-called savages were, in fact, not so—and had ruled with relative peace for three times as long as the new country had existed, a nation born of violence and recently wracked by a murderous Civil War. Nobility and civilization seemed to lie only with the Indigenous occupants, and savagery with the revolutionaries.

While we do not know how audiences reacted to these early speeches, we are privy to some of this information in the transcription of General Sherman's addresses, for it is included within brackets "[Applause]." Journalists suggested that Sherman, rather than Sullivan, was the main draw. Before the event started, one man described as "badly overcome by beer" ascended a stump and tried to make a speech, finally saying, "I come from Tioga County, Pennsylvany, and I got here before daylight. I come to see General Sherman, and I'll be ___ if I go home until he comes!" leading to loud applause. As the journalist concluded, "Everybody seemed waiting to see Sherman."[72]

Sherman spoke twice, on two different stages, cracking jokes at first about his age. His discourse was brief, but he also immediately cleared up the now-blurred "savage/civilization" binary and restored Washington's reputation. He started by reminding everyone that they were on a battleground, however minimal the losses. Wherever one man fell, "the ground becomes sacred," and thus everyone will be "better patriots and better men, because you have come here to recognize the fact that you have stood upon the battle-field, where fell even but four men."[73]

He promised he wouldn't speak long ("I am conscious that you look upon me simply as one of the curiosities of the day") then launched into his primary message, a blunt and unapologetic rallying cry for settler-colonialism, unsurprising to anyone familiar with his role in directing Indian wars. He announced to those present, "But, my friends, we are all at war. Ever since the first white man landed upon this continent, there has been a battle. We are at war to-day—a war between civilization and savages. Our forefathers, when they first landed upon this continent, came to found an empire based upon new principles, and all opposition to it had to pass away, whether it be English or French on the north, or Indians on the west; and no one knew it better than our father, Washington."[74] At this point, rousing applause followed, and one wonders if maligning Washington hadn't irked some listeners. Which war were they all in? The local press that day had two headlines: the first described the centennial, and the second stated, "Attacked by Indians. Two Freighters have a Lively Skirmish with a Band of Indians—Narrow Escape," regarding the attack on two freighters south of the Cheyenne River near Deadwood.[75] Like President Hayes the year before at Wyoming, who had recognized General Custer, Sherman reminded those present of the ongoing Indian wars he was directing, and linked Newtown with the ongoing conflict.[76] General Sherman also refused to question Sullivan and Washington, or to apologize for their actions. On the contrary, he commended everything that they had done, stating, "He gave General Sullivan orders to come here and punish the Six Nations, for their cruel massacre in the valley of the Wyoming, and to make it so severe that it would not occur again. And he did so. General Sullivan obeyed his orders like a man and like a soldier, and the result was from that time forward, your people settled up these beautiful valleys all around here, and look at their descendants here—a million almost. [Applause.]"[77]

After talking about how the Sullivan Campaign had opened this valley "to civilization," he reminded the listener whose side they were on (implying an entirely Euro-American audience), and reframed the Sullivan Expedition as yet another Indian war. Sherman reported, "The same battle is raging upon the Yellow Stone. The same men, endowed by the same feelings that General Sullivan's army had, to-day are contending with the same causes and the same races, two thousand miles west of here; not for the purpose of killing, not for the purpose of shedding blood, not for the purpose of doing wrong at all; but to prepare the way for that civilization which must go along wherever yonder flag floats. [Applause.]"[78]

Sherman confronted the ambiguity developed in previous speeches with a blunt binary logic, sharpening the distinctions between them and us, friends and enemies, civilization and barbarism, with Native Americans lumped together in the latter camp. He reinterpreted the Newtown conflict as part of an ongoing war between "races." In the process, he spelled out an evolutionary replacement narrative, arguing that "civilization" would inevitably replace "barbarism." In his second speech, he told listeners that he found meaning less in the Newtown battle or the expedition itself and more in its later results:

> I do not suppose the incidents of that battle, interest us much here, who remember battles of much larger extent, though probably none of such importance, for the battle here, though almost bloodless, I think only four white men were killed, and probably half a dozen Indians, nevertheless, it opened for settlement the valley of the Chemung, and probably all the sources of the Susquehanna river, probably one of the most beautiful in the world. . . . Had it not been for the battle fought on this ground, it perhaps would have been long, before your ancestors could have cultivated the farms, which you are now possessors of.[79]

Sherman, who had directed some of the more notorious campaigns of the Civil War, was familiar with battles with hundreds of thousands of dead. Rather than ridicule Newtown, he found meaning in its end results, which to him was white settlement and removal of Native people. It is noteworthy that whenever he touched on such a message, he received tremendous applause.

Replacement through Just Warfare

Sherman was not the only speaker to recognize how most people there had benefited from the departure of the land's prior inhabitants. A similar "replacement through fair fight" perspective emerges at the conclusion of a long speech given by the Honorable Steuben Jenkins of Wyoming, Pennsylvania (the lead initiator of the Wyoming battle centennial, chapter 1), a speech that perpetuates the erroneous declension narrative discussed in the introduction to this book:

> Until that day, the Indian power over the whole of this vast region of country was supreme. On that day, that power was broken forever, and the country passed from the possession and dominion of the Indian, to that of the white man. Until that day, a wilderness crowned these hills, and crossed this valley, except at a few spots where the Indian had planted his corn, beans and melons. Where there were but a few small clusters of wigwams, are now, large and flourishing towns and cities, which sprang into existence, almost as at an enchantress' wand.[80]

There are so many mistakes in this presentation of the past, but let me emphasize how in this framing, the Sullivan Expedition is presented as responsible for allowing "replacement" to occur. It is this transition that we should celebrate, Sherman and Jenkins tell their audience. Never mind the details; the ends here justify the means.

Perhaps the most interesting speech was a short one made by General Slocum of Brooklyn, who reminded all present of the short time that had passed since the Civil War. He started by explaining his own ignorance of Sullivan's campaign: "I know very little about the campaign of General Sullivan. I know, as most of you do, far more about Sherman's raid through Georgia and the Carolinas, than I do about General Sullivan's raid through New York." He explained to his audience, "As I have sat listening to the speeches, to-day, I have drawn a parallel between those two expeditions."[81] In his view, Sherman's march was longer, but he had advantages over Sullivan and his troops, such as roads that were already built. But "the spirit" was the same: "It was bold and daring, and, although there was no great loss of life effected in either, yet the results of both were far greater than many battles, in which lives, by the thousands and ten thousands, were lost."[82] Which was worse? While he agreed that "our southern friends" had charged Sherman's expedition with atrocities, his men's actions pale in comparison to those of Sullivan's men: "Sherman's army never committed the atrocities which were committed by General Sullivan's."[83]

Concluding Remarks

The Elmira Newtown festivities were a complicated affair. Carried out a mere fourteen years after the end of the horrific Civil War, and involving veterans and the bereaved of that awful slaughter, it gathered people to celebrate a quite different event. Crowds congregated to recognize a military victory, but the battle of Newtown involved few losses (thirteen dead) and represented just a moment of a much longer campaign, which had lasted for many months. Some of the speakers clearly had the crushing loss of life of the recent Civil War in mind. The relative insignificance of the Newtown engagement, as measured in war dead, seems to have given the most famous participant, General Sherman, some pause.

The wider mission they were commemorating was a strange sort, mostly carried out in the absence of enemy fighters. As Barbara Graymont observes, the "business of this campaign would prove a strange task indeed for men at arms—a warfare against vegetables."[84] Because of the scorched-earth nature of the campaign, celebrating Sullivan meant celebrating a kind of genocide, a fact that many people present understood, on some level, well before the coining of that term. Several speakers found the campaign's methods terrible to recount and difficult to reconcile within the prevailing "civilization versus barbarism" binary of the era. While politicians like Sherman repeated this simplified binary in spontaneous orations, the speakers versed in the historical details were troubled, and troubled over so many of the confounding elements: the barbarism of Sullivan's activities, a barbarism that was ordered by the highest command, which contrasted so strikingly with the high level of "civilization" of the adversary, the Iroquois Confederacy, as measured by a relatively comfortable standard of living, oratorical skill, and political and military might.

We can see too that by 1879, the declension trope, the story of the alleged rise and fall of the great Iroquois empire, was firmly in place, with the Sullivan Expedition presented by some speakers as the beginning of the end for the land's Indigenous inhabitants. That Iroquois decline occurred, there was no doubt;

accounts varied mainly in whether this demise was to be lamented or celebrated. Finally, we have seen how the celebration had to be manufactured. Of course, any historical commemoration is invented and reinvented to meet the exigencies of the day. In this case, even public interest had to be generated. As boosters were well aware, the battle was poorly known by local residents, and they had to sort out what to celebrate and how, and even what to call it.

In his masterful study of the evolution of Newtown battlefield commemorations, Brant Venables discusses the potential stakeholders in the story of the Battle of Newtown. He points out that there were several possible interested communities: descendants of white Continentals, for whom the battle was a victory; descendants of the Oneidas, who had provided scouts for Sullivan's troops; pro-British Haudenosaunee and Delaware allies; and Loyalists.[85] Three of these groups were completely absent that day (and it is unclear how many of the white Euro-American attendees were battle veteran descendants). Venables rightly points out how poetry and speeches reinforced the fantasy of the "vanishing Indian."[86] Some Native Americans did take part, for the Indian Silver Cornet Band of Cattaraugus accepted an invitation to play music and lacrosse at the event.[87] Just what members of the band made of the whole event remains to be determined.

I end with the text developed for the centennial monument. In addition to the competing perspectives reflected in the speeches, the Newtown event is characterized by multistate cooperation. Although initiated by residents of New York, the Newtown commemoration had a broader focus: the executive committee involved representatives from multiple Pennsylvania counties, speakers included national officials, and the governors of several states attended. The marker they developed also reflects this broader focus as it includes the names and states of American generals involved. This multistate focus and the ambivalence evident in the centennial speeches would largely disappear when New York's education department took on the direction of the sesquicentennial festivities in 1929, the focus of the next three chapters.

Near this spot,
on Sunday, the 29th day of August, 1779,
the forces of the Six Nations, under the leadership of
JOSEPH BRANT,
assisted by British Regulars and Tories,
were met and defeated by the Americans under the command of
Major General JOHN SULLIVAN, of New Hampshire,
whose soldiers led by
Brig. Gen. James Clinton, of N.Y., Brig. Gen. Enoch Poor, of N.H.,
Brig. Gen. Edward Hand, of Pa., And Brig. Gen. Wm. Maxwell, of N.J.,
completely routed the enemy and accelerated the advent of the day
which assured to the United States their existence as an
INDEPENDENT NATION.
1779. 1879.[88]

FIVE

Inventing "Sullivan-Clinton" for New York

I n the summer of 1929, New York was abuzz with Sullivan sesquicentennial fanfare. A new Sullivan postage stamp sold out in Binghamton the first day it was on sale.[1] Schoolchildren marched in parades, towns held marker dedications, and people participated in a massive pageant held at three different locations, each involving a cast of thousands.[2] These festivities were the culminating events of an eight-year-long statewide program designed to commemorate the Revolutionary War. Similar celebrations were occurring across the country, and some affairs, like the Philadelphia sesquicentennial of 1926, were lavish and costly.[3] The interwar years have been characterized as times of intense patriotism, modernism, and antimodernist nostalgia, and a vogue for bringing history-making to the people in an effort to "democratize tradition."[4] The sesquicentennial events in New York followed this "democratizing" impulse, with a program carefully orchestrated by state officials that, in the end, was largely the work of a few men. Their activities illustrate how state politics can influence public memory over the long term. In an effort to create a new tradition around the Sullivan military operation, New York authorities developed a unique justification for state hegemony that remains frozen in monumental form today. In this chapter, we consider the state's development of a particular reading of the Sullivan story as part of its grand celebration of the Revolutionary War. In chapters 6 and 7, we turn to silences and omissions in this Sullivan story and the Haudenosaunee response.

A Road-Man's Vision

Like many of the other commemorative activities discussed in this book, the vision and energies of single individuals set the direction of New York sesquicentennial fanfare. In New York, the efforts of industrialist and road advocate W. Pierrepont White were pivotal (see figure 17). The son of a railroad man, William Mansfield White, and the nephew of Canvass White, early engineer of Erie Canal, Utica lawyer W. Pierrepont White had made a name for himself by energetically promoting New York road construction. In his role as president of the Mohawk Valley Historical Society, he continued to think in grandiose terms. In August 1922 he united representatives of seven historical societies to pass a resolution calling on the state legislature to record and observe "New York State's magnificent Revolutionary record."[5] White seemed motivated at least partly by New York boosterism. His proposal followed the massive Massachusetts three-hundred-year anniversary of the Plymouth landing of 1921, and he included estimates of other states' sesquicentennial expenditures and tallied Revolutionary War battles to demonstrate that more conflicts occurred in what became New York (ninety-two) than any other state.[6] His concluding statement sounded the New York–chauvinism call: "When our 10 years' work is done, New York state historic spots will be as correctly and effectively marked as those in Massachusetts, Pennsylvania and Canada."[7] It was high time the state received the recognition it deserved in the national pantheon of Revolutionary War events.[8]

Governor Smith passed a bill on May 24, 1923, granting a fraction of the requested funds ($5,000) to the New York State Historical Association (NYSHA) to make a "preliminary survey and report, for the appropriate celebration of the 150th anniversary of the important events in this state occurring during the revolution period." There was no consensus regarding which events the state should commemorate, however.[9] The NYSHA formed a "Committee on the 150th Anniversary of the American Revolution" and set it to work. The committee sent a letter in July to hundreds of historical and patriotic societies across the state solic-

FIG. 17. William Pierrepont White, courtesy of Oneida History Center, Utica NY.

iting information on the "time and places for appropriate ceremonies."[10] Respondents proposed a remarkable 457 local historical
events and sites as "worthy of recognition"; by the time the committee completed its draft report, the number had grown to 640.[11]

With hundreds of events meriting recognition, how to decide

among them? The committee proposed an ambitious plan that very much resembled White's initial proposal, with the establishment of a ten-year "Revolutionary Anniversaries Commission" requiring $9 million in overall funding.[12] Even the composition of the proposed commission was daunting, with twenty-five to fifty citizens to represent the state, twenty-five to fifty citizens representing historical and patriotic societies, and a subgroup of twenty-five trustees who would carry out the commission's affairs.

The grand proposal failed. Governor Smith rejected the bills seeking to create a *new* state commission at a time when the legislature had just passed a proposal to amend the state constitution to *reduce* the number of state bodies.[13] To meet these objections, the committee regrouped and developed a much more modest proposal, offering to work through the existing Regents of the University of the State of New York, and to focus on events that occurred during the "most important years of the Revolution, namely, 1776 and 1777."[14] This proposal passed in May 1926 with funding granted for battlefield development, participation in the Philadelphia sesquicentennial, and 1926 sesquicentennial activities.[15] The Regents formed the New York State Executive Committee of the 150th Anniversary of the American Revolution (hereafter, the "150th Committee") with newly appointed state historian Alexander C. Flick, a medieval European history professor at Syracuse University, serving as chairman. Supervisor of public records Peter Nelson served as executive secretary.[16] In 1926 Flick, Nelson, and their committee members began preparations for marker dedications and battle reenactments across the state.[17]

Concerned that historical observances would "evaporate in noise and show without leaving results that are either permanent or uplifting," the 150th Committee endeavored to promote "solid historical addresses," establish "permanent markers," and develop "instructive, realistic pageants."[18] Since much of the work for the various Revolutionary commemorative activities was to be carried out at the local level, in 1926 the state historian published *The American Revolution in New York*, a 371-page monograph for a popular audience, and distributed fifty thousand copies to schools, libraries, and organizations across the state.[19] He also sent a letter to more than "1000 local and county historians," encouraging them to take a "prominent part" in arranging local celebrations, and prepared "Program Suggestions for 150th Anniversary of the Revolution," which offered guidance for event organizers.[20] The state's residents responded positively to these ideas, and for the next eight years, schoolchildren and civic organizations engaged in a Revolutionary War commemorative fervor that involved local activities and large celebrations of such landmark events as the signing of the Declaration of Independence (July 9, 1926), battles (Long Island, Harlem Heights, Fort Washington, White Plains), and the adoption of the state constitution (Kingston, April 20, 1777).[21] The "crowning event" was a massive pageant held October 8, 1927, to commemorate the Battle of Saratoga.[22]

Inventing the "Sullivan-Clinton Campaign"

The Sullivan Expedition was not a focus of the state's initial Revolutionary War programming. Only one paragraph of the state-published monograph was dedicated to the expedition, and it is summarized with six lines in the book's twenty-page "Chronology of New York in the Revolution."[23] By the end of 1927, as celebrations of the events of 1777 were winding down, state historian Alexander C. Flick had a change of heart. He began lobbying the state for funding to include the 1779 expedition in future programming, writing, "next to the Burgoyne campaign, the Sullivan expedition was the largest military operation within the Empire State during the Revolution."[24] Flick underscored the mission's geographical spread, writing that it involved "twenty or more" of the present counties, and thus "both the magnitude and importance of the operation justify the observance of its sesquicentennial in order to acquaint the youth of our Commonwealth with its historical significance."[25] In his annual address to the legislature on January 4, 1928, Governor Smith repeated this rationale, noting that previous Revolutionary War commemorations had been "restricted to the eastern, northern and central portions of the State," while "the people of the southern and western sections are interested in observing in 1929 the 150th anniversary of the Sullivan Campaign which was planned by Washington, authorized by Congress and carried out on New York soil."[26] The legislature approved $70,000 for the proposed Sullivan activities.[27]

Building interest in his plans, Flick gave speeches across the state in 1928 educating residents and framing the expedition for public consumption. Correspondence of the era suggests that he was trying to tackle some misgivings within the non-Native community.[28] One of his first tasks was a matter of branding. Until Flick's involvement, the expedition had been known popularly as the "Sullivan Expedition" or "Sullivan's March."[29] He wrote that although Washington and Congress had referred to the operation as the "Indian Expedition," after it was over, "it came to be known as the Sullivan Expedition," nomenclature that "endured for 150 years." He asserted that it was now "more correctly designated as the *Sullivan-Clinton Campaign*." *Campaign* and not *expedition*, due to its extensive geographical scope and multiple major and minor "operations."[30] General Clinton's name was added as well, ostensibly because he was "second in command," personally conducting "one major and one minor movement."[31] They were given equivalent status on each marker heading, as follows:

New York State markers:

ROUTES OF THE ARMIES OF

GENERAL JOHN SULLIVAN

AND

GENERAL JAMES CLINTON

1779

For comparison, the Pennsylvania State marker heading:

THE SULLIVAN EXPEDITION

AGAINST

THE IROQUOIS INDIANS

1779

The fact that General James Clinton was the brother of George Clinton, the first governor of New York, likely prompted this shift in nomenclature. This renaming, unique to New York, not only demoted Sullivan to "General" (he was a major general) and elevated Clinton above the other generals of the same rank, but also served to minimize the roles played by troops from other states. This was in marked contrast to the message on the 1879 plaque established for the Battle of Newtown centennial or even the Tioga Chapter DAR's 1902 marker in Athens (see chapter 2). Clinton led the New York brigade, and the leaders of the other brigades were William Maxwell (New Jersey), Enoch Poor (New Hampshire and Massachusetts), and Edward Hand (Pennsylvania). On New York monoliths, the expedition became the "Sullivan-Clinton Campaign," and not that of "Sullivan, Hand, Poor, Maxwell and Clinton," granting the festivities a New York–centric flavor. Markers established in Pennsylvania the same year commemorate "The Sullivan Expedition."

Turning a many-months-long mission of devastation into a set of celebratory events posed a challenge no matter what it was named. There were only a few military engagements during the four-month-long journey. Rather than engaging in "commemoration-friendly" battles with colorful British soldiers, soldiers spent their time burning villages and fields, activities that were more a source of embarrassment than celebration, as we saw with the awkward comparison made at the Newtown centennial between Sullivan's raids and Sherman's March to the Sea. Flick seemed to adopt a defensive posture at the annual meeting of the Livingston County Historical Society in Geneseo in June 1928. He explained that Sullivan's was of "more importance than it generally gets credit for," admitting that although Sullivan did not reach Niagara as intended, he did "conquer the Indians and forever stopped their depredations" (a patently false assertion). In case the attendees at the historical society meeting that day found something distasteful about sanctifying a mission of devastation, Flick told them that "next year's celebration is not to be for the commemoration of the military victory gained by Sullivan but more for the results of the campaign and its significance afterward." He emphasized the historical nature of his plans: the goal was to survey historic places "along the line of march" and establish markers. He wanted not to celebrate destruction, but rebuild, and told the audience he "would like to see an Indian village built just south of the Boyd and Parker lot, with true models of Indian homes, growing crops like they had, and even domestic animals if they should be found practical."[32] Early news stories sometimes mistakenly reported that there was going to be a reenactment of the entire journey; at a meeting in February 1929, Flick was asked if he had abandoned his "original plan of forming an army and marching over the exact route of Sullivan's Expedition." Flick quickly responded, "We never had planned to march over the entire route. It was merely suggested. But it has been dropped, for we could not ask men to march from Tioga Point through the heart of New York." He added, suggesting that this had indeed been contemplated, "And if we used buses it would mar the effect."[33]

In the end, Flick's committee broke the campaign into seventeen elements that could be celebrated, spread out among the various counties. The expedition had occurred in the summer months, and the committee encouraged communities to carry out commemorations as close to the original calendar dates as possible. It added that "special consideration as major events" should be associated with the Battle of Newtown, the Ambush of Groveland, and the Canandaigua-Geneva area.[34] The first two "major" events involved instances of combat between opposing sides; the latter region was, surely, where many villages had been burned and, not coincidentally, the base of a powerful multitown tourism board, the Finger Lakes Association, which was an enthusiastic early partner in the state's plans.[35] These three locations ultimately hosted the Sullivan-Clinton pageant held in September, the centerpiece of the summer's activities (see chapter 7).

The development of permanent historical markers had been part of the 150th Committee's plans from the start, and the state historian and Dr. George F. Kunz, of the American Scenic and Historic Preservation Society, served as a marker subcommittee.[36] The executive committee agreed to fund no more than half of the cost of each marker (and to spend no more than $500 on each one), which meant that Flick's committee had to work extensively with local organizations. Over the next two years, state historian Flick and his executive secretary, Nelson, were busy assisting communities wishing to organize events and communicating regularly with patriotic organizations and historical societies about marker proposals, design, and text wording. Not all marker proposals were approved, and because communities were encouraged to take charge of local commemorations, programming varied. Sometimes patriotic organizations involved their offspring or Sullivan descendants in monument dedications, while others celebrated with parades of hundreds of schoolchildren.[37] Historical marker dedications were often the centerpiece of local events and commenced with a benediction, the singing of patriotic songs ("America" was in fashion), addresses by the leaders of the patriotic organizations that cosponsored the marker and which often secured access to the land, historical addresses by Flick, Nelson, or a local historian, and a closing religious statement (see figure 18). The press reported on these events in detail. Despite little prior popular focus on the Sullivan story, the state's attempt to generate local interest in its public history-making programming worked, for the most part. On some occasions, however, the state and local community's interests did not align, exposing cracks in a seemingly seamless public history-making extravaganza.

Celebrating a "Colossal Blunder"

The state's foray into large-scale commemoration was not completely trouble-free. A friend warned a marker dedication organizer not to push himself as the stress "killed the Geneva chairman."[38] The case of a marker placed south of Syracuse that recognizes Colonel Goose Van Schaick's raids on the Onondagas reveals the challenges of shared marker development.[39]

The Van Schaick expedition was a surprise attack on the Onondaga Nation from Fort Schuyler in April 1779. It received little mention in the popular textbook Flick prepared in 1926, identified only as "April 20 1779 Expedition against Onondagas."[40] At this point in the war, the Onondaga Nation was still endeavoring to maintain neutrality, although some Onondagas were assisting Oneidas in supporting the rebels.[41] Since Van Schaick was setting off from Fort Schuyler, where Oneidas regularly visited, keeping Oneida allies from learning about the mission against the Onondagas was difficult. Historians Joseph Glatthaar and James Martin note that a large group of Oneida men and women visiting the fort in mid-April saw "obvious signs of an impending cam-

FIG. 18. New York State 1929 Sullivan-Clinton Campaign marker closeup. Photo courtesy of the author.

paign" and asked if they could participate. Colonel Van Schaick deceived them and insisted that there was no expedition afoot.[42] When Oneidas decided to initiate their own expedition against the British at Oswegatchie, Van Schaick provided them food, ammunition, and even over thirty of his men to help further the ruse.

The day after the Oneida group departed the fort, Van Schaick and 558 soldiers left in the opposite direction for Onondaga territory.[43] They burned two villages to the ground, including the longhouse that held the council fire symbolizing the Confederacy, and killed twelve to fifteen Onondagas, captured thirty-three people, including women and children, slaughtered livestock, and destroyed foodstuffs, returning "triumphantly" to Fort Schuyler three days later. Multiple sources conclude that Onondaga women were violated before being killed.[44]

The Van Schaick raid achieved the opposite of what had been intended. The Onondagas had played the role of peace brokers since the start of the Revolution, negotiating between Oneidas and Tuscaroras on one side, and pro-British Iroquois on the other, and some Onondagas were starting to side with the rebels. Van Schaick deceived his Oneida allies and caused the Onondagas to flee their ancestral lands; some 125 people sought shelter with the Oneidas, but most left for the British side and Fort Niagara.[45]

Not long before Flick's involvement, a critical stance on this raid appeared in local media. In 1921 a Syracuse news article stated, "Historians have not minced matters much by calling what happened in the vicinity of Onondaga Valley and Dorwin Spring, 142 years ago this week, the 'massacre of the Onondagas.'" The article explained how Van Schaick left Fort Schuyler "on a mission of retaliation for what later appeared to have been an imaginary belief that the Onondagas were aligned with the British and responsible for attacks on the American patriots." A historian is cited as remarking, "If it was not a breach of faith . . . it certainly proved a colossal blunder."[46] In 1928 George Fryer, the director of the Onondaga Historical Association (OHA), a county historical society, condemned the attack. After White contacted him to suggest an anniversary commemoration, Fryer replied in a letter dated September 21, 1928, that he had been watching with "much interest the work of the Committee appointed to commemorate the Burgoyne Campaign." He wrote, "We have felt for a long time that our patriotic people in this vicinity should do their show to commemorate <u>the glorious work performed by Colonel Van Schaick in subduing its Onondaga</u> commencing with its battle fought near Mickles Furnace." However, this underlined passage is crossed out. A new date, November 9, was added to the top of the letter and, at the bottom of the letter, Fryer added, "upon further investigation, I feel ashamed of Colonel Van Schaick."[47] The OHA seemed determined that this was one event better left uncelebrated.

A few months before the April 1929 anniversary of the raid, there were no plans to move forward with a Van Schaick marker. The Syracuse press began making inquiries to committee members at the same time that the remains of the 1750s Fort Johnson were located. In response to a query from Fred Dutcher, editor of the *Post-Standard*, Secretary Nelson replied that there was a good chance that the state might support a marker at Fort Johnson, adding, "I wish that we might have some definite suggestions for location and character of such monument from the people in your county."[48] Nelson soon got his wish. Local white settlers unhappy with the state's nonaction on a Van Schaick celebration brought their grievances to the local press. The *Post-Standard* published an op-ed, "Onondaga's Neglected Past," arguing that "Syracuse salons, and officers of the Onondaga Historical society alike, have shown marked indifference to the anniversary as far as any suitable recognition of it is concerned. Are they so poor readers of history as to regard this one activity of the war which touched Onondaga County insignificant?"[49] Another op-ed piece, "Fighting Indians, 150 Years Ago," discussed the "raid of retribution" against the Onondagas and the raising of troops in March 1779 that made the "battle" of Syracuse possible; however, "there is no announcement of ceremonies of any sort," nor were there plans to mark the Onondaga raids. The author concluded, "The state historian and his department are interested. Why are not those, here at home, who profess a special interest in Syracuse history?" Finally, "Region's Part in Revolution to Be Ignored in Program" explained that there was "little likelihood Syracuse will observe the sesquicentennial of the only part this vicinity played in the American Revolution when, on April 21, 1779, American troops attacked the Onondaga Indians, allies of the British, killed 15 of them and took 34 prisoners, besides destroying their fort and their village." The author noted that although "state funds were provided for the purpose of marking historic sites in connection with the sesquicentennial, no action had been taken by the city or any organization."[50]

While the OHA could decline participation in a Van Schaick commemoration, it couldn't block other organizations from forging ahead, and in midsummer, after a gathering of many hereditary patriotic societies, the *Post-Standard* announced, "Anniversary of Raid will be Observed."[51] There are intriguing clues in the archival record suggesting that Flick and Nelson tried to distance themselves and official state involvement from this new plan. While the marker looked like the others in that it included the identical seal depicting Sullivan and Clinton, and even carried the usual state attribution, unlike the other monuments, it was funded entirely by a chapter of the Sons of the American Revolution.[52] In addition, Nelson seemed determined to remove himself from all marker planning activities. In response to regular queries from the commemoration secretary, Mamie Spring, he politely kept his distance again and again. When dates conflicted with his schedule, he explained: "There is, however, no necessity for your depending on our presence and it will be entirely satisfactory to us for you to go ahead and make arrangements for your meeting without our attendance."[53] When Mamie asked for input on their plans, he replied, "I have no suggestions or plans for your meeting, as we wish to leave that entirely to your committee to arrange." In terms of expenses, he explained that he would pay his way if he attended, "but we are looking to you to care for any other expenses in connection with your dedication from your local funds."[54] Nelson continued to apologize for Flick's inability to attend on the date that they chose. Regarding requests for approval of their program, Nelson explained, "I have no suggestions to make for your printed program as I understand you were going to print this locally and provide for it out of local funds so that it is entirely in your hands." Remarkably, when Mamie asked for some visual aid or maps, Nelson informed her, "We have no map that would be of any particular value for a printed program related particularly to Syracuse."[55] It could be that, by this time in their sesquicentennial programming, Nelson was overwhelmed by his competing obligations. However, a distancing even followed into the archival record. On the side of the archival folder regarding this event are handwritten notes: "Syracuse, N.Y."; "No other correspondence found"; "Can not find applications; not mentioned among numbers of markers" (underscore in the original).[56] Even though it is included in some tallies of the state's 1929 markers and includes the standard commemorative imagery with busts of Sullivan and Clinton, the state historian and his staff removed themselves as best they could from this particular commemorative activity and did not fund it.

The ceremony held at the Van Schaick site was bizarre. Mixed reviews of the proceedings appeared in local media, one stating, "Today's anniversary is that of Gansevoort and his 100 men stopping to rest on their way back east after fighting in other parts of the state, but the real event of importance here was the attack on the Onondagas and the burning of their fort, the destruction of the heart of the Iroquois confederacy." The article offered indirect criticism of the event by pointing out that the observance was "five months late," and the inscription on the monument was wrong. (It identified the date as April 22 when it should have stated April 21.)[57] However, in describing the military raid, the article did not mince words, stating, "The Onondagas were attacked on the morning of April 21, 1779. Their fort and homes were burned, their crops and cattle destroyed, 13 men killed and 34 taken prisoner. . . . The expedition was out five days, traveled 180 miles and did not lose a man."[58]

The printed program Mamie Spring and her societies prepared for September 22, 1929, mentioned none of this history, but instead advertised the event as the "Dedication of Monument Marking Site of Fort Johnson," referring to the fort built by Sir William Johnson in 1756 but long ago vanished.[59] The ceremony was short and sparsely attended compared to others. It involved the singing of "America," addresses by "Chief David B. Hill [sic] Onondagas" and Peter Nelson, executive secretary to the state historian, the unveiling of the monument by two children, a prayer, and closing remarks (see figure 19).

FIG. 19. David R. Hill (Onondaga) at Van Schaick marker unveiling. Image courtesy of Onondaga Historical Association, Syracuse NY.

Publicity of this relatively minor event was enhanced by the participation of a Native American leader, David Russell Hill. It is unclear why David Hill decided to attend. Hill was the son of Avis Jacob Hill (1836–1927), a Tuscarora woman who married William Hill of the Onondaga Nation and had ten children. She held the position of nominating woman for the Onondagas until she converted to Christianity in the late 1800s.[60] David had lived away from the area for many years: he attended Hampton Normal School in Virginia, and he taught for eleven years at federal Indian schools (two years at Teller Institute in Grand Junction, Colorado, one at Fort Lewis, in Colorado, and eight years at Mt. Pleasant, Michigan). He was an accomplished musician and served as a clerk for Onondaga council chiefs and as an interpreter in state and federal court, and he had recently served on a New York Indian commission (see next chapter). At the time of the sesquicentennial, he was forty-one years old.[61]

The media made a big deal of Hill's participation. One newspaper proclaimed, "Ancient hostility between the Red Man and the pale faces as a result of Sullivan's memorable raid through the valley was forgotten and buried forever as the descendants of the two groups mingled at the unveiling of the marker."[62] The *Post-Standard* offered an over-the-top assessment, proclaiming, "Tribe Forgets Bitterness of Sullivan Raid," with the subhead, "Indians and Whites Clasp Hands as Monument is Unveiled."[63] According to the newspaper, "Descendants of the Onondaga Indian tribe and of American pioneers clasped hands yesterday afternoon in a genuine manifestation of the permanent friendship that will endure among the offspring [of] the original inhabitants and the American colonists." It is a two-sided monolith with the standard state Sullivan-Clinton plaque on one side. The opposite side features a plaque inscribed with the following:

COLONEL GOOSE VAN SCHAICK

and 588 men of N.Y., Mass., Penn. and the Rifle Corps here completed the first movement of the Sullivan Campaign. Along the Onondaga Creek were the Indian villages and cornfields, objectives of the expedition, destroyed April 22, 1779.

COLONEL PETER GANSEVOORT

and 100 men arrived here September 22, 1779. They had gone from Canajoharie to Tioga with General Clinton's Brigade, then under General Sullivan had fought at Newton, marched through the Finger Lakes country to Genesee Castle, and were returning to the Mohawk Valley.

OLD FORT

About 400 feet east stood the stockade and blockhouses off the fort built by Sir William Johnson in 1756.

Erected by Syracuse Chapter, Sons of the American Revolution, and the State of New York, 1929.

The monument that announces Van Schaick's raid and the destruction of Onondaga villages and the council fires is poorly known today. Even the attendant at a large cemetery directly across the street did not know it was there when I visited in June 2017. It is an odd marker, commemorating the site of a British fort from the French and Indian War; a military operation in April 1779 led by Col. Van Schaick, which by the early 1920s was described in the press as an unprovoked massacre; and troops marching by, led by Col. Gansevoort, at the end of the Sullivan Expedition in September 1779. It credits the state even though the state did not provide funding. State distancing from the Van Schaick commemoration calls into question the wider commemorative agenda, however. If Van Schaick's raid was considered shameful in the 1920s, why wasn't the larger "Indian Expedition" viewed similarly?

The case of the Van Schaick marker exposes the potential hazards of joint commemorative programming. Although there was a mismatch here between state and local interests, since the state's committee had established a procedure for determining the scope and focus of local commemorative activities, and had included Van Schaick in its earliest missives, it could hardly prevent patriotic societies from celebrating it. When no marker was forthcoming, these societies turned to the press to pressure state officials to act. Flick and Nelson were in an awkward position between historical society representatives such as Fryer, who expressed shame at Van Schaick's actions, and hereditary patriotic organizations such as the SAR (of which Fryer was a member) that funded the marker and programming. Ironically, the publicity associated with the marker's dedication achieved one of Flick's goals, for it was one of the few marker dedication ceremonies in which a Native person participated. The difficulties state officials faced in garnering the participation of other Haudenosaunees in their Sullivan-Clinton festivities is the focus of the next chapter.

SIX

Celebrating Sullivan in Indian Country

W hen the New York state historian was developing plans to commemorate what he called the "Sullivan-Clinton Campaign," there were multiple Haudenosaunee communities within state borders with which he might engage. Members of the 150th Committee recognized this on some level and outlined the inclusion of "the Iroquois" in their initial proposal to the Regents in 1927, stating, "The purpose of the memorialization of the 150th anniversary of the Sullivan-Clinton Campaign is to obtain an intelligent understanding of its meaning and results in the history of New York State and the American Republic, and not to revive old hatred or to gloat over defeated foes, consequently representatives of the Iroquois, of Canada, and Great Britain should be cordially welcomed to take part in the commemoration."[1] The committee did not indicate how Iroquois representatives might be included, however. Inviting Sullivan's foes to join in such celebrations seems in poor taste today and, despite his repeated efforts, Flick had little success in convincing Haudenosaunees to take part in the fanfare. In this chapter, we consider why.

Memories of the horror wrought by Sullivan's troops are found in early Haudenosaunee accounts and persist in oral history, as we consider in part 3 of this book. Adding insult to injury, the interpretation of the expedition that the state historian was developing had flaws that most Haudenosaunee observers would recognize immediately. The state's 1929 marker plaques read as follows:

Routes of the armies of
General John Sullivan
and
General James Clinton
1779
An expedition against the hostile Indian
nations which checked the aggressions of
the English and Indians on the frontiers
of New York and Pennsylvania, extending
westward the dominion of the United States.
Erected by the
State of New York
1929.

This text, repeated on each of the state's thirty-five monoliths, outlines the significance of the Sullivan Campaign for New York. It develops a replacement narrative that claims that the Sullivan-Clinton Expedition represented the end of conflict with Iroquois foes ("checked the aggressions") and expanded New York State and the country westward ("extending westward the dominion of the United States"). It can be summarized as asserting that it was the Sullivan-Clinton operations that made New York State possible.

This text promotes outright falsehoods. For one, Iroquois attacks on frontier settlements after 1779 were even *more* devastating than before. As historian Colin Calloway documents, the scorched-earth campaigns only strengthened Iroquois resolve:

> Fifty-nine parties totaling almost 2,300 men went out from Niagara between February and September 1780. They killed 142 Americans and took 161 captives, destroyed 2 churches, 157 houses, and 150 granaries, and drove off 247 horses and 922 cattle. In New York, the raids led by Brant, Butler, and the Seneca war chief Cornplanter that spring destroyed 1,000 homes, 1,000 barns, and 600,000 bushels of grain. Pennsylvania fared little better. The Susquehanna Valley . . . suffered at least thirty-five separate raids from 1780–1782.

Calloway concludes: "Washington's war on Iroquois homes and food generated more, not fewer, raids on American settlers."[2] The

1929 plaques also do not mention that all but approximately two thousand Iroquois returned after Sullivan's devastation, and at the end of the Revolutionary War held all of western New York, most of central New York, much of northern and western Pennsylvania, and large parts of Ohio.[3] Beth Ryan documents substantial postwar settlements and finds that Euro-American travelers in the Finger Lakes region from 1780 to 1810 consistently came across Native Americans on the road, concluding, "This was still Indian territory."[4] Even when villages were relocated, Haudenosaunees still used nearby land for hunting and gathering and visited resting places of the dead.[5] In her recent study of Haudenosaunee settlements near Buffalo Creek into the 1840s, Alyssa Mt. Pleasant reports on thriving communities with rich farmlands and a high standard of living.[6]

The message on the stone monoliths neglects to note that it was well after Sullivan's raids that Haudenosaunee nations lost vast stretches of their homeland. After the New York State legislature tried to seize Iroquois territories as military bounty lands before the Treaty of Paris was signed in 1783, and state Indian commissioners evaded state law by concocting a private company that made fraudulent 999-year lease arrangements, the federal government asserted its authority. It enacted several important treaties, including the Indian Trade and Intercourse Act in 1790, which mandated a federal agent, Indian consent, ratification by the Senate, and a presidential signature to purchase Indian land legally, and the federal Treaty of Canandaigua of 1794, also known as the Pickering Treaty, which recognized Haudenosaunee sovereignty in two-thirds of the state. Haudenosaunee leaders and activists continue to recognize these treaties to this day.[7]

Despite these federal laws, New York speculators and political leaders persisted in their pursuit of Haudenosaunee territory, pressuring Haudenosaunee nations into twelve separate land disposition agreements from 1783 to 1796.[8] Entrepreneurs and leading state politicians openly conspired to obtain lands held by Oneidas, Cayugas, Onondagas, and Senecas to benefit from transportation revolutions that were transforming the state.[9] Politicians used the threat of further land loss to force Haudenosaunee leaders into exploitative land deals. By the mid-nineteenth century, Haudenosaunee nations had lost most of their homeland, and in the 1920s, they were living in scattered tiny reserves, or had moved to Canada, Wisconsin, or Oklahoma. Cayugas had lost their land base, and many were living with Senecas at Cattaraugus or other reservations. Many Mohawks were living in Canada, and many Oneidas moved to Wisconsin or Canada by the mid–nineteenth century. Threats of allotment and removal persisted for much of the nineteenth and twentieth centuries.[10] It was almost anyone *but* Sullivan who was responsible for seizing Haudenosaunee land. Why, then, this misleading narrative placing the blame (or the credit) on Sullivan? Contemporaneous Haudenosaunee challenges to state sovereignty may have played a role in encouraging state officials to narrate their story the way that they did.

The Everett Commission and Land Claims

In 1922 New York was rocked with a land-claims movement that put much of the state's legal foundation into question.[11] "Is White Man's Title to More Than Six Million Acres of One-Time Indian Land in New York State Threatened?" asked Albany's *The Knickerbocker Press* in a dramatic full-page spread on April 30, 1922. This uncertainty was raised by the findings presented by a New York State Indian commission chaired by assemblyman Edward A. Everett from Potsdam.[12] Everett's commission was created in May 1919 in response to an Oneida land-claims case that had raised jurisdictional confusion.[13] The New York State Legislature hoped the commission would determine once and for all whether the Six Nations of New York were under federal or state control.[14]

The Everett Commission held hearings with each New York–Haudenosaunee nation and with the Six Nations in Canada (see figure 20). Over the course of these meetings, commissioners confronted the fact that the lines separating state and federal power had never been clearly drawn, and multiple state treaties had not followed federal law.[15] Through these discussions, Everett determined that the tenure of much of New York State, including whole cities such as Buffalo and Syracuse, large industrial centers, power plants, railroads, the Erie Canal, and more, was

FIG. 20. Edward A. Everett; his secretary, Lulu G. Stillman; and three Cayuga leaders on the steps of the capitol building in Albany NY. *Left to right*: Alexander John, Ernest Spring, Edward A. Everett, Edwin Spring, Lulu G. Stillman. This photograph was likely taken in February 1922, when Everett presented his commission's findings to the legislature (Graymont, *Fighting Tuscarora*, 1973). Image courtesy of Six Nations Iroquois Cultural Center, Onchiota NY.

uncertain, asserting that the Six Nations in New York State "have title to lands estimated at 6,000,000 acres and valued at approximately $2,500,000,000."[16] When Everett presented these radical conclusions to the New York Assembly in February 1922, the other commission members refused to sign onto his report, his report was never forwarded to the legislature, and his commission's work was almost completely buried.[17] But Everett had also released his findings to the Haudenosaunee nations with whom he had met.[18]

The Iroquois began to meet at the center of the metaphorical longhouse (Onondaga) to consider a response, and New York presses were noticing. "Six Nation Remnants Seek Return of Old Holdings," the Rochester *Democrat and Chronicle* announced on November 30, 1924, continuing, "The Six Nations are out on the war path. Not with tomahawk and sharp pointed arrows for the heart of an enemy, but with lawyers and ancient records." On February 22, 1925, the *Buffalo Courier* announced: "Land on Which Buffalo is Situated Sought by Tribes of Six Iroquois Nations." The story of bringing together disparate Haudenosaunee nations and subfactions in the 1920s for the massive Six Nations land claim often centers on the figure of Laura (Minnie) Cornelius Kellogg, a Wisconsin Oneida leader and activist who mounted a flawed fundraising effort to support it.[19] In spite of the drama she fanned, Haudenosaunee leaders managed to form a coalition, hire a legal team, and bring the momentous land-claims case to federal court on June 6, 1925, starting with a case against a power company that plaintiffs argued was occupying land that belonged to the Mohawk Nation.[20] The New York attorney moved to dismiss the case on the grounds that the federal court had no jurisdiction—since the 1924 passage of the federal Indian Citizenship Act, plaintiffs and defendants had been citizens of New York. Appeals were soon filed and refiled, into April of 1929.[21]Although the outcome was ultimately a disappointing one for the Six Nations plaintiffs, it was while the future of a huge swath of New York was in question that the state historian was planning his Revolutionary War commemorations. In 1928, when Flick was traversing the state to garner interest in his Sullivan-Clinton programming, appeals and amended appeals were still in play; the deadline for appeal was August 6, 1929.[22]

Coincidence or Something More?

While we can assume that the Haudenosaunee land claim movement was of general interest to Haudenosaunee nations, can we also assume that it was as visible to non-Native New York residents? More to the point, can we link the land claim movement to the Sullivan-Clinton celebration? It is tempting to see the state's decision to celebrate the Sullivan-Clinton Campaign with historical markers as a response to the uncertainties generated by the lawsuit.[23] I have sought correspondence between the main actors on this matter, to no avail. However, it is worth noting that some people with close connections to the state's Revolutionary War programming were aware of Haudenosaunee claims and even advocated on their behalf. W. Pierrepont White raised the alarm early on. Just a few days after Governor Smith approved White's 1923 proposal, White began writing the trustees of the New York State Historical Association to bring their attention to the Haudenosaunee land case. White, who was president of the Mohawk Valley Historical Association, wrote to Rev. Frederick Richards of Glen Falls transmitting an article he had written about New York land tenure law and stating the following:

> At the present moment, there is being held on the Onondaga Reservation, near Syracuse, a gathering of the Six nations, with representatives from Wisconsin and Brantford. The subject of their conference is the wrongs done them by our State and Nation, through breach of treaties. The Sioux Indians are now before the Court of Claims, asking for $700,000,000 from the U.S. for breach of treaties made with their Nation. It is not improbable that a similar uniting of the claims of the Six Nations will be accomplished. New York and MA dealt directly with the Indian tribes. Damages, not ouster from the land, are asked by the Sioux.
>
> New York State has a remarkable history, and our busy populace so engrossed in commercial enterprise can scarcely pause too often to consider the sources of its prosperity and the history of the movements and events that have made New York the Empire State. Let it be hoped that the native red man will have his part properly depicted and that his position as a constructive factor in the development of the state be emphasized at least as much as his acts of hostility. The time has come when our people can afford to understand the red man in other light than that of prejudice.[24]

One of his interlocutors, New York Humane Association (NYHA) trustee William O. Stillman, president of the American Humane Association, wrote to White on June 7, 1923, responding to what we can assume was a similar letter:

> Dear President White,
>   Your very kind favor of June 6, 1923 is duly received; also the clipping which you enclose. I am heartily in sympathy with the

proposition that the descendants of the native Indians in this State shall be dealt with justly and fairly by our State and National Government. Residents of the United States cannot afford to be unjust or unfair with those from whom land has been taken and important privileges secured.

I earnestly hope that New York will go on record as doing the right thing to the Indians. The subject is being actively agitated at the present time. My friend, George Wharton James, of California, has been publishing some valuable discussions of this subject. There should be no legitimate ground for discussion of the questions as to whether we should be honest, whether we should be just, whether we should be decent. With kind Regards, . . . Stillman.[25]

While further research may shed more light on this intriguing communication, correspondence between White and NYHA trustees seemed to end as soon as it began.

A Haudenosaunee Rebuff

Flick and his executive secretary, Peter Nelson, were inviting Haudenosaunee members to take part in a celebration of a military victory over them. What is more, their public monument and speeches misrepresented the import of Sullivan's raids, suggesting that the Iroquois lost their lands in 1779, and all this when Haudenosaunee leaders were arguing that they were never legally ceded. It is no surprise that Flick's solicitations to Native leaders were getting nowhere.[26] In February 1929, while the fate of the lawsuit was still unclear, Peter Nelson made an official visit to Cornell University, during the twenty-second annual Farms and Home Week, to offer invitations to Six Nations leaders gathered there. Rather than a welcoming, Nelson encountered one of the clearest demonstrations of Six Nations opposition to the state's Sullivan-Clinton anniversary fanfare expressed.

Nelson was meeting with that year's "Cornell Indian Board," an organization that had emerged out of the Indian Extension work established by Erl Augustus Caesar Bates, a doctor of obstetrics. Bates helped establish Cornell University's College of Agri-

FIG. 21. Six Nations Delegates (Indian Board precursor) and Winter Course students at Cornell University during Farmers' Week. Source: *Extension Source News* 4, no. 5 (May 1921): 23, Ithaca NY: New York State College of Agriculture at Cornell University, 1921.

culture Indian Extension program in 1920 (see figure 21). New York's Indian Nation Councils selected representatives to travel to Cornell to assist in selecting Haudenosaunee students for college courses, and groups of these councillors became known as "boards."[27] That year, sixteen men and women were gathered for the meeting's concluding "powwow," including head chief Andrew Gibson of the Six Nations.[28] The Board's chair was Walter "Boots" Kennedy, a Seneca man from Killbuck, New York (Allegany Territory), elected in December 1927.[29] Kennedy was an outspoken defender of Haudenosaunee rights, whose presentation at the Everett Commission meeting in Allegany in 1920 was a tour de force.[30]

When Nelson tendered a formal invitation to the Six Nation leaders to participate in the Sullivan-Clinton festivities that fall, Kennedy gave Nelson "an earful of Indian grievance," a journalist observed.[31] Kennedy explained to Nelson that "the Six Nations of the Iroquois did not feel that conditions warranted their participation in the [Sullivan-Clinton] program."[32] Why? Because "the white man had broken his part of the agreement." As Kennedy put it, at the end of the Revolutionary War, "the Iroquois reserved for themselves certain pieces of land of two characters. One was lands now embraced in their reservations in Niagara, Genesee, Erie, Allegany, and Cattaraugus counties and the other pieces reserved were the burial places of their ancestors in Chautauqua, Wyoming, Livingston, Orleans, Monroe, Wayne and Ontario counties." Kennedy explained that the Indians had "the solemn promise of George Washington, himself, that these burial places would never be disturbed," adding, "When we made our treaties, George Washington promised that the spade and plow of the white man would never molest the sleeps of our fathers." This is not what happened. Kennedy continued, "Now in Chautauqua County and in other places the white men have thrown up the bones of our fathers and they are bleaching in the sun and snow at this moment. We understand that these white people send their collections of arrow heads and copper beads taken from the graves of our ancestors to the museum in your department. The graves of our fathers are as sacred as the bones of your white people and we rigorously protest against this practice." He also brought up loans of family heirlooms that were never returned, adding pointedly, "Some of this material is now in your museum cases at Albany."[33] This was a powerful and well-placed critique, for the New York State Museum he was referencing was under the direction of the education department, the same state agency overseeing the Revolutionary War programming. The head chief, Andrew Gibson, and "16 others of his tribesmen who were seated in solemn council" nodded in agreement. According to journalist Leroy Fess, an Onondaga man "told of plans his people had to dig in white men's cemeteries and scatter the bones around unless this careless practice is stopped."[34] The next day, the Cornell Indian Board went a step further to pass a resolution condemning the desecration of Indian graves and sent a copy to the New York legislature.[35] It is interesting that it was the invitation to participate in the public Sullivan-Clinton events that yielded this unanimous resolution and that Flick's extensive clippings file includes nothing related to these meetings or this standoff. For their part, rather than directly challenge the boastful nature of the Sullivan-Clinton festivities, Haudenosaunee leaders used the opportunity to turn the tables and raise a matter of great collective concern.

Performing at Sullivan-Clinton Festivities

Public events in New York in the 1920s often included Haudenosaunee performers, so Flick and Nelson's difficulty in securing Haudenosaunee participation was unusual for the time.[36] A notable exception was the performance by a Cayuga-Seneca group at a marker dedication at Great Gully, the site of the former "Cayuga Castle," an event organized by Auburn lawyer Richard C. S. Drummond. Drummond planned a dedication event he advertised as the "last Council fire of the Cayugas," and he prepared an ode to these imagined "last" Cayugas.[37] To carry out this dramatic performance, he needed to be speaking to Cayugas, and it took him some time to locate people willing to play this role.[38] He ended up inviting Dr. Wilbur Clifford Shongo, a well-known Seneca man from Buffalo. Son of Moses and Alice Ellen (Pierce) Shongo, he served in the New York Seventy-Fourth Infantry National Guard (1902–7, 1907–12) and was described as the "only physician in New York state authorized to practice medicine without a state license."[39] It is unclear how Drummond first connected with Mr. Shongo, but it was likely through Arthur C. Parker, director of the Rochester Municipal Museum (now the Rochester Museum & Science Center).[40] Parker and Drummond were in communication before the events, and Parker sent grave goods that had been excavated at Great Gully to be put on public display in the windows of the Empire Gas and Electric Company during the festivities.[41] The only Cayuga man identified by name was James Crowe.[42]

The ceremony was preceded by a massive procession through the city of Auburn involving 3,500 children from public and parochial schools, "clad in gay raiment," accompanied by school officials, teachers, and national guardsmen. The parade was described as the "climax of the celebration for the City of Auburn," and news coverage detailed the colorful outfits worn by the schoolchildren. At the rear of the parade came the "Cayuga Indians," who "marched in full war paint and feathers, giving a vivid reminder of the days when General Sullivan's men cleared this section for homes and schools."[43] Local press coverage suggested that, in fact, the parade was the main attraction for most participants, noting, "There was the closing event at Great Gully to follow, but that was to be less local and less fascinating to the crowds of Auburn parents, uncles, aunts, cousins and friends of the young folks who lined the streets three deep this afternoon."[44]

At the Great Gully dedication, Haudenosaunee participants had to endure speeches made by two Christian leaders about their churches' missionizing efforts among the Cayugas in previous centuries. Bishop Hamilton, a Moravian leader from Bethlehem, discussed "plainly of the cruelties practiced by some of the Indian tribes on white settlers and mission workers" and outlined "the repeated efforts" of Moravian missionaries to convert the Cayugas. He was followed by Fr. John E. McCarthy, a Jesuit from Philadelphia, who discussed the Jesuit Order's efforts "into the wilds of the lands of the Cayugas," and who also recounted "the atrocities perpetrated upon them by the Iroquois."[45] When it was Dr. Shongo's turn, he started with "an invocation to the Great Spirit, speaking in his native tongue," then spoke to those present through a translator. The journalist's transcript of the translator's statements suggests that Shongo was responding to the religious leaders who preceded him, as he commenced with, "The chief has given thanks to . . . the Great Spirit, that he has brought us here safely from our home near Buffalo, that you and we have been kept in safety here and asked that we might return safely. We are not Pagans and we never were," he added. "We have never worshipped idols. The Indians' God has always been the Great Spirit. Since we have been told about Christ, we close our prayers in the name of Christ."[46]

Drummond's dedication speech was an over-the-top ode to the Cayuga Nation, starting, "O, People of the Long House! We come to you this day in friendship, with a message of good will." After offering salutations to Mohawks and Onondagas, he turned to the "Cayugas" present:

> And you, Gah-Yo-Gwa-Oh! At the place where once your stronghold stood we greet you. In that former time you were a great nation, mighty in war, powerful in council. . . . But now for more than a hundred years their ancient domain has not seen the Cayugas. By grant from them we hold that land. Once numerous, compact and strong, the Cayugas are few and weak and scattered. As a nation soon will they have vanished from the earth. . . . Accept our tribute. Take back to the Cayugas our message. Tell them that your ears have heard our words, and that your eyes have seen the pledge we give of our sincerity: this monument of bronze and granite . . . upon which, to the end of time, shall be found emblazoned the name, Cayuga–GahYo-Gwar-Ohn'! Oon-eh![47]

Drummond seemed to revel in the remarkable "lasting" paean that he concocted. That Flick was eager for Haudenosaunee involvement of this type can be inferred from his gushing response to Drummond's event, writing, "The exercises at Great Gully were unusually impressive. The presence of the Indians and their participation added a note which, I regret to say, was *lacking in most of our dedication observances*" (emphasis added).[48]

How might we interpret Shongo's decision to participate in this ceremony? Some showmanship was involved, as Shongo's pronouncements were regularly translated into English even though he spoke and wrote fluently in that language. Correspondence between Drummond and Shongo suggests that this was partly a money-making venture for Shongo and his entourage. After an initial discussion, Drummond detailed Shongo's obligations, with a request for "the actual part to be performed by you and your people, as you outlined it to me yesterday, had better not be planned to exceed one-half an hour." He added that he hoped he would accomplish "the best and most dramatic result possible under the circumstance," adding, "All of these things you will guarantee as to your performance, without fail."[49]

Shongo replied with a quick note: "Dear Sir, I am pleased to hear from you and something definite, it means $255.00, 5 meals and lodging for 2 nights, for our party, for services we render on the day of Sept. 24th Tuesday 1929. I am working along the lines we discussed, and have called a meeting for a rehearsal. Do not harbor any thots [sic] of disappointment. We are square shooters. After our rehearsal I will drop you words of great encouragement etc. etc."[50]

There may have been more than financial compensation encouraging Dr. Shongo and his colleagues to participate in the Auburn dedication. After the events were over, Drummond and the local police chief took the men on a tour of the area, driving along the "old Indian trail" and to Great Gully, where they observed mounds that "they are certain are the graves of their forefathers."[51] Four years later, central New York presses made much of the visit of three Cayuga men (David Cook and Chief Charles Fun of Buffalo, and Chief Robert Fishcarrier of the Six Nations Reservation in Ontario) to Albany, where they sought information on parcels of land that they believed belonged to the Cayuga Nation. "A yellowed copy of the Indian treaty of 1784 was brought out of the secretary of state's files early today at the request of three Cayuga Indians seeking to establish a claim to a large piece of land in Western New York," reported the *Jamestown Evening Journal* on Wednesday, September 24, 1934, adding, "Warrior Charles Funn of Buffalo said the land in question 'ought to be about 100 miles square.'" Were some of these men the same people who performed during the Auburn event? We do not know; however, Drummond's colleague, Mr. Searing, former president of the Cayuga County Historical Society, immediately brought the matter to Drummond's attention.[52]

Where Brodhead Turned Back

A final episode illustrating the gulf between Haudenosaunee and state perspectives involved the state historian's attempt to place a Sullivan-Clinton marker on Seneca land. The plaque was to commemorate the Brodhead portion of Washington's "Indian Expedition" (see map 2). Flick's decision to include the Brodhead Expedition in the state's Sullivan-Clinton programming seems odd until we realize that adding this mission would help extend the geographical reach of the commemorative activities. Since Brodhead traveled north from Fort Pitt in Pennsylvania, including the monument would allow Flick to plan joint exercises with his counterparts in that state, and would mean placing a marker near the Allegany Territory of the Seneca Nation of Indians and increasing the likelihood of Native American involvement in public ceremonies.

The Allegany Reservation, where Flick hoped to place a marker, was one of few remaining Seneca territories in the state. After regaining millions of acres in western New York, through the federal Canandaigua Treaty of November 11, 1794, the Senecas lost all but eleven parcels of land in the Treaty of Big Tree in 1797 as the result of dishonest negotiating tactics.[53] By the Civil War, they had only four parcels remaining (the Cattaraugus, Allegany, Oil Springs, and Tonawanda Reservations), and in the nineteenth century, the nation divided into the Seneca Nation of Indians and Tonawanda Senecas.[54] The Allegany Reservation was further reduced by the mid–nineteenth century arrival of several railway lines and six railroad stations established on Seneca lands.[55] Non-Indian settlements were made possible by the establishment of ninety-nine-year federal "leases."[56] Further threats to Seneca sovereignty included the curtailment of hunting and fishing on Seneca lands.[57] Given the lengthy history of the state taking Seneca land, it is possible that state officials viewed taking a small amount of Seneca land for a historical marker as inconsequential. Especially given this recent history, this is not how Senecas would see the project.

A further challenge the state committee faced was poor information about the Brodhead Expedition. Flick and Nelson's earliest proposals had identified Olean Point, New York, as the farthest village destroyed in his journey, but they were unsure of the reliability of their sources.[58] It was a minor footnote in most discussions of the Revolutionary War, and in one early U.S. history volume, it was doubted to have happened at all.[59] It was apparently of little interest to the local white historical and patriotic organizations at the time Flick was planning the monument, for they did not request a marker.

Washington designated Gen. Daniel Brodhead commandant of

Fort Pitt in February 1779.[60] In June, Washington suggested that Brodhead might launch a mission from Pitt "as a diversion in favor of the expedition of General Sullivan."[61] Brodhead left Fort Pitt on August 11 with 605 men while Sullivan and his troops were waiting in Wyoming, Pennsylvania, for supplies.[62] His advance guard battled Senecas and Delawares coming down the Allegheny River approximately ten miles below Conewago. After traveling on a hilltop trail, his troops came to the town of Yoghroonwago and seven other towns along the river. They destroyed 130 houses at these settlements and burned three more villages on the way back, returning to Fort Pitt on September 14. Many of his soldiers returned barefoot, with plunder that they sold for $30,000.[63] According to this account, Brodhead's troops never crossed into New York.

The earliest recorded Seneca accounts concurred that Brodhead's men stayed in Pennsylvania. During his research trip to Allegany and Western Pennsylvania in 1850, historian Lyman C. Draper collected Seneca accounts of the Revolutionary War and recorded oral testimonies of the Brodhead mission from Chainbreaker (also known as Governor Blacksnake) and Cornplanter's son, Charles O'Bail. After describing the encounter on the Allegheny River between the Seneca hunting party and Brodhead's advance guard, Chainbreaker attested, "At Kinzua resided a few Delawares, who ran away upon Brodhead's approach: The Americans then advanced as far as the Cornplanter town & burned it— the Indians living there having taken their gathered corn & other valuables to the east side of the river & buried them for security. Cornplanter then did not reside there, nor had he yet removed to the Alleghany. The town was called Du-no-sah-dah-gah, or The Burnt-House—from the circumstance of an Indian house having long before been accidentally burned there."[64]

Charles O'Bail's recollections were similar.[65] Draper noted: "O'Bail thinks Brodhead did not go above Broken Straw–that the Cornplanter town had Indian sentinels out, & were momentarily expecting the Americans."[66] "Broken Straw" is one of many names for a former Seneca village based at the mouth of Brokenstraw Creek and is the site of the present town of Irvine, Pennsylvania.[67]

We do not know if the state historian read the Draper manuscripts, but he certainly did not rely on Brodhead's report. In his September 16, 1779, letter to Washington at the conclusion of his expedition, Colonel Brodhead was quite precise about his troop size (605 "Rank and File including Militia & Volunteers") and movements, reporting that they traveled as far as Yoghroonwago.[68] Yoghroonwago was a Seneca village on the Allegany River near Croydon, Pennsylvania. By his own account, Brodhead never crossed into New York.[69]

In the nineteenth century, amateur historians had stretched Brodhead's trip well across the New York line, however, replete with authoritative-looking maps that showed journeys that crossed into New York, one suggesting that troops went all the way to Olean Point.[70] Flick and Nelson were proposing a monument to a military expedition they knew little about, trying to place the marker where the expedition had not occurred, in a community that did not want it, and all this after the embarrassing meeting with Six Nations leaders at Cornell in February. It is no wonder they ran into difficulties. They carried on nevertheless. One month after his encounter with the Cornell Indian Board, Nelson contacted New York state legislators to inform them of their plan to "put a marker at a place near Red House . . . and possibly to hold the celebration well within the Indian reservation; the dedication of the marker to take place at the site itself but to be very brief." They hoped this would happen August 31, as close to the "actual date of Brodhead's northernmost advance as we can determine," and involve three speakers, one from Pennsylvania, one from New York, and "one from the Indian community if that seemed desirable."[71]

By late March, Flick had begun writing letters to local Senecas seeking their blessing for this plan. He even contacted Walter Kennedy, as if the incident at Cornell had never happened. These letters are remarkable. In them, Flick reveals his hazy grasp of the geography of the 1779 expedition and his inability to imagine how commemorating the raid might be viewed by Senecas. "My Dear Mr. Kennedy," he started, in a letter dated March 21, 1929. He explained that they hoped to "erect a beautiful monument calling attention to the Brodhead Expedition from Fort Pitt."[72] He confessed that he was not sure where the monument should be located:

> It is a little uncertain in my own mind as to just how far north Brodhead got in his invasion of the Seneca country, and also what route he took on his return. I am writing to you, therefore, to ascertain what the traditions are among the Indians as to how far north Brodhead came. The only map I have found which pretends to mark his route shows that the northern extremity was at Buck Tooth, which I presume is West Salamanca.[73]

Flick wanted Kennedy to tell him where Brodhead may have traveled and sought reassurance about his plans. He explained that he had been told the "appropriate place" for a monument would be somewhere near the Old Council House, and he asked Kennedy what he thought about that location. Finally, he asked Kennedy, "Would it be possible for you to provide a brief address on the Indian traditions relative to Brodhead's invasion?" He added, in a polite imperative, "When I visit your reservation I should like to have a talk with you on the subject, but meanwhile would be pleased to have you write me on the points raised above."[74]

On March 21, 1929, Flick sent a similar letter to prominent Allegany Seneca elder Sylvester Crouse:

> This year 1929 marks the 150th anniversary of Colonel Brodhead's invasion of the Seneca country from Fort Pitt in 1779. The states of New York and Pennsylvania are planning to hold some kind of a joint meeting in order to better understand the facts about Brodhead's Expedition. In connection with that meeting the State of New York wishes to erect a beautiful monument at some suitable place near a well-traveled highway. It has been suggested that where the road forks near the Council House would be a good site. Would it be possible for you to obtain permission from the Indians to allow the State to erect such a monument at that point? Just what spot would you yourself recommend as most suitable? In our exercises dedicating the monument I believe that the Indians should be represented. Would you consent to take some part

in the ceremony? For instance, it would be highly appropriate for you, as the leader of the Indians, to accept the monument from the State of New York in your official capacity. I should also like to have you tell me what the Indian traditions are as to the northernmost point reached by Brodhead when he invaded the Indian country. The only map which I have seen attempting to represent his route shows that the expedition ended at Buck Tooth. Is that in harmony with Indian tradition? I shall be glad to have a letter from you with your views relative to the monument and the Brodhead Expedition.[75]

This correspondence mixes ignorance and coercion, a rapid firing of questions, and an indirect command ("I shall be glad to have a letter from you with your views"). Flick's use of the passive voice throughout ("it has been suggested") masks his role in developing these very plans. Mr. Crouse never replied; he passed away before Peter Nelson could meet with him that summer. For his part, Kennedy decided it best to direct this attention elsewhere:

Dear sir:

Would say: In reply to yours of March 21st, 1929; I would refer you to the President of the Seneca Nation of Indians: Post-Office address: Ray Jimerson Irving N.Y.

Who is the proper person for you to take up the Matter with, As I am not connected Officially in any capacity with the Seneca Nation of Indians at the present time, Therefore would not have any authority to grant the right to any person to erect or place a marker upon the domains of the Seneca Nation of Indians. Yours very respectfully, Walter Kennedy, Killbuck, NY.[76]

Traveling to Salamanca

A trip to Salamanca was in order. On Monday, July 29, Peter Nelson traveled there and consulted with state senator DeHart Ames, executive secretary of the Allegany State Park Commission in Red House.[77] According to Nelson's meeting notes, they met with Edison Crouse, treasurer of the Seneca Nation, Jonas and Jerome Crouse, "elders in church on proposed site," and Reverend P. F. Hawthorne, white missionary.[78] Local newspapers described the project as designed to "mark the approximate point at which Colonel Daniel Brodhead's expedition against the Iroquois Indian confederacy turned back," hardly a laudatory event.[79] Each proposed monument location posed challenges.[80] The Olean *Times Herald* noted the development of "opposition among certain of the Indians to placing of the marker on the reservation, some of them evidently interpreting it as a reflection of themselves."[81]

Nelson's visit propelled local state senators Lehigh Kirkland and DeHart Ames into action. The senators' first move was to insist that the date for the proposed marker dedication be pushed back several months, citing Seneca concerns. Kirkland wrote to "Hon. A.C. Frick" [*sic*], "If we are to recommend a place for this tablet, that a little time to find just what the sentiment of the Indians was regarding the same might have a bearing on our recommendation."[82] It appears that they learned what that sentiment was almost immediately, for the next day, Ames wrote to Nelson suggesting the Veterans Memorial Park within the town of Salamanca as the location and expanded with a subsequent letter.[83] Their rationale was that this new location had the advantage of being "where many thousands of people would see and could read the tablet every season." Ames also suggested that it might be nice to have a small tablet on the reverse side "pertaining to the American Legion mentioning the earliest war as well as the latest war."[84] They fixed a date, the first Saturday in October. Perhaps so that there would be no chance of any confusion, Ames wrote to Nelson while Kirkland wrote to Flick that they were "in hearty agreement."[85]

Kirkland and Ames were clear in their correspondence that the proposed Sullivan-Clinton marker was not going to be welcomed by local Senecas. What they may have been too polite to tell the state historian and his secretary was that the proposed marker venue, Veterans Memorial Park, was booked for Labor Day, the weekend Flick and Nelson originally suggested. The park had been created through a series of annual Labor Day fundraising activities, and once it had been built, Labor Day festivities held there were large all-day affairs that drew upward of 2,500 people.[86] It seemed that marking Labor Day, not Sullivan-Clinton, was what mattered there.

After local control was ceded to Senator Kirkland and the event set for October 5, Flick decided not to attend and sent Nelson in his stead. Nelson prepared a speech, but as late as September 25 still had no program details. He wrote Kirkland to ask when the event would start, and "who the other speakers may be and their topics."[87] It turns out he was the only speaker. (In other regions of the state, multiple speeches competed for attention during monument-dedication exercises.) Kirkland responded with a minimalist program, adding that everyone taking part would "limit themselves to five-minute talks."[88] The program he outlined was as follows.

Band
Chorus of school children
Prayer Dr. Elliot
Address of welcome by Mayor Hunt
Apreciation [sic] of monument by Park Pres. Fred Benz
Pledge of care Representive [sic] of Legion
Adress [sic] by yourself
Baseball

Nelson had prepared a much longer speech and wrote back right away: "I understand from this that the entire program is not to take up more than approximately one hour. I am not quite sure as to whether you wish me to limit my remarks to five minutes as well as the other speakers but shall be very glad to fall in line with any plans that you have and to cut them to that limit if you desire."[89]

In the end, the 1929 event to recognize Brodhead's destruction of Seneca villages was a brief affair, with the main attraction a baseball game held immediately after the marker dedication. The Salamanca school band played, a school chorus sang, and Reverend A. C. Elliott of the First Congregational Church said a prayer. Mayor Bert L. Hunt welcomed the audience, John Thornton, past commander of the John D. Hughes American Legion Post, pledged to care for the marker, and Nelson gave his five-minute address, after which a Brodhead descendant, Mrs. Mary Brodhead Hudson, of Kittanning, Pennsylvania, unveiled the marker.[90]

The Seneca Nation made sure that the Brodhead marker was established nowhere near the heart of Seneca social, political, or spiritual life. As a result, the October commemoration of the Brodhead raids in no way matched the state officials' original vision. Flick and Nelson had hoped to place the six-foot-high, three-ton granite slab at a prominent location on the Allegany Territory and to involve both Native Americans and dignitaries from Pennsylvania in the festivities. They had also hoped to time the dedication to occur roughly the same day Brodhead's troops had destroyed Seneca settlements in that location 150 years earlier. Instead, the marker was placed far from anywhere anyone thought Brodhead had traveled, the dedication occurred a month later than planned, and even the desired joint state exercises never materialized, despite Flick and Nelson's repeated outreach efforts to potential representatives starting in March.[91] As Flick later wrote to PHC secretary Frances Dorrance, "It seemed quite difficult to awaken any interest in the Expedition in that part of the State."[92]

Senecas and their allies likely found the whole exercise amusing, if not alarming. In his memoir, *Allegany Oxbow, A History of Allegany State Park and the Allegany Reserve of the Seneca Nation*, Charles E. Congdon, attorney to the Seneca Nation of Indians, addressed the question of how far Brodhead traveled. In his view, the creators of the "stories" about Brodhead's New York journey were ill-informed, and he noted, "The authors of the stories that Brodhead came as far as Coldspring and went back by way of Randolph, or that he reached the vicinity of Salamanca or even Olean, had not read the statements taken down by Dr. Draper from men who were members of the expedition nor the report made by John Butler to Col. Bolton, which is preserved in the British Museum."[93] In another section of his memoir, Congdon wrote that "since the publication of the Draper manuscripts by the Wisconsin Historical Society, no careful student is likely to claim that Brodhead cross[ed] the State Line."[94] Congdon discussed Flick's plan to put the monument at Coldspring with what can only be interpreted as amazement: "It is easy to understand why the Seneca Council in 1929, refused permission for the N.Y. State Historian to erect one of his Sullivan-Clinton monuments at Coldspring. That is the reason it stands in the Veterans Park at Salamanca." He added, "You might as well ask Congress for consent to erect a monument to Ross and Cockburn in front of the Capitol in Washington," referencing the British men who set fire to the Capitol during the War of 1812.[95]

Conclusion

At a time when New York–Haudenosaunee relations were especially fraught, the state historian developed a celebration of a military campaign that had devastated the Haudenosaunee homeland, and invited Haudenosaunees to participate in the festivities. Only a few Native people agreed to take part in the dozens of Sullivan-Clinton marker dedications held across the state, and at least one of these performances was insulting, framed as the "last" appearance of remnants of a vanishing society. We should again consider the performative dimensions of commemorative events. Dedication organizers like Drummond seemed to find it irresistible to orchestrate "lasting" rituals, and they looked far and wide to find Native actors to play carefully scripted parts in their dramas, dressed as if they were ripped from another era and speaking through unnecessary translators, and they paid them to do so. Was staging "lasting" rituals of this kind a type of wishful thinking on the part of the dedication organizers? Were they alarmed by "modern Indians" armed with legal teams, or rendered uneasy by the land claims that threatened titles in vast stretches of the state?

When Six Nations leaders received an official invitation at a public meeting, they refused to participate and condemned the state with eloquent charges of hypocrisy. We might ask how we should interpret the Haudenosaunee response to the state historian's invitation. Should we view it as a form of resistance to state officials' grotesque insensitivity? At the time, Haudenosaunees were battling the imposition of citizenship, educational policies, and hunting and fishing regulations against a formidable foe, as well as organizing to mount a collective suit against the state. Rather than discussing Haudenosaunee resistance to the Sullivan-Clinton extravaganza, we might view the Sullivan-Clinton events as a reaction to that activism. "See, this really is our land," the plaques seem to claim. "We really won this land fair and square in the Revolutionary War." We might read in the state's exercise in mass public patriotism an effort to address the challenges to the state's honor that the land claim case represented. It is in the pageant that we see the full message of the Sullivan-Clinton Campaign laid out in plain language for 1929 non-Native New Yorkers, and it is to the pageant that we now turn.

SEVEN

The 1929 *Pageant of Decision*

I n the summer of 1929, New York state historian Alexander C. Flick and his executive secretary, Peter Nelson, were putting the final touches on a massive pageant reenacting the Sullivan-Clinton Campaign. The *Pageant of Decision*, subtitled *Why the Westward Republic Grew*, was held three times, with separate casts, in Leicester, Geneva, and Elmira on September 14, 21, and 28.[1] While historical monument dedications were attracting dozens of participants, the pageant drew tens of thousands of spectators at each of its three performances. "75,000 Witness Pageant, Mark Twain Park Audience at Pageant Greatest Gathering in History of Elmira," the *Sunday Gazette* announced at the conclusion of the final production. Dr. Flick described the day as "successful beyond anticipation." Why so successful? In his view, this was because "the weather was perfect. The parking facilities were excellent. The seating and standing spaces were inadequate to accommodate comfortably the enormous throng of people who came to see the colorful outdoor drama retelling the beginnings of the white man's invasion of Western New York."[2]

The *Pageant of Decision* was the culmination of the state's Revolutionary War program, and it furthered the replacement narrative developed on the state-sponsored plaques. By fixing the expedition as the source of state sovereignty, it removed from view 150 years of state-led expropriations of Indian land that occurred after the Revolutionary War.

"Pageantry Craze"

It may seem odd to recognize a military operation with a dramatic performance; however, the *Pageant of Decision* reflected the era's commemorative mores. Starting as an antimodernist movement in rural England at the turn of the century, during the Progressive Era, a "pageantry craze" swept the United States.[3] At its heyday, the movement spanned the ideological spectrum as hereditary patriotic societies, like the Daughters or Sons of the American Revolution, and progressive workers, educators, artists, and drama professors worked together with the grand goal of building community and advancing society by putting on historical dramas.[4] Pageant advocates argued that the past was best absorbed through active engagement and role-playing and believed that performing in a pageant could bring a community together.[5] Pageant masters, like William Langdon, even believed that creative historical pageants could provide townspeople a way to imagine a better *future*, an experience "through which they could visualize solutions to their current social and economic problems."[6]

Because of the extensive temporal sweep of these community history dramas, they often engaged, in a crude way, the strategies of "firsting" and "lasting."[7] Community history pageants invariably started with a "pre-history" phase, one that acknowledged Native American predecessors in such a way that it was made clear that this past only set the stage for the arrival of the "first" people, the white settlers. The transition from Indian to settler appeared as seamless and untroubled, sometimes enacted in dance form or carried out through the device of a "Medicine Man" or prophet who foretold "his race's decline."[8] If there was any contact between Indian and settler societies, it came either in the form of Indians attacking settlers (never the other way around), or through peaceful land transactions. Pageants thus offered what historian David Glassberg describes as a "conservative evolutionary approach to social change."[9] Indian residents thus dispatched, white pioneers appeared and community pageants then shifted into celebrations of "firsting," narrating the story of the "first" (white people's) houses, town governments, schools, and churches.[10]

The historical sweep of these early pageants was typically quite long as they often had a goal of linking contemporary inhabitants to the values and contributions of a community's earliest white pioneers. At the same time, pageant writers avoided difficult or potentially divisive topics. They minimized internal ethnic or class conflict, and few pageants depicted overt war scenes. Even the Civil War was alluded to with depictions of sad farewells to brave departing heroes or the return of wounded men.[11] Since the community history pageant was also meant as an exercise in community building, organizers sought participants through a diversity of local organizations, including historical societies, churches, and ethnic and fraternal organizations.[12] Many pageants were inclusive in the text if not in casting, depicting waves of immigrants who settled in the area.[13]

The *Pageant of Decision* was developed at the end of this movement, at a time when a return to community history pageants after World War I was accompanied with a new fashion for historical accuracy.[14] Like other pageants of the era, it incorporated a wide swath of the local community. It was unusual for its scope in that the imagined subject and audience of this community history was not a single town, but an entire state and its residents. Moreover, rather than addressing replacement of Native people obliquely or in a prelude to the story of the white community, the plot of the *Pageant of Decision* was almost entirely centered on the transition from a Native to a white population. The state historian found, in a Revolutionary War–era story, a way to develop a unique replacement narrative for New Yorkers at a time when questions about early land deals New York had made with Indian nations had dramatically resurfaced.

Commemorating the Revolutionary War

Pageantry was already a hallmark of New York's Revolutionary War commemorative activities. As Flick's committee proclaimed, "Nothing will arouse more interest than this, and it has the further advantage of using large numbers of all ages from the community."[15] Their goals were as ambitious as those of the pageant advocates at the height of the pageantry movement. Flick hoped that by educating the public about the local past in this way, he would be helping to create better citizenry, writing, "The impressions received through the eye and ear as a result of the art of pageantry will never be forgotten. Our youth will, as a result, take more interest in their origins, have more pride in their localities, and become more responsive and more responsible citizens."[16] The 150th Committee held pageants to commemorate the adoption of the Declaration of Independence by the provincial congress at White Plains, the founding of the state constitution, and several battles.[17] A Sullivan-Clinton pageant would stray from the previous battlefield pageants, however. How might this story be told? In February 1929 Flick made a pitch to the mayor and people of Elmira, suggesting an all-out reenactment of the Battle of Newtown, one in which local Indians would play a role. This battle "will be enacted in full costume," he claimed, adding, "arrangements are now being made with the Iroquois Indians on the state reservations to take part, representing their forefathers who fought under Joseph Brant, Mohawk war chief."[18] In April, when touring potential pageant sites in Elmira, Flick explained that "arrangements will be made to leave standing a field of corn near the battlefield" and proposed burning the corn and a reconstructed Indian village to illustrate the aftermath of the Battle of Newtown.[19] Apparently, this idea was met with local enthusiasm, and the burning of crops became the climax of the four-hour-long event.

The state hired Ware and Francis, a Boston pageant production company, which commissioned George V. C. Lord to write the text. Lord was a Harvard University drama coach who also produced Broadway shows.[20] He based his text on materials prepared by Flick, who also reviewed and approved the script. Mr. Percy Jewett Burrell, who had directed the Saratoga pageant, was brought on as general pageant director, and Charles W. Ware became official costumer because of his past success in putting on the Saratoga pageant. He had the ambitious task of managing the preparation of period costumes for some 7,500 people.

Much of the work was in the control of local communities, led by executive committees composed of directors of histori-

FIG. 22. Vast parking lot created for pageant spectators. Mark Twain Park, Elmira NY, September 28, 1929. Photographs of Observances of the 150th Anniversary of the American Revolution, New York State Archives, Albany NY.

cal societies, newspaper editors, and boosters. These individuals managed dozens of separate committees that concerned themselves with all manner of details: casting, caring for the animals in the pageant, transportation, and safety. (For a sense of the scale of these pageants, see figure 22.) The massive casts and crews were drawn from a wide area. The Elmira executive committee decided to farm out the casting process to the city's civic organizations. Members of the Elmira Junior League and Elmira College selected 150 girls to perform in the Albany Minuet scene; the Loyal Order of Moose was in charge of portraying the Easton market day scene; the Catholic Daughters of America participated in the Indian Council scene; and members of the more elite civic institutions, such as the Sons of the American Revolution and the Masonic orders, chose men to play members of the Continental Congress.[21] Indian-themed clubs helped staff the Indian roles. The Red Men society, an all-white fraternal order, was assigned

FIG. 23. Playing Indian women for Elmira Pageant, September 28, 1929.
Photographs of Observances of the 150th Anniversary of the American Revolution,
New York State Archives, Albany NY.

to pick 75 men to portray Indians in an Indian village, and the
Daughters of Pocahontas selected Indian women.[22] The Elmira
press joked that casting was to be carried out by hair color: "Most
everyone who is willing to do his or her bit in the pageant will be
gladly accepted by the directors," explaining, "while the blondes
will yield to brunettes as Indians, squaws and girls—the same
applying to men as well as women—the fair-hued will have their
innings as the ladies and gentlemen of the colonial villages, taking part in the grand military ball and reception which was held
in Albany prior to the Clinton campaign."[23] There was a bur-
lesque quality to some of the images taken in Elmira on pageant
day (see figure 23).

At a "mobilization meeting" held in Elmira in August, over
one thousand people showed up at the state armory, where they
learned of committee composition and heard pep talks by William J. Francis, pageant company codirector as well as former state

senator of Massachusetts and veteran of the Spanish-American War. According to the news account, Francis told the gathering of pageant workers and actors that they should consider themselves soldiers: "You are pledged to war on your own volition. It is a war to the finish. It is up to you to make this the greatest thing that has ever happened in your city. You have enlisted like soldiers, and you must serve like soldiers, obeying the orders of your commanders."[24]

By all accounts, the community that "enlisted" in pageant activities was a decidedly non-Native one. The lack of Haudenosaunee involvement is notable given Haudenosaunee participation in other pageants of the same period (such as a centennial celebrating the Underground Railroad that was held in 1927 in Jamestown, New York).[25]

Pageant Day

As pageant day neared, pageant directors Flick, Nelson, and the general pageant director, Mr. Percy Jewett Burrell, crisscrossed the state, meeting with local committees to help determine pageant timing and location.[26] Pageant producers Ware and Francis brought their sons Theodore Ware and W. J. Francis Jr. to help them in a "fleet of four automobiles," driving "nearly 100,000 miles."[27] Local officials often expressed concern about the logistic challenges associated with safely orchestrating a gathering the size of a large town, while historically credible staging was often Flick's overriding concern.[28] Interest was raised by press releases prepared by the Office of the State Historian that emphasized the Indian-war aspects of the drama. Discussing a rehearsal of the Cherry Valley Massacre scene, Elmira papers wrote, "'The Indians are on us!' If real Iroquois had descended with tomahawks upon the Horseheads Citizens' Group participating in the first rehearsal for the Sullivan Sesquicentennial pageant Wednesday evening, the scene could not have been more effective. It sounded like the real thing when the women and children ran shrieking around the Armory, besieged by imaginary Indians."[29] Another reported, "Back of the pageant stage, a small cornfield is now well tasseled and workmen are busily engaged erecting an Indian village of 15 Long Houses, cabins and huts."[30] The day before the presentation, newspapers announced, "The war-whoop of bronze skinned Indians, equipped with muskets, knives and tomahawks, the rattle of musketry, the boom of six-pounders, the flash of a hundred different rich colored costumes, and the Indian village backstage, all unite to present a picture 150 years old."[31] News stories also discussed practical matters such as parking, policing, and the general welfare of the influx of people, and especially the weather. "Natives to Return for Celebration," the *Mount Morris Post* reported August 30, 1929, with no irony whatsoever, as it discussed the return of white settlers for the festivities.

Even though aspects of the pageant seemed designed to entertain and drew from cowboy-and-Indian popular culture, pageant materials also reflected the interwar fashion for historical accuracy. This emphasis is apparent in the published brochure distributed gratis at each pageant: the script contained copious footnotes, and included was a scholarly treatise on the expedition.[32] Press releases announced that the text closely followed the "actual facts" and described the pageant as a "dramatized textbook," one that was "devoid of symbolic dances and grandiose speeches."[33] Its focus on a curtailed time frame helped foster a myopic treatment of its subtitle, "Why the Republic Westward Grew."

The massive event went well at all three productions. Each of the pageant days was organized similarly. Factories, shops, and stores were closed to facilitate the full enjoyment of the populace; mayors declared the day a civic holiday.[34] While some officials tended to the morning marker dedications, the action was at the pageant grounds, where thousands of people gathered for hours to secure seats.[35] Public safety systems were busy in Elmira, with more than fifty-five emergencies ("heat prostration, sun stroke, heart attacks, lacerations and bruises") but no major incidents. Volunteers restored seven lost children to their families.[36]

The pageant scale was challenging. The drama lasted well over four hours, twice as long as reported in the schedule printed in local papers. With a pageant stage close to a half-mile long, it was difficult to discern the activity (see figure 24).[37] As one observer noted, the stage was "so long that music played by the band at the

FIG. 24. The crowd waits on Pageant Day. In the distance can be seen the pageant director's viewing station. Elmira NY, September 28, 1929. Photographs of Observances of the 150th Anniversary of the American Revolution, New York State Archives, Albany NY.

west end reached the crowd at the center through the amplifying horns quicker than the air," and binoculars were in high demand and passed around by the spectators trying to catch a glimpse of their friends.[38] The Rochester *Democrat and Chronicle* suggested that sitting through it was an endurance test: "As the strains of 'America' were amplified through the huge horns in the center of the field, the crowd rose in a body and stood throughout the number and then settled down for more than four hours before the pageant was finally brought to an end."

Sullivan and the Empire State

What story did thousands of spectators observe? The pageant was a jubilant celebration of settler-colonialism expressly designed for non-Indian residents of the "Empire State." When we turn to the text, we see that it lauded westward expansion (more specifically, the "white man's invasion") and served as a community history writ large. Composed of fifteen acts, the *Pageant of Decision* starts, like many community pageants, with a prologue involving a "symbolic dance" depicting "The Wilderness." Unlike other community pageants, however, Indians don't vanish at this point, but reappear in Act I, "Indian Life at the Beginning of the American Revolution." The script explains, "The noble Red Man lives at peace, unspoiled by civilization."[39] Trouble arrives in the form of Tory emissaries, who try to entice Indians to help them in their war with the colonists, explaining that the "rebel horde would steal from you your lands and drive you forth with fire and with sword." A proffered alliance with the king of England is refused by the Indian chief, who says, "Tell your King we want but peace."[40] Colonists arrive on the scene with "the simple request that Red Man remain neutral," and the chief accepts a "peace belt" guaranteeing that they will remain at home. But the Tories return, promising an easy win and payment for scalps. The chief asks his people what they should do, and they agree to join the king after all, thus breaking the peace treaty they had just made with the colonists.[41]

This opening act is a gross simplification. For years, the formidable Iroquois Confederacy endeavored to stay neutral as hostilities began between the British and the "patriots." Maintaining this neutrality became increasingly difficult as British and patriot envoys used increasingly lavish gifts, threats, and "vast quantities of Rum" to convince them otherwise.[42] The drama also neglects the agreements made in 1763 and 1768, establishing boundaries to separate populations, which were regularly broken by white pioneers.[43]

This fateful decision made, the next act, "The Causes of the Campaign," relates the Cherry Valley Massacre. This act depicts Joseph Brant and other Indians attacking individual militia men and scalping them, then a "general melee" in which men, women, and children are killed and the rest of the white settler civilians are marched away. Cherry Valley was one of many settlements sacked during the shift in warfare strategies after British losses in 1777, and this was one of the losses the Continental Congress had in mind in ordering Washington to respond.[44] Footnotes pin down exactly how many civilians were killed.[45]

In Act 3, "Appeals to Washington," we witness George Washington, at the headquarters of the Continental Congress, receiving word about the incident at Cherry Valley. Washington makes the following statement: "Our frontiers must be protected and the only way to do it is to send an expedition into the Indian country. Our claims must be staked down for westward expansion when the time comes to make peace."[46] These statements attribute to Washington an anachronistic vision of Manifest Destiny.[47]

The next act depicts the Continental Congress resolving to send three thousand men to carry out an Indian expedition proposed by Washington. There is a bit of drama here when a "member from Pennsylvania" stands up to "protest against this measure," which he views as "unwise, impracticable" and likely to produce "no lasting results whatsoever." Gouverneur Morris, an elite New York delegate to the Continental Congress known for his lengthy speeches, challenges the Pennsylvanian, describing his remarks as "cowardly, unwarranted and absolutely indefensible." He reminds the members of the group of "the horrible massacres at Wyoming, Cherry Valley, Minisink and the numberless, horrible atrocities" describing then, in grotesque detail, the mutilation of women and children.[48] Morris, in this rendition, is a visionary of the future Empire State: "This proposed expedition is a practical, a sensible solution of our frontier difficulties." He turns prophetic, proclaiming, "And now for a moment glance with me into the future. See the thin red barrier which bars our Westward expansion melt away. See the fair lands west to the Mississippi dotted with homesteads unharrassed by savage or Tory and the mighty wave of American Civilization rolling onward to the Western coast."[49]

By this point, it has been made clear to the audience who the heroes are in this simplification of the past: "good" characters include the colonists, especially Gouverneur Morris, Sullivan, and Washington. The Indians, too, are mostly "good" (but clearly a subhuman people who are called "savages" and further dehumanized as a "thin red barrier" in Morris's speech), while the British, Tories, and the supposed pacifist from Pennsylvania are the villains.

In Act 5, Washington gives the command to Sullivan. Act 6 offers the diversion of a ball in Albany before the departure of

Gen. James Clinton, with the general and his brother, Gov. George Clinton, side-by-side, visually connecting Sullivan's expedition, through General Clinton, to New York's political leadership. Act 7 shows people gathering at the market in Easton, Pennsylvania, where Sullivan first gathered his troops. Act 8 shows Clinton traveling to Otsego Lake, and Act 9 depicts Sullivan and Clinton meeting up at Tioga Point.

The turning point of the whole affair happens at an imaginary Indian Council at Canadesaga, the event of Act 10.[50] This council of Indians, "stripped to their waists," includes Red Jacket, Joseph Brant, Little Beard, "and other chiefs" on one side, and John Butler, his son Walter, and other Tories on the other. Famed Mohawk leader Brant starts right out with a dramatic speech, "My brothers of the Long House! Tonight, you must decide a great question. Whether you will take the hatchet from the heads of the rebels of our great Father, the King, to whom you justly owe allegiance, and go to your homes until the war is over, while the rebels destroy your houses, crops and cattle, so that you starve and die next winter or whether you will remain on the warpath and drive these cruel destroyers from our land."[51] Butler makes a strong plea for them to stay on, describing the rebel colonists as "but a lot of weak old women with blood like water." His speech is impassioned and immediately followed by Queen Esther, who brags about having torn fifteen scalps off the heads of the rebels, saying, "And why? Did not these eyes watch my castle burn and all my village?" She turns into a maniac, shouting, "Go out! Strike!! Kill! Kill!! Kill!!!"[52] The decision to maintain allegiance to the British is made, Sullivan's troops have no choice but to carry out their orders.

The inclusion of Queen Esther, a woman made famous in early white renditions of the 1778 Battle of Wyoming, Pennsylvania, is pure fantasy. Pageant boosters knew it and discussed this fact in their publicity, stating, "With the exception of the introduction of bloody Queen Esther into the plot, the pageant follows accurately historical fact."[53] But as an image of Indian barbarism made famous by Wyoming battle lore, this icon of the "savage Indian" captured audience interest, and historical accuracy was cast to the winds.

The Battle of Newtown (Act 11) follows. The Groveland Ambuscade, the focus of Act 12, was a well-known ambush that was elaborated in local white settler commemoration at a site of supposed Indian barbarism.[54] In the pageant rendition, Tories are about to kill two ambushed men, Thomas Boyd and Michael Parker, but Indian leader Joseph Brant spares their lives as they are members of the same secret society. Tory Walter Butler comes over and begins hitting the two men and orders the Indians to avenge themselves on them. The men are crippled and dragged off. Sources remain conflicted over how Boyd and Parker were killed, by whom, and how gruesome their deaths may have been.[55]

If there were any remaining feelings in the audience that Sullivan and his men were behaving immorally, Mary Jemison sets them straight in Act 13 (see figure 25). Mary Jemison was a Scots-Irish immigrant captured in 1758 by Shawnee and eventually adopted by two Seneca women. James Seaver first published an account of her life in 1824, and it became a classic in American literature.[56] She is likely included in the pageant because her story was well known by this time. What is perplexing is just how far the pageant strays from her famous book. She reported then that as Sullivan approached, the Senecas "sent all their women and children into the woods a little west of Little Beards Town, in order that we might make a good retreat if it should be necessary."[57] But the pageant version of Mary Jemison criticizes the Indian chiefs for leaving the women and children behind: "Brothers!" she shouts, "The white man is not cruel. He will spare your lives if you surrender and agree to remain by your camp-fires."[58] There is a poignant moment at the end of the scene when Mary Jemison looks back, saying, "Farewell, beautiful Genesee!"[59] This is remarkable. While Jemison may have fled with other Seneca in advance of Sullivan's army, she returned and lived in the area until 1823, as her popular narrative makes abundantly clear.[60]

The shortest act (14) is the one that depicts the actual activities of the Sullivan Expedition, reduced to one event, the "Destruction of Genesee Castle." The mock Indian villages and cornfields are destroyed: "Troops are seen in the distance, busily destroying the corn and other crops and burning the houses." After a bugle cry indicates that the destruction is complete, the expe-

FIG. 25. "Mary Jemison" appealing to two "Indians." Leicester Pageant, September 14, 1929. Photographs of Observances of the 150th Anniversary of the American Revolution, New York State Archives, Albany NY.

dition is over, there are three "rousing cheers," and "the return march is begun."[61] In the much longer Act 15, there are celebrations and toasts.

The epilogue, titled "Washington's Dream Comes True," offers a glimpse into the time of the pageant: "Across the broad expanse of the Empire State come throngs of settlers to claim the wonderful country, teeming with untold wealth and resources, made possible of habitation by the Sullivan-Clinton Campaign," concluding, "To the strains of 'Onward, Christian Soldier' they come—on and on—they pass, on and still on, without abating, the throngs of happy, eager, God-hewn pioneers, secure at last in assured prosperity and peace still roll on—and our story ends."[62] The pageant closes with this patriotic "Manifest Destiny" gloss on U.S. history in its final scene.

Unpacking the Pageant

Couched as historically accurate, developed and approved by the state historian, the pageant's rendering of the Sullivan Expedition would have appeared to most of Flick's audience as authoritative. The inclusion of a historical essay in the pageant booklet and use of footnotes in the pageant script further lent a scholarly air to the production. Pageant readers likely assumed that anything presented without disclaimer was grounded in historical documentation.[63]

Despite these authoritative trappings, the pageant text involved gross simplification, fiction, and lying by omission. There was the fanciful inclusion of Queen Esther and a cast of just those Indian leaders best known to white settlers. Flick's attribution of a vision of westward expansion to the Pacific Ocean to Washington was conjecture: scholars of the Revolutionary War stress the precarious nature of popular support for the war and argue that he rarely had the luxury of long-term planning.[64] When Flick published "New Sources" on the Sullivan Campaign, he made a similar claim regarding Washington's vision, and yet he never revealed sources that made these views clear.[65] Many other elements, such as the imaginary congressional debates or the Indian Council dialogue, were creative compilations developed from multiple such events. At the same time, the pageant was not so crude as to depict the Indians as thoroughly immoral. Aside from Queen Esther, Indians appear as "noble savages" with their tragic flaw a continued loyalty to the British. The ignoble characters are the Tories, especially Walter Butler and, adding a bit of New York chauvinism, the unnamed "man from Pennsylvania."

Most significant is the special replacement narrative the pageant developed. Compared to most community histories, in which the transition from Indian- to settler-dominated space is a prelude to a story about the non-Indian community, in this pageant, the transition from Indian to settler *is* the story. This point is worth developing further. Those who win out often share a great desire to explain to themselves, their children, and outsiders how they came to be on the land, as settler-colonial scholarship asserts. Prior community pageants had often presented this transition obliquely, vaguely, as inevitable, or through an evolutionary logic. The *Pageant of Decision*, in contrast, targeted this transition directly by attributing "untold wealth and resources" to the Sullivan-Clinton Campaign. In this version of the Sullivan story, the shift from Indian to white settler occurred because of a set of difficult decisions that were taken—by the Indians themselves. In this framing, members of the Iroquois lost the land because of a fateful decision they made when they decided to join the wrong side in the Revolutionary War. This decision is also framed as one in which they broke a treaty made with the American side. In an amazing twist of historical facts, especially given the legacy of treaties broken by white settlers and their governments before and after the Revolutionary War, it is not the white settlers who are depicted as breaking treaties in this pageant, but the Indians. In the pageant text, it is only after they do so a second time, after the Newtown battle and the fabricated Council with the Tories, that Sullivan's troops begin to destroy fields and homes. And in the pageant rendition, the troops' destructive activities are collapsed to one moment, while in actuality the troops were destroying crops and towns throughout the four-month expedition.

What is most damning about the pageant text is not what was said but what it served to erase. Flick engaged in a magical sleight of hand. By implying that the Haudenosaunee nations were removed from the land by Sullivan, never to return—which was patently not the case—he was able to erase through omission the whole sordid history of New York State's dispossession of its Iroquois populace, which occurred well after the Revolutionary War was over. Federal treaties, notably the Treaty of Canandaigua of 1794, had promised secure title to vast stretches of the state fifteen years after the Sullivan Expedition. Perhaps most directly related to the pageant text is the Seneca ceding of hundreds of thousands of acres of rich farmland in the Genesee Valley, land reserved for them by both the Canandaigua Treaty of 1794 and the Treaty of Big Tree in 1797. Land and canal speculators became rich by convincing Mary Jemison to sell her vast holdings in deals of 1817 and 1823 that were never ratified by the U.S. Senate, as mandated by law.[66] The pageant, however, depicted the well-known heroine sadly waving goodbye to her beloved Genesee Valley while troops began their destruction, falsely implying that she and her adopted Native brethren left, once and for all, in Sullivan's wake.

Flick's neglecting to mention these federal treaties is all the more remarkable because these treaties were the basis of the Haudenosaunee land claim threat that was causing turmoil in the state in the early 1920s, as we saw in the previous chapter. It is worth briefly reviewing the timing of both the pageant and the lawsuit. In response to the Everett Report's conclusions, a Haudenosaunee coalition organized and brought a suit to federal court on June 6, 1925.[67] After the state's attorney moved to dismiss the case, the Haudenosaunee coalition filed appeals. Throughout the entire Sullivan-Clinton sesquicentennial planning period, this claim was hanging in the balance; Haudenosaunee plaintiffs' deadline for appeals was August 6, 1929, not long before the pageant performances.[68]

An Opposing Narrative

New York's sesquicentennial marker and pageant texts may have inspired a courageous piece of writing by Arthur C. Parker, Seneca director of the Rochester Municipal Museum.[69] "The Indian Interpretation of the Sullivan-Clinton Campaign," published by the Rochester Historical Society in 1929, confronts the dominant narrative the state historian was disseminating. It also provides an excellent illustration of how interpretation shifts when one alters the periodicity of a war story. Parker begins his piece by stating that little can be understood "unless we understand thoroughly the initial conditions precipitating the conflict."[70] We have seen how "initial conditions" in settler-colonial war stories typically involve one Native misdeed or another. In contrast to the pageant, Parker's "initial conditions" date to well before the arrival of Europeans on the continent to the formation by five Iroquois nations of a government, The Great Law of Peace.[71] He relates key Iroquois beliefs and practices such as mandated reciprocity and the belief that "all created things were endowed with life and feeling." He also discusses the corn plant as one of the three sisters and points out it was a "mortal sin to burn corn."[72] His primary focus is the Confederacy nations as architects of peace.

This peace was disturbed well before the Revolutionary War by settler actions. Parker recounts British superintendent of Indian affairs Sir William Johnson's struggle to maintain peace in the 1760s as Euro-Americans repeatedly defied prior agreements. Six Nation leaders repeatedly alerted the Crown about these transgressions, but British authorities could not stop the mayhem, and Parker provides a litany of damning colonist misdeeds, including the murders of "Indian women and children."[73] Parker writes that his goal is not to discuss the merits of this country but rather to consider, "Which party the Iroquois will choose to help, and which they will fight against"?[74] Parker then rephrases his own question: "Let us reverse the inquiry: *Is it humanly possible that these Indians will rush to the aid of the settlers who harmed them so much, and repudiate the powers that protected them?*" (emphasis added).[75] He explains that these questions will be answered differently by different Confederacy nations, with wrenching consequences.[76] Rather than seeing Sullivan's raids as just desserts after some Iroquois pledged continued support of the British, as the pageant alleges, Parker commences with so many instances of treaties and promises broken by the Euro-Americans that left Haudenosaunees in an impossible predicament.

Parker also challenges the standard ending to the Sullivan story. Sullivan was wrong to think that he had destroyed all Iroquois towns, Parker explains. While the large town of Little Beard was "in ashes," Sullivan's troops never discovered the nearby settlement of Canawaugus, which was full of refugees; "something was left."[77] He continues, "It has been said often that the power of the Iroquois was broken by Sullivan's raid and that they never recovered. This is not entirely true, for several flourishing towns had escaped and there were buried food supplies." He seems to be speaking directly to the state historian here. After the horror of the winter of 1779, refugees returned: "Hamlets were not difficult to rebuild, and tribal life soon became normal."[78] Parker wants to remind us that planting started up again. He recounts the vengeance that followed the next year. Their towns were charred and their fields emberred, and "all about them were the crushed and bleached bones of their people." He describes the Haudenosaunee as "filled with a desire for revenge." This anger fueled attacks on frontier villages that continued for several years.[79] Writing when the New York historian's project was unfolding in all its glory, Parker penned one of the only published accounts of that era that dismantled the perspective being formulated by the sesquicentennial fanfare, reenacted en masse by the pageant, and summarized on the historical markers going up all around him.

Conclusion

In *Firsting and Lasting*, Jean O'Brien notes New Englanders' propensity to emphasize their just property transactions, stating that "nothing symbolized modernity more powerfully for New Englanders than their imposition of their own system of ownership over Indian homelands."[80] The state-sponsored pageant and markers achieved a similar effect. Performed at a time when New York–Native relationships were particularly fraught, the pageant assisted in presenting New York as white space. Pageant and marker texts broadcasted a replacement narrative that told New Yorkers that it was the Sullivan-Clinton Campaign that paved the way for the "white man's invasion" of New York. This replacement-by-just-warfare construct explained to white settlers why they lived on Haudenosaunee lands and helped lay to rest any remaining concerns about the legality of their dominion, asserting New York's innocence.[81]

Tens of thousands of non-Indian people in New York dramatized this message in a mass public performance that can only be considered a pageant of erasure and a celebration of white supremacy. In looking back at his pageant, Flick commented, "It is safe to say that never before in the history of New York, were so many persons interested in the observance of an historic event. Thousands of them learned for the first time the significance of the Sullivan-Clinton Campaign and its relation to the western portion of the Empire State."[82] Flick and his fellow committee members hoped that the Sullivan-Clinton Campaign sesquicentennial activities would have a lasting effect, and they likely did.

The pairing of the pageant and the authoritative-looking historical markers was a powerful combination. The pageant instructed
those present into a specific understanding of their relationship
to the land as well as to their Native American neighbors, whose
ancestors, it suggested, made a decision that sealed their fate. It
offered a plausible and palatable justification of white settler occupation by rooting that occupation in the heroic Revolutionary War
past. The roadside markers, established at the same time across
the state and presenting the same narrative, reiterated this perspective on the past. It is here that the Indians once lived, they
instruct the public, and now they are gone. This region is no longer Indian country, the markers inform the tourists passing by,
and we owe that fact to Sullivan and Clinton.

Aftermath

New York's Sullivan-Clinton dedication exercises wound down just
weeks before the market crash that ushered in the Great Depression. In the 1930s state officials installed dozens of metal roadside
signs that further detailed the locations of the Native settlements
and orchards destroyed by Sullivan and Clinton's men, and it is
these signs that today are most immediately visible. Journalists
periodically promoted their use as roadside attractions for historical tourism.[83] Passersby sometimes wrote to state officials, asking for a guide to the markers, and as we saw in Pennsylvania,
in the wake of grand commemorative projects, the next generation of bureaucrats found it difficult to keep track of them all.[84] By
1955 the new state historian, William Tyrrell, had enough, and he
began writing every town historian in the vicinity of the markers
asking for information on the Sullivan-Clinton markers, including their precise locations.[85] Offering further sense that priorities
had shifted within the state's education department, Tyrrell's initial memos featured the wrong dedication date: 1927.

EIGHT

A Tale of Two States

The historical plaques and other reminders of the Sullivan Expedition that cross parts of Pennsylvania and New York appear to be elements of a common, coordinated unit. Certainly, that is what some tourists think as they attempt to retrace Sullivan's steps by traveling from one marker to the next, on their own or with a driving tour.[1] Yet when they decide to "follow Sullivan's trail" they must hunt for the markers, for no one authority oversees this commemorative complex, and there is no single guidebook with all its elements featured.[2]

This history of the Sullivan commemorative complex provides an important corrective to the common assumption that the very presence of authoritative-looking stone markers reflects coordination, federal endorsement, or public consensus regarding the meaning of the celebrated event or its significance. Consensus, in particular, is often assumed. In his landmark discussion of U.S. sites of violence and tragedy, *Shadowed Ground*, geographer Kenneth Foote observes that many such sites have undergone a long process of what he terms "canonization." In the immediate aftermath of a tragedy, a site may be rectified (put back into reuse) or obliterated (as when razing a building after a disastrous fire), but if people later decide to note the site (designation) it may become "sanctified."[3] Sanctification involves setting the site aside as a "sacred" space, often with the construction of a durable reminder such as a monument, and the site's ritual dedication.[4] Foote asserts that "the key to success really revolves around rallying support within a larger community. Without a relatively broad base of support, sanctification will not succeed."[5] When he considers sites that "seem as if they should be marked but are not," he suggests that "American society itself has yet to reach consensus" on these episodes.[6]

This question of consensus is worth revisiting. In so many instances outlined in the preceding chapters, broad consensus regarding the meaning or import of the Sullivan story did not precede the development of a particular marker or other public history project, but was generated after memory entrepreneurs decided to act. These entrepreneurs worked hard to publicize their commemorative ceremonies, as we saw ahead of the Wyoming and Newtown centennials in 1878 and 1879, in New York state historian Alexander Flick's travels across New York to garner interest in his programming, and in his securing an expert publicist, who wrote exciting "cowboy-and-Indian"–style press releases to fan public interest in the pageant.

Foote also identifies a standard sequencing of events in the commemorative process. He notes that some markers are established a century or more after an event and, in these cases, "annual rituals came first, then designated sites, and then monuments—often with peaks of activity corresponding to significant anniversaries at ten-, twenty-five-, fifty-, and hundred-year intervals."[7] In the examples presented here, this template applies only to the Wyoming Monument, which had its start with annual ceremonies. Most of the other elements of the Sullivan commemorative complex stray from this pattern; in most cases, it was the upcoming anniversaries that sparked interest and not the other way around. Before the Newtown centennial, the locations of the battleground and Sullivan's path were mostly lost in local collective memory. Boosters debated which county should host the Newtown commemoration and even the battle's name.

This part of the book exposes some of the consequences of the extreme decentralization of our national public historical apparatus, particularly before the 1930s. As Loewen precociously observed and as we have seen, so much of the U.S. public commemorative landscape was developed by elites working locally who wielded an outsized influence, with projects that have endured for decades. By connecting the local community and its concerns into a national story, memory entrepreneurs did not merely add texture or perspectives to that story. Instead, local interests shaped how the national story was told, and when we travel across state lines, we encounter distinct renditions of a common event.

Before reviewing the contrasting Sullivan stories developed in Pennsylvania and New York, I would like to address features common to both states. In constructing this book in the way that I have, I have likely overemphasized distinctions between the states to the neglect of interstate interactions. In both states, marker aesthetics and commemorative practices followed national trends. Until the advent of the abbreviated metal roadside highway marker, Sullivan memorials were almost always made of stone, with texts on bronze or copper plaques. Several monuments were in the form of an obelisk (the Wyoming and Sullivan monuments, Martha Phelps's Laurel Run marker, and a monument to the graves of soldiers killed in an ambush located in Groveland, New York).[8] The obelisk became a favored monumental form for both private and public memorials with the Egyptian revival movement of the early nineteenth century, and especially for Revolutionary War monuments starting with the Bunker Hill memorial (1825–42).[9] Most memorials in the Sullivan commemorative complex consisted of metal plaques affixed to uncut, natural boulders, a tradition that makes the marker appear indigenous and age-old, an interesting choice for settler-colonists trying to secure a place for themselves in a new land.[10]

Grand centennial ceremonies were held in each state in the era of centennial enthusiasm, with the 1878 centennial at Wyoming, Pennsylvania, and the New York 1879 commemoration of the Battle of Newtown. Each of these affairs attracted tens of thousands of people including several governors and state dignitaries. The structure of marker inaugurations organized by patriotic organizations, like the Daughters of the American Revolution, solidified into a fairly set form, involving religious and political leaders, children, the singing of patriotic songs, and the participation of veterans of the Civil War. Both New York and Pennsylvania marked the sesquicentennial in 1929 with mass marker productions that responded to the growth in automobile travel, and the two states' respective bureaucracies even tried to team up on some ceremonies. Each state dutifully noted the Sullivan bicentennial with smaller ceremonial events, school programs, and special newspaper issues.

I have not been able to cover every commemorative plaque in each state. In each state can be found unique, if not strange, commemorative projects. These include a roadside attraction alongside a "torture tree," where two of Sullivan's men allegedly met their demise in Livingston County, New York; and Wilkes-Barre's "General Sullivan Memorial," developed by the Wilkes-Barre Historical Commission out of a huge 6,800-pound block of natural anthracite that was donated by the Lehigh and Wilkes-Barre Coal Company, and the associated "Wilkes-Barre-Sullivan Trail" motorcade along a new highway named after General Sullivan.[11]

Memory entrepreneurs in both states incorporated Native American men dressed in "traditional" garb in their historical marker unveilings, a common fashion of this era. I have already discussed the inclusion of Delaware leader War Eagle as a kind of "lasting" performance, and I would like to elaborate further. These displays of Native people dressed as if from another time and speaking only their native tongue, as we saw with Chief Shongo's use of an interpreter in Drummond's Great Gully performance, may have been standard practice of the time; they also follow the imperatives of the logic of elimination. They foster a settler replacement fantasy by reassuring white settlers that Native people are from a past time and place. If Native people were to participate in marker dedications dressed in their everyday clothing, their contemporaneity would pierce this settler fantasy. In the settler-colonial imaginary, "modern Indians" is an oxymoron, unexpected, or treated as a form of "chronological pollution."[12] Memory entrepreneurs in both states insisted on creating ceremonies that featured "time-traveling" Natives instead.

Sullivan's name can be found on roads in both states (Sullivan Road, Sullivan Trail). Paul Wallace notes that Sullivan followed known Indian trails, namely the upper road of the Pechoquealin Path (from present-day Bartonsville to Wyoming); the Great Warriors' Path (from Wyoming to Tioga), and the Forbidden Path into the Chemung River valley. Approximately thirty miles of trail had to be altered to enable the passage of wagon trains, however, a project that took well over a month. In the late nineteenth century, some of the former route was visible on the land, however Garrick Harding points out that "the long continued distinctness of the track of this road is less attributable, probably, to the passing and repassing of Gen. Sullivan with his army, than to the fact that for twenty-nine subsequent years, or until after the completion of the Easton and Wilkes-Barre turnpike in 1808, it was the only wagon way from Wilkes-Barre over the intervening mountains."[13] Today, the route from Easton to Wind Gap is called Sullivan Trail; there are additional stretches in the Pocono Mountains that still retain that road name and several bridges and hills bear his name.

The politics of settler place-naming practices is a fascinating and well-covered subject that merits its own focus. In a settler society, naming practices are all too often renaming practices and ongoing ones at that; as Linda Tuhiwai Smith writes, "The renaming of the world has never stopped."[14] Commemorating Sullivan through road-naming projects was sometimes more random than one might think, however. When plans were underway to build a highway in Pennsylvania from Harrisburg to the New York State line in 1917, road boosters hoped to call it the "Susquehanna Trail" but were stymied because the name had already been claimed by another road organization. The committee deliberated and came up with "The General Sullivan Trail" as a second choice. Because the new road did not exactly follow the path Sullivan's troops had taken, this road name was mocked by some in the local press.[15] Finally, commemorative historical markers and road names are blurred categories, with historical markers sometimes established to designate where a road had been (see figure 26).

Memory entrepreneurs in each state were likely more influenced by each other's events than I have been able to outline here. The Wyoming centennial helped inspire Warner to promote a similar celebration, which evolved into the Newtown centennial, as I have shown. The *Pageant of Decision* did not appear out of thin air. Not only are influences of national pageant enthusiasts evident in Flick's writings, but he hired a famed pageant director for

FIG. 26. Sullivan Road roadside sign. Photo courtesy of the author.

both the Saratoga and Sullivan pageants: Mr. Percy J. Burrell, who also directed the pageant held at the Wyoming Sesquicentennial in 1928. Burrell's prior Wyoming experience may explain the inappropriate inclusion of the Queen Esther figure in New York's *Pageant of Decision*. State residents and officials also scrutinized their counterparts' public history programming. The editors of the *Wilkes-Barre Times Leader* compared New York's marking of thirty-five sites to Pennsylvania's smaller number: twenty-two. They admitted that the "monuments of each state are somewhat similar," but went on to suggest that both states took inspiration from Wilkes-Barre's 1927 Sullivan Trail motorcade.[16] When the column discussed New York's pageant, they found it to pale in comparison to their Wyoming Sesquicentennial the year before.[17] Cross-state correspondence in preparation for the sesquicentennial events often revealed how people in the different states were working with different scripts; for instance, Wilkes-Barre, Pennsylvania, papers noted New York's inclusion of Clinton on their 1929 plaques with real surprise.[18]

We should briefly review the performative aspects of the dedication ceremonies and their evolution under state management. DAR memory entrepreneurs endeavored to encourage participants to connect to the Sullivan story emotionally and sought to foster patriotic sentiments. They wove into their rituals recitations of national liturgy such as the national anthem and Pledge of Allegiance. Their inclusion of these verses in their printed programs reveals their pedagogical ambitions. They also helped participants "return" to this past moment by soliciting descendants of historical actors to play key roles. Descendants sometimes read ancestors' very words in their performances. We see a shift over time as state agencies hired professionally trained historians, who focused less on ancestry and more on timing, as we saw in both states' efforts to time sesquicentennial marker dedications on the same calendrical dates as the historical events under commemoration. We should note that the most extensive repetition of language of the past was carried out not under DAR oversight but by Easton's Northampton County Genealogical and Historical Society (NCGHS). As part of its sesquicentennial celebration, the NGHS recreated the "Thanksgiving" service given to Sullivan's troops by Rev. Israel Evans on the army's return to Easton in October 1779. The man playing Evans repeated his character's words to the letter, including an invitation to the staff and townsfolk "to attend a reception in the parsonage." After the actors left the church at the end of the reenactment, the audience did not. This led to real confusion until finally the present-day pastor mounted the stage to "explain that the invitation was made 150 years ago and 'we are all dead and gone now' so that the 'show' was over."[19]

Despite these commonalities, borrowings, and influences, the narrative of Washington's Indian Expedition, as developed in these different settler-colonial public history projects, varied regionally, as we have seen. Pennsylvania projects remained very much in the shadow of Wyoming throughout the period discussed here, while New York renditions emphasized the role of the Sullivan-Clinton Campaign in seizing land for the state. In the process of narrating the story of the Sullivan Expedition for residents, memory entrepreneurs were also offering plausible replacement narratives, helping to explain to settler-colonists why they were here.

Replacement narratives will vary with colonial contexts, as we have seen. The New England local histories that Jean O'Brien discusses in *Firsting and Lasting* took great pains to show that English settlers came to the land in a just way, with "all variety of land transactions" being a frequent item of discussion.[20] Replacement was made possible through alleged fair and honest dealings, in this perspective. The origin story of the state of Pennsylvania resembles these New Englander accounts in that the founding myth of Quaker William Penn's "Peaceable Kingdom" also emphasizes an exceptional religious ethos and the "peaceful" acquisition of land.[21] A different replacement narrative is developed in the same state with the Sullivan memorials. Pennsylvanian memory entrepreneurs understood the Sullivan operation in relation to the Battle of Wyoming. It is there that the settler story started, a perspective that removed from view thousands of years of Indigenous habitation, the whole history of the British-Iroquois Covenant Chain, the Yankee-Pennamite War, and so many other incidents that preceded that battle. With this past "contained," segregated out of sight, the Sullivan story starts with an instance of alleged Native American barbarism against which contemporary Euro-American society is contrasted. The settler-colonists, in this view, established a moral presence by having ancestors who suffered at the hands of Natives. In this rendition, the fact that the attacking Natives were participants in the Revolutionary War is muted, as is the entire Yankee-Pennamite conflict. Indian vanishing is not mourned but is celebrated, and the Sullivan operation becomes a mission of righteous vengeance for a barbaric Indian massacre. When the Pennsylvania Historical Commission began to wrest control of the state's public history apparatus from Yankee-dominated patriotic societies, its narration of the Sullivan story became more neutral, with a series of plaques focused on campsite locations. However, more recent markers and associated dedications continued to repeat the savagism so prevalent at Wyoming "Massacre" ceremonies, as we saw with the twentieth-century Queen Esther plaque.

New York's replacement narrative is more explicitly tied to the Revolutionary War, with that war helping to mask the real role of the state in dispossessing Haudenosaunee nations. The initial message as developed in Newtown centennial speeches was more ambivalent, and the text of the first Sullivan Monument plaque recognized generals from multiple states. After the marker collapsed in 1911, a new plaque, installed with the 1912 Sullivan Monument, began to assert a "westward expansion" theme, which was elaborated and consolidated by the time of the sesquicentennial extravaganza.[22] The "white invasion" Flick mentioned in relation to the pageant is presented as the happy consequence of Sullivan's raids. Sesquicentennial markers, orations, and pageants falsely proclaimed that the land was seized by military conquest in the noble fight against the British; white New Yorkers established a moral presence by connecting their settlement in the region to their ancestors' involvement in that noble war. By portraying Sullivan's raids as the turning point, this replacement narrative neglects the sordid saga of fraud, trickery, bullying, removals, and threats of removal that led to successive dispossessions, which occurred well after the 1779 military expedition.

To fully capture the stakes involved in settler-colonial public history projects, we need to consider the local context. While settlers continue to try to grapple with a sense of belonging in their new homes, and use history as a resource to do so, they always carry out their commemorative projects with local as well as broader politics foremost in mind. Having traced some of these politics, we can now turn to the question of their lasting effects. One imagines that local boosters were seeking to advance themselves socially and politically by these projects; their projects, in turn, have endured on the landscape. Did these projects have any lasting effects on the historical consciousnesses of the next generations? Having considered the origins of several elements of the Sullivan commemorative complex across two states, it is time to consider their long-term reverberations. Should we worry over plaques disseminating yesterday's language and ways of thinking? Do the original framings of the Sullivan story have any bearing on how residents discuss or view this past? We now turn to contemporary times to explore what roles the markers play a century after their installation.

PART TWO

Reverberations

The Revolutionary Past in Contemporary America

NINE

Dueling Celebrations

W hat roles do centuries-old boulders with fading copper plaques play in the historical consciousness of Americans today? In this section, we turn to contemporary times to ask how the Sullivan story reverberates, if at all, in the parts of Pennsylvania and New York where memory entrepreneurs fixed elements of the Sullivan commemorative complex. Does the story still matter and, if so, have its meanings evolved? These chapters are developed from ethnographic research, starting in 2012, which involved my immersion in towns along what some residents call "Sullivan's Trail," my observations of reenactments, marker unveilings, and public commemorations, and my formal and informal interviews with event participants and people living nearby. I found both a dimming relevance of the Sullivan story for some and lasting distinctions in how the Sullivan story is framed in the two states. Two popular commemorations of Revolutionary War battles encapsulate these distinctions, and I start this section with a detailed description of each. These include the reenactment of the Battle of Newtown (August 29, 1779), a semiannual event held in late August in Elmira, New York, and the commemoration of the Battle of Wyoming (July 3, 1778), held almost continuously in Wyoming, Pennsylvania, since 1778. While each event attracts a comparable number of outside participants, their structure, tenor, and the image they offer of "the Indian" diverge significantly. They offer an excellent window into the meaning and relevance of the Sullivan story in present-day Pennsylvania and New York.

Reenacting the Battle of Newtown

The Chemung Valley Living History Center (CVLHC) has organized an encampment and reenactment of the Battle of Newtown in New York State for over two decades. When the 1879 monument collapsed and was replaced with a stone obelisk in 1912, the surrounding land became the Newtown Battlefield Reservation. (It is now called the Newtown Battlefield State Park.)[1] The reenactment is held at that park. The two-day event I attended in August 2015 drew 350 and 400 spectators, respectively, and its 2019 rendition was even more popular, with the number of reenactors increasing from 170 in 2015 to 300.[2]

Newtown Battlefield State Park is hilly and wooded with large birch, walnut, and oak trees. When I arrived with my family at about 9:30 a.m., in 2015, traffic into the site was heavy, and the area around the monument had become an immense parking lot, where reenactors were putting on their gear and heading into the woods to prepare for battle. Women in long muslin dresses and bonnets directed us to pay an entrance fee. Reenactors were waking up and making breakfast by their plain white tents dressed in period costumes. At one encampment, a toddler wearing only a cotton smock started running after his siblings holding a giant musket, which we suspected was real and loaded, for his father, also only dressed in a muslin shift, burst from their tent to rescue the gun before it shot off. More white tents peddled Revolutionary era crafts and children's toys (see figure 27). The most popular stands sold goods to reenactors, such as knives, used clothing, and beeswax candles.

Events held before the 2:00 p.m. reenactment included an eighteenth-century church service, a musket-loading demonstration, and a militia drill for children. At lunchtime, while attendees purchased food from vendors, a group of reenactors dressed in finery ate a meal on pewter plates in the rustic lodge. A young boy went up to the open window and asked in awe, "Are you the British?" to lighthearted laughter. At the other end of the park was the "Indian Village." Here, too, people were relaxing near their tents, which were adorned with animal skins. A few men

FIG. 27. Trying on goods for sale, Newtown Battlefield State Park NY. Photo courtesy of the author.

were completely covered in black grease paint. A white man with light blue eyes, lounging against a pine tree, told me that he was one of Butler's Rangers and a member of Mohawk leader Joseph Brant's group, the best unit to be in (figure 28). Other reenactor groups that year included units from the Continental line, the

FIG. 28. Butler ranger reenactor, Newtown Battlefield State Park NY. Photo courtesy of the author.

Royal Greens and other Loyalists, and a group of women in the red military uniforms of the NJ British Brigade.

As the time of the reenactment neared, people jammed into school buses to travel to the battle site in the woods. The vast majority of the attendees were Euro-Americans attending in family groups with children. We were instructed to stay on the road, not to go off the trail, and to make sure to keep walking. Skirmishes deep in the woods, with multiple explosions, grew closer until it seemed we were surrounded. It was confusing and we never knew which side was where. Toward the end, we came across reenactors lying down dead, or dying in gruesome ways. I overheard a middle-aged man saying that he thought they were taking it too far, and when one of the reenactors saw some little children looking distraught, he explained that they were all just "play-acting."

While there I spoke at length with one of the founding members of the Chemung Living History Center, Mark Andrew. He and another man, dressed as Native people, were serving as ambassadors of sorts at their encampment near the parking lot. They

FIG. 29. Reenactor at Newtown Battlefield State Park NY. Photo courtesy of the author.

sported shaved heads, face paint, and traditional mixed frontier dress (see figure 29). Their tents, covered with furs, drew much interest. When a middle-aged woman with a salt-and-pepper perm came up to them and exclaimed, "You are the real thing!," Mark replied, "No, no, I'm one-fourth Abenaki."[3] When I asked him if the event drew so many visitors because of local interest in the Sullivan story, he shook his head and replied, "Ask twenty people on the street, I think you'll find out, it's not very known." In his view, it was a pivotal battle in that it gave Sullivan's troops forward momentum, but the devastation they wrought was horrible and gave him pause: "They plundered their villages, they'd burn their villages, they'd burn their crops, they'd wreck their orchards. The casualties [at Newtown] were thirteen people, I mean, that's not, in . . . in today's standards, that's a little skirmish."

For Mark, the goal of the reenactment is to educate young people about the Revolutionary War and especially about Native Americans. "What we're trying to do," he said, gesturing to his tent site with an iron kettle over a fire, "is to get the message across about the Native American. They were here, they were thriving, and what's happened? We've lost them. Try to go out and research Northeastern Woodland Indians, I'm sure you know, it's difficult." In his view, a Native American vantage point is missing on the contemporary landscape. As he put it, "The winner writes the book. And unfortunately, the Native American didn't write the book." In a later interview, Mark explained that he used to teach fourth and fifth grade in the Sayre, Pennsylvania, school system, just over the border. He also spent years developing the Newtown Battlefield State Park's Indian village with AmeriCorps students. Since his retirement, he does storytelling programs in character for schoolchildren with audiences of up to five hundred people. As he explained it, "My mission is primarily to enlighten anyone who would listen to me on aspects of the Native American. Because there are many contributions that come from them." After discussing the many foods and medicines pioneers learned about from Native Americans, he added, as an aside, that he is now eighty-four: "This is what I have taken as my mission for whatever the Great Spirit will allow me to live."

"Are Newtown battle reenactors a particularly patriotic bunch?" I later asked Dave, a reenactor in his thirties. He disagreed and explained that they represent many different historical societies, units, and militia groups. He pointed out that many Newtown reenactors played the part of the "other side," as British soldiers, Loyalists, or Native fighters. He didn't know if any people "playing Indian" were actually Native American but said they try to "look the part" by smearing charcoal or black walnut dye over every inch of their skin. Orchestrating this two-full-day event was a big undertaking, and he recounted that much of the action occurs long after the spectators leave, when reenactors engage in mock battles late into the night. The annual event was clearly part historical reverence and part social event for them.

Like Mark, Dave is an educator. He has a degree in therapeutic recreation and uses wilderness therapy to treat troubled youth. He usually embodies the character of a seventeenth-century French explorer who lived with the Huron for five years and spoke several Native languages fluently. This character allows him to teach children how to live off the land and about the natural world. Dave is not a fan of the Sullivan Expedition, and he knew a fair amount about its consequences for Seneca and Cayuga nations. He found it alarming that his hometown sports a plaque to the man who founded the town, a man who, as one of Sullivan's soldiers, was responsible for burning the local Native village first.

Commemorating the Battle of Wyoming

Ninety miles south, in Wyoming, Pennsylvania, a quite different ceremony takes place, now on July Fourth, to commemorate the Battle of Wyoming. This is one of the longest continually running historical commemorations in the United States, and it has persisted relatively unchanged since the nineteenth century. Like the Newtown event, most participants at the 2015 and 2018 ceremonies I attended were Euro-Americans in multigenerational family groups, and much of the focus was on educating the next generation. The tenor was much more formal, however. It was cold and rainy in 2015, and when I approached the monument before the event, cars were already parked up and down Wyoming Avenue, and people were racing to shelter at the monument grounds. Large floral arrangements were placed on the lawn in front of the monument, and under a huge tent were four hundred chairs set up with an aisle in the middle (see figure 30). There was a podium, a mic was set up, and a band was playing patriotic tunes. Under their own shelter were reenactors, men and women representing the families of the Twenty-Fourth Connecticut Militia, the unit most decimated in the battle.

The atmosphere was festive despite the weather. Almost every chair under the massive tent was occupied, and additional spectators stood at its perimeter under umbrellas. Many attendees sported red, white, and blue attire. The ceremony had the structure and components of a military or religious service, with a benediction, the presentation of standards with a standard guard, and veterans in uniform in attendance. After a half hour of a patriotic medley, the band shifted to a song composed of the anthems of different military units (army, coast guard, marine corps, and so on). At each shift, the bandmaster announced the unit to be recognized, and veterans of that unit arose to immediate cheers from the audience. At the end of the medley, the band started playing the national anthem, and everybody present stood up and burst into song without any outside prompting.

We heard welcomes from state officials, the president of the Wyoming Monument Association (WMA), managers of the site, and the president of the Wyoming Commemorative Association (WCA). Then the presentation of "floral tributes" began. This is, in many ways, the highlight of the event each year, and the bulk of the printed program delineates each organization presenting floral arrangements and their representatives that year. That year's participating organizations included historical societies, Catholic mutual aid societies, and ethnic organizations, as well as several chapters of the Daughters of the Revolution, among other patriotic organizations.[4] The largest category by far, however, was that of descendant groups of battle participants and victims, such as "Descendants of Zebulon Butler," eleven such organizations in total. As each group was announced, their representatives marched down the center aisle toward the monument carrying their floral contributions.

The main address in 2015 was by Dr. Lewis, a Wyoming High School graduate and art historian at Williams College. Lewis discussed the monument's aesthetic features and told the audience that it was placed "where the bones were found," referring to the bones of the men whose lives were lost in the battle and which are buried at the base. He went on, "Our subject today is the witness of those bones and what they have to teach us. . . . [Their location] gives us a fixed reference point to orient ourselves with all of the testimonies since those first breathless survivors . . . choked out their shocking stories." These stories "shock" because of alleged Indian atrocities. As Lewis explained, "Every early account agrees that patriot prisoners captured by Indians were put to death. These atrocities weren't incidental to the Wyoming Massacre; they were the central event: that is the reason why in this valley, we don't refer to the *Battle of Wyoming,* but the *Wyoming Massacre.*" According to Lewis, the "bodies laid [sic] strewn about this battlefield, scalped, ripped, rotting, unburied." When residents gathered the

FIG. 30. Floral arrangements at the base of the Wyoming Monument. Photo courtesy of the author.

remains at the monument in 1832, the exhumed bodies were, in Lewis's words, "Gruesome." He continued: "Every single one of them bore the marks of the tomahawk, the act of scalping." This speech revisited the anti-Indian sublime (see chapter 1), and the printed program repeated this theme with a back cover reproducing the *Massacre of Wyoming* by Alonzo Chappel, a print that depicts a white-haired man, with his hands raised in surrender, being tomahawked from behind and, in the foreground, a Native man scalping a victim.

Ritual, Reenactment, and Embodiment

Participants in these commemorations of the Revolutionary War return to the past using similar strategies.[5] They hold their events at approximately the same date as the battle in question. The Wyoming battle commemoration is more strict, and the ceremony now occurs every July 4 without fail. (The battle was July 3.) Participants mimic what they imagine were the actions of historical actors from centuries gone by. At Newtown, reenactors wake up in the same kinds of tents, teach children how to carry and march with obsolete firearms, and copy clothing and material accoutrements down to the very last button. At the Wyoming dedication, people say the same words, sing the same songs, and follow strict standing and seating protocol. Family groupings sharing the same patronyms walk down the same aisle to place flowers at the obelisk each year, acts that connect them to their ancestors who carried out these same movements generations before. The printed program links participants to names on the monument, and speakers read statements their ancestors made at ceremonies generations earlier.

These commemorations offer quite different ways of engaging with the Revolutionary War, however, and recreate different kinds of communities through their public events. The Newtown battle reenactment seemed more entertainment than patriotic reverence and involved a loose-knit group of reenactors from multiple states. It was more theater in that visitors were not incorporated into the actual battle reenactment but kept out of the action, off to the sides (see figure 31). If this ritual was constituting a community, it was unclear who was on which side. Reenactors dress as any number of characters with no relation to gender or ethnic/national lines, throwing the genealogical dimension of the rhetoric of reenactment to the winds. The Wyoming commemoration, in contrast, is a more tightly organized ritual with a structure that has stayed almost identical from one year to the next. Lineage is key here. The ceremony has the tenor and structure of a large family funeral, with multiple generations brought back to the fold each year. It is clear who is participating, for a prominent place in the program is dedicated to identifying the people offering floral arrangements. Family linkages to battle victims and participants are paramount, and children wear clothing identifying them with the name of their hallowed ancestor. The program identifies in black and white who the "we" is, reconstituting that same community year after year. While outsiders are clearly welcome, the ceremony recreates a community of Wyoming "martyr" sympathizers each year.

FIG. 31. Newtown battles in the woods, Newtown Battlefield State Park NY.
Photo courtesy of the author.

Related is the contrasting image of the Native American developed at each commemorative event. At Wyoming, participants are reminded that named battle dead are the heroes in whose honor they are gathered, while unnamed Natives are the barbaric enemy, with the alleged barbaric acts spelled out in great detail. At Newtown, there is more nuance. Although there was much "playing Indian," as Native roles are typically played by non-Natives, the reenactors I met displayed some knowledge of Native American history, were able to identify Haudenosaunee leaders present at the battle by name, unit, and individual nation, and expressed sympathy not with Sullivan's troops but with his Haudenosaunee foes. In this Sullivan story, Native people are humanized. The community being recreated is one of colonial history buffs of unclear affiliation.

These two public rituals orient us to the different ways the Sullivan story is understood in these two states, distinctions that are partly related to the ways the story was set out in initial public history programming and frozen in marker texts. The distinct nomenclature persists. New Yorkers often corrected me if I referred to the military engagement as the "Sullivan Expedition," for there, Alexander Flick's "Sullivan-Clinton Campaign" label is accepted as the operation's official title. (Readers from New York have likely bristled at my employment of "Sullivan Expeditions" throughout this book.) From my very first days in the archives of Bradford, Luzerne, and Wyoming counties in Pennsylvania, on the other hand, docents, visitors, and archivists regularly reminded me to include the Wyoming battle in my research, presenting these as connected operations, two parts of a whole. A Connecticut Yankee cultural identity appears to persist in regions of Pennsylvania settled by the Susquehanna Company and is reinvigorated each year at the Wyoming battle commemoration. I never heard Pennsylvanians mention General Clinton on a par with Sullivan, and the one time the "Wyoming Massacre" moniker came up in New York, the speaker was challenging the massacre appellation as misleading.

These states differ in another critical fashion: in the presence (or absence) of federally recognized Indian nations. There are Native people in both states, certainly, and we will hear voices of self-identified Native people in what follows. However, federally recognized Lenape nations are based far from their Pennsylvania homelands: in Oklahoma (Delaware Nation, Delaware Tribe of Indians); Wisconsin (Stockbridge-Munsee Community); and Ontario, Canada. In New York, there are eight federally recognized nations, most of which are Haudenosaunee (the Cayuga Nation, the Oneida Nation of New York, the Onondaga Nation, the Saint Regis Mohawk Tribe, the Seneca Nation of Indians, the Tonawanda Band of Seneca, and the Tuscarora Nation of New York), who live on part of their ancestral lands. They have been engaged in activism since before the state was formed. I believe this activism plays a measurable role in how the Sullivan story reverberates there. While many Haudenosaunee leaders I met expressed a general feeling of invisibility to non-Native residents in New York, this invisibility is relative. The non-Native residents of New York whom I met seemed far more aware of the persistence of Native American nations into the contemporary era, and of what a Haudenosaunee perspective on the Sullivan memorials might be, than did residents of Pennsylvania. I presented my research topic identically in each state ("I am studying how the Sullivan Expedition is represented in public memory.") In Pennsylvania, this presentation of my research topic raised no alarms, while it was met with outright challenge at New York local historical societies on more than one occasion.

Across years of fieldwork, I met and spoke with anyone interested in speaking with me in both states. In each, I encountered apathy, criticism, and pro-Sullivan responses. I also found that the distinct replacement narratives, as developed in early marker dedications and associated propaganda, live on. Peoples' reactions to the markers shifted with subject position, with Native interlocutors offering the strongest critique. I group these responses by state and by subject position. In doing so, I do not want to overlook the important alliances and networks between Native and non-Native Americans. Moreover, I do not mean to suggest that each group is a monolithic block. Different positions are presented within social categories, and even by the same person on different days. The number of people I interviewed who self-identified as Native Americans in Pennsylvania was small, and a different kind of study is needed to fully capture the complexities of their relationship to the settler past and Indigenous communities. After outlining these diverse viewpoints, I consider the stories of people pushing back, trying to change the narrative. Finally, I turn to Haudenosaunee cultural centers, whose intervention in mainstream hegemonic perspectives is the most profound of all.

Wyoming's Lasting Shadow

T he regions Sullivan's troops crossed in Pennsylvania now
encompass former centers of industry in varying states of
disrepair and reinvention, such as the Scranton/Wilkes-
Barre and Easton urban centers, vast stretches of mountainous
forest in the Poconos, and rolling farmland in the Susquehanna
Valley. The immense size of the granite boulders demarcating the
route made them difficult to move, so most markers remain at
roadsides, sometimes quite precariously situated between parking
lots and busy roads. Marker enthusiasts must hunt them down
in what can turn into a dangerous long-distance scavenger hunt.
Martha Bennett Phelps's Laurel Run marker is reduced in size and
now found alongside a steep thoroughfare, surrounded by poi-
son ivy. The 1929 PHC-sponsored stone monoliths appear to be
overwhelmed by later roadside signs (see figure 32). Bronze and
copper plaques were sometimes missing, and interviewees spent
some time musing over their fates. An elderly woman thought
they ended up in people's basement "rec rooms," while other
people assumed they were sold for scrap. The Colonial Dames'
bridge lost its plaque in the early 1900s, and the stone structure
was moved to storage decades ago. Regional DAR chapters continue to meet and draw large audiences for their events, however,
and the markers they developed are still well-tended.

Many non-Native people I met in towns with these disparate elements of the Sullivan commemorative complex felt that the plaques
and markers did not feature in the daily imaginations of most residents. A Seneca sociologist explained in an interview that there will

FIG. 32. Old and new Sullivan markers compete, Tannersville PA. Photo courtesy of Nathaniel Janssen.

be a subset of people within any community or nation that is more aware of and attuned to history. This assessment was borne out in both states. Ed, a sixty-year-old white man from the Poconos who works in river-related recreation along the Susquehanna River, told me, "Some people have an interest and some people don't. So, the people who have an interest have already read them. There are people who come up primarily just to stop and look at all the historic things. And there's people who drive by them every day without a clue." Two Bradford County, Pennsylvania, high school teachers who lead river trips with Ed connected this lack of awareness to the fact that *local* history is not a focus of school curriculum.[1]

One of Pennsylvania's 1929 sesquicentennial monoliths is in the center of Tunkhannock, Pennsylvania, which has undergone some revitalization in the past twenty years. The local DAR chapter, which had cosponsored it, replaced its missing plaque in 2013 (see figure 33). This is one of the most accessible of the 1929 markers, and I interviewed a dozen elderly people there about its meaning and significance. When I first met "Ida," in her nursing home with her nephew, James, a retired prison guard, she was 101, and still sharp. Since she would have been fourteen at the time of

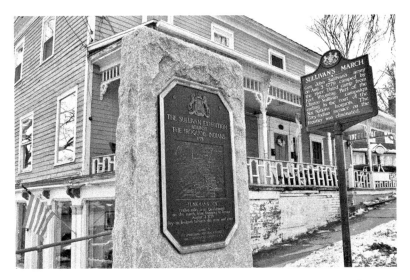

FIG. 33. New Sullivan plaque on 1929 monolith, Tunkhannock PA, 2013. Photo courtesy of the author.

the 1929 sesquicentennial events, James thought that if anyone remembered the fanfare associated with the plaque unveiling, it would be she. But when we asked, her response was immediate: "No, I don't. Sullivan? I don't think so."

James tried again: "She's saying that in 1929 they had a lot of celebrations and they put up some stones and stuff—did you remember any of that stuff?" She shook her head.

"Do you remember going to any celebrations, like for . . . like Fourth of July celebrations? Or any kind of celebrations? Do you remember anything like that?"

"No," she repeated, "Family reunions, yes, I remember, but that, no."[2]

While Ida seemed to have no recollection of the Sullivan plaques, she did enjoy talking about the past, and our two-hour interview was filled with stories about her career history, her husband's tannery accident, which ripped off his arm, and her escapades running the factory for him at night after his injury. Later in the interview, she interrupted our conversation to explain why she did not remember the monuments. "I guess they put them up after I stopped driving" (which was in the 1970s). James laughed out loud, saying, "No, they've been there since 1929. You've been driving right by them on your way to work your whole life!"

I encountered a similar lack of connection to the Sullivan markers in a conversation with three white women in their eighties and nineties, sisters Geraldine and Gertrude and their friend Laura, all three retired schoolteachers who had grown up and still lived in the Tunkhannock area. The sisters' mother and grandmother had been college graduates and members of the Tunkhannock DAR chapter. Despite this immediate family connection, they knew nothing about the plaque that chapter had cosponsored in 1929. "I never knew *who* it was!" Geraldine exclaimed when I told her about the plaque's origins, seeming quite surprised.[3] Their mother had helped the Tunkhannock DAR chapter develop a library, and the sisters outlined in detail her efforts to keep it afloat. Despite this direct family link, the sisters never connected the Sullivan plaque to the DAR or even relayed to me anything about the region's role in the Revolutionary War.

This orientation to the memorials was widely shared. When I met a retired blacksmith of the same generation at breakfast one morning at a local Tunkhannock cafe, he told me, "I've read that plaque a hundred times sitting in traffic, but that's about all I know about them." The marker had little to no relationship to his life.

A woman in her thirties, running the regional tourist office in Tunkhannock, was perhaps the most revealing. As I began to explain to her my interest in the Sullivan memorials and their relevance in the present day, the corners of her mouth started to lift as if she was having a hard time keeping a straight face. When I asked her to what degree this Revolutionary War story features in local people's understanding of the past, she immediately responded, "Not at all." I wondered how often people come through asking about monuments. "Never," she replied with conviction, "Never! I've never *once* had a person come in asking about historical sites or monuments."

History Enthusiasts

Not everyone I met was disinterested in the past. In *The Past Is a Foreign Country*, David Lowenthal observes how the past can become an integral part of some peoples' identities. The past guides and enriches, and it can even offer a form of escape, offering alternatives to an "unacceptable present."[4] He observes that while some people visit the past occasionally, "some prefer to live permanently in the past."[5] I met several people of this ilk for whom the past—the Revolutionary War past, or even earlier times—was truly alive, more alive, it seemed, than their present circumstances. These history enthusiasts included amateur historians and archaeologists, reenactors, memory entrepreneurs who were trying to exploit local heritage to draw tourists to the region, members of DAR chapters, and sometimes self-taught experts whom others thought I should meet. For these people, the Sullivan commemorative complex, the Revolutionary War, or prior times were a central orienting focus. I encountered this perspective before starting this project in earnest. When I first began reaching out to county historical societies in April 2012, a cold call to the Wyoming County Historical Society (WCHS) in Tunkhannock, Pennsylvania, led me to a woman with such detailed knowledge of local Sullivan memorials that I was convinced to move forward with this research.

Because I spent so much time working in local archives, it is likely that I encountered a disproportionate number of history enthusiasts, and sometimes it seemed as if everyone I met in the rural towns of northeastern Pennsylvania was immersed in the Revolutionary War era. On one day in June 2015, after accidentally meeting an amateur historian with extensive experience in the Sullivan story in Towanda, Pennsylvania, I crossed paths with author Jim Remsen in the Wyoming County Historical Society parking lot. He had arrived with copies of his novel, in which the 1902 DAR Sullivan marker in Athens, Pennsylvania, features prominently. I was astounded, and I turned to one of the WCHS staff, exclaiming, "See, this past isn't forgotten: everywhere I go people know all about it!"

Remsen and the staff member laughed and responded that it all depends on *where* you spend your time—if at historical societies, sure, you'll find like-minded folks. The staff member agreed, adding, "It's just a bunch of oddballs who care about this stuff."

Some history enthusiasts sometimes thought that their way of viewing the world was widely shared. Greg, a middle-aged amateur archaeologist from Tunkhannock, is fixated on the Spanish past and convinced that Spanish explorers were in northeastern Pennsylvania centuries ago and that this past has been silenced. When I suggested to him that the Sullivan past is also poorly known, he vehemently disagreed, proclaiming, "You can't grow up living around this river without knowing about Sullivan and his march!" When I responded that it seemed people didn't learn much about it in history class, he challenged me, stating, "I find it hard to believe that Tunkhannock high school students wouldn't hear about this part of the Revolutionary War." He went on to say that down in the Wyoming Valley, *everyone* knows about the Wyoming massacre. "And heck, we live on *Sullivan's Trail.*" He remembered visiting the old granite monuments with his grandfather and great-grandfather. In his mind's eye, they were enormous structures: "Not like the ones we have now, but they were huge." He held his arms about six feet apart, adding, "They were eight feet tall. You couldn't *not* know."

While Greg was asserting Sullivan's great significance locally, a sixty-year-old woman sitting nearby was shaking her head. She countered that the people in her neighboring town could not care less about Sullivan unless they were related to him. Greg seemed taken aback.

Some enthusiasts were not only aware of Sullivan's travels, and convinced, like Greg, that everyone else was, but also knew this past so intimately that they took issue with plaque texts or their placement. Henry, a Tunkhannock metal detectorist who collects Sullivan-era coins and buttons along the Susquehanna River, became animated when we discussed the 1929 PHC-sponsored roadside monoliths. "The markers at Falls are on the wrong side of the river," he exclaimed. "They put the markers where the public would see them, not necessarily where Sullivan traveled!" He added, "I was *stunned* that the state allowed them to put that marker at Black Walnut, for it is totally off."[6] He took out a pad of paper and drew a map that showed one area, and then lines to the river, tapping the drawing with vigor: "You see, what happened was this: when they put the railroad in, you see, they moved the creek. The campsite was really on the other side, over here. So, the marker isn't anywhere near where Sullivan's men camped. Typically, they stayed on this side of the river, for obvious reasons," he said, gesturing outside and alluding to the steep rocky cliffs that line the river on the opposite shore. On days like that, I had to struggle to keep up with interviewees' detailed geographical knowledge and enthusiasm. Henry was intimately acquainted with local geographies both past and present.

Continued Resonance

In former Susquehannah Company towns, DAR chapters continue to meet, repair markers, and travel to present floral wreaths at Wyoming battle dedications each year. DAR members are also proud history enthusiasts. They responded promptly to my queries, sending me copies of early photographs of markers and newspaper articles discussing their unveilings. When I presented my findings at a DAR meeting at the Tunkhannock library in May 2019, the meeting had attracted members of several local chapters, and it was standing room only. The audience was informed and engaged and made sure to correct an error they found in my handouts.

The density of DAR chapters in the former Susquehannah Company towns may explain the large crowds that attended the Sullivan-related events carried out during this research. Such was the case when I was asked to speak about my marker research at the Dietrich Theatre in downtown Tunkhannock (March 5, 2017). I was paired with a well-known amateur historian, and the programming director thought that we might be a draw. She was right. The night before the talk, I learned that they had sold out all their tickets and were expecting a packed audience. My talk was relatively brief and focused on the history of the plaques. My co-speaker decided to offer a more critical view of the Sullivan Expedition, describing in grim detail the destruction of Native villages and the consequences that winter for Seneca and other Native nations. The audience's mood became increasingly somber as he detailed one destructive act after another, and by the end of his talk there was stunned silence. During the Q&A, an elderly man stood up and suggested that the expedition seemed to have been a kind of genocide, something we really needed to further scrutinize. Other audience members deflected the genocide question, however, by challenging both speakers on the fine points of Sullivan's biography after the war, demonstrating their own knowledge of early American history. The wide response to this talk, and the fact that some people had traveled hundreds of miles to attend it in February, indicates that for a strong component of the local population, the Sullivan campaign, Wyoming battle, or Revolutionary War past still resonated.

"Sullivan Was Following an Indian Trail"

History enthusiasts I met in Pennsylvania were not all pro-Sullivan, and several people challenged not the placement of the plaques or their wording, but their very existence. John was a case in point. He was a retired surveyor and self-taught scholar of early local history. I met him on several occasions in Tunkhannock before his early demise. He was working on a book, "Through the Eyes of Surveyors," reconstructing contact-era Native American settlement patterns through a study of the earliest land surveys. He spent his days gleaning clues from the eighteenth-century warrants that he obtained from the Pennsylvania State Archives in Harrisburg. They have "remnants of a history," as he put it. Surveyors were keys to this history, in his view: "*They* were *on the ground*, they made *many* trips because they had to do every piece of property in all of Pennsylvania" (emphasis his).[7] He enthusiastically showed me warrants that carry the notation "Indian shade" as illustration. "It just blew me away, they called it an 'Indian shade.' I guess it was a scaffolding over the trees or something, and they would sit under there, now I don't know if that was the exact purpose, so you're looking from an English or German perspective and seeing something and conveying it."

While poring over these old documents, he tried to imagine early surveyors interpreting Native American structures and, in turn, the Native Americans they were observing. He pointed out the challenges he faced: not only is the handwriting difficult to

discern, but spellings varied widely too. "Just like all the different spellings of all the different creeks were *Indian names*. A lot
of names had changed. Briar Creek down here between Blooms-
burg and Berwick had an Indian name, and I'm trying to glean
out those names too, and put them by my maps to reference the
way we spell the names. Like 'Tunkhannock' is an Indian word,
but we *massacrated* it."

John found plenty of evidence of Indians living on the lands
when the surveyors came through, and he argued that Indian
lands were highly sought, for they were likely the best lands and
could thus bring "top dollar." Sometimes, lacking other landmarks,
these Indians themselves became the landmark. "I came across
one warrant and the surveyor said 'George or Gabriel Allen'—he
was an Indian living just above Berwick, on that side I think it
was, they were describing that area. And, see they would use all
these things as references because . . . you used anything you had
to describe *where* this was. Well this Indian apparently lived there
a long time so they used *him* as a reference."

It was the Indian past that energized John. He took issue with
misleading or touristy renditions like the indiscriminate labeling of *all* local Indian trails as "warrior trails." "*Everybody* calls
them 'warrior trails,' but they were just *trails* to get places," he
insisted. He showed me how some trails led to good sources of
blueberries or jasper, concluding, "These Indians were *all over*."
He found it especially ludicrous that people had named so many
roads after Sullivan. "Sullivan gets all the praise!" he exclaimed
one day in frustration. Some five hundred of Sullivan's men did
clear about thirty miles between Wyoming and Easton, across the
Pocono Mountains, and sections of the former military road bear
Sullivan's name. However, this was a small portion of his troops'
overall path across the land. Whenever they could, they followed
existing trails. John knew this well and told me, "I'm tracing the
Indian trails—but guess, guess what he did, he was *following* the
Indian trails. Once he got to Wyoming, he basically followed the
Indian trails up along the North Branch. *All the way*. That's why
they didn't need the surveyors there." He added, "Once they were
on the Indian trail, which was well worn in, *everybody* knew that

one, I mean, that went from Stroudsburg, or Sunbury—all the way up to Tioga Point in Pennsylvania."[8] It irked him whenever people referred to the road as "Sullivan's Trail," for if Sullivan was not the last person to travel on it, he was certainly not the first.

Some people I met in Pennsylvania volunteered that they found the Sullivan memorials offensive. I attended a public history walking tour of Tunkhannock on a hot June 2016 evening. The many-hour tour concluded downtown in front of the 1929 Sullivan marker. The tour guide narrated the monument's Revolutionary War background, describing in awful detail the girdling of orchards and burning of homes. One of the participants who knew about my research chimed in and told her that I was studying these plaques. The guide was understandably concerned: "Oh no, did I get anything wrong?" she queried. When I reassured her that her facts were all correct, she added, "I think that whole story is really sad. We really gave Native Americans a raw deal. They never came back because there was nothing here for them, but then the Iroquois Confederacy was never the same. We should say more about them in our local plaques. They are so one-sided!" I should note that even while criticizing the expedition, the tour guide fell into the dominant trope positing inevitable Iroquois demise.

When I was working at the Wyoming County Historical Society in June 2016, James, the retired prison guard who had brought me to see his centenarian aunt, Ida, blurted out, "Well, if you ask me, your Sullivan markers are going to go the way of the Confederate flag!" He added, "Really, when you think of it, all of our policy for Native Americans out west came from Sullivan's march. That's when we established our pattern," he asserted. He "confessed" that he was downright sick of all the monuments—there are just too many. He lives on the other side of the river and was thinking of putting up his own sign saying, "East Bank Pride: We didn't allow Sullivan over here!"

James explained later, in a private taped interview, that he doesn't know many people who *are* Sullivan fans, and he pointed out that even soldiers at the time seemed conflicted. "One chapter I read about them destroying the fields up in New York—those guys *then* didn't seem pretty proud of it. They were really sad about it." He continued: "And I don't think there's that many people that even look at it as a sense of pride around here—saying 'Oh, yay, we beat the Indians.' You know what I'm saying? I think more people are sad about it. I think there's more people have turned their opinions."

When I asked James whether or not he thought the markers in New York State that identify each village demolished could be seen as a type of war trophy, he equivocated: "It could be taken either way. They're either honoring the villages, or they're saying, 'Oh yeah, we destroyed that village.' If we think the way political correctness is going with taking down the Confederate flag and monuments down to the soldiers, someday you're gonna say, 'Hey we should probably take these things down,' because it's not politically correct to celebrate Sullivan."

While critical of the markers, James is unsure of the best next steps. He turned to the current Confederate debate as illustration. "I have five people in my family who were in the Civil War, and I don't understand people in the North flying a Confederate flag. I just don't like that, you know? Like we beat them, so, like, why are you celebrating the Confederate flag?" But even if he doesn't believe in flying that flag, he is torn about removing Confederate statues, arguing, "It's part of our history so why not try to learn from it? If you erase it, then people are going to forget." Regarding the Sullivan plaques, he followed the same logic: "I don't know if I necessarily think they should take them down. I don't think they should deny history because then you forget."

"Indigenous" Pennsylvanians

The vast majority of people I interviewed in Luzerne, Wyoming, and Bradford Counties in Pennsylvania were Euro-Americans. Although there are no federally recognized Indian nations based in Pennsylvania, there are Native Americans and people who identify as such living in the state. In Wyoming and Bradford Counties, I encountered several people who self-identified as Native people, and it is no surprise that they take a dim view of the Sullivan memorials. Barbara Seymour works as a drug and alcohol counselor in Towanda, Pennsylvania, and is a member of the Eastern Delaware Nation, Inc., an organization that she explained is for anyone with Indian ancestry.[9] "A lot of our members are descended from the Tuscarora," she explained. She talked about being "hidden in plain sight." She said she does not entirely look Indian but has a brother "that looks so much more Indian than me and people are always asking which one was adopted." But despite her "average appearance," her Indianness is obvious to others. "As Indians, you can always tell," she explained, adding, "A lot of people who were drilling in our area were from the Texas-Mexico border. I had a funny interaction in the parking lot of the Dollar Store one day. These guys were in their truck, they were Mestizo, and they gave me a thumbs up. We recognize each other, you see. You just know."[10]

She told me that while growing up in the area, she was pretty low key, trying to avoid hearing, "Your ancestors were savages!" She explained there is a large group over near Pittsburgh and splinter groups all over the state who did not want to be removed: "These people wanted to stay here, so they hid in plain sight and took on the ethnicity of the people they married into," she maintained. She discussed 1930s eugenics laws. "If you were of color, you could be sterilized so you wouldn't be a burden of the state. This was still going on in the Four Corners area of Arizona in the 1970s," she exclaimed. "So, my mother would not discuss this outside the family. But us kids started examining our heritage." She said this reawakening is a recent phenomenon. "They've been holding the powwows in Forksville for the past twenty-five years. We keep it low key."

Barbara is not a fan of the Sullivan plaques. The expedition came up when she was at a dinner for a volunteer organization, and the annual speaker was working on a book on the Sullivan Campaign. "I couldn't believe what I was hearing. It was really all about celebrating American genocide!"

I heard a similar perspective from Bob, whom I met at a powwow held in nearby Noxen in September 2016. The tiny town is nestled in the mountains about twenty-five minutes west of Tunkhannock. It was a glorious day—bright blue sky, a few puffy white clouds, breezy, and chilly in the shade. The powwow was held at a fairground behind small clapboard and vinyl-sided homes, many of which were decorated with Trump signs. One house sported a huge Confederate flag that served as a curtain, and at another house, one hung on a flagpole. Eerily watching over the scene were gigantic windmills high on the mountaintops, blades slowly whirling. People were gathered under a big awning or setting up booths around the powwow ground. A small fire was burning in a circle of stones in the middle of the grass.

Bob is a strong man, with very tanned skin, bleached blond hair, and clear blue eyes, and a card-carrying union boilermaker. He had just spent two years building the new gas power plant in Wysox and had much to say about Trump, fracking, and trade unions. But he also wanted to tell me about the plaques from a Native perspective, for he identifies as Indian. He explained that he always knew about his Indian ancestry. His maternal grandmother was "half Native," but she never talked about it for she was too busy preparing food. He learned a great deal from her, though: how to harvest sumac, cook it up, and make tea; how to gather dandelions and nettles and prepare them to eat. She prepared big feasts for her neighbors in Tunkhannock, and she knew cures. When I asked if there was anything else that made her seem culturally different, he commented on her appearance: "She had real high cheekbones and a dark complexion. She wasn't real white or anything in the winter."[11]

Bob has been attending powwows for years; his cousin was one of the original powwow organizers. "He would be at every one of these powwows," Bob explained. He noted that many people at the powwow didn't look Native American, adding quickly, "But I wouldn't go up and ask them." His cousin was overt about his identity, on the other hand. "Yeah, he made sure everybody knew. He was *proud* of it."

For Bob, his Indianness was always understood: "I've always had a connection, even when I was a little kid growing up. When the black and white films were on? I was *never* on the cowboys' side, I was *always* on the Indians' side. Even when I was young, and they talked about the settlers killing off Indians, taking their land and all that stuff, I wrote a report in school, when I was very young, about how I hated cowboys."

Bob has strong feelings about the Sullivan monuments, the Wyoming events, and any celebrations of that era. He explained that when people give him "the little history lessons, and start talking about how great these people were that joined the forces to go get rid of the Indians, you know, I get irritated. I don't even want to hear it. I'm like, I wish all the Indians banded together and wiped them all out. I'm not on that side. I'm on the other side." He finds much of the dominant American narrative irritating: "I watch a lot of movies on how these settlers would go in with Bibles open, preaching the Bible, taking hatchets, and just chop the kids, mothers, and babies, while preaching the Bible. You know, these people were *evil*, pure evil. And you don't hear about it in our history, in our American history, it's like all hush hush . . . nobody hears about America slaughtering the Red Man."

Pennsylvanians like Bob and Barbara who identify as Native Americans expressed strong opposition to commemorations of Sullivan, and I found their navigation of their alliances with Native and non-Native communities fascinating. It is beyond the focus of this book to interrogate fully their subject positions, but I offer their voices here as noteworthy examples of people who volunteered unequivocal condemnation of the plaques.

Inertia

Stone monuments last—that is the very point of establishing them. They can become part of the background environment, turning from a purposeful "memorial" to a "locus," a background place we take for granted where everyday life occurs.[12] The fashion that we have encountered of designing memorials out of unfinished blocks of local stone helps to further the illusion that they have always been there. But monuments are sometimes moved or damaged, or "lose" their plaques. Even when their original meaning is lost, some people see them as fixtures of the local environment and are compelled to tend to them, whether out of a sense of civic responsibility or just because they need tending. These people may become memory entrepreneurs almost despite themselves.

Several Sullivan markers in Pennsylvania have been refurbished or repaired recently. In Tunkhannock, the local DAR chapter replaced a missing plaque in 2013, raising the funds and working with the state. Many of the women involved were descendants of the original monument benefactors and were proud of their refurbished marker, perhaps expressing a sense of responsibility fulfilled to both ancestors and nation. More intriguing are the cases when people unrelated to the Sullivan story or the original memorial founders take it upon themselves to repair them. I turn to two such examples in the wooded Pocono Mountains.

Hungry Hill

The elaborate "Hungry Hill" memorial provides an excellent example of the perpetual care demanded by stone memorials and the difficulties in maintaining the historical infrastructure. This monument designates the site of the grave of an unnamed Sullivan soldier killed while building the road through the Poconos. The grave site was first marked with old stones, and later by a marker placed by a Philadelphia unit of the Grand Army of the Republic.[13] The site was surrounded by an iron fence, and in 1929, the Pennsylvania Historical Commission placed a marker there.[14] The idea for a new and rather dramatic construction came from Wanda and J. Elwood Calhoun, who owned a boy's summer camp nearby. They proposed the idea of the monument to the Monroe county commissioners in 1943, leasing the land for that purpose for ninety-nine years for $1.00. The commissioners paid for the construction of a stone wall and ordered a stone cut with historical details.[15] It was dedicated on September 30, 1944.[16]

After the Calhouns passed away, the monument lacked an official caretaker and it fell into disrepair. Eagle Scout chapters tidied up the area periodically, and in 2007, the local community paid two masons from Philadelphia over $11,000 to repair the stonework. In 2013 Tobyhanna resident Bill Mullen took on the charge. When he first encountered the site, it was weed infested and the walls were crumbling. He admitted his ignorance of the memorial's message, commenting that he and his wife "had a hard time finding people who knew the story" behind it, but they worked on clearing weeds and eventually requested funds from the Monroe County commissioners to assist them in making the repairs. Mullen was not a Sullivan specialist but a veteran, and he was moved by the fact that it marks the resting place of an unknown soldier.[17] For him, repairing the Hungry Hill marker was a matter of civic pride and an act of patriotism connected to his love for his own military, but not tied to a specific interest in Sullivan or his mission.

Bear Creek

Another extensive monument refurbishment was completed during my fieldwork. Will Kresge approached me after my talk on March 5, 2017, in Tunkhannock, Pennsylvania, to invite me to a Sullivan marker dedication he was holding that summer in Bear Creek, in the Pocono Mountains. He had received permission from the Pennsylvania Historical and Museum Commission to move two large Sesquicentennial-era monoliths that had been plaque-less for years, one from "Fatigue Camp" (also known as Fort Fatigue), and the second at Bullock's Farm, at the intersection of Laurel Run Road and Route 115, both in Bear Creek Township, where he had grown up and still lived.[18] I attended Kresge's marker dedication on a clear blue summer day in late June 2017 (see figure 34). It was held at the town's new Trailwood Park complex, near a mountain pond surrounded by tall pines. Over a hundred people attended. Because the location had been the homestead of a Connecticut Yankee family, and because I knew Kresge was a member of the Sons of the American Revolution, I expected that Kresge was motivated by Yankee ancestry. I was wrong.

The event Kresge organized followed the structure and content of the DAR plaque installation events I had studied which, in turn, resembled the annual Wyoming battle commemoration. He opened the festivities by discussing the expedition as an example of self-sacrifice and service to the nation.[19] After recognizing the many dignitaries present and thanking community members, he called on the local Boy Scout troop to present the colors. Everyone remained standing for "The Star-Spangled Banner," followed by a mass recitation of the Pledge of Allegiance. A benediction

FIG. 34. New Bullock's Farm monolith, Bear Creek Township PA, 2017. Photo courtesy of the author.

by a Methodist minister emphasized the sacrifices of those who came before and American "freedom" more generally and suggested that God himself encouraged monument building: "Heavenly Father, we are gathered here to dedicate these memorials. We are reminded that from early history you have instructed people to erect monuments at significant events so that future generations might understand your hand working in their lives. As we reflect upon these monuments, we see the lifestyle reflected in the homes around us, the freedom which our children have in the playground, and all these blessings of the father."

The main speaker was lawyer Stephen Killian. Killian explained that his fifth great-grandfather was a Wyoming martyr from Connecticut. His address exemplified the Pennsylvania Wyoming framing of the Sullivan Expedition. After beginning with Lexington and Concord, he turned almost immediately to the Yankee settlements in the region, expending almost 1,400 words on the Wyoming battle and only 400 on the Sullivan Expedition. At the end of his speech, he explained, "So I hope today I placed Sullivan's march in the context of the broader Revolution and the fact that the main catalyst for that expedition was our own Battle of Wyoming." This speech attests to the persistence of a Wyoming-centric framing of the Sullivan Expedition in Pennsylvania.

I want to turn to Kresge's decision to dedicate years to this marker project. He addressed this question in his remarks that day. Rather than a family tie to the Wyoming battle or to the Sullivan story, it was his memory of and sense of indebtedness to a dear friend, Ray Wasilewski, that provided the impetus: "This project began in 1979. At that time, I was chairman of the board of supervisors and Ray Wasilewski Senior was the zoning officer . . . As many of you know, Ray Senior was quite the historian. Remember his newsletters that he sent around about one every other week, and on the back was a history lesson? It got to the point that no one read the Township news. They just were interested in the history lesson."[20]

People were chuckling at the memory of this town figure, who had since passed away. The event began to feel more like a memorial service for Ray, which in many ways it was. Kresge continued, "Ray came to me one day and suggested this memorial park. Little did I know he already had it all worked out. I said, 'Ray, we have to purchase the site!' To which Ray responded, 'Well, I approached the owner . . . and he agreed to donate it to the township.' Well, what could I say?" Ray had already received permission from the Pennsylvania Historic and Museum Commission to move the two plaque-less markers to the new park. Kresge's story continued: "'Okay, Ray, how are you going to get them there?' To which he responded, 'I've already contacted Harvey Neilson, and he said that he would move them with his tow truck.'" Kresge's account elicited many laughs. He continued, "So here comes Harvey down the road in a few weeks barely being able to steer the truck because the front wheels keep coming off the ground with the monuments on the back. The Beverly Hillbillies had nothing on this spectacle. On steep hills he had people sit on the front bumper!" His talk then took a thoughtful turn. "Ray passed away, and I got out of office before we could get this place finished. Last fall I was traveling past the park, and it suddenly hit me just as if Ray had spoke to me. He said, 'Look at that place, Will. You've got to finish the park before you and I are having a one-on-one conversation about it.' And I knew what he meant by that." With this folksy and self-effacing statement, Kresge touched on mortality and friendship, and credited the day's activities to his close friend Ray.

When we met in his home a year later, I asked if he was always aware of Sullivan's journey through the area. He replied, "I did, but I didn't—I couldn't put it all together." He had learned about the Revolutionary War in school, but he explained, "All the battles I ever heard of were down in Yorktown, and Virginia, and other places like that. I couldn't understand how there was a battle and a campaign up through here."[21] On the other hand, the Battle of Wyoming was well known. As he put it, "Now, I knew about the Wyoming Massacre, but I couldn't put two and two together that *this* was a—somewhat of a retaliation for that."

The state's 1929 monuments were in place while Will was growing up and, at first, still sported their plaques. He had read them but, "I—it still didn't dawn on me . . . the importance of it." He explained that until he started working on the plaques, he had not even been aware that Washington had directed the Sullivan Expedition.

My original assumptions about Kresge's connection to Wyoming were incorrect. Yes, Kresge was a member of the Sons of the

American Revolution, but he joined only a month before the festivities, and through a German ancestor from the Brodheadsville area of Pennsylvania, not Connecticut Yankees. When I asked why he decided to work on the markers, he explained that it was hearing the voice of his friend. He added that he was passing those big blank stones, with no plaques, almost every day. "I almost got used to them being there without anything on them. But I got thinking, you know, we never finished that job. There's nothing. The stones are there, and it doesn't say what it's for or anything else."

Huge stone monuments have a physicality and gravitas that can draw people to care for them. For that reason, there is a built-in conservatism in the national memorial landscape. I am in no way calling into question Kresge's patriotism and dedication to his community or to his country. It is important to note, however, that he was drawn to this project partly out of loyalty to a close friend and because the blank stones seemed to be calling to him. It is also important to note that, regardless of this initial motivation, Kresge's dedication ceremony followed a set of patriotic rituals—presentation of the colors, formal roles for children, standing for "The Star Spangled Banner," recitation of the Pledge of Allegiance, and a Christian benediction—that resemble those of the Wyoming battle ceremony, and the main speaker interpreted the Sullivan story very much through Wyoming-centric framing.

Conclusion

In this region of Pennsylvania, the Sullivan Expedition usually conjures up the Battle of Wyoming and its annual commemoration, which persists almost unchanged to the present day. The DAR- and state-sponsored stone monuments and later roadside markers designating campsites of Sullivan's soldiers garner somewhat less attention. The Pennsylvania residents I met expressed a range of perspectives on the Sullivan markers, from apathy to strong, positive attachment, to strong antipathy. Peoples' views certainly sorted by ethnicity in that all the Pennsylvanians I met who self-identified as Native found the memorials offensive. Unsurprisingly, people who expressed the strongest views, both positive and negative, were history aficionados. I often encountered members of both camps at historical societies, making these places sites of sometimes quite passionate debates. Yet, along with these different orientations on the Sullivan story, most white settlers I met in Pennsylvania understood the expedition, as outlined in the Easton DAR marker in 1900, as a mission of "revenge," with the primary cause the Wyoming "massacre." We find a very different interpretation when we cross the state line.

ELEVEN

New York's Conflicting Voices

N ew York's education department followed the thirty-five Sullivan-Clinton monoliths with dozens of blue-and-gold roadside signs. Today, these various roadside markers read like victorious war trophies scattered from one lakeside vista to the next (see figure 35). When I first traveled to central New York to study them, I hadn't anticipated their pairing with so many anti-Indian signs on private yards. The summer before the 2016 election, along with Trump signs, many lawns were decorated with placards that blared, "Say NO to the Cayuga." Oversized wood-framed signs in red, white, and blue trumpeted, "No sovereign nation, no reservation." The bucolic rural landscape of the Finger Lakes region seemed to bristle with pockets of hate.

And yet New York is also alive with Native presence. While waiting to meet with community members in Syracuse in July 2017, I came across a newspaper article announcing the arrival of replica Columbus ships to the Finger Lakes. I was not the only one to take note. As the activists later explained, members of the Onondaga Nation were already organizing a protest, and the next week, news reports published the image of a sign hung over a highway bridge stating, "Columbus didn't discover anything. Thousands of Native Americans were already here."[1]

Haudenosaunee nations survived the Sullivan Expedition and the aftermath of the Revolutionary War, albeit with a greatly diminished land base, and conflict with the state has been ongoing since Sullivan left. The 1920s collective land claim case prompted by the Everett Commission (*James Deere v. St. Lawrence River Power*), dis-

FIG. 35. New York roadside sign, New York. Photo courtesy of the author.

cussed in chapter 6, had collapsed by 1929; however, activism and land claims continued. Since World War II, Iroquoian peoples had been waging wars on multiple fronts, fighting termination threats and over 1940s and 1950s taxation, and battling land sovereignty issues with highway construction, Salamanca leases, the Kinzua Dam, the Saint Lawrence Seaway, and a Niagara power plant.[2]

Land remained a focus. The Oneida Nation had long believed that the State had violated the Indian Trade and Intercourse Acts of 1790 and 1793 as there were no federal commissioners present at their 1795 "treaty," or at twenty-four of the twenty-six "treaties" New York made after 1798, as had been mandated by the 1790 and 1793 acts.[3] The January 1974 Supreme Court decision to sustain the Oneida land claims case and send it back to federal courts was a momentous one. As Hauptman observes, it "opened up the federal courts to the Oneidas as well as to other Indians seeking to get back land" in New York and the other original thirteen states.[4] The Cayuga Nation followed soon after. In the mid-1970s, with titles to so much land hanging in the balance, there was real economic uncertainty in the region and growing anti-Indian sentiment.[5]

This troubled atmosphere may have muted the tone of New York's bicentennial events surrounding the Sullivan-Clinton Campaign. Richard Allen, the program director of New York State's bicentennial commission, argued that the emphasis should be on commemoration, not "celebration," adding, "Any ceremonies should be dignified and not offend modern sensibilities."[6] A Sullivan-Clinton bicentennial planning meeting held in June 1978 had to be canceled due to lack of response, and the Cayuga County Historical Society chairman wrote that "no re-enactments of battles or disturbances will be scheduled. No emphasis upon the conflicts of the day will be re-cast. The theme of peace and brotherhood will take the place of conflict and bloodshed in the story represented."[7] Even anniversary publications played it safe. The "Bicentennial Remembrance of the Sullivan-Clinton Expedition 1779 in Pennsylvania and New York," published by the New York State Bicentennial Commission and the Chemung County Historical Society, mainly reprinted items prepared by Alexander C. Flick in 1929.[8] Richard Allen's speech given on the anniversary of the destruction of Cayuga Castle on September 22 was not widely known. There was "virtually no publicity" preceding the meeting because of the Indian land claims issue. As one member explained, "We didn't want any pickets."[9]

A public official's slip in the heat of the moment suggests that the 1929 public history program was successful in shaping New Yorkers' understandings of how it was that they were living in Haudenosaunee homelands. When information about negotiations underway with the Cayuga Nation was leaked in August 1979, pandemonium ensued. A meeting in Seneca Falls the next month attracted over fifteen hundred people. At one point, Waterloo supervisor LaVerne Sessler repeated the narrative found across the state on the 1929 markers when he exclaimed to all present, "I thought when Clinton and his troops marched through here in the 1700s that the Indian problem was taken care of."[10]

The anti-Haudenosaunee signs that I saw on people's yards were remnants of land claims agitation. Many of the cases lingered into the early 2010s, and they were a topic of vigorous discussion among the Haudenosaunee leaders I met. In February 2001 the Cayuga Nation was awarded $36.9 million, and on October 2, 2001, Judge Neal McCurn added $211 million in interest. The Onondaga Nation, meanwhile, filed a claim on March 11, 2005, seeking recognition of title for 4,000 square miles of land, and environmental repair of damaged lands. On March 29 of the same year, the U.S. Supreme Court ruled that the Oneida Nation couldn't reestablish sovereignty on lands they were buying back. Bad news continued when the Second Circuit Court of Appeals reversed the Cayuga claim decision, nullifying the $247 million settlement and leaving the tribe with "no currently recognized legal remedy and no land." On August 9, 2010, the Oneida Nation's land claim was dismissed by a U.S. district court, using an antiquated concept of "laches" to argue that they had "unduly delayed" their filing of this claim, and the next month, the Onondaga land rights case was dismissed due to its "readily identifiable disruptive nature." The Onondaga Nation filed an appeal, but on October 15, 2013, the U.S. Supreme Court refused to take the case, which ended the matter.[11] The publicity associated with this Haudenosaunee activism and the associated anti-Indian backlash made it difficult for New York residents living in the region of the markers to not know about the persistence of Native nations in that state, and likely shaped how the markers reverberated there.[12]

Apathy

As in Pennsylvania, I encountered a layer of apathy in New York toward the Sullivan commemorative complex. For many New Yorkers, the Revolutionary War was ancient history. A seventy-five-year-old DAR member from Waverly, New York, knew about the Sullivan Expedition ("Well, he marched up through here and wiped out the Indians," she told me), but didn't think many other people did, saying, "Up here I'm sure people don't know what Sullivan's march is all about." She added, "A lot of people aren't that interested in history. I think a lot of people don't care; once the monuments are established, they are just there." Mark Andrew, whom I met at the Newtown reenactment, made a similar point. A ninety-year-old historical museum docent, Joan O'Dell, concurred. She starts each tour at her town museum with a discussion of how the town of Horseheads, New York, got its name. This grim story recounts the demise of many of Sullivan's pack-horses, euthanized at that location at the end of the grueling expedition. According to local white settler lore, their heads were later assembled by Native Americans, and the sight of so many horses' heads led to the town's name. She told me that at most, 15 to 20 percent of the museum visitors had ever heard of Sullivan before she recounted that story. She conceded that most of the people she leads through the museum are not necessarily historically minded; they are returning home after moving away and are looking for high school yearbooks, or their parents have died and they are looking for something to do "in between viewings."

Patriotism

I also encountered patriotic perspectives among white New Yorkers, and Joan O'Dell is a case in point. She is so connected to local history endeavors that several people put us in touch. When we first met in June 2017, she presented me with a stack of fifty-nine photographs of different Sullivan plaques across the state, carefully marked with location details. She told me she took on the project after her husband died, adding, "I've always been a historian. I mean, from the time I was a kid, I was a collector of anything old. And since I retired, which is twenty-five years ago, I sort of leaned toward doing history. I wanted to do something."[13]

When I asked about the role Sullivan plays in the local imagination, she insisted that Sullivan concerns *everyone*, whether they know it or not. Her understanding of the relationship of the expedition to white settlement accorded with state historian Flick's 1929 framing, and she repeated the replacement narrative exemplified by the *Pageant of Decision*, asserting that there would be "no settlement, no towns, no farms, dairies, industry, no cities in the area if it weren't for him [Sullivan]." On another occasion she said the expedition "probably made this place [her small town of Horseheads] happen." She believed that it was only after Sullivan that "the settlers began to come in and felt safe. And that's when the surveyors came and laid out plots of land and that was in the 1790s." On some level, O'Dell knew that Native Americans still lived in the region long after the expedition, for she relayed a story of a smallpox epidemic of 1801 that decimated their numbers. She nevertheless attributed white settlement to the Sullivan-Clinton Campaign.

Joan has also been a member of the Chemung chapter of the DAR (through a Massachusetts patriot) since 1967, and like other DAR women I met, was focused on the Revolutionary War more generally. One afternoon we took a tour of the small burial grounds in the Chemung River Valley area. We were seeking both Sullivan plaques and gravesites of veterans of the Revolutionary War. It turned out there were far more graves than plaques. Like the history enthusiasts we encountered in the previous chapter, Joan could tell me precisely how many Revolutionary veterans are buried at each burial ground. When we talked about the men buried at the Knowles Cemetery near the Newtown Battlefield State Park, she relayed the aftermath of the Battle of Newtown as if she had been there herself: "They were put in the ground quickly because the Indians would have taken the buttons off their clothes, and dragged them around. So, they buried them quickly." When we talked about the Sullivan Expedition, she could imagine the soldiers on the landscape, walking right by her front door. But Joan's fascination with the past is not limited to Sullivan or the Revolution. While we drove around looking for local Revolutionary War veterans' graves, she also recounted stories about Elmira's heyday and economic decline. She narrated the biographies of buildings as we drove by old brick factories, train stations, and glassworks. She talked about the town's heyday in the mid-1950s and the relentless population decline since. We looked at tobacco-drying barns that were still in use in the late 1940s, and she showed me where the canals came in to bring coal on barges, and one of the largest concrete buildings in the state, a former A&P packaging plant that closed in 1980, putting "a ton of people" out of work. She pointed to the site of a prisoner-of-war camp where Italian prisoners were held during World War II. While interested in the Sullivan story, she is so thoroughly engaged by later historical eras that they collide in a whirlwind of stories whenever we meet.

"It Can Never Be an Honorable Nation"

I also encountered several Euro-Americans in New York who criticized the Sullivan-Clinton markers. Dick Cowles is a case in point. A history enthusiast who has thought and written about the expedition since he was a child, he was ninety-two when I first met him in 2015. His father, Ellsworth Cowles (1897–1992), grew up in Waverly, New York, and served in World War I. (Dick served in World War II.) Despite never finishing high school, Ellsworth rose in the ranks as an engineer for Ingersoll-Rand. He was a well-known local amateur historian and archaeologist and even worked with Louise Welles Murray at the Tioga Point Museum.[14]

Dick has family ties to the Battle of Wyoming as one of his ancestors was Lebbeus Hammond ("he was my great-grandfather's great-grandfather," he explained), one of the two men who allegedly escaped from Queen Esther at the battle's end. Dick told me that story in detail. I was always struck by the balance in Dick's views, however. He said he was proud to be descended of people from "both sides" of the Wyoming story, and he said he would join the United Empire Loyalists' Association of Canada if he could locate the requisite family connections, for he knew he had Tory relatives who left the region after the war. On more than one occasion, he emphasized that the Wyoming battle was not technically a "massacre," referring to it as "the Battle of Wyoming, which they called a massacre."[15] As he explained, "If you had been a part of the army that was being overrun, if you were dumb enough to go out, you were being outnumbered three to one, straight into a classic ambush—what a bunch of dummies!" He quickly conceded, "Well, they did fight bravely, and held together for a while. But, within no time, somebody shouted an order to back up or to do something, it was interpreted as retreat, and it turned into a mad panic, everybody, on their own, in a panic through the woods." He admitted, "If I were running in panic, I'd be inclined to call it a massacre, because it sure felt like a massacre, and most of their friends—there were very few survivors that ever made it back to the fort. So, in that sense it was a massacre. But the people [civilians] were not hurt. The British colonel kept his promise." Despite his personal tie to Wyoming, his critique of the massacre label was the clearest I heard:

> You read the early histories of Wyoming, the early writers that wrote about it, I've got 'em, some of them, and it's strictly, "That was a massacre, and these were just savages, it was our land, and they . . ." Well, baloney, it was *their* land. If they [Native Americans] are guilty of anything it's trying to protect their homeland, the same as we get so excited about homeland protection. It's exactly the same although the roles are reversed.

Through their writing and everyday discourse, Dick and his father, Ellsworth, challenged the dominant version of the Sullivan story. We can see this in his father's series of articles about the Sullivan Expedition that he published in the *Corning Leader* leading up to the bicentennial of the Battle of Newtown in 1979. While describing the expedition as a military success, rather than recycling largely one-sided heroic reports of previous eras, Ellsworth Cowles inserted a unique angle. His first article discussed the defeat of Gen. John Sullivan by the British on August 29, 1778, at the Battle of Newport, and his victory over the combined British-Indian forces one year later, on August 29, 1779, at the Battle of Newtown. Ellsworth Cowles highlighted the presence of 125 Black soldiers at Newport, of whom "over 30 were freemen," and outlined their valor: "The outcome of the hard-fought action in which the Negro regiment so distinguished itself, held back the British advance long enough so that Sullivan could execute an orderly retreat."[16] He suggested that without their courage, which helped secure Sullivan's survival, local history would have been different, "since there would have been no battle on the field of Newtown exactly one year to the day later." He then pointed out that while there is no record of Black troops in Greene's command at Newtown, when Sullivan told his Black valet that "they were going with the army to fight for liberty, the man replied that it would be a great satisfaction to know that he was indeed going to fight for his liberty."[17] Not only did Cowles bring race and slavery into his discussion of these early battles of the Revolutionary War (and suggest that Sullivan had an enslaved Black valet), but he ended the article with a nod to Sullivan's Indian foes: "And while we are at it, why not commemorate the bravery of the few hundred Indians who fought so valiantly at Newtown against almost one third of all General Washington's Continental Armies, to preserve their own homes in their own homeland—and lost."[18] In his last article of the series, "Last Bonfire of the Sullivan Expedition," published in the *Corning Leader* on September 20, 1979, he described the Native peoples as "homeless in their own homeland" and detailed their retreat to Fort Niagara during the severe winter, leading to so many deaths from starvation, and illness from poorly preserved meat and insect-infested flour, causing hundreds to die of scurvy. He concluded by describing the mission as a "practical failure:"

> Militarily, the great punitive expedition against the sprawling Iroquois confederation was a strategic success. During the following two years, however, well-organized raids by both large and small groups of revengeful Indians and embittered Tories against the frontier settlements proved the Sullivan Indian campaign a practical failure.
>
> It did, however, open a long hey-day of vast and illegal activities by "Land Grabbers." Abandoned by their British allies at the peace table, the Indians are only now, 200 years later, beginning

to receive *long overdue recompense* and justice from a Congress ready to make amends (emphasis added).

Rather than concluding his article series with one-sided praise of the patriots, he offered a nuanced discussion and expressed no small measure of compassion for the Native American "enemies." Referring to the region as the Indians' homeland drives home a particular political orientation, as does his hopeful nod toward a "long overdue recompense," which he wrote while the 1970s land claims movement was in full swing.

Ellsworth's son, Dick Cowles, also wrote a booklet, "Why Sullivan Marched," that he sells at a local museum. In it he grapples with how it was that Native American relationships with white settlers devolved so. He explains the origin of his essay in this way:

> It was happening about *this* time of year, before Christmas. Somehow or other, the line out of "Oh little town of Bethlehem," "The hopes and fears of all the years." And that, over and over, "the hopes and fears of all the years." Between the highest hopes of William Penn and the worst of fears, with the Paxton Boys, all in just a couple of generations. The irony, the tragedy, the ironic tragedy of that story.[19]

He placed the onus on Congress, telling me that after the Wyoming battle, "Congress was really all hepped up, 'We gotta do something, and we do it *now*.' And Washington was appointed, and then by the time they got into the wintertime, they couldn't wait! They wanted Washington to get an army going, and Washington and Sullivan had to say 'Wait, wait, wait, you're talking nonsense!' . . . But it was like after 9/11. We gotta do something and do it fast, and now."

Like James, the Pennsylvania prison guard, Dick didn't have a lot of positive things to say about Sullivan or his "march," even though, like Joan, he felt completely indebted to that side of the story as it led to his ancestors' ability to flourish where they did. He put it this way: "I'm a mix. I've got this history, I've got, you know, they're part of my ancestry. But I see, on the other side of that, I personally think that the United States of America can

never be a nation of honor . . . until we face up to the Indians."
I asked Dick to elaborate on this point. What would it mean to
"face up to the Indians?" He replied first by outlining what he felt
our pattern of stealing Indian land has done to the national soul:
"I personally think that the United States of America can *never
ever* be a nation of honor the way we like to say it in our hymns,
all this, 'we're such great honorable people.' That's all hypocrisy
until we face up to the Indians. Somehow or another we got to
come to a point in time where we face honestly that we stole this
land from them. And people don't want to listen to that." When
I asked him to expound, he replied: "Right, it can never be the
honorable nation that it thinks of itself and likes to sing about
and so forth. On this specific issue what can we do with the Indians?" I ask if he's thought of an answer. "Oh, I've thought about
that," he responded, and launched into his ideas:

> Obviously what happens is this: it's going to cost us establish-
> ment people, we're going to have to forfeit probably some land,
> probably some money, and it's going to be costly. We're going to
> have to face up to the fact that we can't be honorable any other
> way. Restitution is a fact of life. And now, to get down to details.
> See that? I'm still talking in abstractions. Here's something that's
> not abstract. Here we've got Allegheny State Park, and the Allegh-
> eny National Forest, it's a huge block of land. Who would suf-
> fer? What white man there? Nobody has any private property
> there, I don't think, right next to the village of Salamanca. Inci-
> dentally, Salamanca has an interesting history. It's gone back to
> the Indian now, boy a lot of Salamancans, there was a near rev-
> olution out there. They had to start paying taxes like, a little bit
> more than the rent that was put on them a hundred years ago.
> Give the Allegheny State Park to the Seneca. Get some of a simi-
> lar chunk of land for the Cayuga, all of them [referring to the six
> Haudenosaunee nations].

Dick has spoken with some Native Americans about his ideas:

> I've said this amongst the Indians, and they agree with me. That if
> a group of men with their hearts in the right place really sat down

with each other and say, "We're going to work something out, and our primary goal is to work out justice once and for all," they'll be able to do it. And I'm not going to sit here and tell them the details of what that plan is. That will be figured out by right-minded men with the will to do it. But you *have* to come to a reckoning.

Dick and his father are not alone in their discomfort with the dominant narrative. While it is outside of this book's purview, I should note that the private Pomeroy Foundation's solicitation of subjects for new markers to the Sullivan-Clinton Campaign, in preparation for the 250th anniversary in 2029, yielded cries of both celebration and despair among the people I was interviewing. The foundation has begun to develop new signage that is beginning to dot the New York landscape, often under a "Native Voices" rubric.

"The People You Are Occupying Never Forget"

How do descendants of the Iroquois, who feature on the 1929 New York plaques as "hostile nations," view the Sullivan-Clinton markers that cross their homelands? My interviews with Haudenosaunee leaders in charge of cultural centers offer a vital corrective to dominant perspectives. I include these comments here with a caveat, for I recognize that my own positionality as a white settler outsider makes this research challenging. In these interviews, this subject position was often a topic of conversation. Native interviewees sometimes shifted pronouns from "we" to "you," identifying me as a white member of dominant society and placing the plaques in my domain, as we saw in the introduction to this book. A Seneca man, once involved in the Seneca-Iroquois National Museum (SINM), corrected me after I asked him what "people in Salamanca" thought of the Sullivan plaques. He told me that I needed to be more precise in my language. My questions were vague, he explained. *Which* Salamanca people was I interested in, he wanted to know? *Seneca* people? *Non-Seneca* people? *White* people?

When I characterized the Sullivan plaques as "odd" in another conversation, with a Seneca resource specialist I met at Tim Horton's in Salamanca, he countered that celebratory markers could be found all over the country, referencing Civil War markers. He is the man who stated, almost as a kind of warning: "the people you are occupying never forget, never." Part of never forgetting is noticing the vainglorious markers and their lies and omissions. The apathy I found among so many non-Native inhabitants, especially of Pennsylvania, indicates the relative invisibility of the Sullivan plaques to them; this is not how they are viewed by the Haudenosaunee people I met.

I confronted a very different temporality in these conversations and at the cultural centers. The ways Haudenosaunee and non-Haudenosaunee accounts mark out time contrast, for good reason. The temporal horizon for most Euro-Americans is short, often starting the year Europeans arrived at the continent, as scholars of other settler-colonial societies have observed. Alternatively, the national story starts with a foundational event: the Revolutionary War.[20] For Native people who have been living in their homeland for time immemorial, claiming either moment as a starting point would be nonsensical. Sullivan's raids do not represent the start of their story nor its end; instead, they comprise one of many such episodes in a long saga of dispossession and resistance that continues into the present day. More significantly, in these conversations, the Sullivan story was not connected temporally to other moments of an era labeled the "Revolutionary War," but to other instances of white aggression leading to land loss. For this reason, our conversations were wide ranging temporally and involved a full complement of actors, shifting from Sullivan to the French invasion of the seventeenth century, to New York State seizing land for thruways, to Ruth Bader Ginsburg's use of the "laches" concept in a land claims case in a twenty-first century Supreme Court ruling, with dizzying leaps across centuries of time, making my discussions with even the most informed non-Native Revolutionary War buffs seem limited and parochial indeed.

Language also shifted in these conversations. Jaré Cardinal, a Euro-American who had directed an early iteration of the SINM in Salamanca, once interviewed Seneca elders about the Kinzua Dam. She explained that the Seneca people she interviewed referred to Sullivan not as an "expedition" but as an "invasion." She, too, employed "invasion" as a matter of course, for instance when she told me that "after the invasion, families traveled together." In fact, I do not remember ever hearing the word "expedition" in my conversations with Native leaders. For people in Indian Country, the operation was a disaster that arrived from outside and was experienced as an intrusion, an invasion.

These speakers also took a wider view of the practice of marking the land with plaques and monuments, suggesting the cultural specificity of this placemaking practice. Seneca sociologist Dr. Randy John mentioned a Salamanca park that hosts a plaque to Simón Bolívar and asked why it is there. Did he own the railroad? Jaré Cardinal laughed and added that you can't take many of the signs as accurate; a lot of them are outright wrong. Her favorite was one in Tonawanda; it was a place-name called "Washington's Crossing," after a Native American man named Washington who crossed there; the state mistakenly put up a sign saying that it was crossed by George Washington. Seneca faithkeeper G. Peter Jemison pointed out that Newtown Battlefield State Park was so named "even though it's not located where the battlefield is." The final straw is the use of that site by reenactors not of that battle but of the Civil War. "They would have Civil War encampments, apparently. How bizarre!"[21]

Many Native people and their allies viewed setting up markers to the military victories in or near Indian country as in such poor taste as to be comical. When I shared with Dr. John and Dr. Cardinal what I had learned of state historian Flick's attempts to convince the Allegheny Seneca to host the Brodhead plaque at Cold Springs, they found the prospect hilarious, imagining what local Seneca peoples must have thought. They imagined him stating, "We are going to celebrate where we killed Indians and took your land!" But as they laughed, Jaré pointed out this isn't behavior restricted to the deep past. She remembered that when she was working at the SINM, she fielded a call from people wanting to involve Native representatives at another Sullivan ceremony, adding, "Imagine that, going around to Native nations asking if they want to take part." This was seen as unbelievable.

"That Becomes the Story for Our Region"

The role the Sullivan markers play in dominant American memory and cultural practice was a popular topic in these interviews. Jemison noted that many of the Sullivan plaques went up around the heyday of automobile tourism:

> When you think about it, the public is, in the thirties, they're really just beginning to really motor more, get in their cars, and go places, and go to a lake, to go for a picnic, and camping, and whatever else. And so now you've got something historical for them to go and read and see. So I guess that was part of it, you know, is this the mobility of the American and the creating of these monuments now to tell a story, a select story.

We talked about how putting a monument in a little town encouraged tourists to travel to that place, take a detour, buy ice cream, and otherwise support the local economy. Jemison said, "And there's a monument there to go see. And they go all the way across the state—you know, from Elmira to here. And then some parks are [built] around that subject, you know, like the Newtown Battlefield."

A central problem for Jemison was the fact that the markers transmit a partial story, and the rest of the story is never taught. As a result, the average passerby doesn't know how to evaluate or critique the information that is there. As Jemison put it, "People living around the signage are aware of it, and know *something* because of the signage that is there," but he expressed concern that they are being misled because the signage is so clearly one-sided. As illustration, he brought up the example of a monument to a Mohawk leader named Kryn, who assisted the French in the 1687 attack on Seneca villages Gannagoro and Totiakton. The markers were established in the early twentieth century by a local man who happened to own a foundry and was a "big lover of Jesuits." He decided to "create monuments for every Jesuit mission that he could in this region," Jemison explained. "So he cast these signs, plaques, that he mounted on various things, sometimes stone. So what he did, basically, was he commemorated a guy by the name of Kryn who actually led the French here to attack us. And he touted the fact that this guy was a 'good Christian Indian,' who, you know, was trying to, in essence, get rid of the 'savages.'" The problem is that these one-sided or partial markers were never corrected. As Jemison reported, "So that monument is still standing down at the corner of Maple Avenue and Route 96, right in the center of the village here. And we are just now in this conversation about what to replace that with because we want it down." The marker expresses a position diametrically opposed to the Seneca Nation and the museum that Jemison helped found. It celebrates a Mohawk man who led an attack on the Seneca, but it neglects to mention that he carried out this mission under terrible duress:

> We live with a monument down there that still touts the achievement of this guy who, the story goes (that we have heard from many of the Mohawk people living in Kahnawake, outside of Montreal), their families were basically being held as prisoners. Unless these guys served that French Army, the penalty would be, "If you're not going to do that, we're going to take your children and your families and ship them off to France! They're going to be working the galleys of the French ships." And so, what choice do you have? You know, you do what you think has to be done to save your family. So, again, he's celebrating this guy who led them, and that becomes the story for the region.

Jemison found it amazing that the "story for the region" was inscribed on the landscape by a random non-Native foundry owner who had the technical skill, and perhaps the financial and social capital, necessary to mark up the landscape however he wanted. Jemison asked, "Did he have to go get permits in these different towns? I doubt it. They probably just said, 'Oh, go ahead.' Just because he had his own foundry, because he had the financial wherewithal, he could go around and put these monuments up. And they're still around, you know?"

The mistakes the markers make are more than ones of labeling or placement. Speakers felt they communicated half-truths and were more about mythmaking than anything else. Jemison said that many Seneca people find the Sullivan plaques infuriating. "For some of our people, you know, it still makes them mad, really. When they really, fully grasp—what happened, you know."

Cardinal talked about how white Americans get so caught up in local lore and the general narrative of American history that they stay trapped by it all, and they aren't even doing this intentionally. She noted that in the 1870s, people were trying to create all these myths to celebrate American culture for the immigrants, trying to create a common culture, and she felt that this mindset persists today. In her view, these roadside markers provide a window into how the dominant society used to think. And still thinks. She added: "It's all about myths, the creation of myths. They talk about 'conquering' Indians, but it was an 'invasion,' and we need to start thinking that way. It's all part of that early educational mission to create an 'American' culture. We have created this culture with all these blinders so that we can live with ourselves after all that we have done. The monuments, then, are part of the blinders."

Jemison described this dominant perspective as "from the perspective of the American Army, the American effort to settle the West [he pauses] . . . whatever that was. You know, manifest destiny, or whatever they were thinking of." He does realize that there are some people with a more critical eye, and who "understand that it was really a very, what would you call it? a racist-driven campaign." The plaques thus speak from a specific white settler vantage point:

> Take an area down south of here . . . it becomes a historical visit for people who are interested in the Revolutionary War. And there are other locations, too, south of here, where towns were, you know, down the Genesee River. But I would say the view is not, "the poor Seneca." I mean, the view is, *"This is how we got these towns, and this land, and how our economy developed,"* and whatever else you want to see. But the view isn't, "Was this justified?"

Part of the problem is that the full Sullivan story is not taught to schoolchildren, so they can't evaluate the signage all around them, Jemison explained. "Right now, that story is not available in elementary school. It's not in high school. It really isn't in college, either, unless you are really focused on Revolutionary War history and, you, yourself are doing the research. . . . You are really not going to find course work on that." As he summed up the situation, "Our school systems don't teach the stories that serve us."

Jemison wants to rethink how the Revolutionary War is narrated more generally, and he brings up the question of land. "This is another thing that I always say is that this idea that the Revolutionary War was about taxation without representation, you know, tea, and about housing soldiers, or any of that crap." He starts to laugh at these explanations, continuing, "To me, it's about land. The bottom line is land. Who has the right to claim that land? Who has the right to get that land? To me, that's what it's about. Okay, because that's certainly the way it played out. And, so—it's not an accommodating view. It's not a view that people want to hear. And the—the *less* I say it, the better, you know?"

In Jemison's view, the Sullivan Campaign had been understood as something to celebrate—until the Geneva Convention.

> One of the things I was told was that . . . that there was a period when the Expedition was [viewed as] a glorious campaign. And it was really celebrated as something, you know, very important—more attention was paid to it. And then, when the Geneva Conventions came out in the end of the 1940s, at the end of the Second World War, and people really began to discuss genocide, they saw the campaign in a different light. And if you were going to continue to portray it as this, you know, this great example of how to expand your empire, or how to tame the wilderness, or whatever you're going to call that, you have to include that it was really directed at men, women, and children indiscriminately. It was directed at an entire population.

From the perspective of these Native American leaders and their allies, the Sullivan-Clinton markers are wrong on so many levels. They are badly worded, are misplaced, blame the victim, celebrate land theft, are symbolic of an ongoing colonial relationship, justify genocide, and provide one of many examples of a dominant group putting half-truths on the land.

Conclusion

As I found in Pennsylvania, the New York residents I met expressed an array of positions on the Sullivan markers, ranging from apathy and disconnection to patriotically embracing them. However, the overall sentiment in New York was far more critical, as we have seen, a critical stance I attribute at least partly to the persistence in that state of multiple active Native American nations who have been working to preserve what land, sovereignty, rights, and recognition that they can. This activism seems to have influenced non-Native New Yorkers, as they expressed more informed views about the memorials and seemed to have a basic understanding of Native American actors, history, and perspectives. One man volunteered his plan for giving land back.

When we are considering how national history is displayed in public spaces, what constitutes an intervention? Is talking back in private settings enough? I heard criticism of the markers in both states and, in many regards, criticizing the dominant narrative that is found on roadside markers could be viewed as a kind of resistance, a way to start changing the public narrative, and may even reflect shifts in the wider historical consciousness already underway. Over the course of this fieldwork, I encountered white people who, either working alone or with Native American allies, have taken this resistance one step further. In the next chapter, I review these interventions before turning to the Native cultural centers, which are making the greatest intervention of all.

TWELVE

Changing the Narrative

T he roadside markers, street names, and monoliths that
span two states and celebrate the Sullivan story can remain
invisible to people who do not know enough of the historical background to take a position on them. When they learn
more, however, some people become upset. We have seen examples of people who "talk back," who criticize marker texts in public or in private asides. Are there other tacks to take? When does
one intervene in the memorial landscape, and how? Marker revisionism was in the news while I was conducting this research,
and people like James from Tunkhannock, Pennsylvania, compared the Sullivan memorials directly to Confederate symbols and
debated their removal. Both the impressive scale of the markers
in the Sullivan commemorative complex and the extreme decentralization of memorial-making in the United States lead to difficulties in confronting them, however. Whom does one contact
regarding a marker an elite white woman put at the edge of her
property in a previous century?

Problematic roadside markers do not go unnoticed, however,
and people over the ages have pursued both official and unofficial methods of righting what they perceive as terrible wrongs.
We have seen creative acts of iconoclasm expand over the past
several years in the wake of the Black Lives Matter movement. At
the end of his landmark *Lies Across America*, James Loewen discusses "snowplow revisionism," a less dramatic response, and
he offers examples of markers that were updated after their accidental damage, suggesting that many more merit the same fate.[1]

"Unofficial" approaches to problematic markers occur, but they can be difficult to research as perpetrators often seek anonymity. In these cases, motives can only be inferred. The meaning of a red handprint placed in the middle of a Sullivan-Clinton plaque in New York may be transparent to Haudenosaunee passersby and their allies.[2] Similarly, many wooden markers along "Crook's Trail" in northern Arizona, marking the journey of a military general during the Apache wars and now bordering the White Mountain Apache Reservation, have been defaced and some even set on fire, presumably by people unhappy with Crook's role in the subjugation of the Apaches. Yet the motives of other such attacks are more difficult to interpret. Take, for instance, the defacing of DAR-established markers denoting the path of the Santa Fe Trail, one of which was broken from its base, "dragged to face northwest," and used for target practice.[3] Was this a political act, or merely a pragmatic one?

In a recent article, James Osborne discusses monument removal as examples of "counter-monumentality." Memory inscribed in stone is fragile, he writes, "Despite their outward appearance of strength and permanence, monuments additionally render the memory of their creators vulnerable and open to contestation."[4] Comparing the cases of a Confederate memorial statue in Baltimore, Maryland, and colossal Iron Age royal statues from the Near East, he argues that such monuments promote a memorial agenda that is fragile "precisely because of monuments' enduring material status, not in spite of it."[5] The examples of counter-monumentality he considers include the installation of thematically opposed artwork near an existing monument, and other anti-monumental practices like defacement.[6]

The very materiality of the Sullivan monuments, often weighty granite monoliths, has had the opposite effect, in my examination. Their heft makes them difficult to tackle, and their official-looking appearance and labels indicating state sponsorship conspire to present a misleading message of continuing consensus and official approval when in fact, as we have seen, few people were consulted or had strong views about the commemorations before they were developed. The interventions I encountered differed from Osborne's examples.

"Another Killing Monument": Pennsylvanians Intervene

Amy is a retired white seventh grade English teacher from the Wilkes-Barre area whom I met through a local writers' group. She is working on a novel for young adults that provides a different side to the Sullivan story. Her wider goal is to educate and bring to life the past for young adults in her community, and she decided to feature the Sullivan Expedition to counter local Wyoming-centrism. "There are so many things here about Sullivan and nobody even knows who Sullivan is. A friend of mine for years said, 'Which Sullivan are you talking about?' And I said, 'Sullivan's march!' And she said, 'Oh, you should have said that.' Of the two topics, I thought it would be much easier to write about Sullivan's march for young adults than it would be to detail the Wyoming Valley Massacre. I didn't want to get into the massacre."[7]

I asked her if, in her experience, young people in this part of the state did not know this story. She was adamant: "No, no idea. They've been to Philly, New York, Washington, but nobody around this end of the valley knows that much about Sullivan or the [Wyoming] Massacre." She has found that people from out of state who come to work in "the Valley" learn only then about the Wyoming battle. "The girl who came to take my job, I told her, 'When you're teaching the kids make sure you include the Wyoming Valley Massacre,' and she said, 'Oh my God, was there a massacre in Wyoming?' and I said 'Yeah, about two hundred years ago.' She had *no idea*. Neither did the social studies teacher at that time. Now he knows a lot about the Wyoming Massacre."

Amy's goal is not so much to intervene as to balance out the story that is already inscribed on the plaques. I asked if she wanted to set the story straight. "Not necessarily set the story straight," she replied, "but to try to get young adults into that time period." Specifically, she wants her book to offer middle- and high-school students an empathic understanding of the Indian side of local history, which in her experience as a lifelong middle-school teacher is desperately lacking. Students know so little about local history, and about the Indians who lived right in the vicinity.

They *all* know Geronimo, you know? But they don't know that right above them there were so many Indians that had ownership of this land as much as Indians own anything. We took it. We took everything. *The Warrior Trail* was the first time I was very cognizant of the Indians as far as what Sullivan was doing and what a brutal policy we had towards the Indians. In his introduction, he says you have to look at it from both ways. Nobody looks at the Indian side.

I pressed her about her book: "When people read this book, you're hoping they'll get a sense of . . . what's the final message?" Her response was immediate: "We were right, and we were wrong, they were right, and they were wrong. Does a one-day massacre justify scorched earth? Or is that one-day massacre what caused that horrible hatred? It *was* horrible. And the Indians were *not* the ones instigating."

She discussed the difficulties she was facing in humanizing both the troops and their foes as her research led her into a thicket of characters and mythologies. She had been trying to understand the sounds and smells of the Sullivan Campaign, what roles the women on the march played, and whether or not children were present. Some larger-than-life figures also pose problems: "One of my biggest problems in the book is Queen Esther. You can't get a straight story on Esther Montour."

We discussed how the historical markers differed in New York. After some thought, Amy announced, "The monuments are a problem for me. Are there monuments through the south about Sherman's march? No. The fact that we defeated a people, who we completely subjugated, and then we put up monuments?" When I relayed to her the roadside signs in New York identifying locations of so many destroyed villages and orchards, Amy was appalled. "Is it said in *praise* of Sullivan?" When I said it was, she asked, "What are we bragging about?" She considered how many monuments are really about death and destruction, what she calls "killing monuments." "Are there any monuments where peaceful things happened?" she asked. She had attended a marker dedication in Scranton, Pennsylvania, a decade ago that commemorated a railroad strike where workers were killed in the street. "I was there when they put it up that day. It was pretty impressive to see it. But it was another killing monument." Amy asked if there were any pro-Indian monuments along "Sullivan's trail." I told her I knew of none. That seemed to resolve the question for Amy, and she declared, "So I'm officially coming out and saying the markers aren't fair. They're not fair. When I write I will try to give equal points of view."

Monuments helped motivate another writer to take on the Sullivan Expedition. After taking a close look, for the first time, at the Sullivan and other Bradford County monuments he passed during a driving tour of his home state of Pennsylvania, it dawned on retired journalist Jim Remsen that he had never studied the region's role in the nation's history. He decided on the device of a novel and published *Visions of Teaoga* in 2014. He explained that this format would allow him to present a range of views through the perspectives of his characters. His novel follows two female protagonists, one in the present day and another from a previous century, and the novel moves back and forth between two storylines.

The protagonist in the contemporary storyline is a teenage girl, Maddy, from Texas, who travels to Athens, Pennsylvania, to spend time with her father. Much of the novel involves her discovery of local history by encountering historical markers, and through her relationship with a schoolteacher. At one point, she encounters the 1902 Athens marker and reads the plaque text:

Maddy gulped, letting her fingertips linger above the jarring words. Her eyes hopscotched over the rest: "FOUR BRIGADES . . . RIFLEMEN . . . 250 SOLDIERS," but kept returning to "DESTROYED SAVAGERY." She looked over at Curtis, who refused to come closer. His hostility, along with the musty air and cemetery atmosphere, were giving her the creeps. "You understand it, don't ya," he frowned. "George Washington sent General Sullivan and his troops to burn down whole lots of Iroquois towns from here up into New York.

We're Keystone, New York is Empire. We're civilization. You can figure out what the savagery meant. Tommy and I hate this thing. I call it the hissing stone."

Maddy thinks to herself, "So that's what they thought a century ago. Savagery. Civilization. Yikes, so black and white."[8]

Over the course of her time in Athens, and through her encounter with a history buff who runs a summer camp where Maddy works, Maddy learns more about local history and becomes increasingly critical of its portrayal on the land. She also has mystical experiences that connect into Remsen's second storyline, which features perhaps the most vilified woman in Pennsylvania settler public memory, Esther Montour. In this book, Queen Esther is an old woman, brought to Athens in 1790, by Sagoyewatha (Seneca chief Red Jacket), to assist in a 1790 peace council designed to console two Seneca families whose sons were killed by whites. Remsen has Esther narrate her life story to Tutelo women gathered at the treaty grounds awaiting the arrival of other treaty participants. Esther narrates a life of movement, meeting her husband, the Munsee chief Eghohowin, their life at Assinissink and local resettlement at Sheshequin after Assinissink's destruction in 1764, and finally the establishment of what became known as "Queen Esther's town." She describes living there as a time of "uneasiness."[9] Through this device, Remsen imagines Esther returning to her former home over a decade after it was burned by Hartley:

> She yearned to see the promontory where her home had stood, the wood-frame home, which the whites called Queen Esther's Castle. . . . She knew what she would see: the settler Snell had claimed her high ground as his own and built his cabin there.
>
> As the procession passed the settlers' new wharves and approached the landing, curious yengwes [white people] lined the Teaoga bank to stare. The Indians now numbered nearly 100, four or five per vessel. What a sight we must be to them, thought Esther. Native leaders sat high in their long boats, displaying their finery of beaded headbands, feathers, and long bright ribbons.[10]

This fictional imagining calls into question any simplistic replacement narrative readers might have, and it shows how for a time, white settlers and Native peoples were coexisting in the same time and place. This era is contrasted with chapters taking place in contemporary times as Maddy learns the backstory from a history buff and museum director, Mrs. Tulowitsky: "So it's said that Esther's castle was the largest building, in full view of the Point. One of the accounts says her home—here, I'll read it—'was long and low, built of hewn logs and planks, neatly done, with a porch over the doorway.'"[11]

These sections provide readers less versed in the sprawling story of Esther's life necessary background information. Remsen also retells the Wyoming battle story through Esther's eyes. She tells the women about the loss of her son right before the battle and her being blinded by grief, suggesting that the manic killing attributed to her by later settlers may not have occurred. In an afterward, Remsen offers further details of Timothy Pickering's 1790 Peace Council and lets readers know that while there is no evidence that Esther returned to Teaoga for the treaty, she was presumably alive in 1790 and would have known about the treaty meetings.

Remsen's primary mission in publishing this book was much like Amy's in that he hoped to bring young adults to a more nuanced view of the past. He told me he wanted Esther to be able to tell her story, rather than being a "demon of history."[12]

The book is rich in images—not only depicting the Esther and Sullivan markers, but also Tioga Point, Pickering, and Red Jacket. It also includes some gruesome Wyoming Massacre illustrations, drawing readers in to interrogate these events and how they have been portrayed. On the back of the book, Remsen encourages readers to consult his website for further study, where he has included original maps and primary sources, a bibliography, recommended reading, discussion questions, author's notes, and links to related websites.[13] He spells out his main goal in clear terms: "The author offers up his own deep wish. It is that *Visions of Teaoga*, his ode to a lost world, succeeds in bringing local history fully alive for the reader."[14]

When we spoke in December 2017, I asked Remsen if he had received any negative responses. He said no, and he was actually pretty surprised about that. "I gave forty public talks and a number of them were right up there, the Spalding Library (Athens, Pennsylvania), the Sayre schools. I was braced for someone to say it was unpatriotic history, but I never got that. I never did. Maybe it's just a matter of who shows up at these talks. It was a surprise."[15]

We discussed his critical look at the Sullivan markers, and what he thought should happen next. "I'd be fine if the markers never existed. I thought in the book there could be a bulletin board where people could post their thoughts. But seriously, a lot of places people have put up storyboards. In my view, we shouldn't erase history but give a fuller understanding. I think it would be good to have something there that talked about the DAR's outlook at that point in time that would keep the monument there but broaden the perspective."[16] Broadening the perspective and engaging youth in the complexity of local history were his main goals.

In the cases of Jim and Amy, the historical markers definitely reverberated. Jim, in particular, discusses quite clearly having an epiphany after reading the texts on 1929 PHC Sullivan Expedition and related historical plaques. He decided then and there to embark on this project. Independently, they both decided to insert a different perspective on the local past into the "public theater of history."[17] They each addressed this goal with creative writings. Similar to the memory entrepreneurs we discussed in the first part of this book, both authors find it vitally important that a revised message be transmitted and have identified schoolchildren and young adults as their target audience. Whether or not their publications reach these young minds and what will be the effect on wider settler-colonial historical consciousness remains to be seen. However, in these examples of personal interventions, the markers were noticed and have had real effects in galvanizing these writers to write back.

Righting the Wrongs through Information

The only people I met who successfully changed a historical marker were members of NOON, the Neighbors of the Onondaga Nation, an activist organization in the Syracuse area. NOON emerged in the context of rising tensions between Natives and non-Natives during the land claims era. It was created by the Syracuse Peace Council, an antiwar and social justice organization that dates to 1936. NOON's mission is to "promote understanding of, and respect for, the Onondaga people, history, and culture, to provide accurate information about the Onondaga Nation's issues of concern," to "challenge racism towards the Onondaga people through education," and to "advocate for just and fair treatment of the Onondaga people at all levels of our own government."[18] They articulate this agenda in an eighty-page booklet, *Neighbor to Neighbor Nation to Nation, Readings about the Relationship of the Onondaga Nation with Central New York, USA*, that translates Onondaga philosophical tenets and historical and contemporary concerns. NOON endeavors to embody a model of respectful inter-community relations found in Onondaga philosophy and exemplified by the seventeenth-century "Two Row" wampum treaty. In Haudenosaunee oral tradition, the "Two Row" (Guswénta) treaty belt records a treaty made between the Dutch and the Haudenosaunee in the early seventeenth century.[19] NOON describes it as the "first treaty made by the Confederacy with European settlers [and] . . . understood by the Haudenosaunee to be the basis on which all subsequent treaties were made . . . a model of relationships between peoples."[20] The *Neighbor to Neighbor* cover depicts an image of a treaty belt replica woven by Tony Gonyea, Onondaga artist and faithkeeper. This shell belt has a white field symbolizing peace and friendship, and two purple rows represent the "separate but equal paths of two sovereign nations." As the NOON booklet explains, "These two rows will symbolize two paths or two vessels, traveling down the same river together . . . we shall each travel the river together, side by side, but in our boat. Neither of us will make compulsory laws or interfere in the internal affairs of the other. Neither of us will try to steer the other's vessel."[21]

To follow the spirit of this treaty in their initiatives, NOON members focus on reaching out to the non-Native community, serving as translators and go-betweens with other local residents on behalf of the Onondaga Nation. NOON member Sue explained this tack as follows, "Basically, our mission is to support Onondaga leaders, and to—we decided, the best way that we could do this was to educate people in *our* community about who *they* are. So, we go out and give talks, we go to clubs . . . We would take them with us to Kiwanis clubs, and, so, people would meet them and ask questions."[22] Another white member, Gail, explained their approach as follows, "We can hear things that might be insulting to an Onondaga person, and explain it, in a way because we kind of come from that place ourselves—we can explain it in a way where the Onondaga person doesn't have to say it over and over again for the five hundredth time." Sometimes their goal is to simply disseminate information, or "tabling," reaching hundreds of people at a time. The women agreed that this work represents their own efforts at a kind of redress. Sue explains, "I'd have to say we're—we're trying to right some of the wrongs." "Through information," Gail adds.[23]

Gail has a nuanced view of the white communities they are trying to reach and spoke of the need to tackle these issues with real empathy: "Sometimes people do things out of ignorance, you know? That they wouldn't do if they knew. I mean, there are people who are, you know, actively evil, but that's another issue. But, you know, to help people who . . . who don't want to, don't want to be culturally insensitive, or don't want to be rude to others, but just are because they don't have any information, because their origin stories are different."

NOON members insisted that since the Sullivan and other historic markers were initiated by members of the white community, the white community is responsible for them, not the Haudenosaunee. When I discussed this question with Andy, another NOON member, he replied using the "two row wampum" principles. Referring to his Onondaga allies, he told me, "They feel like those signs are in our boat, they're our responsibility, not theirs. While some young folks might decide to go take their pickup truck and mow them down on their own, collectively, their leaders would feel like it would be inappropriate for them to even approach towns or villages or counties and say, 'These signs are wrong.' You know, that's overstepping their commitment to this agreement. This is a model of living in parallel, in peace and mutual respect."[24]

NOON has taken on the marker issue as one of their major initiatives, resulting in a marker program unlike any I have seen. It was not hard for members to explain to me how and why they started getting involved in this way. To them, changing local historical consciousness is a necessary element of their wider mission to confront ignorance and racism through education. As Andy recounted, "What it makes sense to do now is to a large degree based on what our understanding of the history was. Did we collectively do things wrong? Do we have some responsibility?" Originally they wanted to just document the Sullivan-Clinton and related signage. As he explained, "The initial plan was, let's document them all and be able to share that with the public, put it all on the website so people are aware of it. And, provide some context, debunk it if it was something to be debunked. The idea was to identify what were the key ones, what were the ones that seemed like we might be able to get changed more easily."

Sue and Gail took on this program with gusto. They worked from the few lists they could find identifying all the markers in Onondaga and Cayuga Counties and proceeded systematically: they went to the field, determined the locations of markers and roadside signs, and documented them with images. They built a database with this information that commented on what was erroneous or missing in the texts.[25] This work was carried out in consultation with Onondaga historians. Some markers were simply in the wrong place, but often the texts were completely fanciful. They spent time identifying problematic language. While they didn't mention Jean O'Brien's work to me, they were well aware of the need to confront the "firsting" and "lasting" language found on so many New York markers.[26] As Sue explained, "We might write something as simple as, 'Despite the fact that this sign says the first resident here was so-and-so, there were Natives here long before that.' But others are much more complex." As Gail put it, the markers are all about "creating the mythology." She referenced a plaque that discusses an early settler "carrying the grindstone for his mill on his back, fjording a river, you know? What is that about but creating a mythology of someone who has extraordinary strength? You know, did he *really* do that?"[27]

This research was painstaking but rewarding, and Gail and Sue are pleased that when someone googles "Sullivan markers" today, their website is one of the first to appear. Realizing that not everyone will find their website, they prepared a handy one-page flier, "Historic Markers," designed to get people thinking, which they bring to their tabling sessions. The flier provides NOON contact information, introduces the historic markers project, and reproduces "Ten Questions to Ask at an Historic Site," from James Loewen's *Lies Across America* (1999), including the following:

> 1. When did this site become a historic site? (When was the marker or monument put up? Or the house 'interpreted'?). How did that time differ from ours? From the time of the event or person commemorated?
> 2. Who sponsored it? Representing which participant group's point of view? What was their position in [the] social structure when the event occurred? When did the site go 'up'?
> 3. Why? What were their ideological needs and social purposes when the site went 'up'?
> 4. Who was the intended audience?
> 5. Did they have government support? At what level?[28]

Their brochure also highlights many words to watch for, offering an informative and helpful unpacking of such potentially loaded terms as *wilderness, empty land, discoverer, settle, settled, settlement, first settlers, civilization, civilized, uncivilized, progress,* passive voice with no subject, *massacre.* For instance, regarding the term *massacre,* they write the following: "Sometimes markers use the word to describe a situation when Indigenous people were defending their own homes and the numbers of deaths were small. The word 'massacre' is often used to describe deaths of early immigrants. The indiscriminate use of the word 'massacre' contributes to the belief that all Indigenous People are savages." Regarding the use of the "passive voice with no subject," they present markers to Sullivan and Clinton as examples: "One marker says that Clinton and Sullivan 'were commanded' to attack the Indians. The sentence conveniently leaves out the fact that General George Washington gave the order to initiate the military campaign."[29]

NOON is the only organization I have encountered during this fieldwork to have successfully replaced a marker, which speaks to the challenges inherent in such an undertaking. The marker in question was a historic sign found in Onondaga Lake Park, along a popular Syracuse biking/walking trail. When I first met Sue and Gail, they had me meet them at the park so we could walk directly to the new sign. "Number 19," Sue remembered, repeating the marker's identification number in their massive database. "I've never forgotten the number. Number 19."

This project was complicated. They first brought the existing wording to a gathering of Onondaga leaders to see if they found it problematic and, if so, to learn what they thought should be changed. As Sue explained, "What I did was make a copy of the sign and blow it up on a big sheet of paper, and we just put it on the table, and said, 'Please read this and let me know what bothers you about it.' And so they wrote around it. It took up about a quarter of that sheet, and they wrote around it, what their issues were."

The original marker text, with the problematic language in bold, is reproduced here:

The northeast shore of Onondaga Lake has traditionally been recognized as the site of the **founding of the Iroquois Confederacy in the late 16th century. Hiawatha, revered by the Iroquois as "the Peacemaker,"** was responsible for bringing together the Five Nations in a political and **military league.** The Confederation allowed the Iroquois to develop the most sophisticated political system in North America by the time European colonization began. **The military power of the Iroquois expanded as well.** At its peak in the late 17th century, the Confederacy was able to **assert itself over native peoples** from New England to the Mississippi and from the St. Lawrence Valley to Virginia. The Iroquois remained a significant power in North America until **their defeat** in the American Revolution. The strength of the Confederacy forged by Hiawatha is still evident. **Despite military defeat** and the **loss** of their lands, the Iroquois nations continue to hold council in Onondaga County as they have for **nearly 400 years.**

I should note that the original marker text already used more contemporary language than many of the Sullivan markers discussed in this book. It did not reproduce the "civilized-savagery" binary or "Indian extinction" mythology so prevalent in many early plaques. It recognized the continued existence of Iroquois nations and described the early Iroquois political system as "sophisticated." However, there was an array of errors Onondaga leaders felt needed correcting: "Hiawatha" was not the "Peacemaker"; the league was founded by both Haionwhatha and the Peacemaker. In addition, the original plaque made it appear that the Confederacy was advanced only in relation to other people in North America, and it emphasized Haudenosaunee loss and defeat.

Sue worked with different Onondaga leaders, including Clan Mother Wendy Gonyea, to develop more accurate language and determine the visuals of the new plaque. She then took the new language to the Onondaga Lake Park superintendent, who was enthusiastic. An artist at Syracuse Cultural Workers, Karen Kerney, did the artwork gratis while the park department paid for the structure and the sign (see figure 36).

The new sign has words and images on both sides. It details how the Haudenosaunee Confederacy worked, explaining that "this democratic system of government was developed centuries before the Europeans arrived." Rather than highlighting defeat or loss, the new plaque foregrounds the political and economic significance of the Haudenosaunee Confederacy and its formidable power. It includes a passage about the Sullivan Campaign, making it clear who gave the orders: "In 1779 General George Washington ordered their destruction. The scorch and burn military campaign against their villages, granaries, and people was devastating. However, the strength of the alliance formed by the Peacemaker is still evident." The "nearly 400 years" from the first iteration is replaced with the following concluding sentence: "The Haudenosaunee continue today with one of the oldest recorded forms

FIG. 36. NOON's new plaque, Liverpool NY. Photo courtesy of the author.

of representative government in the world, still meeting in council at the Onondaga Nation, 10 miles south of here, as they have for over 12 centuries." This additional language helps localize the Onondaga Nation and its meetings, thus making the plaque more relevant to contemporary Syracusans who may be walking by. The striking visuals include a purple-and-white border, immediately recognizable as Haudenosaunee colors, and images of local Onondaga leaders, further humanizing the plaque's subjects.

The new side of the plaque relates the Haudenosaunee Confederacy to the political structure of the United States. This side confronts non-Indian assumptions of Aboriginal primitivism with a statement made by Onondaga chief Canassatego about the Confederacy, given at a treaty council in Lancaster, Pennsylvania, in 1744: "We are a powerful Confederacy; and by your observing the same methods our wise forefathers have taken, you will acquire such strength and power." There is an image of Benjamin Franklin, and a discussion of Franklin's 1754 Albany Plan of Union ("the first document to propose what would become the United States governmental structure . . . borrowed heavily from the Haudenosaunee example"). A discussion of Haudenosaunee symbols "borrowed" by the U.S. government includes visual depictions to allow viewers to make clear connections.

Sue attributed their success with this project to their pragmatism. They started with a marker that *could* be changed. As she put it, "You have to pick and choose where you can accomplish something." This sign fell under the jurisdiction of the city parks and recreation division, which they felt might be more easily approached than the State of New York. Luck was a factor: the fact that "that particular superintendent was cooperative." But whatever the reason, after several years of work, a problematic marker was replaced and a revised story told.

A Marker Mystery

I want to end this section with another successful marker revision, this time by unknown actors on some unknown date. The 1929 New York State marker recognizing Brodhead's northernmost destination ended up in Veterans Memorial Park in Salamanca, New York, as we saw in chapter 6. This park and the city itself are in the Allegany Territory of the Seneca Nation of Indians. When I went to photograph it, I learned that the original plaque was missing and a new plaque was in its place (see figure 37).[30] Was this a case of snowplow revisionism? While the full story of this plaque replacement remains to be written, I'd like to end this chapter with an image of the new plaque. It offers a model of inclusivity that we have not yet seen in the settler-colonial public memory projects discussed here.

Conclusion to Part Two

The memorials to Sullivan and Clinton that were established in the nineteenth and twentieth centuries are sometimes overlooked, but when noticed, their appearance commands respect. Their physicality, and their material qualities as unmovable blocks of granite, with words engraved in stone or forged in durable metal and attributions to state agencies, convey an aura of permanence, stability, and official sanction. They were unveiled with grand ceremonies. What happens over time when the next generations grow up with these memorials as features of their everyday environment?

FIG. 37. New plaque on old stone, Veterans Memorial Park. Photo courtesy of Randy A. John.

The elements of the Sullivan commemorative complex are "memorials," places of memory created consciously to commemorate a person or an event. In *How Modernity Forgets*, Connerton contrasts the memorial with another kind of place, the "locus." The locus is a place where people live and work, a place that over time gathers memories. Drawing on emplacement theory, Connerton argues that the locus and the people who live there are co-constructed. Imagining the home as a locus, for instance, he explains that "the life history of the house is interwoven with the life history of the body."[31] Because people and loci are co-constructed, the locus is an important carrier of "place memory" as it is embodied and thus integrated into a sense of self.[32] It is for this reason that displacement and changes in the built environment can cause such lasting psychic damage to people living there.[33]

What happens when a commemorative stone persists for so long that it shifts from being read as an overt call to remember, a memorial, to being part of a backdrop for everyday life, part of a locus? Can memorials become parts of one's locus? If so, might not changes to a monument-turned-locus be as troubling as changes to other elements of one's locus, one's neighborhood or home? Given the relentless change wrought by shifts in the capitalist economy, sometimes historical markers are the only structures that last, as we have seen in the images in this book, with ever-shrinking markers caused by the ever-rising roadways. Could this be why in other settings, people may see an assault on a historical marker as akin to an assault on their very bodies? This may help explain why I found people compelled to repair the damaged Sullivan markers, even when they had little personal connection to the message they proclaimed, as we have seen in the Bullock's Farm and Hungry Hill markers. Ironically, it may be markers' unchanging persistence on the land—and their very loss of commemorative function—that cause some people to resist their alteration by later generations.

In white communities in New York and Pennsylvania, one can encounter an array of perspectives on the Sullivan commemorative complex, ranging from apathy, to critique, to enthusiastic support. The annual celebration of the Battle of Wyoming is the best known commemorative event in the area, and the Wyoming revenge narrative it disseminates reverberates widely there. It is noteworthy that the new Sullivan marker dedication I attended in Bear Creek followed that ceremony's language and performative practices in striking fashion. I encountered more ambivalence in New York, starting with the Newtown reenactment, where people cross-dressed liberally, and where Native actors and perspectives were more widely known and shared. New York's "replacement-by-just-warfare" message, as relayed on the plaques, remains in force in some circles. However, I encountered several people who were critical of the dominant story and the nation's relationship to Native Americans more generally.

The fact that Sullivan markers have become invisible for some people indicates their consonance with a wider hegemonic historical consciousness, a settler-colonial "common sense." What is seen is their linkage to the Revolutionary War; their colonial nature is masked or even viewed as unremarkable. These colonial qualities are not ignored by people directly subjected to U.S. imperialism, however. For the Native Americans I met and their allies, the markers are all about dominance, claiming land, possessing it. The message they announce is read as an affront. The markers can never become invisible.

Over the course of my discussions with leaders of Haudenosaunee cultural centers, conversation sometimes ventured into how the existing memoryscape might be addressed. G. Peter Jemison couldn't see many good options for New York state officials:

> And to place all those signs around, and—to not have gone back at some stage and said, "It would probably be good if we put on some additional information here about how this all . . ." but that would definitely not be in the state's interest! That would be awfully difficult to justify, you know, how on the one hand, you said that, and now you're saying this. It would be *too* inconsistent. So how do you justify it? How do you live with it?[34]

Changing historical markers is a daunting task, as we have seen with the Herculean efforts NOON members made to change the text of a single historical marker. And changing minds by writing historical fiction and meeting with youth also takes time and dedication. I discussed these questions with former SINM museum directors Dr. Jaré Cardinal and Dr. Randy John. At the time, Cardinal was helping state officials narrate Seneca history along the Genesee River, and she and Dr. John discussed the challenges inherent in such a project. She wondered aloud how one can tell the story about the significance of any historic site with just a small sign. She noted that they decided they needed something bigger, the size of a kiosk, but even that scale was proving inadequate as there are so many details to incorporate. In Dr. Cardinal's view, historical knowledge is sorely lacking in American society, and she felt a need for more signage because some people will pay attention, and if they don't have Native input, people will get a whitewashed view, the perspective of "manifest destiny," as Jemison described it.

Dr. John challenged her, explaining that the Senecas wouldn't put up a little historical marker like that; they'd put up a museum instead. That's a measure of the same thing, he explained, museums are put there to take care of some of that need. It is to contemporary Native-run museums and cultural centers that we now turn.

PART THREE

Interventions

Indigenous Histories of Settler Colonialism

THIRTEEN

Haudenosaunee Historical Consciousness

The False Reporting of True Genocide

When Onondaga Nation member Haiwhagai'i (Jake Edwards) spoke at a public forum on the Sullivan-Clinton Campaign in October 2020, he discussed Onondaga views of the maelstrom while commenting on the three previous talks given that afternoon, my own included.[1] Jake Edwards often attends events at Skä•noñh–Great Law of Peace Center, one of the cultural centers that we will consider shortly, and which cosponsored the forum. After introducing his Onondaga and English names, he started right in, talking about genocide and truth: "The story you've been hearing about the Sullivan-Clinton Campaign is true genocide, it's the false reporting of true genocide." Over the course of his talk, Edwards emphasized the need to tell the truth: "One of our messages to the world is to understand truth in the history of America. Understand truth in the survival of the Indigenous people. And understand that you don't teach your children untruth. Because they grow up living in a world of untruth." The truths that he wanted to set straight that day had to do with the content of the dominant Sullivan narrative as exemplified by the Sullivan commemorative complex, as well as historical epistemology: how history is made, and how it is that we know what is true. Speaking to an audience of 250 people, his discourse was measured and deliberate, perhaps reflecting the weight of the topic. In this section of the book, we consider the place of the Sullivan story in Haudenosaunee cultural centers. I begin with Jake Edwards's statements, for he offers a distinct orientation on that story, and outlines a different way of understanding the past, distinctions we will encounter at the cultural centers.

There are many reasons to expect that Haudenosaunee and settler-colonial approaches to the Sullivan story will differ. For Haudenosaunee and other Native peoples whose homes and crops were destroyed by the 1779 raids, the story is one of horror that would never be the subject of celebration, a point Edwards makes clearly. The first part of this book explored the consolidation of a dominant colonizer's point of view as exemplified by celebratory memorials, a diametrically opposed stance. In addition, different societies' understandings of time and pastness will be inextricably linked to different cosmologies, understandings of themselves as human beings in relation to the natural world, their languages, and other cultural features, distinctions Edwards's discourse also touches upon.[2] But first, I want to emphasize the unbroken nature of Haudenosaunee accounts of this time.

Edwards introduces stories he heard from his grandmother, who heard them directly from her great-grandmother. Some of these stories have not appeared in the dominant settler-colonial writings: "And I'll start out—some of the people that were in that campaign did not even want to be there. Some of the people that were carrying out the orders did not want to do what they were instructed to do. We don't know that side of what would happen to them if they refused." The memorials and associated fanfare never present Sullivan's soldiers as having had misgivings, and this is a perspective that remains undeveloped in historiography.[3] Edwards brings up how much rum was likely involved in the actions of the "five thousand white guys coming through the forest," rum involved "in all of these decisions." He also emphasizes his relatives' return to the land right after the raids:

Did you hear about reestablishing gardens, *right away?* When we hid as people from these invaders? Our elders used to tell us exactly where they hid, their hiding spots, and what they had with them. It was just like our creation story of the Sky Woman bringing down what she planted, the Three Sisters. When they took off running, they grabbed beans, and corn, and squash seeds, and hid them with them. Right over there, right over that hill (he points). When our people hid from these invading peoples, soldiers, they're called, we were running to the Cayugas to see if they can help. We had a runner come tell us, they said the same thing was happening over there. It's a pandemic in Haudenosaunee territory, a pandemic of genocide.

Edwards's statements are informed by Haudenosaunee cultural traditions as he draws parallels between Sky Woman's actions and the Haudenosaunee people saving seeds while they escaped from the troops.

A shift in orientation found throughout Edwards's discourse is evident in a shift in word choice. In the Sullivan commemorative complex, military terminology infiltrates almost as if by an unseen hand, and it is usually not called into question.[4] Whenever Edwards uses any of the standard labels in his discussion, there seems to be a subtle pause, a distancing. When he says, "When we hear about this—Sullivan Campaign," it is as if the name itself has quotation marks. He discusses that time in other ways, referring to it as "that starving time," referencing the period of famine that followed the destruction of most subsistence sources. In the passage above, when he describes his relatives hiding, it is from "these invading peoples—'soldiers,' they're called." He calls out the generic military terminology that invades most texts about the Sullivan-Clinton raids and brings into question words like "battle." So many of the markers I have covered in this book commemorate this or that "battle," such as the so-called Battle of Chemung. Yet the Chemung raids, and so many of the events comprising the Sullivan "Campaign," were in fact surprise attacks on villages. Van Schaick's April 1779 raid on the Onondaga Nation is a case in point, and Edwards frames these attacks differently: "Onondagas were never conquered, you can't conquer a neutral nation, a peaceful nation; those are called 'massacres,' 'invasions' and 'massacres.' They were documented as 'battles,' they called them 'battles.' They weren't battles! We've got families sleeping comfortably, and you wiped them out. You just won a battle? Come on! Let's teach the truth here and explain to America what geno-cide is." Part of telling the truth, then, is using the appropriate words. This was not a military operation; this was an act of geno-cide on people "sleeping comfortably." Come on, people, let's tell the truth here, he proclaims.

A Haudenosaunee perspective on Washington's raids can be viewed as an unbroken stream, one central to Haudenosaunee historical consciousness, and which has erupted sporadically into settler-colonial awareness. Haudenosaunee oral tradition spans a far greater time span, of course. The basis of Haudenosaunee cultural teachings has arrived to the present day from word of mouth and includes accounts of the founding of the Iroquois Confederacy and The Great Law of Peace, events that date well before the arrival of any Europeans to this continent, and which are encoded in sacred belts of wampum beads.[5] Haudenosaunee commentary on the Sullivan raids was recorded by white chron-iclers as early as 1790 and 1794, including statements made by Seneca leader Cornplanter and others, as we have seen.[6] Mary Jemison's account of returning to the Genesee region after Sulli-van narrates the famine of that time, and her story was published in 1824. Published oral testimonies include accounts of women and children hiding in Great Gully as soldiers burned Chonodote (Peachtown), destroying a massive peach orchard. Their terrified screams echoing off the gorge walls convinced soldiers that they were about to be attacked, and the gorge itself is credited with saving the Cayuga people.[7] The cicada is credited with saving the Onondagas, for it provided a needed food source "that first year of rebuilding," according to stories recounted by Dehowäda:dih.[8] Additional oral testimonies were recently gathered by The Public Archaeology Facility, Binghamton University, in projects funded by the National Park Service. G. Peter Jemison (Seneca) empha-sized that Haudenosaunee were especially "horrified by the wan-ton destruction of plants," reminding the reader that "the corn, beans and squash are like sisters to the Seneca people."[9] Richard W. Hill Sr. (Tuscarora) documents stories of brutality and notes that the "attack on the corn and the destruction of the sacred crop has had the most enduring impact on Haudenosaunee oral history. People are still puzzled about what kind of people would do such a thing."[10] Narratives of these times traveled with the people who experienced them; since many of the towns the troops destroyed were multinational, stories of these raids likely persist in Native communities across North America (see map 2). The ways this traumatic event has shaped people's memories of the Revolutionary War and their future relationships with each other and the non-Native settler society remain to be fully analyzed.

One might be tempted to frame this Indigenous perspective on Sullivan's raids as a "counter-memory," a version of the past formed in opposition to a dominant or officially sanctioned rendition.[11] I want to push back against such a framing to emphasize that we cannot posit a dominant memory existing *prior* to an Indigenous memory, which the Indigenous memory then counters. Unlike the white settler memory, which was discontinuous and had to be invented and reinvented within white settler society, as we have seen, the Native memory of this time can be viewed as a continuous, unbroken stream. Yes, Sullivan's soldiers remembered their activities the summer of 1779, and many wrote down their experiences in their journals.[12] These men were a subset of colonial society, however, members of a new community, still under construction, from people originating all over Europe and beyond, and these men and their journals were scattered to disparate locations across a vast territory after the war. Their separate accounts were brought together into a unified story only much later by memory entrepreneurs. They were consolidated around the centennial in 1879, long after most of their authors had died.

Let us contrast this experience with that of Sullivan's foes. Living in their homeland, settled at known, named village sites in family groups traced back since time immemorial, these multi-generational communities and their places were co-constructed. If anything, having experienced a common traumatic event would only further tie them to each other and to these home places, even if they were forced to leave for a time.[13] They engaged in continuous storytelling down the generations, maintaining their alternative history. I want to return to the Seneca consultant I discussed in the introduction who reminded me that the people "you are occupying never forget, never."[14] Continuing to keep an alternative version of the Sullivan story alive despite the rampant misinformation and erasure can be read as an act of defiance, a form of resistance, with storytelling and "never-forgetting" as purposeful acts that perpetuate community. "Never-forgetting" exemplifies what Gerald Vizenor (Chippewa) has termed "survivance." As Vizenor writes, "Native survivance stories are renunciations of dominance, tragedy, and victimry."[15] The Haudenosaunee Sullivan story, too, persists, survives, as is confirmed by Edwards and many other sources.

I want to return to Jake Edwards's talk that day to introduce two more points. All through his discourse, he brings up questions of historical epistemology, how we know the truth about the past, and which sources are credible or trustworthy. The title of the forum was "Revisiting Washington's Assault on the Haudenosaunee 240 Years Later," and the talks that preceded him included a historical overview of the campaign and the destruction wrought by the troops, and my discussion of its commemoration by white settlers. He admits that he found it difficult to listen to these accounts: "But this campaign of genocide against my people. It's hard to listen to again. It's hard to listen to it from non-Indigenous persons' writings. Because our elders passed down from generations that witnessed it, had different stories that were passed down from the generations that witnessed it."

There are two aspects of his statement "It is hard to listen to it from non-Indigenous persons' writings" that I want to address. When he added, "Our elders passed down from generations that witnessed it," he was succinctly capturing a specific understanding of how we know about the past, the belief that we know about the past from accounts of people who were actually there. Stories transmitted from one person to the next are the ones that are credible; stories transmitted orally are the ones that we can trust. The immediacy of the past communicated from one person to the next contrasts completely with that in which paper, documents, and books are intermediaries, which come "from non-Indigenous persons' writings." In discussing oral accounts, he lays out the chain of transmission, much like footnotes in a document, as if to say that this is what makes his accounts credible. "My grandmother was interpreting the oral teachings of her great-grandmother, who ran up alongside Onondaga Creek, right out here." (He points outside while he is talking.) "She tells us about that, what her great-grandmother told her, what she did, and where she hid. My uncle, he showed me where it was." Credibility is guaranteed by the security of face-to-face discourse and further cemented by the story's rootedness in place, and he knows right where that place is. He contrasts this with the approach to history-making we call historiography: "And to listen to these elders' stories, and hear about the locusts, the message that they brought us from the earth. A reminder to us at that starving time, to have gratitude for what Mother Earth still provides for us. Through that hard time, to share gratitude is powerful, very powerful. *It's not something you can read in a book, somebody's journal*" (emphasis added). Listening to the powerful story that has been put together from pieces of disparate soldiers' journals is a very different kind of experience. Even the way he says, "in a book, somebody's journal" feels bracketed, like the words *battle* and *Sullivan*. Their truth value is questionable. As he first stated, "It's the *false* reporting of true genocide."

The statement "It's hard to listen to from a non-Indigenous person's writings" brings in another dimension of this epistemology. Oral sources are important, surely, and who you hear the story from really matters. Right after Jake says, "It's not something you can read in a book, in somebody's journal," he continues in this way:

> In those oral teachings, we hear we are not to trust the white man, not to be with that person alone. You take always two, so that you can watch over that shoulder, watch his back and he can watch over your shoulder, watch your back, as you are talking to a guy who appears to be trustworthy and friendly. Like the Dutch did to us, or like Columbus' crew did everywhere they landed. They have instructions from their church to subdue, enslave us. They carried those teachings into the next centuries, to the next centuries. Wait a minute, where are we now, 2020? In Washington down there, they are doing about the same thing today to the

Indigenous people looking for fresh drinking water on the southern border of what they call the United States. It's going on today.

The teachings Jake learned about the Sullivan raids are wrapped up with teachings about white people more generally, teachings about trust, safety, and survival. Be careful of people who appear to be trustworthy and friendly. You are not to be with that person alone. He brings these lessons into the present day. When reflecting on how white people have treated Indigenous people from the earliest times, it occurred to him that these patterns continue, and he reminded the audience of the ways the U.S. government, at that minute, was treating people crossing the international border.

The need to be vigilant appears many times in this discourse. Edwards talks about showing his great-great-great grandmother's hiding spot to Onondaga youth the previous summer. He then tells the audience, "I give gratitude to my ancestors who helped us to be here today. We had this spot. I know where the hiding spot is, but I'm not going to tell everyone though, it might come back."

"It might come back." That statement may give pause. There may be no better way to capture the lessons of the Sullivan story for the Haudenosaunee than to consider the word used for Washington, and for president of the United States, Hanödaga:nyahs, literally "he who destroys towns."[17] In the introduction to this book, I included an excerpt from Washington's orders in which he instructed Sullivan to instill terror: "Our future security will be in . . . the terror with which the severity of the chastisement they receive will inspire them."[16] That terror was achieved and it is remembered. It is remembered in Edwards's stories of fleeing and of hiding, in others' stories of being saved by canyon wall echoes, in the warnings about white people who might look trustworthy, and in the Seneca language. As Cornplanter and other chiefs told Washington in 1794, "When your army entered the country of the Six Nations, we called you the town destroyer; and to this day, when that name is heard, our women look behind them and turn pale, and our children cling close to the necks of their mothers."[18] Calling all future American presidents "town destroyer" is an efficient and lasting means of communicating across the generations an experience of horror and identifying the man, institution and, by association, the colonizing population responsible.

Memories of Sullivan's destruction of Haudenosaunee homes, lands, and gardens hold a central place in Haudenosaunee historical consciousness.[19] Moreover, these stories provide a powerful pedagogical resource, instructing the next generations about the wider social world within which they now live, a world of white colonizers. This brings me back to my own positionality and why, in this book, I focus on *public* manifestations of the Sullivan story. I chose not to enter Haudenosaunee homelands as a colonizer anthropologist asking about times of horror. To ask people to recount a trauma is already a kind of violation; to do so knowing that I am someone they should guard against would be grotesque. There is real power to these stories, and it is not my place to decide which ones should become public knowledge. This is a question for Haudenosaunee and other Native people to determine for themselves.[20]

This detailed look at Jake Edwards's presentation introduces us to an alternative Sullivan story, one persisting into the present day, and a different epistemology, which are also reflected in the Haudenosaunee cultural centers in the vicinity of the Sullivan commemorative complex. Haudenosaunee historical consciousness differs from the settler-colonial perspective in at least one other important way, as we shall see, for it encompasses a much deeper timeline that upends dominant periodicity.

Interrogating the Museum

The seizure by Native Americans of representational sovereignty is a watershed intervention in museology that is having lasting effects. Museums (and the discipline of anthropology more generally) have long played a powerful role in shaping how non–Native Americans understand their past and the place of Indigenous peoples in it, disseminating indelible stereotypes, often through exhibits of material culture. For many Native people, the museum itself is "intimately linked to the colonization practice."[21] In his article "'Our' Indians: The Unidimensional Indian in the Disembodied Local Past," James Nason (Comanche) puts the spotlight on the local history museum, stating that two-thirds of the museums in the United States are history museums, making them "the most accessible of all museums"; they are small; they have limited funding; and most display Native American material.[22] Whether material cultural objects are organized as geographical or ethnological collections, as "life groups," or in "open storage," these exhibits rarely concern contemporary Indigenous peoples. As Nason puts it, "Indians are virtually always presented as elements from the community's past."[23]

W. Richard West Jr. (Cheyenne), founding director of the National Museum of the American Indian, describes the new vogue in museology as a "radically different approach," one that includes authentic Native voices and Indian-run institutions, with an emphasis on cultural continuity.[24] This new approach places dialogue and collaboration with Indigenous communities at its center.[25] While some people have associated this new approach with theoretical developments in museology, Amy Lonetree asserts that we cannot discount Native American activism of the 1960s and 1970s, which led to the landmark Native American Graves Protection & Repatriation Act (NAGPRA) decision in 1990, and which included a tribal museum movement. When she published *Decolonizing Museums* in 2012, there were some two hundred tribal museums.[26]

There are multiple cultural centers that treat Haudenosaunee culture and history in the United States and Canada. In this section, I briefly discuss four such institutions, three in detail, all in the vicinity of the Sullivan memorials. They are Shako:wi Cultural Center, based in Oneida, New York; Skä•noñh–Great Law of Peace Center (Onondaga), in Liverpool, New York; Onöhsagwë:de' Cultural Center, Allegany Territory, Seneca Nation of Indians; and Seneca Art & Culture Center at Ganondagan, near Victor, New York (see map 1). Each of these cultural centers merits full book-length treatment, and what follows can only be seen as a snapshot in time.

How these centers treat the Sullivan Expedition and the Revolutionary War must be considered within the context of the Haudenosaunee nations' respective histories before, during, and after the Revolutionary War. The Onondaga Nation had endeavored to remain neutral during the war, but some members were drawn into the conflict as it proceeded, particularly in the wake of Van Schaick's devastating raids on Onondaga villages in April 1779. Oneidas, on the other hand, found themselves increasingly surrounded by white settlement and chose to become allies of the patriot cause, as did Tuscaroras. A few Oneidas served as scouts for Sullivan, and the Oneida Indian Nation recently recognized its Revolutionary War service by donating $10 million to the National Museum of the American Revolution.[27]

These centers also have different institutional structures and origins. Skä•noñh involves a unique collaboration between the Onondaga Nation and a preexisting historical society, and Ganondagan was first a state park and is now a New York historic site. Two are tribally owned and operated. The Seneca Nation of Indians created the Seneca-Iroquois National Museum (SINM) with funds from a federal settlement after land was seized to build a dam, and SINM has been succeeded by Onöhsagwë:de' Cultural Center. Shako:wi, the Oneida Cultural Center is run by the Oneida Indian Nation. The latter two centers were developed with resources associated with gaming revenues.

Despite these distinctions, common themes are immediately apparent. In what follows, I consider how each center addresses or counters the Sullivan story as developed by the celebratory settler memorials. In what ways do they intervene with the story that is told by the public markers and with settler-colonial public history? For a people established in North America since time immemorial, the Revolutionary War is not the start or the end of any story. At these centers, we find that this war and the Sullivan operation are recontextualized, reduced to a briefer moment of a much longer history, or missing altogether.

Skako:wi Cultural Center, Oneida Indian Nation

Each time I visit the Shako:wi Cultural Center, women are beading in the large entrance room. Created in 1992, the center is named after Richard Chrisjohn (Oneida, Wolf Clan), whose name in Oneida is translated as "he gives."[28] It is built out of large peeled white pine logs. In front is a log cabin and former Oneida residence. Permanent displays focus on Oneida basketry, wampum and its role in the foundation of the Haudenosaunee Confederacy, lacrosse, and "Oneida Industries," life-sized figures from a museum display created by Arthur C. Parker that was once in the state museum in Albany.

The Onyota'a:ká, the People of the Standing Stone, became known in English as the Oneidas. Their homeland on the eastern portion of Iroquoia placed them in early and regular interaction with Dutch and English colonists with their centers near Albany. Many Oneidas eventually assisted the patriot side in the Revolutionary War. After the Fort Stanwix Treaty, Oneida settlements were under threat, for they were on the eastern side of the treaty line. Surrounded by settlers, the Oneida Nation faced annihilation as the war proceeded.

Despite their service to the United States, Oneida loss of their land base was rapid after the war. Situated at a transportation crossroads, their land was coveted by the new state's entrepreneurs.[29] In the postwar Treaty of Fort Stanwix, Oneidas were granted a vast territory, but in 1788, New York gained 5.5 million acres of their land, leaving the Oneidas 300,000 acres, which was further reduced.[30] By the 1820s many Oneidas had started to move to Wisconsin, and another group left for Ontario, Canada.[31] Allotment of Oneida lands in 1843 led to a reduction of their land base to thirty-two acres.[32] By the time of the 1877 dedication at the Battle of Oriskany, they had become the United States' "forgotten allies."[33]

Museum director Kandice Watson explained that the "Oneida Nation is very proud of the fact that we are America's first allies," and she pointed out that they never fought against the United States.[34] Some Oneida served alongside the Revolutionaries in the Battle of Oriskany of 1777, and even today, when it is commemorated on August 6 at the battlefield, the Oneida Nation sends representatives. A National Park Service ethnographic study of the Oriskany battlefield in contemporary memory found that many Haudenosaunee interviewed found it "a sacred site where events contrary to the Great Law occurred," where divisions between different members of the Confederacy led to armed conflict between nations. For many it is described as "a place of great sadness" that "should remain a place for remembrance and reflection."[35] Watson discussed Oneida involvement at the annual event: "It's a solemn ceremony. And then usually our people will give some type of offering to the soldiers, you know, that died that day. In our culture, we usually give food. So we usually will put a plate of food at the base of the monument, just to kind of appease any unsettled business that they may have, or anything like that."

The depiction of Oneida cultural history at the Shako:wi Cultural Center is remarkable. While the cultural center has many of the trappings of an ethnographic museum, with material cultural items such as baskets in open storage cases, a subtle shift in signage has a radical effect. Traditionally, ethnographic collections connect objects to a cultural group and approximate era ("Seneca, 1920s"). This approach more easily relegates the items to a distant past and severs them from people living in the present. At Shako:wi, in contrast, material items have full provenance traced to present-day Oneida families. A beaded bag, for instance, is identified with its artist, clan, Haudenosaunee nation, and full names of their contemporary relatives. This practice brings Native artists and their products into the contemporary era and turns the center into a repository of creative work made by local community members and their families. The curators followed this practice with the diorama figures they retrieved from a New York State Museum exhibit that Arthur C. Parker had developed from living models, by identifying the people by name. This signage grants the cultural center a cozy community feel. Since this information is fully intelligible only to members of the community, the signage is evidence of community and helps to create community, while non–community members may feel a bit on the outside as they will have no clue who the Oneida people referenced might be. This labeling practice took conscious effort. The museum director explained that they were fortunate in still knowing the provenance of many of the objects, and in having the resources needed to hire researchers to uncover the full provenance for others.

The Sullivan-Clinton Campaign is featured in the Broken Treaties exhibit. Its placement there reduces it in significance as it is part of a much longer discussion of the state's breaking of treaty promises by taking Oneida land. It is that story that is front and center. I discussed the Sullivan-Clinton markers with the cultural center museum director and the Oneida Indian Nation archaeologist. They were dubious about the benefit of trying to replace or change the plaques and suggested that if one wanted to start carrying out such a task, the reaction would be quite predictable: "You'll get accused of rewriting history. Sometimes it's easier to not talk about some things than to try to explain them. Otherwise, one is stuck in a defensive posture: it is easier to leave the markers than to try to correct them. Watson added that the marker problem reminded her of the mascot issue and, as she put it, "We can only worry about one thing at a time." The archaeologist brought up another problematic dimension of the Sullivan-Clinton signage: pothunting. Many of the New York markers identify sites of former Native villages and can encourage pothunting and desecration of Native burials. Calling attention to the markers today could have unforeseen negative consequences, such as accelerating burial ground disturbances.

"We're Trying to Be Very Proactive"

The Sullivan Expedition is almost an aside here: education is their method and their mission. Watson spoke at length about a much more recent mission of destruction, that of the boarding school, which purposefully interrupted intergenerational ties and thwarted cultural transmission. She spoke at length of the effects of the boarding school era on Oneidas and on Native peoples more generally:

> The boarding school era really did a number on our people in regard to our culture and our traditions, even our family structures, all kinds of damage . . . Basically, they robbed us of our—our culture and history. We were not allowed to practice these things at the schools. So when the kids got out of the schools, after spending ten years or so there, returned home to their reservations and had their children—for one, they were certainly not going to teach the language to their children. And they didn't really know a lot of the

cultures or the traditions anymore. So, these people really found themselves living, you know, really between two worlds, they did not belong in either one of them, because they were full-blooded Indians, but had no idea about their culture, traditions, history, religion, language, any of that. And they were not accepted, they weren't really accepted on the reservation, and then they were not able to just move into town and get a house, because nobody wanted Indians living next to them in town.

Watson related the emotional damage the schools caused, especially with their horrible teacher-student ratios: there would be "one matron who is in charge of fifty children, so it's going to be very difficult for her to establish any type of bond with any of these kids, so these kids really grew up with certainly no affection, no love, no—no mother, no aunties around, you know, none of that."

The denigration of Indian culture at the schools and the prevention of traditional religious practices meant that "this generation is really the first time that we've been able to practice our culture openly, practice our religion openly. You know, we're really the first generation that we're allowed to practice our religions and our cultures."

Watson feels the pressure of trying to make up for so much lost ground. The center has a huge task ahead of it:

So, we have been tasked with teaching this stuff to our children but also to our elders. Many other communities can go back to their elders and get that information—their elders have that. They can go back and get their language. They can go get their culture and their religion. We don't have that luxury. Certainly not every elder went to boarding school; there are some who know how to make crafts, or how to speak the language, but they're very elderly. We utilize these people to come into our classes and teach. We've had our 4D department, which is a production company, come in and film them, so that we have them on film, making these crafts. We're trying to be very proactive so, in the future, if we're ever in the same situation again, we can always consult these tapes and figure out how to make these things.

Teaching the language is a key piece of their Oneida cultural revival program. Watson is proud of the progress made so far, but they were successful only by adapting to the circumstances at hand. They brought Oneida speakers from Canada as instructors, for instance. Several women became fluent, so they are now teaching it in their community. Watson adds, "We are actually paying our members to learn the language." She explained the thinking here: "You know, for a long time, we struggled, trying to get people to attend language classes. It's real hard to learn a language, you know, just two hours on a Wednesday night. You know, it just isn't going to happen. So we finally had to make a decision and changed it to where it is their full-time job. Monday through Thursday, eight hours a day, that is their job." Casino revenues have allowed them to follow this tack, but not without some raised eyebrows: "We did get some criticism from other nations who feel that people should want to learn their language on their own; they shouldn't need to be paid. That may be true, but really, the bottom line on that issue is, we have the money, and it's that important to us, so why not?"

Healing the Nation(s)

The center is helping to heal not only intergenerational rifts but also breaches among the three main Oneida communities. Oneidas from Wisconsin and Canada visit the center regularly. The Canadian Oneidas bring their sixth-grade graduates down each year to visit the "homelands," Watson explained. After visiting battlefield sites such as Oriskany, they'll travel around to "just visit different sites in the area to kind of see where their people came from." They often don't know the local history: "They don't really even know how they got to Oneida, Canada. So we tell them what happened," she added. People sometimes trace family connections to each other through these visits:

> We had a group come down from Canada, and we went to the Oriskany battlefield. We were walking around and talking about different people. And, my mother's father is from Oneida, Canada. I had mentioned his name to one of the ladies and she said, 'Hey, that's my uncle.' So, we were related! My grandfather was

her uncle! And, so definitely, when they come down, we try to talk to them, see who their family is. I have friends that live up there. You know, we have people who do go from community to community, back and forth.

"We Are People"

A second major mission of the center is teaching non-Indians about the Oneidas. This appears to be their biggest challenge due to an incredible ignorance among non-Natives. Like many people interviewed for this book, Watson described the ignorance of most Americans about their own history as "astounding," and their ignorance about Native Americans as even more so. She explained, "There are certain things that, you know, mainstream Americans are just not taught about our own history. It's easier to not teach it because then, you know, you have to answer questions, and you have to be accountable for that history." Many of the people who come to the center are locals, which adds another dimension to this problem: "They grew up in this area and have no idea, because it just was not taught in history books." She used herself as an example: "I have lived here my whole life. I attended school in Stockbridge, and I never learned *anything* about the Oneida Nation. Not one thing."

After decades-long activism, all fourth graders in New York public schools learn about the Haudenosaunee nations and Shako:wi makes a point of hosting school groups as part of this curriculum.[36] This is a big part of Watson's responsibilities:

> They come in here and I tell them about, you know, how the five Nations joined together, how they became the Iroquois Confederacy. I teach them a little bit about our culture and different things. . . . They also make a no-face doll. They hear that legend, why she has no face, and they get to make a doll, which they all love. The kids really seem to enjoy it. It seems to be one of their favorite field trips, even compared to a theme park. This is where they want to come.

If Watson has any frustration, it is with those school systems that don't bring their students in. She relates this to long-standing animosities. She spoke with candor about the difficulties moving forward:

> We've struggled for so long in this issue, you know, because it's . . .
> [She pauses] You know, I have lived on this reservation pretty much
> my whole life. I moved here when I was about five. And so for
> years, I mean years, twenty years, we lived here and we had a lot
> of bickering, in-fighting, and just ridiculousness going on here . . .
> And when the outside community sees that going on, it's more
> or less, "Oh, those dang Indians just can't get it together." And
> I'm sure this talk was going on in the community for years. But
> when that same community that you're used to bashing and look-
> ing down on suddenly gets a little bit of money, the people start
> working, the drinking is at an all-time low, this feels like a revolu-
> tion to them. It feels like "These oppressed people are coming up
> into our level." It's almost like they have to quell this revolution
> that's going on. I mean, it really does feel that way sometimes.
> You know, they can't share in our success.

Watson's goals in this regard are very modest ones: "The most we
can do is try to show the local community that we are people. We
are people. We are just trying to do the best we can here. We're
not trying to take anyone's land; we're just trying to exist and be
a nation, a successful nation, you know, so that future generations will have a land base, so future generations will have jobs,
so future generations will be able to learn their culture and traditions without fear of reprisal from anybody." At the same time,
she hopes people will feel comfortable enough to ask whatever
questions they have. When people come in, she explains, "I make
sure that people understand that they can ask me *any* question; it
will not offend me. I would rather you ask me that question than
walk out of here and say, 'Jeez, I wish I had asked this question.'
And I always let people know that we do a lot of tours here with
fourth graders. So if their question is stupid or silly, believe me,
a fourth grader already asked me!"

The Oneida Indian Nation tries to build bridges across the community in other ways as well. Along with the casino being a major
regional employer, their community hosts a Veterans Day brunch

open to Oneida and non-Oneida veterans alike. She said this has been surprisingly popular: "That brunch has become so popular with non-Indian veterans in this area because there's not a lot of events for simply veterans. You know, they may get a discount at their meal at some restaurant or something. But there is no real breakfast or dinner that's specifically put on to honor these veterans. And so we do have a lot of non-Indian veterans that come to that event; they've actually had to move it to our casino because it was too big for our elders' dinner."

Watson found that one of her primary missions is simply to foster Indian–non-Indian communication, in as many ways as possible:

> We do what we can in this area, really just to foster some better relationships. And by working with young fourth graders, getting them when they're nine years old, maybe we can change their conception of Indian people, because a lot of times, people—you could go your whole life without ever meeting an Indian person. And so for most people, they really don't, I don't think, believe they even still exist. They think they're extinct. You know, "there are no more Indians left, right?" And, that's not their fault. It's usually just from where you live, you know?

Much of their underlying goal is to simply show people that the Oneida Nation still exists. As Watson puts it, "We just have to keep reminding people that we are still here and that we're still practicing our culture, still teaching our culture, we still practice our religion."

Skä•noñh–Great Law of Peace Center

Skä•noñh is a striking new museum and welcome center located behind a wall of rushes along the shores of Onondaga Lake outside of Syracuse, New York (see figures 38, 39). "Skä•noñh" is an Onondaga welcome greeting meaning "peace and wellness."[37] The center offers an introduction to Haudenosaunee and Ononodaga history and philosophy that places oral testimony front and center. It also represents a remarkable example of what can be possible with the transformation of an antiquated site.

FIG. 38. Skä•noñh–Great Law of Peace Center, Liverpool NY. Photo courtesy of the author.

Skä•noñh is at the site of a former county museum depicting a seventeenth-century Jesuit mission. The current iteration is the culmination of years of effort.[38] French Jesuit missionaries had built a fortification on Onondaga Lake in the seventeenth century that they used as a base as they attempted to convert Onondagas. They were there a scant two years, leaving in March 1658.[39] In the 1930s, almost three centuries later, Syracuse officials claimed the site as a county park, and a public works project reproduced the mission, naming the site Sainte Marie de Gannentaha, after the Jesuit mission.[40] The museum underwent several iterations until it went bankrupt and closed in December 2011.[41] At this point, the Onondaga Historical Association took over site management and hired Philip Arnold, chair of the Department of Religion at Syracuse University, as founding director. Arnold, in turn, developed a partnership with the Onondaga Nation to develop a "radically different public learning space" emphasizing Haudenosaunee perspectives.[42]

FIG. 39. Onondaga Lake from Skä•noñh, Liverpool NY. Photo courtesy of the author.

Bringing together the Onondaga Nation and a local historical society to map out a new direction in narrating the past carried unique challenges. County and other historical societies in the contemporary era of neoliberal cost-cutting are often in a chronic state of budgetary shortfall. Moreover, Euro-American elite have comprised the majority of these societies' founders, presidents, and board members, and these organizations have tended to elevate the actions of the founders' families, if only because these are the same people who donated the items that formed the basis of the societies' museum collections to begin with. As a result, historical society exhibits often participate in a kind of "firsting" and "lasting" by default, emphasizing the story of the local white community donors, and relegating Native peoples to a "prehistory."[43] The Onondaga Historical Association was no different. Formed in 1863, this is the organization whose director, George Fryer, tried to stop the creation of the state's 1929 Van Schaick monument, writing that he was *ashamed* of Van Schaick (see chapter 6). While Fryer appeared relatively enlightened compared to other actors that we encountered in that chapter, he also made his living working for the Solvay Process Company, one of the companies that polluted the sacred Onondaga Lake, reminding us that local historical societies are embedded within local political economies and colonial practices. In fact, during the period of center planning, the Onondaga Nation requested the return of human remains and sacred objects stored at an OHA warehouse in downtown Syracuse, and the OHA complied with public and private repatriation ceremonies.[44]

Shifting the focus of a site that had celebrated a Christianizing mission into one that now reflects Onondaga and Haudneosaunee values and cultural precepts was a lengthy and hard-fought process, and museum directors had to work on several fronts at once.[45] Some of the public looked fondly at what they called the "old French fort."[46] Center staff published op-ed pieces in the local press discussing how the Sainte Marie historical site had commemorated a "narrow slice of history," involving the often violent conversion of Native Americans to Catholicism, and arguing that it was time to tell a different story, time to shift focus to celebrate why Haudenosaunees consider Onondaga Lake to be sacred.[47] Oral historical sources recount that this is where the five warring nations of the Iroquois Confederacy accepted the Creator's Great Law of Peace, buried their weapons, and founded a lasting democratic union.[48] In September of 2012 the OHA announced that it would develop a Haudenosaunee cultural center, keeping the replica of the French fort in place.[49]

This shift was not without some public grumbling. An August 2015 article that mentioned the museum's one-million-dollar cost generated negative anonymous comments. "MyOpinion" thought it was "another ridiculous waste of tax dollars."[50] OHA director Tripoli replied that most of the funds were coming from private sources, including local foundations, and that 25 percent was from the room and occupancy tax, which residents never pay (unless they live in a hotel). "neveryou" asked how much of the funding came from the Onondaga Nation; Tripoli responded that they provided the largest individual component of private funding (but would not specify a dollar amount).[51] In the meantime, an academic collaborative was working to develop the vision for the new center. This robust collaborative includes representatives from the Onondaga Nation, the OHA, Le Moyne College, the State University of New York College of Environmental Sciences and Forestry, Empire State University, Onondaga Community College, and Syracuse University.[52] Rick Hill (Tuscarora) was commissioned to help develop an overarching narrative, and representatives of the Onondaga Nation, including faithkeeper Oren Lyons, Tadodaho Sidney Hill, and Clan Mother Frieda Jacques, worked at reenvisioning the site.[53] The end result is remarkable; in their study published in *The Public Historian*, Debora Ryan and Emily Stokes-Rees describe it as a "bold departure" from its former iteration.[54]

Skä•noñh–Great Law of Peace Center, opened on Saturday, November 21, 2015. Abundant press, including a feature in *Indian Country Today*, emphasized the center's innovative ways of treating the local past, explaining that the story of the Haudenosaunee has "generally been told through a white Eurocentric lens, and as a written story."[55] The new museum tells the story from an Onondaga perspective with an emphasis on the oral transmission of knowledge.[56] Onondaga faithkeeper Oren Lyons described the museum opening as a landmark moment, explaining that "the American public is just not taught . . . the history of Native people here. So this is a good beginning . . . this is where the Tree of Peace was planted a thousand years ago, and I think it's going to grow. Hopefully other nations will join in and the true history will come."[57]

Voicing Tradition

Skä•noñh is a cultural center with public meeting space, a gift shop, and two floors of exhibits. In each room, a large screen displaying videos of Onondaga elders discussing the room's focus draws the visitor's eye, and this renders the objects on display secondary to Onondaga voices. In an orientation room, the visitor is welcomed by photographs and videos of contemporary Onondagas speaking in the Onondaga language and teaching them the meanings of words such as *Skä•noñh*. Visitors receive the Onondaga greeting *Nyaweñha sgé:noñ',*"I am thankful that you are well." The scope of the center's mission is even broader than simply introducing people to Haudenosaunee beliefs: "Our goals are to inspire people to action through contemplation of Haudenosaunee values and worldview, to nurture the Good Mind."[58] Woven throughout the exhibits are central tenets of Haudenosaunee philosophy. Visitors learn about the *Ganonhanyonh* (Thanksgiving Address), which is often recounted in Onondaga and then English at the beginning and end of public events held at the center. The Haudenosaunee Creation Story is recounted and depicted with original artwork by Indigenous artists. As visitors travel up the stairs, they pass a large Tree of Peace and learn about The Peacemaker's Journey and *Gayaneñhä' go:nah*, The Great Law of Peace, the center's primary focus. According to oral tradition, the Peacemaker traveled from the Mohawks to the Oneidas to the Onondagas, "spreading this word of peace."[59] He traveled to the Cayugas and Senecas, and leaders from these nations approached the Tadodaho, a powerful leader who was controlling the Onondaga, and convinced him to support his mission of peace, ultimately leading to the unification of the five original nations of the Haudenosaunee. The exhibit emphasizes the "power of the Good Mind," stating, "The Peacemaker united with 49 Chiefs to use the power of the Good Mind to transform Tadodaho's thinking from a seeker of death to a maker of peace." After discussing how this transformation was achieved, the text connects this lesson to contemporary visitors: "The lesson for all of us is that no matter how demented one may have been in the past, the mind has the capacity of being restored. Once we apply our minds in the way it was intended, we will naturally find ourselves in Skä•noñh—the state of peacefulness and wellness."[60]

It is only in a section on the controversial subject of European–Native American contact that we find mention of the Sullivan-Clinton Campaign. One set of texts discusses the raids, accompanied by an image of one of the 1929 New York plaques, information that appears in an accounting of a much longer history. Panels discuss treaties, highlighting the seventeenth-century

Two Row Wampum treaty with the Dutch and the 1794 Treaty of Canandaigua, as well as the Doctrine of Discovery, which served as the basis for European land claims; and Jesuit missionary activities; followed by Sullivan-Clinton. The Sullivan story is followed, in turn, by an extensive discussion of the Indian boarding school movement of the late nineteenth century and its consequences, and the timeline appears open-ended as it moves into the present day. Placing Sullivan-Clinton within a much longer account of European attacks on Native sovereignty challenges the "declension" narrative featured on the state's 1929 plaques and renders the raids as one of many ordeals, all involving outsiders' attacks on Indigenous peoplehood. The fact that the timeline stretches into contemporary times gives one pause.

Further framing Sullivan is a final exhibit, "Continuance and Contributions," that discusses Haudenosaunee resilience and contributions to the wider world. As the visitor's guide explains, this room is designed to demonstrate that "despite many attempts to remove them from their homeland, they remain strong in their original belief system and oral tradition today."[61] Rather than emphasizing Haudenosaunee assimilation to white culture, it demonstrates the reverse. We learn of the widespread adoption of Haudenosaunee foods, for instance ("60 percent of the food eaten in the world today was developed over thousands of years by the Indigenous peoples of the Americas"). We learn of the Haudenosaunee contributions to the structure of American democracy and the women's movement, and the part Haudenosaunee leaders continue to play in advancing international diplomacy and global environmental concerns, with imagery depicting visits by Deskaheh to the League of Nations in the 1920s, followed by delegations in 1977, 1991, and 2007.

Public Encounters

The center's use for public events on Native American–related topics is remarkable. I have attended several public lectures and two multiday workshops, a symposium on the Doctrine of Discovery, and a virtual discussion of Washington's assault on the Haudenosaunee. Each time I have been struck by the robust draw of both Native and non-Native participants. Onondaga members and other Haudenosaunee participants seemed as engaged in these discussions as were their guests, and I observed several open, honest, and sometimes difficult debates held across community lines. One night, a non-Native historian presented his research on long-term consequences of Indian boarding schools and suggested that some students chose this path to pursue personal or community goals. Native people in the audience who had attended boarding schools spoke up, challenging the speaker's suggestion that anything good could have come from the experience, and bringing to public awareness the harm the experience had caused them or their relatives. While difficult at times, the conversation that followed was powerful, honest, and heartfelt.

Is the open, accepting atmosphere at these events because meetings there typically start with a full recitation of the Thanksgiving Address in Onondaga and English? Are center members trained somehow in interpersonal communication? Whatever the reasons, I always leave feeling that this center is doing more for Native–non-Native relations that nearly any other educational programming I have encountered, for people are engaging with each other with honesty and respect across many group boundaries.

Seneca Art & Culture Center at Ganondagan

I first drove to the Seneca Art & Culture Center at Ganondagan through a dramatic summer thunderstorm with blinding lightning, roiling dark clouds, and downpours. The center is in a rural area about twenty miles southeast of Rochester, New York. When I reached the parking lot, the storm had passed. The sleek gray building was visible through a profusion of blooming purple thistles, daisies, and delicate Queen Anne's lace growing in a meadow bordering the parking lot (see figure 40). Yellow finches darted around the flowers. It was a lovely sight.

The Seneca Art & Culture Center is based at the Ganondagan State Historic Site, the site of a large seventeenth-century Seneca village, "Gah-a-yan-duk," then a large settlement and the regional granary.[62] The French troops who encountered it in 1687, under the Marquis de Denonville, described it as a huge palisaded vil-

FIG. 40. Seneca Art & Culture Center at Ganondagan, Victor NY. Photo courtesy of the author.

lage filled with an estimated over one million bushels of green and dry corn. They burned it all. Setting aside the land for a state historic site was a long process that commenced in 1959 under the impetus of J. Sheldon Fisher, county historian.[63] In the 1950s the area was drawing the attention of amateur archaeologists and real estate developers. As Fisher began spreading his vision for the site and worked with Seneca leaders, he mobilized a growing group of interested parties who helped fundraise. He even fought off opposition from two state senators.[64] I met with site manager G. Peter Jemison, Seneca faithkeeper and artist, who worked for years at the site. Jemison recounted:

> In the 1980s, the Bureau of Historic Sites and New York State Office of Parks began to think about actually interpreting this site and doing something about it. So they assembled an advisory group of Haudenosaunee people. And they began to meet and discuss how this story should be told between the publications, signage, obviously some kind of a visitor center, this very

small building we had renovated, a film that would be shown to visitors. That was sort of the beginning.

Jemison doesn't take credit for these ideas; when he became involved at the site in the mid-1980s, he inherited the advisory group's master plan and was charged with carrying it out. After laying out trails, they needed to attract visitors. "So, the next thing was the bark longhouse," he recalls. "The bark longhouse really did prove to be the thing that fourth graders were the most interested in." Also, part of the site development involved a name change from "Gannagaro," a Mohawk word of undetermined meaning and origin, to "Ganondagan," as suggested by Tonawanda Seneca chief Corbett Sundown.[65] Ganondagan means "town on a hill surrounded by the substance of white," the white referring to a "blossom of an edible fruit." The color white is associated with peace for Haudenosaunee, and the name could be translated as "town of white" or "town of peace."[66]

Cultural programming first revolved around the longhouse replica and thus was restricted to the summer months.[67] A shift to a year-round facility took years of hard work. Jemison had an architect develop drawings and a model; then he met with colleagues to sell the idea to the state. "You know, I had to convince the Parks that that was something worthwhile and then I began to get interest, financial support." He attributes his ultimate success to luck: "I was very lucky. I had almost unwittingly made friends with some of my main supporters—before I really knew I was going to have to call upon them to do something."

The center was completed in October 2015, after decades of planning, fundraising, and organizing. It is built for year-round use and is ready for the foreseeable future. It includes fifteen exhibit spaces, which offer beautiful and well-narrated programming, as well as an auditorium with theater-style seating, galleries, offices, and even a caterer's kitchen. The structure incorporates green building design features such as geothermal heating and cooling.[68] It is capable of hosting large events and material-culture conferences. I attended an Iroquois Studies conference that was held there in October 2018, and it hosts a regular winter festival and concerts. In a Rochester *City Newspaper* article, Jemison described the grand opening as a "dream come true," and site historian and interpretive program assistant Michael Galban explained the unique mission of the center: "On one level, Seneca people themselves are our most important audience. We have a responsibility as caretakers of culture to the Seneca people." He added that in doing so, the center will become an asset to the wider community, and a "bridge between the Seneca people and the rest of the world."[69]

The Seneca Arts & Culture Center confronts the dominant historical narrative, as exemplified by New York's 1929 Sullivan-Clinton plaques, albeit on its own terms. The first point to make in this regard is that the site was developed in consultation with a Haudenosaunee advisory committee, and today proudly announces on its official website that it is the only New York State Historic Site dedicated to a Native American theme.[70] As Jemison told a reporter in 2015 when it opened, here, "Seneca people are able to tell their own story."[71]

Visitors are encouraged to start at the Orientation Theater and watch a film narrating the Iroquois Creation Story. This award-winning film involves Seneca, Tuscarora, and Mohawk dancers in a dramatic recounting of the complex narrative involving Sky Woman, Baby Girl, Turtle Man, and the creation of humanity and all good and bad things. For a non-Native visitor steeped in a Judeo-Christian framing of the past, it certainly reorients. The visitor learns basic information about key beings in Haudenosaunee cosmology and a wholly different way of understanding the start of humanity and the beginning of time. At the same time, the film is covertly informing visitors, "This is our museum; we are telling you about ourselves, in our way." It is a powerful film, and a very powerful experience.

The exhibits that follow may feel familiar in that they involve glass cases, artifacts, images, maps, and text, but the story they tell differs from the relentlessly depressing tale of "loss and once was" that permeates too many accounts of Indigenous America. Like the other cultural centers discussed here, exhibits instead emphasize Seneca survivance. This is perhaps most evident in the excellent lacrosse exhibit, which is ostensibly about sports, but also "about sovereignty, self-determination, independence, the right to self-govern from a Native perspective."[72]

Most significant for the present discussion is the absence of any direct discussion of Sullivan and his mission of destruction. Jemison explains this absence in a matter-of-fact manner: "Well, of course, we're dealing primarily with a much earlier time period. Ninety-two years earlier, actually. We're dealing with a French campaign that comes here to basically do what Sullivan and Clinton were going to do—try to do—wipe us out. But, obviously, we are telling this story from the perspective of the Seneca and not the perspective of the French, and not the perspective of the Jesuits." The fact that Jemison spontaneously cites precisely how many years after Denonville's raid the Sullivan Expedition occurred indicates a keen awareness of the Sullivan story. He also defends his museum's *not* taking on the Sullivan story due to pedagogical and resource constraints. Their goal is to educate about a lesser-known period of time:

> The main thing that I have noticed is the average person knows nothing about the seventeenth century, nothing at all. So, this is really an enlightening thing to them because their first thought is, "Oh, this is about the French and Indian War." No. This is *not* the French and Indian War. And it's not the Revolutionary War that we're describing here. We're describing something that happened 92 years before the Sullivan Clinton campaign. And so we really didn't have—we had not chosen that subject to really be a part of our exhibit.

I added, "I noticed that. Sullivan's not in there at all."

He agreed. "It's not in there, right? Well, we knew there was a limited amount that we could cover in that exhibit space. And we had to decide what were the stories that we knew we had to tell about Ganondagan."

"How This All Finally Concludes"

We have already encountered Jemison's views about historical markers and their role in mythmaking. The New York replacement narrative exemplified by the 1929 plaques asserts that it was Sullivan who removed the Native people in New York, "clearing" the way for the white settlers. The Ganondagan exhibits confront this dominant mythology head-on. Jemison wants to explain his way of treating this story by showing me another exhibit. As we walk down the hall, he tells me, "When I saw this, I realized it gave us another opportunity—an opportunity to do another kind of interpretation, which gets into the Sullivan Clinton Campaign. We have one more thing down the hallway, which I'll show you in a minute, that kind of ties it all together, or ties it up, I guess I would say." He takes me down the hall to look at an exhibit with a huge painting at its center, *The Treaty of Canandaigua*, by historical painter Robert Griffing and commissioned by the Wegmans Food Markets. He discusses the process by which they developed this exhibit:

> The artist, Robert Griffing, kind of became a friend of ours. He then took photographs of us individually. And then we got together as a group, and he photographed the group. And then he built his painting from that. So that is literally me holding the wampum belts there, in the middle. And then I could name the other people that are in the painting, you know—all of whom are either Seneca or Cayuga and so forth. So this is the signing of the Canandaigua Treaty. This is [pointing], this is Pickering coming and negotiating, you know, here in Canandaigua, and, them reaching, finally, an agreement after, you know, several months of discussion [the artist] imagining, at least, what this might have been like.

Also in this room is a huge time-lapse map that illustrates quite clearly Six Nation territories according to the 1794 treaty, and then the successive losses of land, through various deals, over time. There is a life-sized reproduction of the Canandaigua Treaty. "It stands on that easel, there." He points to me. "So now we have—here's the treaty, here's this image, so we can talk about how this all finally concludes." He goes on to explain:

> How does the Revolutionary War, for us, end? Because it's certainly not the Treaty of Paris [1783]. We're not included in that at all. And it's not the Treaty of Fort Stanwix [1784]. It's the Canan-

daigua Treaty [1794] that finally kind of brings to an end, this—
this era. I don't know [how] much you saw this map across the
hallway. It shows you the land diminishing, and it shows you what
the Canandaigua Treaty promised, and all of that. Again, as far
as really getting into the Sullivan Clinton? *This* is how *we* do it.

In Jemison's view, the way to challenge the widespread settler
mythology that the Sullivan Campaign was the endpoint of Indian
settlement in New York is to discuss what happened *after* the Revolutionary War, to highlight the Treaty of Canandaigua, and to
show, visually, that what mattered most in removing Seneca from
their lands was not Sullivan's destruction, but the series of land
deals, many fraudulent, that occurred afterward. If that treaty had
been respected, the destruction of homes and crops, while horrific, would have been less consequential and more easily overcome. Certainly that destruction would not be commemorated
on the landscape at all, or at least not in a celebratory fashion, for
much of the land would still be under Seneca control. It would
all still be Seneca country.

I'm trying to take this all in and summarize it back to Jemison. "So you mean, what you're saying here is that . . . *that* is the
main story. Like, if you had a map of land, that should be—this
whole half of New York State [I gesture] should be your country?"

He agrees emphatically. "Exactly! It would be our country and,
you know, even down to the flooding of the Kinzua Dam—so *this*
is the—at least one way for us to address, um, you know, the *real*
history." By emphasizing the seventeenth-century French invasion and the 1794 Canandaigua Treaty, Ganondagan shatters the
straightjacket the dominant Sullivan narrative imposes. By not telling the Sullivan story, Ganondagan is able to tell so much more.
Seneca, Haudenosaunee, and Native American land loss was not
limited to one period of time, but has been a long-term process
involving more people than just John Sullivan.

Conclusion

I conclude this section with a discussion of a Seneca cultural center located in the Allegany Territory of the Seneca Nation of Indi-

FIG. 41. Seneca-Iroquois National Museum, Allegany Territory, Seneca Nation of Indians. Photo courtesy of the author.

ans. The original museum, the Seneca-Iroquois National Museum (SINM), was established in 1977 with funding secured from a federal settlement that followed the construction of the Kinzua Dam on Allegany Territory (see figure 41).[73] The fight to prevent the building of the Kinzua Dam has been narrated in several important sources; despite popular outcry and hard-fought community action, the Army Corps of Engineers built the dam from 1960 to 1965, flooding one-third of the Allegany Territory of the Seneca Nation of Indians and most of the contiguous Cornplanter tract, the only land reserved for Native people in Pennsylvania.[74] It displaced 550 people from 160 families.[75] This forced removal was described by the Tribal Council of the Seneca Nation as "a great tragedy inflicted upon the Seneca People as a whole," and it continues to animate Seneca political and social life.[76]

I visited SINM in July 2017 and October 2018, before the new center was built. In the original museum, a fascinating exhibit outlined the fight to block the Kinzua Dam project and presented oral testimonies from people who had been displaced. The exhibit was emotionally wrenching. The Sullivan raids were referenced in the exhibit description but not as a central story, more as a way of reckoning time, appearing "after the devastating invasion." The Sullivan story was folded into a much longer narrative of loss, disruption, and community repair. While both the Sullivan and Kinzua events involved displacements, the Kinzua trauma and the betrayal it represented by the federal government were front and center.

Kinzua is the most recent major removal story for Allegany Senecas, and it holds an important place in the new center as well. During the fieldwork for this book, the original building was closed and a new cultural center built; the new center thus merits a far deeper treatment than I can provide here. The new center is housed in an impressive new structure and renamed the Onöhsagwë:de' Cultural Center (see figure 42). Onöhsagwë:de' comes from the Seneca word "onöhsogaën," which means "house opening" (referring to a doorway, window, or chimney), and honors Richard Johnny-John, a beloved Seneca language and culture teacher, whose nickname was Gwë:de'.[77] The exhibits are organized around Seneca concepts, which are presented first in the Seneca language. The first room one enters is called *Agwastiadiya'dade'*, which means "the distinct community." Visitors are oriented by listening to the *Ganönyök*, the Thanksgiving Address, while standing under a giant-sized *gustoweh*, a men's ceremonial hat. The museum's signage explains that "the Onöndowa'ga:' (Senecas) are very thankful people. We give thanks for everything before we meet, or when we gather together in groups. As we speak the *Ganönyök* we make our minds one." When the feathers on the *gustoweh* move, they clear the person's mind from dust and give them good thoughts. This symbolism is powerful, and when new visitors are brought to the center and are being introduced to the culture, it is as if they are encouraged to center themselves with good thoughts, a stance they may carry with them as they travel through the center's many exhibits.

Ending with the old and new centers at Allegany reminds us to keep the future in mind. The Onöhsagwë:de' Cultural Center is a large building with room to grow, offering spaces for archives and more. Ending with the old and new centers at Allegany also reminds us of the necessarily open-ended nature of any such study: all the institutions mentioned here are living centers, and every center I discuss here will likely continue to change as community interests and needs adapt. Finally, I would be remiss if I neglected to emphasize that this is a subset of the museums that emphasize Haudenosaunee culture and traditions in New York. Other noteworthy centers include the Six Nations Iroquois Cultural Center in Onchiota, a collection established by Ray Fadden, which includes drawings narrating the Sullivan raids and many other important events of Haudenosaunee history, and the Akwesasne Cultural Center in Awkwesasne, New York. Additional centers can be found in Wisconsin and Oklahoma, and across the international border in Canada.

In *Decolonizing Museums*, Amy Lonetree argues that museums can serve as sites of decolonization by challenging stereotyped representations, honoring Indigenous knowledge, serving as sites of memory for their communities, and "discussing the hard truths of colonization in exhibitions."[78] In her view, outlining the "hard truths" such as genocidal acts committed against Indigenous people can turn sites of "colonial harm into sites of healing."[79] Washington's Indian Expedition certainly constitutes an example of a "hard truth." Why do we not see it play a more central role at these cultural centers? I believe it is partly by *not* making these raids central that these cultural centers intervene in the white settler mythmaking exemplified by the Sullivan commemorative complex. These centers reposition the raids within a much longer timeframe and much deeper context. If the Sullivan "Expedition" is mentioned (and it would likely be renamed an "invasion" or act of genocide), it is presented as one of many efforts by outsiders to disrupt the long-standing Haudenosaunee presence on the land. The invasion of the Haudenosaunee homelands did not start with Sullivan, and prior incursions by French troops and Jesuit priests are relayed at all these centers. Exhibits emphasize broken treaties, for it was the nefarious dealings with Native communities after the Revolutionary War—often with Euro-American elites or political leaders employing deceitful divide-and-conquer practices, in defiance of federal law—that

FIG. 42. Onöhsagwë:dé Cultural Center, Allegany Territory, Seneca Nation of Indians. Photo courtesy of Randy A. John.

severed Haudenosaunee people from their territories. This history postdates the Revolutionary War and is ongoing, now well over two centuries after the Revolutionary War. Along with land grabs came other challenges: cultural losses and intrafamily rupture caused by boarding schools, and efforts to thwart the practice of customary law, religion, and language, all topics that feature prominently. These discussions are grounded in a completely different epistemology, reflecting a different cosmology and ontology.[80] They emphasize stories from the earliest times, the times of Creation and the Great Law of Peace, and stress human relationships with the natural world. Oral transmission of knowledge is foregrounded, and at some centers, participants learn by listening to voices in Native languages and in English.

The text on New York State's Sullivan-Clinton monoliths suggests Haudenosaunee decline and constructs a statewide replacement narrative, with the expedition serving as a turning point in state history. The centers disrupt that narrative head-on by proclaiming Onondaga, Oneida, Seneca, and Haudenosaunee survivance, by existing as true community centers that look to the future. The Sullivan story is certainly not forgotten, and for many, it may provide a vital cautionary tale. The trauma caused by Washington's assault on the Haudenosaunee and the removal of Haudenosaunee from their ancestral home is a central element in Haudenosaunee historical consciousness. Keeping this cautionary tale alive is not incompatible with survival but may ensure it. Knowing when to tell these stories and to whom thus also matters greatly. While welcoming the outside visitor, these are, first and foremost, Indigenous community centers that serve Haudenosaunee nations. They proclaim to themselves and the outsiders unabashedly, "We are here." They foster pride and hope, and look to the future, with concern for wider humanity and Mother Earth.

These centers contribute to healing within nations by bringing distant cousins back into the fold. They also foster dialogue between subject positions. For, of course, the white visitors to such centers are aware, on some level, that the dominant settler narrative, what Rose calls the "story we tell," is deeply problematic. While a way forward for someone of a white settler persuasion is not entirely clear, it certainly requires a shift in perspective and a wholly different understanding of the past, and as someone of that ilk, I feel that the place to start is at these centers.

FOURTEEN

Epilogue

Americans are discovering that they live in a monumental landscape that celebrates white supremacy. Grand
statues, historical signs, and names of towns and uni-
versities memorialize prominent white slave owners and their
business partners. So many of these memorials are now under
attack, for as people address a crisis of racial oppression, historical
markers are targeted as well. This is because the historical landscape matters. Place-names and historical markers help secure
a dominant mindset, whether telling us which races have value
or whose country this is. In this book I have tried to show that so
much of the U.S. memorial landscape is also profoundly shaped
by the country's settler-colonial beginnings. Even memorials to
a relatively obscure component of the Revolutionary War reflect
and help construct a point of view in direct opposition to a Native
one. They play a key role in establishing a settler-colonial historical consciousness and collective identity.

Galvanized by scholarship on such diverse settings as French
Algeria, Canada, South Africa, and Australia, scholars in American, Native American, and Indigenous studies are exploring
the American "settler-colonial present," considering how American literature, geographies, and cultural practices are shaped by
the country's colonial nature. Understanding "settler common
sense," as Mark Rifkin puts it, means understanding how Indigenous peoples and geographies remain "unseen."[1] Patterns in
settler-colonial historical consciousness help to perpetuate this
"unseenness," and I have identified the roadside markers and other

commemorative memorials as fruitful sites for exploring dominant understandings of the past. Historical markers disseminate what can appear to be rather innocuous or even boring messages, announcing bland and generic histories. As I have shown, however, these histories and their associated commemorative performances work to construct an imagined "we" that does not—and indeed, cannot—easily include a Native perspective. The stories these projects communicate are partial and myopic and help create a landscape of forgetting.

This land was wrested from its original inhabitants through nearly continuous conflict.[2] There is no easy way to relate this violence in a storyline that includes opposing sides together within a common "we." Like the print media that Benedict Anderson argues helps construct an "imagined community," texts on historical markers create an imagined settler-colonial community that excludes the country's Indigenous people.[3] By participating in commemorative ceremonies, settler-colonists are socialized en masse into specific "mnemonic traditions" that feature certain heroes and morals and that teach only certain points of view. The protagonists of this version of the past are newcomers, "pioneers," "founding fathers," and by starting the nation's chronometer at point zero, previous histories are erased, whole pasts mnemonically obliterated.[4]

The stories settler-colonists tell must grapple with their place on the land and their relationship to its Indigenous peoples. Invaders of an inhabited land who come to dominate it will need to explain how and why they came to be there, and have a limited number of possible explanations, and an even smaller subset that allow usurping narrators to retain a positive self-image. Either the newcomers were welcomed and happily "merged" into the existing community, or the first peoples left voluntarily. Original inhabitants may be framed as unfit in some way, as having committed atrocities, as having to be destroyed. The tale of the replacement of a barbaric order by a civilized one has been animating human history since the earliest times, and many of these themes can be found in the stories Euro-American settler-colonists have told about themselves, built upon worn tropes and stereotypes that include racialization, Othering, savagism, and the regularly "vanishing Indian." Typically missing in the stories settler-colonists tell is an acknowledgment of their own role in the drama. Instead, conflicts occur without settler instigation; Indigenous people get upset, massacre others, or die for no apparent reason. The authors of these self-centered autobiographies that masquerade as national histories cannot see their own power, do not want to acknowledge their own action in the drama, and narrate it indirectly, often in the passive voice. Heroes and heroines blindly stumble into untold bounty innocently, accidentally. When they engage in violent acts, it is always someone else's fault.

Erasures and distortions in the settler historical consciousness stem from a basic settler-colonial dilemma, the logic of elimination. In the process of trying to develop what Deborah Bird Rose describes as a sense of belonging in their beloved homes, settler-colonists conjure up what Jean O'Brien has called replacement narratives, settler fantasies that explain how they inherited that new land and replaced its inhabitants. Land transactions are central features of the stories New Englanders tell; stories about the Sullivan Expedition add another rationale for white settler ascendancy: the "natural" logics of war. Rooting a story of settler replacement in a foundational period of U.S. history further insulates the actors from blame. Sullivan and his men were simply following military orders developed by national demigod George Washington himself. The land they later enjoyed is understood in this telling as their just deserts, the spoils of war—with war featuring as a regrettable circumstance, but in the case of this war, what were the alternatives? The Revolutionary War features as inevitable, necessary, and right. The Pennsylvania variation on the Sullivan story adds a revenge component. Sullivan's Expedition, in this reading, was a response to the barbarism that preceded it at the Battle of Wyoming, and more specifically the *Indian* participants in that Revolutionary War battle.

A fuller inventory of the nation's replacement narratives awaits development and systematic comparison with those in other settler societies. In other regions of the United States, these stories are centrally about race, as we see in Andrew Denson's fascinating *Monuments to Absence*, which relates white southerners' narrations of the Cherokee Trail of Tears removal story.[5] In other settler-colonial societies, narratives of Indigenous barbarity and settler-colonist victimhood feature prominently in national monumentality with striking parallels to the Wyoming drama developed here, with rituals that may foster similar emotions among participants.[6] And, of course, replacement stories are not just about settlers. As Philip Deloria observes in *Playing Indian*, from colonial times to the present day, "The Indian has skulked in and out of the most important stories various Americans have told about themselves."[7] Using any manner of devices—silencing, disavowal, mnemonic decapitation, and twisting the story into falsehoods—settler-colonists keep trying to tell a story of themselves in relation to the Indigenous population and in relation to the land, a story of replacement, a settler fantasy of wishful thinking.

The placemaking practices considered here are not unique. The tendency of settler societies to recognize and mark out explorer and military routes is so pervasive it seems almost pathological. In the United States, the Sullivan commemorative complex represents one of many such "journeys" marked out by stones or other permanent markers, several of which have gained national recognition. It is no surprise that most of the U.S. National Historic Trails (NHT) directly relate to colonization. Aside from one recognizing a civil rights march (the Selma to Montgomery NHT) and another interpreting Hawaiian culture (the Ala Kahakai NHT), they mark out military routes, the paths of forced migrations of Native peoples, explorer trails, or settler trails.[8] What does it say that these are the journeys we most revere?

This marking out tracks onto the land in perpetuity is also a way of placing claims on it, holding it in reserve, as others have observed.[9] Place-naming offers another form of place-claiming.[10] Renaming practices are common with regime change; what people may forget in a settler-colonial society is that place-naming practices are almost always renaming projects, a renaming that never ends, Linda Tuhiwai Smith observes.[11]

The land-claiming aspects of historical markers are further clarified when we include marker inauguration rituals in our focus.

The first Sullivan marker dedications often included participation by active or veteran military units, Boy Scout troops, the blowing of bugles, the singing of the national anthem, and the flying of the national flag. Many of these rituals resemble long-standing practices associated with conquerors' rights, practices carried out in a conscious manner in the early United States by such explorers as Lewis and Clark. Roberta Conner notes that Jefferson ordered Lewis and Clark to follow well-known rituals for applying discoverer's rights, such as mapping, taking physical possession of the land, carving names in rocks, erecting improvements on it, and naming places and waterways, all actions carried out strategically so that anyone trying to preempt U.S. interests would know Americans had already been there.[12] Sullivan memorials also involve taking possession of a piece of land, marking it permanently by carving names in rocks or constructing other lasting materials, and inaugurations involving flag-planting and public pronouncements by dignitaries. For the land's first inhabitants, the meaning of these acts is clear, as Alice, a Kugluktuk elder, told Emilie Cameron regarding a historical marker in Canada: markers mean her people "can't use that land."[13]

The Locus, the Memorial, and Settler Colonialism

We have considered settler-colonial placemaking and the historical marker as ways to narrate a morally acceptable past, claim land, and create a sense of belonging. I want to turn to Connerton's two models of place, the locus and the memorial, for they further elucidate the settler-colonial predilection for memorializing. In Connerton's model, the locus is the taken-for-granted place, the backdrop for everyday life, the place where people live. The memorial, on the other hand, involves a purposeful placement of a story about a past event or person; it is an overt call to remember.

Paul Connerton's central concern in *How Modernity Forgets* is to understand the rapid proliferation of memorials in the modern world. He relates this to the loss of loci and an associated fear of forgetting.[14] Rapid transformations of the built environment associated with capitalist expansion and modernity have led to relentless change in the places where people live and work, severing people from their loci, leading directly to memorial-making. While it is clear that the destruction of the locus can have profound effects, what is less clear is if settler-colonists might be especially afflicted by memorial-making. One might connect the Sullivan commemorative complex to modernity and relentless changes to local landscapes associated with American capitalist expansion. This may be part of the story, and it is noteworthy that the high point of U.S. monument development dates to 1870 to 1930, a time of rapid industrialization and social change. I want to focus on the disruptions specifically caused by settler-colonial processes, however. This social form's underlying logic sets into play a series of disruptions of people and their loci, and the loss or disruption of place memories. By leaving their homes, voluntarily or not, settler-colonists severed themselves and subsequent generations from the places in which they had been embedded, their landscapes animated by spiritual beings and historical references.[15] It is not my intention here to investigate specific examples of settler place-loss and the damage this may have caused, but rather to situate this rupture as a crucial starting point.

These unsettled people didn't resettle in any old place but often sought out Native places in particular, directly causing a mass severing of Native peoples from *their* places, a forced dislocation with damaging consequences impossible to fully relate. In her study of the Australian town of Kuranda, Queensland, Rosita Henry explores the effects of Australian settler placemaking on Aboriginal place attachments. By removing Aboriginal peoples to mission stations, settlers erased or, in her words, "mutilated" Australian Aboriginal place memory, for removal from their home places denied them ways to pass down place memory to the next generation, especially since place is a fundamental mnemonic tool for them.[16] Aboriginal place mutilation was furthered by settler-colonial renaming practices, which fostered the erasure of "Aboriginality" from the land.[17]

White Australian settlers were well aware of Aboriginal settlement sites and trails.[18] They didn't simply move nearby, "but appropriated Aboriginal pathways and chose to occupy sites they cleared" and soon after began to rename these places.[19] Paul Carter also notes that whites in Australia employed Aborigines as guides, followed Aboriginal tracks, and were assisted by them in learning about the land and its resources—before removing them. Even though there was a chance for long-term cooperation, it wasn't pursued: "This was the universal pattern: aboriginal cooperation followed by usurpation of aboriginal resources," Carter writes.[20] Similar examples abound in North America, and we need look no further than the aftermath of the Sullivan Expedition. The villages Sullivan's troops destroyed were loci for Haudenosaunee and other Native inhabitants, sites where people and place were co-constructed, sites that had generated generations upon generations of place memories, as many have observed.[21] Destroying these places was not enough, however, and after the Revolutionary War, some of the soldiers returned to the very village sites they had destroyed, claimed them, and renamed them. The "new world" settler-colonists built was established not on a logic of cooperation and collaboration, but one of elimination and replacement.

The severing of Haudenosaunees and their Indigenous allies from their loci was damaging and unforgiveable, yet there is ample evidence that despite these disruptions, Haudenosaunee people either returned to many of these places, or have kept knowledge of their home settlements alive, revisiting them in narrations across the generations.[22] The loci live on in the cultural memory, and new loci are added to the already richly storied land.[23] Research on displacement and memory often finds that a site of displacement can serve to unite long after exile. In *Rebuilding Shattered Worlds*, Anna Eisenstein and I found that even after a whole neighborhood was obliterated through urban renewal, the remembered locus served as a focus of community building. It was in narrating this missing place, by returning to their place memories, that Eastonans rebuilt their shattered community.[24] Despite repeated experiences of place-loss, Haudenosaunee place memory, too, is strong, and community after community is rebuilt in the physical realm as well as in storyscapes, as we have seen.

How great the contrast is with the myopic memory of the settler-colonist. After severing themselves—willingly or not—from their homelands, this "mutilated place-memory-people" attempt to make themselves at home in another people's land in part through incessant intentional placemaking. There is almost a frenzy in their memorial establishment. Rather than the stories growing organically out of these places, out of a long-term human connection with them, their stories are slapped down almost willy-nilly, resembling the "onomastic megalomania" Carter observed in Australian place-naming practice. Despite their incessant renaming, shaping and reshaping, placing markers, planting and saluting flags, settler-colonists are not settled.

Haunting

Settler-colonists face many problems with their attempts to indigenize themselves and make a foreign land their home.[25] Despite all this placemaking, the wishful "firsting" and "lasting," and attempts to fuse family history to the land, there are reminders all around that somebody else was here first, and that this replacement is a fantasy. The pseudo-tranquility offered by erasures and mnemonic myopia is pierced by the regular unearthing of material evidence of the long-term inhabitation of the land by others. These material clues "haunt." This idea of the haunting by material remains is elucidated in a remarkable ethnography, *The Make-Believe Space*. Anthropologist Yael Navaro-Yashin explores the aftermath of the partition of Cyprus for Turkish Cypriots. She presents northern Cyprus as a "phantomic" space, for Turkish-Cypriot inhabitants of the northern part of the island live among the things they perceive as "connected to the Greek Cypriots" who used to live there and who were forced out in 1974 in the aftermath of war. At the time of the partition, people were "separated from their personal effects, from the materialities and environments with which they identified or with which they were associated." The objects left behind—homes, fields, trees, personal belongings—carry associations with the people who left, and she argues that Turkish Cypriots lived with a phantom presence: "phantoms or ghosts appear or linger in a slice of territory in the form of 'non-human objects.'"[26] Greek Cypriots remained there, not physically but through their material objects, their dwellings, and their fields, and thus exerted an "enduring affective presence" that was often a subject of conversation. A doctor said, "You know, the earth under our feet here is full of corpses. All Turkish Cypriots know this; Greek Cypriots know this too."[27] One of his patients wakes up at night "and thinks of all the Greek Cypriots lying dead in the fields close to his house."[28] He argues that if people don't discuss this openly, "the anxiety is there." They have collected some of the objects left behind, calling it *ganimet* (loot, or property taken from the enemy), a term that implies self-criticism.[29] Loot is everywhere, and how it is discussed signifies the violence against the other party carried out during the war, a violence people "know and remember."[30] People even live in the other party's homes. She considers what it means to inhabit a home that belongs to another people, writing, "There is guilt over having appropriated someone else's ancestral property and an attempt, through hanging family photographs on living-room walls, to inscribe the incoming family's ancestral links and genealogy in the space of the home."[31]

I see establishing memorials to the Sullivan Expedition as a similar process to hanging family photos in someone else's home. Evidence of the land's first peoples may be removed, carefully organized and displayed in museums, or set on fire and destroyed but, as Raymond Williams observes, rewriting a past is a dangerous ground on which to build a new hegemonic order because the real story can always be uncovered.[32]

Setting the story straight is difficult within the white settler toolkit. What is the best way forward? I was inspired by the tremendous efforts a few Euro-Americans have taken in trying to rewrite a complicated past in novel form, a labor decades long. Others have engaged in an even longer process of tackling the markers directly, and revel in the one marker that they have established that gets it right. Confronting the Sullivan plaques on their own terms, by either revising, replacing, or addressing the monuments, takes effort. Members of NOON are certainly aware of their own positionality and spend their time on the matters most essential to their Onondaga neighbors. They are trying to tackle the very ground on which the national story is built by starting with the hearts and minds of nearby non-Natives, a daunting daily task that makes the direction taken by critical academics like myself seem frivolous.

FIG. 43. Sign for dejódiha:'kdö:h (Great Valley), Allegany Territory, Seneca Nation of Indians. Photo courtesy of Randy A. John.

A completely different take on the Sullivan story comes from outside the settler-colonial community. Haudenosaunee cultural centers address Sullivan differently, tangentially, or not at all. They already know that story, and detailed accounts of the trauma are repeated across the generations and may serve as a cautionary tale. One way to challenge the myopia in settler-colonial historical consciousness is to stay true to one's own alternative storyline, and disregard the artificial containment imposed by standard periodization practices embedded in the American English language, with everyday phrases such as "Founding Fathers," "prehistoric," or "New World." To stop telling a story of "Iroquois declension," one must stop telling the story of Iroquois declension, and go back to narrating one's own history in one's own way. For a people living on or near their homeland for thousands of years, there is so much more to say.

FIG. 44. New signage, Allegany Territory, Seneca Nation of Indians. Photo courtesy of Randy A. John.

I asked a Seneca colleague one day how Senecas might address the problematic nature of misleading historical markers and other memorials. He thought for a moment and said that they would do things differently. He asked me to go look at the new road signs recently installed in the Seneca language. I end this book, a lengthy intervention of my own, with the beauty and power of these signs.

NOTES

Note on Terminology

1. Hill, *The Clay We Are Made Of*, 5.
2. John, *Seneca People*, xi–xii.
3. Grumet, *The Munsee Indians*, 13, 47, 232, 293n10; Schutt, *Peoples of the River Valleys*, 3; Weslager, *The Delaware Indians*, 33, 46–47, 232.
4. Mt. Pleasant, Wigginton, and Wisecup, "Materials and Methods," 207–36.
5. Mt. Pleasant, Wigginton, and Wisecup, "Materials and Methods," 207–36.
6. Useful discussions of the need for decolonizing lenses in interpreting historical sources can be found in Smith, *Decolonizing Methodologies*; and Hill, *The Clay We Are Made Of*, 7–10.
7. John, *Seneca People*, 445.

Introduction

1. Rose, "New World Poetics of Place," 228.
2. Smith, "Settler Sites of Memory"; "Settler Historical Consciousness"; "Place Replaced"; "Mormon Forestdale"; *Colonial Memory and Postcolonial Europe*.
3. Kammen, *A Season of Youth*, 256.
4. See McDonnell et al., *Remembering the Revolution*, 1–2. See also Kammen, *A Season of Youth*.
5. Raphael, *Founding Myths*.
6. Kammen, *A Season of Youth*, 259.
7. Allen, *Tories*; Taylor, *American Revolutions*, 2–6.
8. McDonnell, "War and Nationhood," 21. A review of scholarship on the American Revolution would fill this volume. Along with sources already cited, I found most useful Taylor, *American Revolutions*; Countryman, *Enjoy the Same Liberty*; *A People in Revolution*.
9. Calloway, *The American Revolution in Indian Country*.
10. "George Washington to John Sullivan, May 31, 1779, with Instruction," gwp. This letter can also be accessed online: https://www.loc.gov/item/mgw3b.009/.
11. Excellent summaries of the expedition can be found in Graymont, *The Iroquois in the American Revolution*; and Calloway, *The Indian World*, 235–59. See also Calloway, *The American Revolution*; Fischer, *A Well-Executed Failure*; Mintz, *Seeds of Empire*; Williams, *Year of the Hangman*. Journals of Sullivan's soldiers were published by the state of New

York: Cook, *Journals of the Military Expedition*. For a full sense of the scope of the literature, Folts, "Sullivan Campaign"; and Ingalsbe, "A Bibliography." See also NBP and CBP. Additional sources introduced below.

12. The Pomeroy Foundation has begun establishing new markers in preparation for the 250th anniversary. As this is an unfolding project, it is beyond the focus of this book.

13. Because the mission involved the deliberate destruction of foodstuffs and dwellings, it would be defined today as an act of genocide according to the Geneva Convention. Article 2 of the Geneva Convention on the Prevention and Punishment of the Crime of Genocide, adopted by the UN General Assembly on December 9, 1948, included "deliberately inflicting on the group conditions of life calculated to bring about its physical destruction in whole or in part.'" This point was raised by G. Peter Jemison in an interview with the author, July 12, 2017, Victor NY.

14. Veracini, "Settler Collective."

15. Seneca consultant in discussion with the author, August 13, 2017, Salamanca NY. Aside from public officials and directors of public museums, all names are pseudonyms.

16. Prochaska, *Making Algeria French*.

17. Fanon, *The Wretched of the Earth*, 51, 83.

18. Amato, *Monuments en exil*. Acts of iconoclasm and revision continue in postcolonial spaces worldwide. Elago, "Colonial Monuments," 276.

19. Blee and O'Brien, *Monumental Mobility*; Colwell-Chanthaphonh, *Massacre at Camp Grant*; Jacoby, *Shadows at Dawn*; Kelman, *A Misplaced Massacre*; Cothran, *Remembering the Modoc War*; Denson, *Monuments to Absence*.

20. Calloway, *The American Revolution*, 1.

21. "Lenape" means "original," "man," or "common," "real person" in the Lenape language; "Delaware" is a 1610 English term devised to recognize the second governor of Virginia, Thomas West, Baron de la Warr, and referred to the bay, the river, and the people living alongside it. By the mid–eighteenth century, European colonists used the term for Munsees and Lenapes. See Soderlund, *Lenape Country*, 5–7; Weslager, *The Delaware Indians*, 33, 36–37, 44–46. Jersey Lenape are sometimes referred to as "Lenopi." Becker, "Native Settlements." My use of encompassing terms does not imply homogeneity or political unity across such an extensive region in early contact times. The ethnonym "Lenape" was rarely used in early sources but has become popular and is used by many living descendants, while other descendants refer to themselves as "Delaware" Indians. Grumet, *The Munsee Indians*, 13, 293n10; Schutt, *Peoples of the River Valleys*, 3; Newman, *On Records*, 10–11.

22. For much of the seventeenth century, Lenapes dominated trade and managed a multinational Delaware Valley society that included Swedish, Finnish, and other European colonists, as described in Jean Soderlund's *Lenape Country*. Penn's "holy experiment" is discussed in multiple sources, including Bronner, *William Penn's Holy Experiment*; Harper, *Promised Land*; Kenny, *Peaceable Kingdom Lost*; Marsh, *A Lenape among the Quakers*; Merrell, *Into the American Woods*; Pencak and Richter, *Friends and Enemies in Penn's Woods*; Wallace, *King of the Delawares*. Munsees and Lenapes established or joined settlements at Wyoming, Wyalusing, Tioga, and Ochquaga along the Susquehanna River. Grumet, *The Munsee Indians*, 251–52. On the multinational nature of these towns, see Folts, "The Munsee Delawares." The history of the Lenape, Munsee, and Delaware involvement in the Seven Years' and Revolutionary Wars is beyond the scope of this book. Today, people

of Lenape descent live in "virtually every state," with concentrations in Ontario, Wisconsin, and Oklahoma. Brown and Kohn, eds, *Long Journey Home*, xxiv–vii.

23. Soderlund, *Lenape Country*, 184–85. The Walking Purchase is the subject of a literature that spans centuries. For reviews of sources, see Newman, *On Records*, chapter 4; Jennings, *The Ambiguous Iroquois Empire*. Soderlund notes that the vast tract obtained by Penn's sons "had preserved a homeland for Munsees and Lenapes as they sold much of central and northwestern New Jersey and southeastern Pennsylvania to land-hungry whites" (*Lenape Country*, 184).

24. "Iroquois" was an ethnonym used by the French, derived possibly from a Mohegan word meaning "real snakes." It was in widespread use in English by the 1700s. "Haudenosaunee" is the preferred autonym. See Hewitt, "Etymology of the Word Iroquois"; McCarthy, *In Divided Unity*, xvi, 54–55; translation of Haudenosaunee in George-Kanentiio's *Iroquois Culture and Commentary*, 9.

25. Hill, *The Clay We Are Made Of*, 3.

26. Hill, *The Clay We Are Made Of*, 5.

27. Hill, *The Clay We Are Made Of*, 5 (list adapted from table 1); Seneca orthography in John, *Seneca People*, x.

28. On the origins of the Confederacy and the Great Law of Peace, see Hill, *The Clay We Are Made Of*; George-Kanentiio, *Iroquois Culture and Commentary*, 9–28. See also Graymont, *The Iroquois*, 6. Classic works also include Fenton, *The Great Law*.

29. Grumet, *Historic Contact*, 334.

30. On the longhouse metaphor rendered in different Haudenosaunee languages, see Fenton, "Northern Iroquoian Cultural Patterns," 320.

31. Confederacy nations endured the Queen Anne, King George's, and the French and Indian Wars. Graymont, *The Iroquois*, 29; Grumet, *Historic Contact*, 344. See Hill, *The Clay We Are Made Of*, chapter 3, for a Haudenosaunee-centered account of contact times. On Iroquois skill at diplomacy, see Oberg, *Peacemakers*; Parmenter, *Edge of the Woods*; Merrell, *Into the American Woods*; Shannon, *Indians and Colonists*; Wallace, *King of the Delawares*; Jennings, *The Ambiguous Iroquois Empire*.

32. The Covenant Chain is discussed by many; a useful starting place is Jennings, *The Ambiguous Iroquois Empire*, 8–10, 43. Jennings reproduces a 1744 Native oral history of the agreement presented by Onondaga chief Canassatego, 357–59. See also Haan, "Covenant and Consensus."

33. Calloway, *The American Revolution*, 31.

34. An estimated sixty thousand whites had violated the Treaty of Fort Stanwix by 1773. Hill, *The Clay We Are Made Of*, 126.

35. The Oneidas faced an existential threat due to white settler encroachment and designs on their territory; the Mohawks, as the easternmost nation, faced the largest influx of British people, and by the mid–eighteenth century had adopted European material culture. The western-based Seneca nation was less hemmed in and utilized hunting grounds as far as the Ohio Valley. McCarthy, *In Divided Unity*, 110–12.

36. At a Council held in October 1774, Confederacy members decided to retain their alliance with the British. After the Second Continental Congress organized an Indian department to compete directly with the British Indian administration, each side held meetings, throughout 1775 and 1776, designed to bring the powerful Confederacy forces to their side of the conflict. Graymont, *The Iroquois*, 39–65.

37. Graymont, *The Iroquois*, 113.

38. Graymont, *The Iroquois*, 138. At least three dozen Senecas were killed at Oriskany, including six chiefs. The Confederacy was further fragmented following a council held in Albany on September 14, 1777, at which Oneidas, Tuscaroras, and a few Onondaga and Mohawk participants pledged to support the Americans. For a detailed look at the Battle of Oriskany, see Abler, *Cornplanter*, 83–91; Glatthaar and Martin, *Forgotten Allies*, 168–69.

39. Graymont, *The Iroquois*, 155–56.

40. Graymont, *The Iroquois*, 193.

41. Calloway, *The Indian World*, 247.

42. "George Washington to John Sullivan," GWP.

43. Glatthaar and Martin, *Forgotten Allies*, 243.

44. Calloway, *The Indian World*, 235–59.

45. Kurt Jordan provides a table of the Seneca homes destroyed by the Sullivan Expedition in *The Seneca Restoration, 1715–1754*, table 6.3, 189. For an effort at quantifying the human and material losses due to Washington's onslaughts, see Koehler, "Hostile Nations." Helpful tallies are also in The Public Archaeology Facility's CBP and NBP. The number of towns Brodhead destroyed was estimated at ten or eleven towns; see Abler, *Cornplanter*, 52; Calloway, *The Indian World*, 255.

46. Norton, *History of Sullivan's Campaign*, makes this point. McAdams, "The Sullivan Expedition," and Fischer, *A Well-Executed Failure*, 6–8, review debates about the expedition's long-term strategic impact.

47. Fischer, *A Well-Executed Failure*. Mintz suggests that Washington's reception of Sullivan was cold and noted that Sullivan resigned three days after the mission was completed. Mintz, *Seeds of Empire*, 154.

48. Downes, *Council Fires*, 259.

49. Graymont, *The Iroquois*, 220, 223–46.

50. Calloway, *The Indian World*, 257.

51. Ryan, *Crowding the Banks*, 1–18.

52. Morgan, *League of the Iroquois*. Wallace, *Death and Rebirth*, and Fenton, "Northern Iroquoian Cultural Patterns," perpetuated this narrative of decline and imagined an "authentic" Iroquois lifestyle relegated to the distant past. Their work has been roundly criticized by many. See McCarthy, *In Divided Unity*, chapter 1; Simpson, *Mohawk Interruptus*, 86–94; Ryan, *Crowding the Banks*, 1–17.

53. Venables, *The Six Nations of New York*, xii; Graymont, "New York State Indian Policy," 376.

54. Mt. Pleasant, *After the Whirlwind*, 89–103; Ryan, "Crowding the Banks." These points are developed further in chapters 5–7.

55. Hauptman, *Conspiracy of Interests*.

56. "The Speech of the Cornplanter, Half-Town, and Great-Tree, Chiefs and Councillors of the Seneca Nation to the Great Councillor of the Thirteen Fires," in Abler, *Chainbreaker*, 238. See Calloway, *The Indian World*, 397–404, for additional context for these meetings.

57. Kent and Deardorff, "John Adlum on the Allegheny," 459; see Cook, *Journals of the Military Expedition*, 279.

58. Glatthaar and Martin, *Forgotten Allies*, 244.

59. Graymont, *The Iroquois*, 219–20.

60. Calloway, *The Indian World*, 253; Graymont, *The Iroquois*, 196.

61. Fischer, "The Forgotten Campaign."

62. Butterfield, "History at its Headwaters," 137.

63. LCHS, *Warrior Road* (CD).

64. The 1929 monolith was first placed on Bushkill Drive but relocated to Sullivan Trail (Route 115) with the construction of Route 22. *Morning Call* (Allentown PA), February 19, 1998, 33.

65. Elkins and Pedersen, *Settler Colonialism*; Johnston and Lawson, "Settler Colonies"; Coombes, ed., *Rethinking Settler Colonialism*; Stasiulis and Yuval-Davis, *Unsettling Settler Societies*; Veracini, *Settler Colonialism*; Veracini, *The Settler Colonial Present*; Wolfe, *Settler Colonialism*; Wolfe, "Structure and Event."

66. Wolfe, "Structure and Event," 103; Russell, *Colonial Frontiers*, 2.

67. Wolfe, *Settler Colonialism*, 163.

68. Wolfe, "Structure and Event," 120.

69. Jacobs, *White Mother to a Dark Race*; Jacobs, "Parallel or Intersecting Tracks?"; Stasiulis and Yuval-Davis, *Unsettling Settler Societies*; Veracini, *Settler Colonialism*; Moses, *Genocide and Settler Society*.

70. Wolfe, "Structure and Event," 103–4.

71. Revolutions in historiography are not always peaceful, and "history wars" often follow paradigm shifts encouraged by new theory. On battles over Australia's past, Attwood, *Telling the Truth*.

72. Dahl, *Empire of the People*; Ostler, *Surviving Genocide*; Hixson, *American Settler Colonialism*; Fujikane and Okamura, *Asian Settler Colonialism*; Blackhawk, *Violence over the Land*.

73. Simpson, *Mohawk Interruptus*, 11.

74. Said, *Culture and Imperialism*, 12.

75. Rifkin, *Settler Common Sense*.

76. Kosasa, "Sites of Erasure," 196.

77. Kosasa, "Sites of Erasure," 196, 197.

78. Palmié and Stewart, "Introduction," 207.

79. The discipline of history developed a methodology that was consolidated in the nineteenth century and which has become an authoritative approach to the past, one that revolves around the systematic amassing of culturally neutral "facts" that are discovered and verified according to scientific methods. Nabokov, "Native Views of History," 3; Novick, *That Noble Dream*. Palmié and Stewart, in "Introduction," discuss the hegemonic place of Western historical methods, which they term "historicism," 210.

80. Samuel, *Theatres of Memory*, 8.

81. Popular Memory Group, "Popular Memory," 207.

82. The English translation of *La mémoire collective* appeared in 1980, and portions of *Les Cadres* were published in the 1992 volume by Halbwachs and Coser, *On Collective Memory*.

83. Halbwachs and Coser, *On Collective Memory*, 57.

84. Important literature reviews include Stewart, "Historicity and Anthropology"; Shryock, Palmié and Stewart, "Introduction"; Munn, "The Cultural Anthropology of Time"; see also Hristova et al, "Memory Worlds"; and Erll and Nünning, *A Companion to Cultural Memory Studies*.

85. Irwin-Zarecka, *Frames of Remembrance*; Zerubavel, *An Invitation to Cognitive Sociology*.

86. That there are multiple memories, multiple forms of historical consciousness, and multiple temporalities (or "temporal multiplicity") is a given in much of this literature. Societies without writing have developed a host of mnemonic devices to assist in

remembering and recording past events, including wampum beads, paintings and other artwork, and specialists trained in skilled orality, who may memorize knowledge verbatim with narrations that can last days and can be preserved across the centuries. See Tonkin, *Narrating Our Pasts*; Bloch, *How We Think They Think*; Basso, *Wisdom Sits in Places*. Mark Rifkin makes an erudite plea for recognizing multiple temporal formations and allowing for Indigenous "temporal sovereignty," which in my view should be a starting point for any serious study of historical consciousness. See Rifkin's *Beyond Settler Time*, 25; on "temporal multiplicity," see Lyons, *X-marks*, 13.

87. Assmann, *Moses the Egyptian*, 9. Examples of long-standing preservation of histories in oral tradition abound. See Tonkin, *Narrating our Pasts*; Shryock, *Nationalism and the Genealogical Imagination*.

88. Popular Memory Group, "Popular Memory," 207.

89. Brow, "Notes on Community"; Hobsbawm and Ranger, *The Invention of Tradition*.

90. Smith, *Decolonizing Methodologies*, 35.

91. Popular Memory Group, "Popular Memory," 207.

92. See "Introduction" in Seixas, *Theorizing Historical Consciousness*. Bruyneel prefers "settler memory" for a similar concept. See "Codename Geronimo."

93. "Historical consciousness" is a phrase with a lengthy genealogy. In some formulations, it refers to a particular stage in Western development as a "marker of Western civilization." See Koselleck, *Futures*; Rüsen, *Western Historical Thinking*, ix. To avoid the evolutionary thinking implied by such an interpretation, some anthropologists prefer "historicity" to "historical consciousness." In his masterful review, Charles Stewart traces the notion that different societies will have different cultural frameworks for "perceiving and representing the past" to Lévi-Strauss (*The Savage Mind*). See Stewart, "Historicity and Anthropology," 81–82. "Historicity" was later used by Marshall Sahlins, who famously wrote, "different cultures, different historicities" (*Islands of History*, x). Emiko Ohnuki-Tierney also points out that "historicity" avoids assumptions of conscious awareness of the past. See Ohnuki-Tierney, *Cultures through Time*, 19. While Palmié and Stewart prefer the term "historicity," they find it similar to "historical consciousness"; see "Introduction," 223. In this book I prefer the latter term for its cross-disciplinary use value.

94. Some scholars apply terms such as "mythology," "folklore," or "memory" to the pasts of non-Western societies, but not their own. The "great divide" between native orality and European literacy is discussed and complicated by Newman's *On Records*, 3–5.

95. Stasiulis and Yuval-Davis, *Unsettling Settler Societies*, 11.

96. Attwood, "Denial in a Settler Society," 24, 29. On violence, see Blackhawk, *Violence over the Land*.

97. Veracini, "Settler Collective," 366.

98. Steven Conn notes that after such a focus of early American scholarship, by the 1890s, "American scholars moved Indians out of progressive history and into cyclical history." *History's Shadow*, 33. See also Bruyneel, *The Third Space*; Deloria, *Custer Died for Your Sins*, 2, 225; Rifkin, *Beyond Settler Time*. Historians keep trying to address systematic erasure of Native Americans from the dominant American narrative. Important contributions include Dunbar-Ortiz, *An Indigenous Peoples' History*; Sleeper-Smith et al., *Why You Can't Teach*. See also Blackhawk, "The Iron Cage of Erasure"; Richter, *Facing East*.

99. Dahl, *Empire of the People*, 4. Wolfe, "Structure and Event," 113; Stoler, *Imperial Debris*, 128.

100. Binarism is discussed at length in colonial studies. See Memmi, *The Colonizer and the Colonized*; Cooper and Stoler, *Tensions of Empire*. A useful synthesis is in Bruyneel, *The Third Space*, 6–8.

101. Documenting this tendency to place Native Americans out of time could fill volumes; the "inability to deal with Indian people" is in Deloria, *Playing Indian*, 5; Deloria, *Custer Died for Your Sins*, 2; Rifkin, *Beyond Settler Time*, 5–9.

102. O'Brien, *Firsting and Lasting*.

103. O'Brien, *Firsting and Lasting*, xv.

104. O'Brien, *Firsting and Lasting*.

105. As she writes, "Whether famous or anonymous, the notion of the solitary Indian survivor captured non-Indian imaginations through the nineteenth century." O'Brien, *Firsting and Lasting*, 116. On the "vanishing Indian" syndrome, Dippie, *The Vanishing American*.

106. Along with other works already cited, a terrific review of studies of settler-colonial literature is in Johnston and Lawson, "Settler Colonies." An excellent ethnography is Furniss, *The Burden of History*.

107. Doss, *Memorial Mania*, 2.

108. The phrase "site of memory" is often associated with French historian Pierre Nora's extensive *lieux de mémoire* project (Nora, *Les Lieux de Mémoire*). Nora's project is less helpful for us here as he makes a distinction between sites of memory of premodern and modern France, and even uses distinct terminology for each type (*milieux* versus *lieux*), suggesting a lurking evolutionary model (Nora, "Between Memory and History"). I find Jay Winter's definition of a site of memory more useful, "physical sites where commemorative acts take place." Winter, "Sites of Memory," 61.

109. Connerton, *How Modernity Forgets*, 11, 35.

110. On the significance of museums and historic sites, see Rosenzweig and Thelen, *The Presence of the Past*, 20, 105; Ames, *Cannibal Tours*; Handler and Gable, *The New History*; Schlereth, *Cultural History and Material Culture*. On the need for theorization of historic sites, see Loewen, *Lies across America*, 15.

111. Michalski dates the rise of the public political monument at the end of the Middle Ages; however, any cursory exploration of global history reveals much earlier examples. Michalski, *Public Monuments*; Kammen, *Mystic Chords of Memory*, 37.

112. Pessard, Gustave, *Statuomanie Parisienne*, (Paris: H. Daragon, 1912), cited in Michalski, *Public Monuments*, 44; Kammen, *Mystic Chords of Memory*, 33.

113. European commemorative and aesthetic trends traveled to the United States, albeit with a time lag of about two generations. Kammen, *Mystic Chords of Memory*, 37.

114. Kammen, *Mystic Chords of Memory*, 44.

115. Kammen, *Mystic Chords of Memory*, 53.

116. Kammen, *Mystic Chords of Memory*, 53.

117. Kammen, *Mystic Chords of Memory*, 54–55.

118. Glassberg, *Sense of History*, 272.

119. Loewen planned to read every historical marker in the country, but stopped once he reached the state of Texas, which had nearly 12,000 markers in 1990. *Lies across America*, 455–56.

120. Loewen, *Lies across America*, 16.

121. Loewen, *Lies across America*, 15–50; Levin, *Defining Memory*; Smith, "Settler Historical Consciousness," 156–72.

122. Loewen, *Lies across America*, 1.

123. Loewen, *Lies across America*, 36.

124. Folts, "Sullivan Campaign."

125. Anthropologist Geoffrey White's ethnographic study of the Pearl Harbor National Memorial, which takes a processual and longitudinal approach, is exemplary. White, *Memorializing Pearl Harbor.*

126. Robyn Autry also develops a concept of "memory entrepreneur" in her excellent work on revisionist historiography in South Africa and the United States. Her application differs from mine in that she uses the concept to refer to revisionist activists who are advancing inclusive agendas. See Autry, *Desegregating the Past*, 27–28.

127. On "undifferentiated elites," see Strange, "The Battlefields of Personal and Public Memory," 198.

128. Some of the memory entrepreneurs in this study defy easy categorization, especially in the early years, when wealthy nonvoting women were involved. My findings complicate the "vernacular" vs. "official" public memory dichotomy developed by John Bodnar in *Remaking America*, for instance.

129. I could not consider every project in this volume. Some sites I do not consider here merit their own dedicated study, including the complex surrounding the "torture tree" in Cuylersville NY.

130. Zerubavel, *Social Mindscapes*, 97.

131. Connerton, *How Societies Remember*, 44, 58.

132. Connerton, *How Societies Remember*, 65.

133. Connerton, *How Modernity Forgets.*

134. Smith and Eisenstein, *Rebuilding Shattered Worlds.*

135. Connerton, *How Modernity Forgets.*

136. My use of *story* is much like *myth* in the cultural memory literature and like that employed by Richard Slotkin in his magisterial work on the frontier myth. For Jan Assman, *myth* is narrative that has consolidated and repeated over time: "History turns into myth," Assmann writes, "as soon as it is remembered, narrated, and used, that is, woven into the fabric of the present." In his work on Moses, Assmann is not interested in whether Moses was, in fact, an Egyptian, but instead examines where, when, and how he was presented as such. He contrasts this goal with that of the classic historian, which "consists in separating the historical from the mythical elements in memory." As he puts it, the "truth" of a given memory lies not so much in its "factuality" as in its "actuality." Assmann, *Moses the Egyptian*, 9–10. Similarly, Richard Slotkin writes that the frontier myths he studies "are stories, drawn from history . . . historical experience is preserved in the form of narrative; and through periodic retellings those narratives become traditionalized. These formal qualities and structures are increasingly conventionalized and abstracted." Slotkin, *The Fatal Environment*, 16.

137. Trouillot, *Silencing the Past*, 27.

138. Trouillot, *Silencing the Past*, 26–7.

139. Trouillot, *Silencing the Past*, 27.

140. White, "Historical Pluralism."

141. Zerubavel, *Time Maps*, 87.

142. Zerubavel, *Time Maps*, 92.

143. Trouillot, *Silencing the Past*. On narrative emplotment, 6; on moments of silencing, 26–27.

144. Zerubavel, *Time Maps*, 93–94.

145. Zerubavel, *Time Maps*, 97–100.

146. Brooks, *Our Beloved Kin*, 6.

147. Brooks, *Our Beloved Kin*, 8.

148. Brooks, *Our Beloved Kin*, 346, 302.

149. Calloway, *The Indian World*, 247.

150. See part 3.

151. Alert readers will have noted that I have already "contained" the story at the start of this chapter!

152. On the flexible ideology of the "noble savage," Deloria, *Playing Indian*, 4; see also Berkhofer, *The White Man's Indian*.

153. Parker, "The Indian Interpretation." Arthur Parker's Seneca ancestry is discussed in chap. 7, note 69.

154. Feld and Basso, *Senses of Place*.

155. DeLucia, *Memory Lands*, 3. She develops Jonathan Boyarin's memoryscape concept, a constellation of spots on the land that have accrued stories over time; Boyarin, *Space, Time, and the Politics*; see also Cardina and Rodrigues, "The Mnemonic Transition."

156. On Haudenosaunee sites of memory, see George-Kanentiio, *Iroquois Culture and Commentary*, 28–30; Anderson, *The Storied Landscape of Iroquoia*; and especially the oral histories collected in The Public Archaeology Facility's NBP and CBP archives.

157. Alonso, "The Effects of Truth"; Popular Memory Group, "Popular Memory," 207.

158. On Ray Tehanetorens Fadden's travels with young Haudenosaunee students, see Broadrose, "Memory Spaces."

159. See CBP and NBP.

160. Ferguson and Colwell, *History Is in the Land*, 6.

161. Cameron, *Far off Metal River*, 27, 15.

162. Rifkin, *Beyond Settler Time*, 26.

163. Smith, *Decolonizing Methodologies*.

164. Alyssa Mt. Pleasant, personal communication, October 10, 2020. The recent public archaeology projects on the Chemung and Newtown battlefields offer important compilations of Haudenosaunee accounts of the expedition. See CBP and NBP.

165. Cameron, *Far off Metal River*, 14.

166. This phrase is from Zerubavel, *Time Maps*, 92.

1. Yankee Insurgency

1. "Gift of the DAR," *Easton (PA) Daily Free Press*, June 18, 1900, 3.

2. Margaret Mildred Stone Conway was born in Fredericksburg, Virginia, where she met Francis March. The couple married in 1860 and moved to Easton, where they raised nine children. March, "Biographical Note," 20.

3. On difficulties getting volunteers for the Pennsylvania militia, see Fischer, *A Well-Executed Failure*, 157–81; Jennings, "The Bicentennial," 299; Craft's "Historical Address" in Cook, *Journals of the Military Expedition of Major General John Sullivan*.

4. Cook, *Journals of the Military Expedition*, 446.

5. Moyer, *Wild Yankees*, 16–17.

6. Mancall, *Valley of Opportunity*, chapter 1.

7. See Mancall, *Valley of Opportunity*, 27–46 for detailed discussions of regional Native settlement histories.

8. Mancall, *Valley of Opportunity*, 30–36; Wallace, *King of the Delawares*, 48–51.

9. Mancall, *Valley of Opportunity*, 39–40. An exceptional discussion of the multinational Chemung Valley region of the Susquehanna that includes village population estimates is Jim Folts, "The Munsee Delawares."

10. Wallace, *King of the Delawares*, 48–50, 53.

11. Bright, *Native American Place Names*, 576.

12. This controversy is discussed at length in Miner, *History of Wyoming*. The Susquehannah Company was a joint-stock company based in Windham CT. They also created the First and Second Delaware Companies. Mancall, *Valley of Opportunity*, 76–77; Moyer, *Wild Yankees*, 16–17.

13. Moyer, *Wild Yankees*, 18.

14. On the Albany Congress, see Shannon, *Indians and Colonists*.

15. Moyer, *Wild Yankees*, 19–20; Merrell, *Into the American Woods*, 15. By the mid-eighteenth century there were clear practices to follow in order to purchase Indian land. Since these lands were considered "tribal trusts," the entire group that controlled them needed to agree. Company envoy John Lydius ignored protocol and instead got a few individuals drunk to sign away the land. Six Nations leaders saw the agreement as fraudulent. Mancall, *Valley of Opportunity*, 77–78.

16. The origins of the seventeenth-century allegation that the Five Nations had won the Susquehanna Valley by conquest over the Susquehannocks is outlined in Jennings, *The Ambiguous Iroquois Empire*, 228–30.

17. Wallace, *King of the Delawares*, 184–85. Teedyuscung was born near present-day Trenton NJ. His epic life story, including participation in the Seven Years' War and protests of the 1737 Walking Purchase, is outlined in Wallace.

18. Mancall, *Valley of Opportunity*, 86–87; Wallace, *King of the Delawares*, 258–59.

19. Wallace noted that although the Six Nations are often blamed for the fire, it was in their interest for him to remain alive to help protect their land. *King of the Delawares*, 259–61; Moyer, *Wild Yankees*, 22.

20. In the Proclamation of 1763, settlers were asked to stay east of the crest of the Appalachian Mountains, an agreement that proved impossible to enforce. Mancall, *Valley of Opportunity*, 90. On the implication of the 1763 treaty in the settler revolt that become the American Revolution, Rana, *The Two Faces*, 5–7; and Dahl, *Empire of the People*, 30.

21. The Fort Stanwix Treaty meeting was a massive affair involving over 2,200 Native people, the superintendent of Indian Affairs, dignitaries, and colonial leaders seeking land in central NY and PA. See Mancall, *Valley of Opportunity*, 90–94.

22. Miner, *History of Wyoming*, 108.

23. Ousterhout, "Frontier Vengeance," 339.

24. Moyer, *Wild Yankees*, 31.

25. Moyer, *Wild Yankees*, 51–52; Ousterhout, *A State Divided*, 245.

26. Kenny, *Peaceable Kingdom Lost*, 19; Ousterhout, *A State Divided*, 247.

27. For a clear account of Penn's land policies, see Kenny, *Peaceable Kingdom Lost*, 18–20.

28. Kenny, *Peaceable Kingdom Lost*, 19.

29. Murray, *A History of Old Tioga Point*, 235.

30. For a discussion of the different kinds of Susquehannah Company land rights, see Murray, *A History*, 230.

31. Rana, *The Two Faces*, 11.

32. This ideology combined ethnic nationalism, Protestant theology, and the seventeenth-century English republican ideals that saw economic independence through land ownership as the basis of free citizenship. As Rana points out, the "engine" of these freedoms was a territorial expansion that required "free" lands obtained by force and deception. Rana, *The Two Faces*, 12.

33. Parallels with the Pennamite-Yankee conflict and that between the Vermont independence movement and New York's landed elite are striking. The writers of the Vermont Constitution declared independence from both New York and the British Empire, claiming that the governors of New York used fraud and deceit to make "unjust claims to those lands." See Dahl, *Empire of the People*, 51–54.

34. Ousterhout, *A State Divided*, 246.

35. Kenny, *Peaceable Kingdom Lost*, 143–44; on the attack on Conestoga Indiantown, 140–46. Merrell, *Into the American Woods*, 284–88. See also Gordon, "The Paxton Boys" and "Yoked by Violence."

36. Meier, "Devoted to Hardships"; Moyer, *Wild Yankees*, 27. After Stewart killed Nathan Ogden, Northampton County deputy sheriff and brother of Amos Ogden, a Pennsylvanian who had a trading post in the Valley since the mid-1760s, the gang hid out in Connecticut, where they were offered refuge and even an allowance. Meier, "Devoted to Hardships," 62; Kenny, *Peaceable Kingdom Lost*, 224–25.

37. Wallace, *King of the Delawares*, 265.

38. The next year the Connecticut Assembly converted Westmoreland into a county located outside the state. Moyer, *Wild Yankees*, 41.

39. Ousterhout, "Frontier Vengeance," 338.

40. Moyer, *Wild Yankees*, 41.

41. Ousterhout, "Frontier Vengeance," 340–42.

42. Ousterhout, "Frontier Vengeance," 339.

43. Ousterhout, *A State Divided*, 239.

44. Moyer, *Wild Yankees*, 51.

45. Ousterhout, "Frontier Vengeance," 344, 347; Moyer, *Wild Yankees*, 51.

46. Ousterhout prefers "disaffected" to "loyalist" as the latter usage didn't appear in Pennsylvania until later in the war, and the former shifts attention from Britain to the colonies. *A State Divided*, 3–5.

47. Ousterhout, "Frontier Vengeance," 337, 348; Ousterhout, *A State Divided*, 5.

48. Ousterhout, *A State Divided*, 240–41.

49. Excellent summaries of this battle can be found in Graymont, *The Iroquois*, 167–74; and Mintz, *Seeds of Empire*, 44–56.

50. Glatthaar and Martin, *Forgotten Allies*, 222.

51. On troops present, see Mintz, *Seeds of Empire*, 55–57.

52. Graymont, *The Iroquois*, 167–74; Mintz, *Seeds of Empire*, 56–57. Zebulon Butler was not directly related to the British officer with the same surname.

53. For a detailed account of the battle, see Miner, *History of Wyoming*, 219–28. Miner, 242–44, includes a list of the dead.

54. For articles of capitulation, see Graymont, *The Iroquois*, 171.

55. John Butler wrote that the only people his men killed were those in arms. He first identified 301 patriots dead, and later, 376. On this discrepancy, see Graymont, *The Iroquois*, 171. On the British side, the losses were "killed one Indian, two Rangers and eight Indians wounded," in Graymont 172; Glatthaar and Martin, *Forgotten Allies*, 222.

56. Parkinson, *The Common Cause*, 412–13.

57. Parkinson, *The Common Cause*, 413, 414–15.

58. Esther Montour is often connected to the Montour family, with Andrew Montour and his mother, "Madam Montour," famed eighteenth-century interpreters and "go-betweens." Esther may be the daughter of Margaret, sister of Catherine, and granddaughter of Madame Montour, although the lineage is in some dispute as Moravian sources describe her as originally Shawnee. Laubach, "Queen Esther Montour of the Munsee Delaware," 48–50. On Andrew Montour, see Merrell, *Into the American Woods*. Miner reproduces oral testimonies he gathered from two purported survivors of these attacks, Lebbeus Hammond and Joseph Elliott. Miner, *History of Wyoming*, 226, appendix 53–55. Two recent theses explore the extant documentary evidence and conclude that stories of Esther's violent acts were likely fantastical tales. Laubach, "Queen Esther Montour"; see also Tharp, "Savage and Bloody Footsteps." On the braining motif found in early American literature, see Newman, *Allegories of Encounter*, 66–73.

59. Silver, *Our Savage Neighbors*.

60. Silver, *Our Savage Neighbors*, 44, 41, 69.

61. Silver, *Our Savage Neighbors*, 45.

62. Silver, *Our Savage Neighbors*, 74, 78

63. Silver, *Our Savage Neighbors*, 80.

64. Silver, *Our Savage Neighbors*, 83.

65. Silver, *Our Savage Neighbors*, 84.

66. Silver, *Our Savage Neighbors*, 86, 94

67. Parkinson, *The Common Cause*.

68. Parkinson, *The Common Cause*, 21.

69. Parkinson, *The Common Cause*, 21.

70. Andrlik, "The Twenty-five Deadliest Battles."

71. Parkinson, *The Common Cause*, 21. The story of the death of Jane McCrea, an American woman presumably killed by Indians outside Fort Edward in 1777, is similar in that some say it fanned enlistments and may have helped win the Battle of Saratoga. Parkinson, *The Common Cause*, 339–50; Engels and Goodale, "Our Battle Cry," 93.

72. Ousterhout notes that while Wyoming Valley historian Charles Miner claimed that many of the disaffected moved to the Wyalusing area *after* the conflict with the British, she foun..d that it was the other way around. Many of these people were on the tax rolls between 1770 and 1776, well before the conflict was underway. *A State Divided*, 244–45.

73. Murray, *A History*, 310.

74. Bradsby, *History of Luzerne County, Pennsylvania*, 114.

75. Ousterhout, *A State Divided*, 244; Graymont, *The Iroquois*, 171.

76. Harvey, *A History of Wilkes-Barre*, 995.

77. Graymont, *The Iroquois*, 171.

78. Taylor, *Susquehannah Company Papers* 7, xvii, 59–62.

79. Pennsylvania authorities approached Congress in November 1779. For a thorough discussion of this trial, see Taylor, *Susquehannah Company*, xvii–xxxiii; Moyer, *Wild Yankees*, 41–42.

80. Murray, *A History*, 227–28.

81. Moyer, *Wild Yankees*, 4–5.

82. Moyer, *Wild Yankees*, 56–60.

83. Moyer, *Wild Yankees*, 57.

84. Moyer, *Wild Yankees*, 78.

85. Moyer, *Wild Yankees*, 79–80.

86. Moyer, *Wild Yankees*, 102.

87. Moyer, *Wild Yankees*, 68.

88. Moyer, *Wild Yankees*, 69.

89. Moyer, *Wild Yankees*, 68.

90. For a riveting account of Pickering's capture and the aftermath, see Moyer, *Wild Yankees*, 65–93.

91. Reconciliation between the Yankees and the state of Pennsylvania was achieved in the courts with cases that concluded in 1827. Moyer, *Wild Yankees*, 179; Murray, *A History*, 233.

92. Even when wealthier Connecticut families were relinquishing claims and purchasing Pennsylvania titles, land agents in the backcountry were still being scared off by gunfire. Franklin was also elected representative to the state legislature multiple times (1795, 1796, 1799–1803). Moyer, *Wild Yankees*, 151, 117–18.

93. Moyer, *Wild Yankees*, 179–82.

94. There are several accounts penned from a Yankee perspective. Miner is unapologetic about his partiality. *History of Wyoming*, 478.

95. Davies, *The Anthracite Aristocracy*.

96. Davies, *The Anthracite Aristocracy*, 26–32.

97. Miner, *History of Wyoming*, appendix, 69.

98. *Wyoming Herald* (Wilkes-Barre PA), July 11, 1832, 2, emphasis added.

99. *Wyoming Herald* (Wilkes-Barre PA), July 11, 1832, 2.

100. This was likely Reverend Nicholas Murray, pastor of the churches of Wilkes-Barre and Kingston from 1829–33. Bradsby, *History of Luzerne County*, 429.

101. Gruesome English practices in early Massachusetts included drawing, quartering, and beheading. Brooks, *Our Beloved Kin*.

102. The Ladies' Monumental Association changed its name to the Wyoming Monument Association (WMA) in 1860. This organization still owns and maintains the monument, which is located on an acre lot at the corner of Wyoming Avenue and Susquehanna Street in the Township of Wyoming. "New Wyoming Monument Marker Will Be Erected by State Board," *Wilkes-Barre (PA) Record*, June 6, 1952; "Wyoming Battle," *Republican Farmer and Democratic Journal* (Wilkes-Barre PA), May 31, 1843, 3. Both in WMF, LCHS.

103. Several graveside memorials to wartime generals took this form, as did many large-scale memorials, starting with the Bunker Hill Memorial (1825–42). The obelisk (rather than statuary) was viewed by many as more appropriate for commemorating universal ideals. Giguere, *Memorial Architecture*, 103. See also Purcell, "Commemoration, Public Art, and the Changing Meaning."

104. Kammen, *Mystic Chords of Memory*, 105–6.

105. "Wyoming Centennial," *Daily Times* (Scranton PA), July 18, 1878. News clipping in "Wyoming Memorial Battle and Massacre Scrapbook, 1778–1878" (hereafter, WMBMS), 2.

106. "Keep their Memory Green," *Daily Times* (Scranton PA), July 4, 1877, WMBMS, 1.

107. "Wyoming Centennial," news clipping, no source, July 18, 1877, WMBMS, 2.

108. "Wyoming's Centennial," news clipping, no source, December 25, 1877, WMBMS, 6.

109. Journal of Lieutenant-Colonel Henry Dearborn, in Cook, *Journals of the Military Expedition*, 64.

110. "Wyoming Massacre," news clipping, no source, November 12, 1877, WMBMS, 5.

111. "Wyoming Massacre," news clipping, no source, November 12, 1877, WMBMS, 5.

112. "Wyoming Centennial," *Boston (MA) Post*, July 4, 1778, 2.

113. "Wyoming," *Record of the Times* (Wilkes-Barre PA), July 4, 1878, 1.

114. "Wyoming," *Daily Times* (Scranton PA), July 4, 1878, WMBMS, 37.

115. "Wyoming," *Daily Times* (Scranton PA), July 4, 1878, WMBMS, 38.

116. Steuben Jenkins, a descendant of Wyoming Valley icon John Jenkins and Rev. W. P. Abbott of New York City, "a descendant of the brave patriots of 1778," gave orations. "Wyoming," *Daily Times* (Scranton PA), July 4, 1878, WMBMS, 39.

117. "Wyoming," *Daily Times* (Scranton PA), July 4, 1878, WMBMS, 37.

118. "Immortal Wyoming," *The Republican* (Scranton PA), July 4, 1878, WMBMS, 57.

119. "Immortal Wyoming."

120. "Immortal Wyoming."

121. "The Fourth," news clipping, unknown source, WMBMS, 87.

122. "Summing up the Result," *Daily Times* (Scranton PA), July 9, 1879, WMBMS, 47; Wyoming Commemorative Association, 3. From 1877 to 1929 presidencies were under the guidance of three descendants of Col. George Dorrance, the person "highest in rank of those who fell in the battle." Wilcox, "The Story of Wyoming," 8.

123. On settler disavowal of foundational violence, see Veracini, *Settler Colonialism*, 79–82, and "Settler Collective."

124. Eviatar Zerubavel, *The Elephant in the Room*, 53.

125. Silver, *Our Savage Neighbors*, 85.

126. Campbell's epic poem, *Gertrude of Wyoming*, helped popularize the Wyoming battle story, and "Wyoming" was adopted as place-name for the territory and later state of Wyoming. Bright, *Native American Placenames*, 576–77.

127. On the enduring stereotypes of warlike Iroquois and their use of the tomahawk in early American writings and artwork, see Stevens, "Tomahawk." Deloria suggests that there may regional "unevenness" in non-Indian expectations about Indians. Continued engagement by Anglo-Americans in ceremonies that disseminate savagist stereotypes may play an important role in determining such variation. See *Indians in Unexpected Places*, 49.

128. Paxton, "Remembering and Forgetting," 190.

129. Engels and Goodale, "Our Battle Cry," 109.

130. O'Brien, *Firsting and Lasting*, 6.

2. Patriotic Women

1. "Mountain Monument. Interesting Exercises on the Wilkes-Barre Mountain," *Wilkes-Barre (PA) Semi-Weekly Record*, September 15, 1896, 5.

2. Kammen, *Mystic Chords of Memory*, 201–4.

3. Davies, *Patriotism on Parade*, 46. By 1895 forty-seven distinct patriotic organizations had been recorded, and this number grew to seventy by 1900. Davies, 44.

4. Davies, *Patriotism on Parade*, 1.

5. Davies, *Patriotism on Parade*, 77.

6. In the earliest years of the DAR, some members wanted to include collateral as well as lineal relatives, but opponents felt that this would open up the organization to Tories. Dissenters formed a splinter group in 1891. At the society's third Congress in 1894, DAR membership was limited to lineal descendants. Strange, "Sisterhood of Blood," 113–14.

7. Lamar, *A History of the National Society*, 31–33. There were two societies of Colonial Dames. The first, The Colonial Dames of America, was created in New York in 1890; a second, the Pennsylvania Society of the Colonial Dames of America, was formed in Phil-

adelphia in 1891. The latter organization ultimately created a national society with a DC headquarters. See Lamar, *A History of the National Society*, 19.

8. Davies, *Patriotism on Parade*, 103.

9. Davies, *Patriotism on Parade*, 77; Truesdell, "God, Home, and Country," 20.

10. See Jones and Meyer, *The Pledge*, 55–74; Morgan, "Home and Country," 7.

11. Kammen, *Mystic Chords*, 188–202.

12. *The Allentown (PA) Daily Leader*, June 18, 1900, 1; NSDAR,"George Taylor Chapter." The George Taylor chapter, named after a local signer of the Declaration of Independence, had been fundraising to purchase his former home. When this goal seemed unattainable, they began returning donations, in March 1900, only to shift gears to develop the Sullivan marker. *The Philadelphia Inquirer*, November 15, 1896, 39; *Harrisburg (PA) Telegraph*, March 7, 1900, 4.

13. "Gift of the DAR," *Easton (PA) Daily Free Press*, June 18, 1900, 3.

14. Morgan, "Home and Country," 161–62.

15. Morgan, "Home and Country," 159–70.

16. Kammen, *Mystic Chords*, 263.

17. Morgan, "Home and Country," 156.

18. Davies, *Patriotism on Parade*, 228–29.

19. Davies, *Patriotism on Parade*, 229–30.

20. Lamar, *A History of the National Society*, 28.

21. Morgan, "Home and Country," 154.

22. Morgan, "Home and Country," 159.

23. Davies, *Patriotism on Parade*, 48–49; Strange, "Sisterhood of Blood," 116, 121; Truesdell, "God, Home, and Country," 19.

24. Morgan, "Home and Country," 49–51.

25. Chujo, "The Daughters of the American Revolution," 160–64; Morgan, "Home and Country," 49–51.

26. Morgan, "Home and Country," 3. Many early DAR members were proponents of women's suffrage, and they may have found in organizations such as the DAR a way to insert themselves politically. Some scholars emphasize the increasingly conservative policies of the DAR in the early twentieth century, and Davies found an increased interest in restricting immigration, but minimal explicit connection to nativist groups. See Strange, "Sisterhood of Blood"; and Davies, *Patriotism on Parade*, 296–367; Truesdell, "God, Home, and Country," 156, 162.

27. "Conference Favors Purchase of Valley Forge Camp Site," *Harrisburg (PA) Telegraph*, October 24, 1901, 1.

28. Harned, *Pennsylvania State History of the Daughters of the American Revolution*, 251.

29. Lockwood and Rivière, eds. *Lineage Book*, 145–46.

30. "Mrs. Katherine S. McCartney," *Scranton (PA) Truth*, April 18, 1914.

31. "Points of Local History Wanted by the Daughters of the American Revolution," *Wilkes-Barre (PA) Record*, August 17, 1891.

32. "The Social News," *Wilkes-Barre (PA) Semi-Weekly Record*, February 26, 1892, 6; *Wilkes-Barre (PA) Times Leader*, July 3, 1895, 2.

33. *Wilkes-Barre (PA) Record*, July 10, 1895, 1; *Wyoming Democrat* (Tunkhannock PA), June 19, 1896, 2.

34. *Wilkes-Barre (PA) Semi-Weekly Record*, June 16, 1896, 7.

35. Public ceremony, Wyoming PA, July 4, 2018.

36. Urquhart, "Masonic Celebration," 56.

37. Urquhart, "Masonic Celebration," 71.

38. Slocum, *A Short History of the Slocums*, 238.

39. "The Fourth. Wyoming's Gala Day," WMBMS.

40. "Martha B. Phelps, Prominent Woman of This City Dies," *Wilkes-Barre (PA) Times Leader, the Evening News*, September 7, 1920, 1.

41. "Martha B. Phelps," *Wilkes-Barre (PA) Times Leader, the Evening News*, September 7, 1920, 1.

42. "Death of John C. Phelps," *Wilkes-Barre (PA) Record*, July 15, 1892, 1.

43. "Mountain Monument." This and subsequent passages are from this article. Jenkins's journal entry, included in the centennial publication edited by Cook, *Journals of the Military Expedition*, does not include these passages.

44. "Mountain Monument."

45. The story of Frances Slocum was a well-known captivity tale. Meginness, *Biography of Frances Slocum*; Buss, "They Found and Left Her an Indian." Martha Bennett Phelps published a book about Frances Slocum in 1906. Phelps, *Frances Slocum*.

46. "Mountain Monument."

47. Charles Slocum described Martha Phelps's great-grandfather, Jonathan Slocum, as a member of the Society of Friends and "kindly disposed toward the Indians," and "from principle a non-combatant." *A Short History of the Slocums*, 124.

48. Her eldest son, William G. Phelps of Binghamton, was designated master of ceremonies, her son Francis A. Phelps read her speech, and her youngest son, Ziba Bennett Phelps, introduced the monument. "Mountain Monument."

49. "The Daughters and the Dames," *Wilkes-Barre (PA) Semi-Weekly Record*, November 6, 1894, 3.

50. Petrillo, *Albert Lewis*.

51. "Historic Spot Marked," *Wilkes-Barre (PA) Semi-Weekly Record*, October 14, 1898, 7.

52. Petrillo, *Albert Lewis*.

53. Petrillo, *Albert Lewis*, 14–24.

54. Petrillo, *Albert Lewis*, 29–30.

55. Petrillo, *Albert Lewis*, 143.

56. Petrillo, *Albert Lewis*, 151.

57. Lewis's first wife, Lizzie Crellin, was the half-sister of Sarah Blakeslee, the wife of railroad magnate Asa Parker. She died in 1885. Lewis met Lillian Constance Westendarp on a business trip in England. She was twenty-eight years his junior. They wed in 1892. Petrillo, *Albert Lewis*, 146–47, 18–20, 44.

58. Petrillo, *Albert Lewis*, 147.

59. "Historic Spot Marked."

60. "Historic Spot Marked." For a detailed discussion of the troops' road- and bridge-building activities, see Harding, *The Sullivan Road*.

61. Petrillo, *Albert Lewis*, 47.

62. Davies, *The Anthracite Aristocracy*. See figures 1 and 2 for illustrations of the kinship ties between Wilkes-Barre elite leaders and their families in the nineteenth century, 45.

63. Davies, *The Anthracite Aristocracy*, 46–49.

64. Davies, *The Anthracite Aristocracy*, 77.

65. McCartney held an annual reunion September 1, 1893, in colonial dress at Bear Creek, at the home of Mrs. Benjamin Reynolds. *Wilkes-Barre (PA) Record*, September 2, 1893, 7.

66. Miner, *History of Wyoming*, 247.

67. The chapters based in more rural communities may have had greater challenges in securing funding. For instance, the Tunkhannock chapter was established in June 1900 and began fundraising for a Sullivan marker the next year but didn't complete this task until 1929, when assisted by State of Pennsylvania cosponsorship. *Wilkes-Barre (PA) Democrat*, April 5, 1901, 3; May 17, 1901, 3.

68. The George Clymer chapter invited members of the Tioga and Tunkhannock chapters as well as the Towanda Sons of the Revolution to their 1908 dedication. The Mach-wi-hi-lusing chapter invited long-standing Tioga chapter member Mrs. Louise Welles Murray to give the formal address at their unveiling of a boulder marking a Sullivan encampment. Hopkins, "Mach-wi-hi-lu-sing Chapter"; Mercur, "The George Clymer Chapter."

69. Connerton, *How Societies Remember*.

70. Truesdell, "God, Home, and Country," 19–20.

71. This is the sentiment in the present day as well. Joan O'Dell (retired nurse), interview by the author, July 19, 2017, Horseheads NY.

72. After developing a database of the charter members of each of the Susquehanna River DAR chapters, I researched each ancestor's war service. Data is drawn from lists of charter members only. Because chapter membership rosters constantly shifted as members died or moved away and new ones joined, I chose charter lists to serve as a snapshot of ancestry composition at one moment in time.

73. "Mach-wi-hi-lusing" was selected for the chapter name as it was purportedly the "old Indian spelling of Wyalusing," meaning "the home of the grand old veteran." DAR, *Pennsylvania State History*, 187.

74. Jonathan Dodge, Oliver Dodge, Henry Elliot (born in Connecticut but served in PA), Joseph Elliott, Elisha Keeler, John Keeler, Thomas Lewis, James Terrell, and John Warner.

75. Louise Welles Murray, "A Memorial of Charlotte Marshall Holbrooke Maurice, Regent and Founder of Tioga Chapter, DAR, Athens PA," n.d., BCHS, 5.

76. Murray, "A Memorial," 6.

77. Murray, "A Memorial," 8.

78. The poor man seemed carried away by PTSD. One journalist wrote, "His graphic portraiture of Kenan's charge at Chancellorsville when the brave 300 Pennsylvanians stood the shock of that rebel host of 25,000 and saved the army from annihilation *was given with such vividness as to arouse the grandest emotions* (emphasis added)." "Markers placed on Soldiers' Graves," November 3, 1901, TPDAR.

79. Louise Welles Murray, "The Fort Sullivan Tablet," *Wilkes-Barre (PA) Semi-Weekly Record*, October 14, 1902, 3; William Elliot Griffis Collection, Rutgers University Libraries Special Collections. Dr. Griffis (1843–1928) was a minister who spent many years in Japan and was the author of over fifty books, mostly on Japan. When he gave the main address at the 125th commemoration of the Wyoming battle the next year, he explained that Wyoming was one of the compelling causes of the Sullivan Expedition. Griffis, "The History and Mythology of Sullivan's Expedition," 10.

80. Murray, "The Fort Sullivan Tablet," *Wilkes-Barre (PA) Semi-Weekly Record*, October 14, 1902, 3. TPDAR.

81. Delegates from DAR chapters of Tunkhannock, Towanda, Elmira, and Binghamton attended the Athens dedication as well as men from the Elmira and Towanda chapters of the Sons of the American Revolution. Murray, "The Fort Sullivan Tablet."

82. "Fort Sullivan," *Athens (PA) Gazette*, September 25, 1902, 1, TPDAR. Vice Regent Sarah Perkins Elmer, Regent Maurice, Miss Perkins, and Edward H. Perkins all lived side by side. U.S. Census 1900.

83. The land was donated by Edward H. Perkins, and the marker was partly funded by his sister, who lived next door. His older daughter, Sarah (Perkins Elmer), was Maurice's vice regent. Edward Perkins's son George donated a cannonball that he and his wife had found on their land. "Memorial Table Unveiled," *Waverly (NY) Free Press*, October 3, 1902, TPDAR.

84. Strange, "The Battlefields," 203.

85. Truesdell, "God, Home, and Country," 19.

86. The Wyoming Valley chapter documented multiple local historical site focused on the Battle of Wyoming. In 1900 their sister DAR chapter, Dial Rock, based in West Pittson (also one of the early Susquehannah Company towns), marked the site of Jenkins Fort, burned during the Wyoming battle. This was again a family affair. John Jenkins was the chapter regent's great-grandfather, and the main address, on the Yankee-Pennamite controversy, was given by William Wilcox, Steuben Jenkins's son-in-law (discussed in the previous chapter). "Revolutionary Fort," *Wilkes-Barre (NY) Record*, October 13, 1900, 7; "The Monument Unveiled," *Wilkes-Barre (PA) Weekly Times*, October 20, 1900, 5.

87. Morgan, "Home and Country," 161–62.

88. Truesdell, "God, Home, and Country," 95–96.

89. Glassberg, *Sense of History*, 187.

90. Truesdell, "God, Home, and Country," 117–18; O'Brien, *Firsting and Lasting*.

3. "Bootleg" Monuments

1. The PHC published report contradicts itself, claiming that there are twenty-two markers and twenty markers, and identifying only eighteen by name. See Pennsylvania Historical Commission, *Fifth Report*.

2. PHC minutes, July 2, 1928.

3. Act No. 777 on July 25, 1913, "An Act providing for the establishment of the Pennsylvania Historical Commission; defining its powers and duties; and making an appropriation for its work." In Pennsylvania Historical Commission, *First Report*, 3–5.

4. Pennsylvania Historical Commission, *First Report*, 3–4.

5. Pennsylvania Historical Commission, *First Report*, 4.

6. Pennsylvania Historical Commission, *First Report*, 5–6.

7. "Appendix B" of *Historic Sites in Pennsylvania*, "What Has Been Done to Mark Them." Pennsylvania Historical Commission, *First Report*, 24.

8. "Appendix B," 24–25.

9. "Appendix B," 24–27.

10. Pennsylvania Historical Commission, *First Report*, 13. This is a great example of the reaction against New England's cultural hegemony that Michael Kammen observes was brewing in the late nineteenth century, exploding into open resentment after 1915. Kammen, *Mystic Chords of Memory*, 379.

11. Pennsylvania Historical Commission, *First Report*, 14. This list of the components of Pennsylvania's populace is interesting not only for the ethnic groups it does not include but also because it mirrored the composition of the committee, and members commended their unique capacity to represent the citizens of the state in this regard. Pennsylvania Historical Commission, *First Report*, 12.

12. Pennsylvania Historical Commission, *First Report*, 15.

13. Pennsylvania Historical Commission, *First Report*, 15.

14. Pennsylvania Historical Commission, *First Report*, 8.

15. Pennsylvania Historical Commission, *First Report*, 9

16. Pennsylvania Historical Commission, *First Report*, 10.

17. Pennsylvania Historical Commission, *First Report*, 10.

18. Pennsylvania Historical Commission, *First Report*, 9.

19. Pennsylvania Historical Commission, *Second Report of the Pennsylvania Historical Commission*, 14

20. Pennsylvania Historical Commission, *Second Report*, 14.

21. Bronner, *Popularizing Pennsylvania*, 2–3.

22. His family was so wealthy that he received the most expensive real estate wedding gift in New York history in 1913. Bronner, *Popularizing Pennsylvania*, 19–20.

23. Bronner, *Popularizing Pennsylvania*, 13–16.

24. Bronner, *Popularizing Pennsylvania*, 42. He served as state archivist, director of the state museum, and member of the state's geographical board, and he became the country's first official state folklorist. Bronner, xvii-xviii.

25. Bronner, *Popularizing Pennsylvania*, xix.

26. Bronner, *Popularizing Pennsylvania*, xix.

27. PHC, *Marking the Historic Sites of Early Pennsylvania*, 14.

28. PHC, *Marking the Historic Sites*, 14–17.

29. PHC, *Marking the Historic Sites*, 24.

30. *Marking the Historic Sites*, frontispiece.

31. "Sites Marked at Wyalusing," *Wilkes-Barre (NY) Record*, November 10, 1928, 15.

32. Williams, *Year of the Hangman*, 143.

33. A vengeance component to the mission is suggested in Hartley's statement "that they may revenge the murders of fathers, brothers, and friends," in Williams, *Year of the Hangman*, 159–60.

34. Graymont, *The Iroquois*, 184.

35. Of the 200 men there were some 150 troops from Wyoming under Captain Simon Spalding, including 58 men from Spalding's Independent Company and 12 volunteers under Captain John Franklin. Sixty members of the Eleventh Pennsylvania Regiment were sent to reinforce Wyoming. Murray, *A History*, 131–32.

36. Williams, *Year of the Hangman*, 162–65.

37. Graymont, *The Iroquois*, 180.

38. Heverly, *History and Geography*, 50.

39. David Craft in Murray, *A History*, 138; Williams, *Year of the Hangman*, 166.

40. David Craft in Murray, *A History*, 129; Indian Hill marker text in Carl, *A Traveler's Guide*, 10.

41. Although it was attributed to the Bradford County Historical Society and the state commission, the Tioga Point DAR chapter "and friends" paid for the marker, and early

DAR press releases explained that the marker would commemorate "the destruction of Teaoga and Queen Esther's Town by Colonel Thomas Hartley and his troop 150 years ago." The PHC provided only a bronze tablet. "Hartley Boulder Will Be Dedicated on November 8th," undated news clipping, TPDAR.

42. Brown descendant Harriet Brown granted the land for the marker. "Sites Marked at Wyalusing," *Wilkes-Barre (PA) Record*, November 10, 1928, 15.

43. Heverly, *History and Geography*, 54–55; Carl, *A Traveler's Guide*, 8

44. Programme, IHB; "Sites Marked at Wyalusing," 15.

45. In the foreword of the 1931 publication, Frank Speck suggests a fortuitous encounter as he thanks Albert Myers of the PHC, who "advised me so opportunely in 1928 to apply to the Historical Commission of Pennsylvania for a research grant the very week the Great Spirit sent Wi-tapano'xwe to my office in search of employment." Frank G. Speck, Witapanóxwe, and PHC, *A Study of the Delaware Indian Big House Ceremony*, 5. Witapanóx'we also worked with Gladys Tantaquidgeon in 1930 recording Delaware medicinal practices. Pennsylvania Historical Commission, *Second Report of the Pennsylvania Historical Commission*, 7; Gladys Tantaquidgeon and PHC, *A Study of Delaware Indian Medicine Practice*. For Speck's relationship with Witapanóx'we and other indigenous collaborators, see Bruchac, *Savage Kin*, chapter 6.

46. Speck and PHC, *A Study of the Delaware*, 9. One local news source states that Witapanóx'we attended both the Haskell Institute at Lawrence, Kansas, and the Chilocco Indian Industrial School in Oklahoma. "Red Men Have Secured Chief War Eagle," *Daily News* (Lebanon PA), October 3, 1929, 1.

47. "Nanticoke Tribe Holds Pow-wow," *Wilkes-Barre (PA) Record*, November 30, 1928, 1.

48. Two different DAR chapters coordinated the unveiling, with the Tioga Point DAR contributing a descendant of John Franklin, and the George Clymer DAR from Towanda choosing a "Simon Spalding" descendant. The Lime Hill marker was unveiled by descendants of Thomas Baldwin and Joseph Elliott, first and second in command of that battle. Programme, IHB; "Sites Marked at Wyalusing."

49. Murray, *A History*, 136, 138.

50. This possibility is suggested by Louise Murray, who wrote in 1908 that, by that time, mostly descendants of "Wild Yankees" lived on Tioga Point. Murray, *A History*, 310.

51. Spalding also led the Westmoreland Independent Company on the Sullivan Campaign, while John Franklin led a company of Wyoming militia on the expedition. Miner, *History of Wyoming*, 268.

52. Miner, *History of Wyoming*, 369.

53. Murray, *A History*, 310.

54. The Committee on the Sullivan Expedition, Sesqui-Centennial Celebration. *Fifth Report of the Pennsylvania Historical Commission*, 19.

55. PA Historical Preservation Office, "Society at 90."

56. The other series commemorated the Battle of Brandywine (sixteen bronze plaques); "The Famous Indian Walk" (four bronze plaques); "the Great Trail of the Minquas" (two monoliths); and the Forbes Road (thirteen monuments). See "Plaques in Series," IHB; *Fifth Report of the Pennsylvania Historical Commission*, 19.

57. *Fifth Report of the Pennsylvania Historical Commission*, 19.

58. *Fifth Report of the Pennsylvania Historical Commission*, 19.

59. *Fifth Report of the Pennsylvania Historical Commission*, 20.

60. The former site of the multicultural Indian village of Shamokin, Fort Augusta, is now located in the town of Sunbury. Approximately 100 soldiers of the Eleventh Pennsylvania Regiment under Colonel Hubley left from this fort to serve under Sullivan.

61. "Markers," typed page, TPDAR.

62. Louise Welles Murray, Letter of February 19, 1929, to Alexander C. Flick, B0566, "Pennsylvania" folder, NYSA; Alexander Flick, Letter of March 15, 1929, to Louise Murray, B0566, "Pennsylvania" folder, NYSA.

63. Louise Murray, Letter of April 13, 1929, to Alexander Flick, B0566, "Pennsylvania" folder, NYSA.

64. "Great Crowd Gathers to See Pageant Commemorating Epic Expedition of Sullivan Army." Newspaper clipping, n.d. TPDAR.

65. "Dedicate Two Markers on Historic Locations," *Elmira (NY) Advertiser*, August 25, 1929, flick clippings, 13912-00, box 1 & 2, Flick, *Sesqui History*.

66. "Easton to Erect Tablet along Line of General Sullivan's March," *Easton (PA) Express*, March 12, 1929, 1.

67. "Unveil Marker at Spot Where Sullivan Began Famous March," *Easton (PA) Express*, October 17, 1929, 1.

68. "Unveil Marker at Spot Where Sullivan Began Famous March," *Easton (PA) Express*, October 17, 1929, 1.

69. Murray to Flick. In Tunkhannock, the PHC sponsored two markers. The local press explained that despite the rain, a "goodly number" of people showed up, but no PHC representatives attended. "Marker Unveiled. Rain Marred the Occasion Somewhat, but DAR Gives Good Program," *Tunkhannock (PA) Republican and New Age*, August 8, 1929, 1.

70. Letter of May 4, 1939, from Mrs. Bolton Coon to Maj. Frank Melvin, and Letter of May 9, 1939, from S. K. Stevens to Mrs. Bolton Coon, 13/100, box 1, folder F, "General Correspondence," PSA. The PHC became the Pennsylvania Historical and Museum Commission (PHMC) in 1945.

71. Robinson and Galle, "A Century of Marking History."

72. Letter of August 5, 1969, from Frederick W. Liegerg, U.S. 6 Roosevelt Highway Association of PA, to James Scandale, Pennsylvania Department of Highways. Bureau of Archives and History, Division of History, Historical Marker Files, Bradford County, Lime Hill Battlefield, folder 5/32 (13/112/6), PSA.

73. This professionalization of the PHMC is discussed in several articles authored by the new director, Stevens, who cannot hide his withering contempt for Shoemaker. See S. K. Stevens, "The Pennsylvania Historical," 147; "Operation Heritage," 3.

74. Letter of July 2, 1973, from A. Henry Haas, Field Coordinator, Historical Marker Program, to Mrs. Harry Tiffany, 13/112 6, folder 5/32, PSA.

75. Letter of July 2, 1973, from A. Henry Haas, Field Coordinator, Historical Marker Program, to Mrs. Harry Tiffany.

76. "Battle Monument on Lime Hill Promised Move," *Rocket-Courier* (Wyalusing PA), March 1975, news clipping, 13/112/6, folder 5/32, PSA.

77. Letter of May 24, 1976, from Helen Harned to A. Henry Haas, 13/112/6, folder 5/32, PSA; "Historical Marker Replaced at Long Last on Lime Hill," October 28, 1976, news clipping, folder "Bradford County," WCHS.

78. Letter of March 29, 1989, from Marilyn Levin, Legislative Liaison to Kenneth Lee, State Representative, 111th District, 13/112, box 6, 5/32, PSA.

79. Letter of December 7, 1982, from Ray Wasilewski, Zoning Officer, Bear Creek Township, to Vivian Piasecki, Chairman, PHMC, 13/100, box 1, PSA.

80. Henry Farley, "Historical Markers: Missing and Misplaced," *Rocket-Courier* (Wyalusing PA) June 10, 2004, 2.

81. Stevens, "The Pennsylvania Historical," 147; "Operation Heritage," 3.

82. Letter of September 21, 1962, from Donald Kent, PHMC, to Elsie Murray, Athens PA, 13/112, box 15, 14/28, PSA.

83. "Colonel Hartley's Career Told," *Wilkes-Barre (PA) Record*, July 4, 1944, 4; "Historian Speaks at Irem Temple Country Club," *Wilkes-Barre (PA) Times Leader*, April 30, 1962, 8.

84. Kammen, *Mystic Chords*, 479.

85. Kammen, *Mystic Chords*, 458.

86. Graham, "The Keystone Markers," 243.

4. Ambivalent Festivities

1. The best work outlining the machinations involved is Hauptman, *Conspiracy of Interests*.

2. Some fifty years after the expedition, white settlers unearthed the purported remains of two Sullivan soldiers killed during an ambush known as the Groveland ambuscade. The remains were reburied in Rochester in 1841 and a monument erected in 1901 by the Livingston County Historical Society; this settler tradition involving allegations of torture merits separate treatment, and an overview can be found in Alden, ed., *The Sullivan Campaign*.

3. A Seneca Falls DAR chapter, the Sa-Go-Ye-Wat-Ha chapter (named after the Seneca leader Red Jacket) developed a few small markers, including one denoting a Sullivan campsite in Seneca Falls, in 1910. "General Sullivan Memorial Fountain," *Buffalo (NY) Courier*, October 2, 1910, 69.

4. These settlements were multinational villages with a strong Munsee Delaware presence. For a detailed accounting of the ethnic groups in upper Susquehannah and Chemung River villages, see Jim Folts, "The Munsee Delawares"; on the towns, see Venables, "The Two Towns of Chemung." Both are in the Public Archaeology Facility, CBP.

5. Three Americans were killed, and one died of his wound. Butler reported five rangers and five Indians killed, while an unknown number died of their wounds. Americans took two prisoners, and some of Poor's men took scalps. In Williams, *Year of the Hangman*, 272.

6. Hurd and Hamilton, *History of Tioga, Chemung*, 110. Obituary, *Tioga County (PA) Record*, November 13, 1890, 3.

7. Warner established Waverly Gas Light Company in 1873, serving as company president for many years. Gay, *Historical Gazetteer*, 103, 346.

8. William Fiske Warner, "The Battle of Chemung: The Proposed Observance of Its One Hundredth Anniversary," *Elmira (NY) Daily Advertiser*, July 20, 1878, SCCF.

9. Warner, "The Battle of Chemung."

10. In Seneca County, in April 1878, civil engineer General Clark, a "zealous student" of Indian history, traveled on an expedition from Elmira to Geneva, along the Seneca River, and the east and west shore of Cayuga Lake, "for the purpose of accurately locating the line of Sullivan's march and the Indian villages destroyed by his army." *Syracuse (NY) Journal*, April 10, 1879. An August 11, 1879, article in preparation for the centennial reported that interest in "Sullivan's expedition all along its line of march is intense, and every effort is making to *clear up whatever may be obscure* in reference to it," *Syracuse (NY) Journal*, August 11, 1879, emphasis added. SCEF.

11. Warner, "The Battle of Chemung."

12. Warner, "The Battle of Chemung" (emphasis added).

13. "That Centennial," August 2, 1978, typescript manuscript version of *Elmira (NY) Daily Advertiser* article, SCCF.

14. Jennie F. Snell, "Sullivan's Expedition: Battle of New Town—Incidents and Anecdotes," *Elmira (NY) Daily Advertiser*, August 15, 1878, SCCF.

15. Kammen, *Mystic Chords*, 105–6.

16. "The Centennial of New Town," *Elmira (NY) Daily Advertiser*, August 30, 1878, SCCF.

17. There were three settlements along the Chemung River at that time: the then-abandoned "Old Chemung," the inhabited "New Chemung," destroyed by Sullivan's troops on August 13, 1779, and "New Town," the site of the August 29, 1779, battle. For a detailed look at the raid on "New Chemung," see Venables, "The Historical Context of Chemung" in the Public Archaeology Facility's excellent report, CBP. Warner, "The Battle of Chemung."

18. "The Centennial of New Town."

19. "The Centennial of New Town."

20. "The Centennial of New Town."

21. "The Sullivan Centennial. Meeting in Elmira Yesterday," *Elmira (NY) Daily Advertiser*, October 3, 1878, SCCF.

22. *Waverly (NY) Advocate*, August 1878, SCCF.

23. "The Next Centennials," *Elmira (NY) Daily Advertiser*, August 16, 1878, SCCF. In the article, the newspaper cited is identified as the *Geneseo Republican*, but it was likely the *Livingston Republican* of Geneseo NY.

24. *A Biographical Record of Chemung County*, 503.

25. *A Biographical Record*, 504.

26. *A Biographical Record*, 506.

27. Gay, *Historical Gazetteer*, 351; *A Biographical Record*, 507.

28. Towner, *Our County*, 200.

29. Towner, *Our County*, 130.

30. He was described as a "Barnburner Democrat," one of two factions of the Democratic party in New York at that time. Towner, *Our County*, 240.

31. Towner, *Our County*, 63.

32. Lowe had been county clerk before the war (1858) and served on the Elmira City Council at the same time as aldermen Charles Langdon and Stephen Arnot, all centennial trustees. Col. Henry C. Hoffman, a farmer near Horseheads, was a member of the Horseheads Board of Supervisors three times. John Arnot was a banker and served as mayor of Elmira in 1870 and 1874; his son, Stephen Arnot, became mayor after the centennial in 1883. Towner, *Our County*, 115–16, 200, 208, 355.

33. Slotkin, *The Fatal Environment*, 5.

34. Hild, *Greenbackers*, 22–23.

35. Baker, "The Gilded Age: 1860–1914," 455.

36. "A Centennial Celebration," *Elmira (NY) Daily Advertiser*, November 26, 1878, SCCF.

37. Warner, letter to the editor, no source, no date, SCCF.

38. "The Sullivan Celebration," August 11, 1879, SCEF.

39. *Elmira (NY) Daily Advertiser*, August 25, 1879, SCCF.

40. *Hornellsville Tribune*, reprinted in *Elmira (NY) Daily Advertiser*, August 21, 1879, SCCF.

41. *Democrat and Chronicle* (Rochester NY), August 30, 1879, 4.

42. *Democrat and Chronicle* (Rochester NY), August 30, 1879, 4.

43. On estimates of attendees, see Thomas E. Byrne, "Sullivan Centennial Drew 50,000 in 1879."

44. Cook, *Journals of the Military Expedition*. As Brant Venables has documented, meanings and emphases in Newtown battle celebrations changed across the years. Venables, "A Battle of Remembrance."

45. Brooks correspondence, *Elmira (NY) Daily Advertiser*, August 18, 1879, SCCF.

46. "How to Get to the Centennial," *Elmira (NY) Daily Advertiser*, August 29, 1879, SCCF.

47. *Democrat and Chronicle* (Rochester NY), August 30, 1879, 4.

48. *Elmira (NY) Daily Advertiser*, August 25, 1879, SCCF.

49. For a brief review of key authors promoting the Iroquois Empire myth, see Richter and Merrell, "Introduction," *Beyond the Covenant Chain*, 5–8.

50. Cook, *Journals of the Military Expedition*, 411, 412–13.

51. Cook, *Journals of the Military Expedition*, 413.

52. Cook, *Journals of the Military Expedition*, 414.

53. Cook, *Journals of the Military Expedition*, 414.

54. Cook, *Journals of the Military Expedition*, 414.

55. Cook, *Journals of the Military Expedition*, 415.

56. Cook, *Journals of the Military Expedition*, 414.

57. DeWitt Clinton, in Cook, *Journals of the Military Expedition*, 414.

58. Cook, *Journals of the Military Expedition*, 415.

59. Cook, *Journals of the Military Expedition*, 416.

60. Cook, *Journals of the Military Expedition*, 417.

61. Cook, *Journals of the Military Expedition*, 417.

62. Cook, *Journals of the Military Expedition*, 420–21.

63. Cook, *Journals of the Military Expedition*, 425.

64. Cook, *Journals of the Military Expedition*, 426.

65. Cook, *Journals of the Military Expedition*, 426.

66. Cook, *Journals of the Military Expedition*, 428.

67. Cook, *Journals of the Military Expedition*, 432.

68. Cook, *Journals of the Military Expedition*, 430.

69. Cook, *Journals of the Military Expedition*, 430.

70. Cook, *Journals of the Military Expedition*, 435.

71. Cook, *Journals of the Military Expedition*, 435.

72. *Democrat and Chronicle* (Rochester NY), August 30, 1879, 4.

73. Cook, *Journals of the Military Expedition*, 439.

74. Cook, *Journals of the Military Expedition*, 439.

75. "The Newtown Centennial" and "Attacked by Indians," *Record of the Times* (Wilkes-Barre PA), August 30, 1879, 1.

76. Venables, "A Battle of Remembrance," 149–50.

77. Cook, *Journals of the Military Expedition*, 439.

78. Cook, *Journals of the Military Expedition*, 439.

79. Cook, *Journals of the Military Expedition*, 440.

80. Cook, *Journals of the Military Expedition*, 455.

81. Cook, *Journals of the Military Expedition*, 442.

82. Cook, *Journals of the Military Expedition*, 442.

83. Cook, *Journals of the Military Expedition*, 442.

84. Graymont, *The Iroquois*, 213.

85. Venables, "A Battle of Remembrance," 148.

86. For instance, Guy Humphrey McMaster's lengthy poem "The Commanders" asserted, "The ancient race must disappear, and hither new men must come." In Venables, "A Battle of Remembrance," 151.

87. "Sullivan Centennial. An Indian Band and an Indian Game of Ball," August 28, 1879, SCCF.

88. Cook, *Journals of the Military Expedition*, 393.

5. Inventing "Sullivan-Clinton"

1. "Postoffice [sic] Deluged by Requests," *Press and Sun-Bulletin* (Binghamton NY), June 17, 1929, 5.

2. "Parade Thrill Lasts; Praise for All Concerned," n.d., clipping file, in Flick, *Sesqui History*, 662.

3. Evensen, "Saving the City's Reputation."

4. Kammen, *Mystic Chords*, 299.

5. "Memorial," No. 1381, to the Senate of the State of New York, February 14, 1923, Introduced by F. M. Davenport, in Flick, *Sesqui History*, 3–8. The other societies represented Oneida, Herkimer, Montgomery, Fulton, Schenectady, and Schoharie counties.

6. "Memorial," 3.

7. White, W. Pierrepont, "Why—A Ten Year Program to Celebrate New York State's Part in the American Revolution on the 150th Anniversary of the Event," speech given at The New York Historical Society, manuscript in Flick, *Sesqui History*, 31–37.

8. "Capitalizing the State's History," *Schenectady (NY) Union Star*, October 25, 1923, in Flick, *Sesqui History*, 52.

9. New York State, Chapter 687 of the Laws of 1923. "An Act Making an Appropriation for a Preliminary Survey and Report by the New York State Historical Association for the Appropriate Celebration of the One Hundred and Fiftieth Anniversary of the Important Events of the Revolutionary Period," in Flick, *Sesqui History*, 10.

10. NYSHA, letter of July 20, 1923, in Flick, *Sesqui History*, 17.

11. Committee on the 150th Anniversary of the Revolution, "Celebration of the 150th Anniversary of the American Revolution," draft report, in Flick, *Sesqui History*. Tallies in Flick, *Sesqui History*, 27, 57.

12. Flick, *Sesqui History*, 28–29.

13. Memorandum filed with assembly bill, May 2, 1924, introductory number 1569, printed number 1787, signed by Alfred E. Smith, in Flick, *Sesqui History*, 74.

14. Flick, *Sesqui History*, 80.

15. $145,000 was dedicated to battlefield purchase and rehabilitation, $100,000 to support New York's part in the Philadelphia Sesquicentennial, and $75,000 for 1926 Sesquicentennial celebrations. Thompson, "The Observance," 61.

16. Thompson, "The Observance," 61.

17. Dozens of landmark events were marked, including the signing of the Declaration of Independence and multiple battles. Thompson, "The Observance," 62–63.

18. Thompson, "The Observance," 61.

19. Flick, *Sesqui History*, 130.

20. Letter to "local historian" by Alexander C. Flick, February 1, 1926, in Flick, *Sesqui History*, 101–2; Flick, "Program Suggestions for 150th Anniversary of the Revolution," in Flick, *Sesqui History*, 133–34.

21. Flick, *Sesqui History*, 94.

22. Thompson, "The Observance," 63–64.

23. Division of Archives and History, *The American Revolution*, 169, 266.

24. Alexander Flick, "The Sullivan-Clinton Sesquicentennial, 1779–1929, General Significance of the Sullivan Campaign," typed manuscript, in Flick, *Sesqui History*.

25. Flick, "The Sullivan-Clinton Sesquicentennial."

26. Flick, *Sesqui History*, 468.

27. Thompson, "The Observance," 64.

28. Richard Drummond to Peter Nelson, April 10, 1929, CSPR. In this correspondence, Drummond comments on a draft of a marker design and suggests that the state use "War Tribes" or "Hostile Nations" rather than "Home Lands," because the latter "will merely give support to the sobby notion I find quite prevalent, to my surprise, that the Expedition represented 'a terrible thing to do to the poor Indians, etc.' I need not say more. If you haven't heard it, let me say that I have heard it, and have had some trouble, strange to say, to combat it."

29. In "Sesqui to Be Supported by Many Groups," the subheading reads, "State to Be Asked to Make Grant for Celebration of Sullivan March." *Democrat and Chronicle* (Rochester NY), January 1, 1928, 5.

30. "The Sullivan-Clinton Campaign in American History," 2, in Flick, *Sesqui History*.

31. "The Sullivan-Clinton Campaign," 2.

32. "Says Sullivan Expedition had Far-reaching Effects," *Democrat & Chronicle* (Rochester NY), June 10, 1928, 4.

33. "Sullivan Army to March Again In Sesqui Celebration Pageant," *Star-Gazette* (Elmira NY), February 22, 1929, 15.

34. "Sullivan-Clinton Sesquicentennial, General Program," typed manuscript, SCSCF.

35. "Sesqui to be Supported by Many Groups," *Democrat & Chronicle* (Rochester NY), January 1, 1928, 5.

36. "Minutes of a Meeting of the Executive Committee," May 28, 1926, 4, *Sesqui History*.

37. "General Sullivan's Kin May Be Here for Sesquicentennial Celebration," *Elmira (NY) Telegram*, August 18, 1929; "Many Descendants of Sullivan's Soldiers Take Part in Pageant," *Star-Gazette* (Elmira NY), September 28, 1929, 18.

38. Frederick Newhall, to Richard Drummond, September 10, 1929, CCHSC.

39. Van Schaick was the son of the mayor of Albany and the head of the First New York Regiment. See Mintz, *Seeds of Empire*, 83.

40. Division of Archives and History, *The American Revolution*, 169, 266.

41. Glatthaar and Martin, *Forgotten Allies*, 240–42; Calloway, *Indian World*, 248.

42. Glatthaar and Martin, *Forgotten Allies*, 241–42.

43. Glatthaar and Martin, *Forgotten Allies*, 242–43.

44. Glatthaar and Margin, *Forgotten Allies*, 243; Graymont, *The Iroquois*, 196; Calloway, *Indian World*, 249; Richard Hill, "The Indian Expedition of 1779 and Haudenosaunee Responses," CBP, 79–80.

45. Glatthaar and Martin, *Forgotten Allies*, 244–45.

46. "This Week is Anniversary of Massacre on Onondaga," April 19, 1921, JF.

47. George Fryer, to W. Pierrepont White, September 21, 1928, SCSCF.

48. Peter Nelson to Fred Dutcher, September 26, 1928, SCSCF.

49. "Onondaga's Neglected Past," undated news clipping, SCSCF.

50. "Fighting Indians, 150 Years Ago" and "Region's Part in Revolution to be Ignored in Program," undated news clippings, SCSCF.

51. Organizations participating in this activity included the General Asa Danforth Chapter, DAR; Ta-whan-ta-qua Chapter, DAR; the Onondaga Historical Association; the Onondaga Chapter of the Daughters of 1812; the Syracuse Colony; New England Women; and the Syracuse Chapter of the Sons of the American Revolution. *Post-Standard* (Syracuse NY), July 10, 1929, JF.

52. "Sullivan Memorial Boulder Will Be Dedicated Today," *Post-Standard* (Syracuse NY), September 22, 1929, JF.

53. Peter Nelson to Mamie Spring, August 16, 1929, "Syracuse" folder, CSPR.

54. Nelson to Spring, August 20, 1929, "Syracuse" folder, CSPR.

55. Nelson to Spring, September 7, 1929, "Syracuse" folder, CSPR.

56. "Syracuse" folder, CSPR.

57. "Marker will be dedicated at Fort Site," unknown source, September 22, 1929, JF

58. "Marker will be dedicated."

59. "Programme," JF.

60. "Mrs. Avis Hill, Born an Indian Princess, Dies," HAF.

61. "David R. Hill, Onondaga Chief, Expires Suddenly" *Post-Standard* (Syracuse NY), October 15, 1950, HDF.

62. "300 Witness Dedication of Valley Drive Monument," unknown source, September 23, 1929, JF.

63. *Post-Standard* (Syracuse NY), Monday, September 23, 1929, JF.

6. Celebrating Sullivan

1. "Sullivan-Clinton Sesquicentennial, General Program," SCF.

2. Calloway, *The Indian World*, 257.

3. Graymont, "New York Indian Policy," 438.

4. Ryan, "Crowding the Banks," 85–115, 91.

5. Ryan, "Crowding the Banks," 201, 247.

6. Mt. Pleasant, "After the Whirlwind," 89–102.

7. Hauptman, *Conspiracy of Interests*, 90–91; Graymont, "New York State," 381–86. For Native American perspectives, see Powless, Jemison, and Schein, eds., *Treaty of Canandaigua 1794*.

8. Jones, *License for Empire*, 180–81; Graymont, "New York State;" Rosen, *American Indians and State Law*, 33–49.

9. Hauptman, *Conspiracy of Interests*, 23.

10. See Hauptman, *Conspiracy of Interests*, 218–19; see also Hauptman, *The Iroquois and the New Deal*, 4–5; Graymont, "New York State." For a detailed discussion of Oneida lands, see Tiro, *The People of the Standing Stone*.

11. Epstein, "Unsettled New York," 47–48.

12. Hauptman, *The Iroquois and the New Deal*, 11–12.

13. A U.S. District Court voted to return land to an Oneida family, stating that New York courts could not remove the Oneida as they were a federally recognized tribe. Hauptman, *The Iroquois and the New Deal*, 11.

14. The Machold Bill (Chapter 590 of the Laws of New York) established the "Indian Commission to Investigate the Status of the American Indian Residing in New York" on

May 12, 1919. Republican assemblyman Edward A. Everett was elected chairman, and it is often known as the "Everett Commission." The most detailed account of the commission's work is in Upton, *The Everett Report in Historical Perspective*. See also Epstein, "Unsettled New York."

15. Hauptman, *The Iroquois and the New Deal*, 11.

16. "Everett Believes Indian Claims Good," *The Courier and Freeman*, February 15, 1922, in Epstein, "Unsettled New York," 74.

17. Upton, *The Everett Report*, 102–3; New York State Assembly (unpublished), "Report of the Indian Commission," commonly known as the "Everett Report." Arthur C. Parker and David R. Hill were on the committee. Parker apparently told the committee in its final deliberations that a decision by the Supreme Court was the only solution. He refused to sign the report. Upton suggests that his being a state employee may have played a role. Upton, *The Everett Report*, 100–102.

18. Upton, *The Everett Report*, 109; Hauptman, *The Iroquois and the New Deal*, 11–12.

19. Laura Kellogg was an author, activist, and Oneida leader who also cofounded the Society of American Indians. Much of the money she raised for the massive claim never went to the intended purpose, and in the process, she "helped factionalize every Iroquois reservation." Hauptman, *The Iroquois and the New Deal*. Hauptman has described her as the "most controversial Iroquois leader of the twentieth century" (*The Iroquois Struggle*, 183). See also Hauptman, "Designing Woman: Minnie Kellogg, Iroquois Leader."

20. The case was *James Deere v. St. Lawrence River Power Company*, brought to a U.S. district court on June 6, 1925. Upton, *The Everett Report*, 124; Hauptman, *The Iroquois Struggle*, 185. On the state reaction to the report, development of the lawsuit, and the Kelloggs' involvement, see Upton, *The Everett Report*, 120–35.

21. Upton, *The Everett Report*, 129.

22. The land dispute case officially ended on May 27, 1929, when claimants decided not to bring the case forward to the U.S. Supreme Court. Upton notes that there was dissent and some Six Nations participants wished to proceed, suggesting that additional appeals were not out of the question. Upton, *The Everett Report*, 129–30.

23. Seed, *Ceremonies of Possession*. Thanks to Dr. Jessica Dolan for this insight.

24. W. Pierrepont White to Frederick B. Richards, June 6, 1923, WPWP.

25. William O. Stillman to W. P. White, June 7, 1923, WPWP.

26. William B. Newell, to Alexander Flick, January 9, 1929. "Indian" folder, CSPR; Frances Dorrance, to Alexander Flick, February 9, 1929, "Pennsylvania" folder, CSPR.

27. Bates, "Founding of Indian Village," EBP.

28. Attendees included Russell Hill, James Jonathan, Inez Blackchief, Aaron Poodry, Mrs. Rose and Mrs. Irene Poodry, and Miss Dorothy Moses (Tonawanda); Mrs. Eli Henry, Mrs. Harriet Pembleton, Mrs. Ella Printup, Miss Gladys Ganesworth, Louise Pendleton, Ray Ganesworth, Harry Patterson, Havemeyer Jack, and Joseph Woodbury (Tuscarora); Mr. and Mrs. Walter Kennedy, Sylvester C. Crouse, Jerome and Edison Crouse, Adelbert John, Hiram Watt, Frank John, Mrs. Joshua Pierce, and Miss Ruth Pierce (Allegany Seneca); Mr. and Mrs. John K. Button, Mr. and Mrs. Theodore Gordon, Mr. and Mrs. Ulysses Kennedy, Frank Logan, and James Jones (Cattaraugus Seneca). Leroy E. Fess, "Relic Hunters' Desecration of Cemeteries Stirs Indians," *Buffalo (NY) Evening News*, February 14, 1929.

29. Kennedy succeeded former board chair and Seneca Nation of Indians president William C. Hoag in 1927. One of his first charges was developing the Indian village estab-

lished at the New York State Fair in 1928. "Elect Kennedy President of Indian Board," *The Ithaca (NY) Journal*, December 17, 1927, 7; "Indian Village for Fair Exhibit," *Times-Herald* (Olean NY), July 9, 1928, 11. See also John, *Who Is Walter Kennedy?*

30. In Hauptman, *Coming Full Circle*, 174–75; see also John, *Who Is Walter Kennedy?*, 7–18 for transcript of Kennedy's testimony during a commission meeting at Allegany on August 16, 1920.

31. Leroy Fess, "Relic Hunters' Desecration of Cemeteries Stirs Indians," *Buffalo (NY) Evening News*, February 14, 1929, 3.

32. Fess, "Relic Hunters."

33. Fess, "Relic Hunters."

34. Fess, "Relic Hunters."

35. Leroy Fess, "Indian Complaint Heeded," *Buffalo (NY) Evening News*, February 18, 1929, 3.

36. "Real Indian Braves Appear in Pageant," *Dunkirk (NY) Evening Observer*, June 4, 1927, 11. The other Haudenosaunee participant I have identified was David R. Hill, Onondaga, who participated in an event recognizing Van Schaick's raids on the Onondaga in April 1779 (see chapter 5).

37. "State Historian Delivers Presentation Address on Site of Ancient Iroquois Village," news clipping, in Flick, *Sesqui History*, 674.

38. Annie Laurie Davis to Richard Drummond, September 11, 1929, CCHSC.

39. Harold Murphy and Bob Dunn, "Hard to Believe," undated newspaper clipping. I thank Terri John for this information.

40. Richard Drummond to "C. A. Parker" [*sic*], July 20, 1928, CCHSC. After the event, Drummond also reported to Flick that the Indians "were very much pleased with the whole ceremony, and with their treatment here, reported promptly to Doctor Parker, at Rochester, and he wrote me a gracious letter expressing his appreciation." Drummond to Flick, October 8, 1929, CSPR.

41. Newspapers stated, "The masks in the window display . . . are attracting much attention. They are perfect examples of the false faces used by Indians for primitive ceremonies of a secret nature. Weird expressions and uncanny features characterize these ancient masks which are shown with the artifacts exhibited by the Rochester Municipal Museum, as part of the sesqui-centennial exhibits in Auburn." "Big Crowd for H.S. Sesqui Rally Tonight Likely," news clipping, in Flick, *Sesqui History*, 674.

42. "Long Sesqui Procession Beautiful and Stirring Climax. Seven Markers on Route of General Sullivan to be Dedicated Thursday," *Democrat & Chronicle* (Rochester NY), June 10, 1928, 4.

43. Students of St Hyacinth's School wore white blouses with red stripes, the Polish national colors; the James Street School children were clothed in white ensembles with yellow sashes and caps; the Seward school, red, white and blue; the girls of St. Mary's were "fetching" in "white and green sashes"; St. Aloyslus children wore purple and yellow, "Long Sesqui Procession"; "Soldier Trail of 150 Years Ago Blazed with Impressive Ceremony"; "Five Monuments Unveiled in Cayuga County Program," in Flick, *Sesqui History*, 674, 650–56.

44. "Long Sesqui Procession Beautiful and Stirring Celebration Climax," news clipping, n.d., in Flick, *Sesqui History*, 674.

45. "State Historian Delivers Presentation Address," n.d., in Flick, *Sesqui History*.

46. "State Historian Delivers."

47. "Original Manuscript of Richard C. S. Drummond. At Dedication of Monument at Great Gully. September 24, 1929." Typed speech. CCHSC.

48. "Dr. Flick Congratulates Cayuga County on Success of Its Sesqui Celebration," in Flick, *Sesqui History*, 663.

49. Richard Drummond to Chief Wilbur C. Shongo, September 6, 1929, CCHSC.

50. Chief Shongo to Richard Drummond, September 9, 1929, CCHSC.

51. "Indians Visit Logan Monument," *Auburn (NY) Citizen*, September 26, 1929, n.p.

52. Mr. M. K. Sniffen, secretary of the Indian Rights Association, conducted research on the case and discussed it with George Decker. Sniffen to Allen, October 4, 1934; Sniffen to Allen, October 31, 1934. Unsigned note to file dated November 19, 1934, states, "These papers were delivered to me by Mr. Searing for perusal in November, 1934," CCHSC.

53. Preemption rights, or the right of first purchase from the Indians, had passed to Massachusetts in 1786 and were resold, with millions of acres passing to Robert Morris. In the 1790s Morris was facing bankruptcy and debtor's prison, and sent his son to negotiate with the Senecas using bribery, alcohol, and other tactics. See Hauptman, *Conspiracy of Interests*, 88–92.

54. An excellent discussion of this wrenching process can be found in Hauptman, *The Tonawanda Senecas' Heroic Battle against Removal*.

55. Hauptman, *Conspiracy of Interests*, 216–18.

56. Hauptman, *Conspiracy of Interests*, 218. These leases led to a significant dispute that was not settled until November 1990.

57. Hauptman, *Coming Full Circle*, 172–82.

58. "Sullivan-Clinton Sesquicentennial," SCSCF.

59. In *A Popular History of the United States*, Sydney Gay and William Bryant write, "Brodhead's expedition is usually considered of little moment, and it has been deemed, or doubted by some writers that it even took place," 7.

60. Brodhead was sent to Fort Pitt with a mission to "reduce Detroit," but he was hampered by low troop numbers, intelligence, and supplies. Appel, "Colonel Daniel Brodhead and the Lure of Detroit," "Colonel Daniel Brodhead and the Problems of Military Supply." I am grateful to Randy John for directing me to this and other sources on the Brodhead Expedition.

61. Washington to Brodhead, in Williams, *Year of the Hangman*, 232.

62. Appel, "Colonel Daniel Brodhead and the Problems of Military Supply," 1; Appel, "Colonel Daniel Brodhead and the Lure of Detroit," 269.

63. Downes, *Council Fires*, 252; Graymont, *The Iroquois*, 218.

64. Draper, *Notes of Border History*, 42.

65. Charles O'Bail was born in 1778 in Conesus town and died on the Cornplanter grant on December 31, 1868. Draper, *Notes of Border History*, 117.

66. Draper, *Notes of Border History*, 123.

67. Other names for Broken Straw include "Buckaloons, Boccalunnce, Bockaloons, Buffler's town," and in Seneca, "Da-gah-she-no-de-a-go," or "broken reed" or "cut straw." It appears on maps of Sir Mandeville (1740) and Bonnecamps (1750). John, *Seneca People*, 393–94.

68. "To George Washington from Colonel Daniel Brodhead, 16 September 1779." Founders Online, National Archives, last modified November 26, 2017. Original source: *Revolutionary War Series*, ed. Benjamin L. Huggins, vol. 22, *The Papers of George Washington: 1 August–21 October 1779* (Charlottesville: University of Virginia Press, 2013), 433–38.

69. John, *Seneca People*, 469.

70. Edson, "Brodhead's Expedition," 655; Stone, "Brodhead's Raid on the Senecas"; Stone, "Sinnontouan, or Seneca Land, in the Revolution."

71. Peter Nelson to DeHart Ames, March 18, 1929, "Salamanca/Cold Springs" folder, CSPR.

72. Alexander Flick to Walter Kennedy, March 21, 1929, "Salamanca/Cold Springs," CSPR.

73. Alexander Flick to Walter Kennedy, March 21, 1929, "Salamanca/Cold Springs," CSPR.

74. Alexander Flick to Walter Kennedy, March 21, 1929, "Salamanca," CSPR

75. Alexander Flick to Sylvester Crouse, Quaker Bridge NY, March 21, 1929, "Salamanca," CSPR.

76. Walter Kennedy to Alexander Flick, April 12, 1929, "Salamanca," CSPR.

77. Peter Nelson to DeHart Ames, July 20, 1929, "Salamanca," CSPR.

78. Handwritten note, July 29, 1929, "Salamanca," CSPR.

79. "Brodhead Slab May be Placed in Salamanca," *Times Herald* (Olean NY), July 31, 1929, 15.

80. "Brodhead Slab."

81. "Brodhead Slab."

82. Leigh G. Kirkland to Hon A. C. Frick [*sic*], July 31, 1929, "Salamanca," CSPR.

83. DeHart Ames to Nelson, July 30, 1929, "Salamanca," CSPR; DeHart Ames to Peter Nelson, July 31, 1929, "Salamanca," CSPR.

84. DeHart Ames to Peter Nelson, July 31, 1929, "Salamanca," CSPR.

85. DeHart Ames to Peter Nelson, August 12, 1929, "Salamanca," CSPR; Leigh G. Kirkland to Alexander Flick, August 12, 1929, "Salamanca," CSPR; "Veterans Park Chosen Site of Brodhead Slab," *Times Herald* (Olean NY), August 24, 1929, 3.

86. "Cattaraugus County Labor Day Celebration at Little Valley Will Attract Large Crowds," *Times Herald* (Olean NY), August 23, 1927, 3; "Plan Running of Marathon Rain or Shine," *Times Herald* (Olean NY), August 31, 1928, 4.

87. Peter Nelson to Leigh Kirkland, September 25, 1929, "Salamanca," CSPR.

88. Kirkland to Nelson, September 30, 1929, "Salamanca," CSPR.

89. Nelson to Kirkland, October 2, 1929, "Salamanca," CSPR.

90. "Unveil Memorial to Gen. Brodhead at Salamanca NY," *Kane (PA) Republican*, Saturday, October 5, 1929, 2.

91. Peter Nelson to William Stevenson, March 23, 1929; Peter Nelson to Frances Dorrance, March 23, 1929, "PA folder," CSPR.

92. Alexander Flick to Frances Dorrance, October 14, 1929, "PA folder," CSPR.

93. Congdon, *Allegany Oxbow*, 33.

94. Congdon, *Allegany Oxbow*, 18.

95. Congdon, *Allegany Oxbow*, 33. In August 1814, Rear Adm. George Cockburn and Maj. Gen. Robert Ross burned many federal buildings including the State Department, the War Department, and Congress.

7. The *Pageant of Decision*

1. In Flick's notes and press releases, the pageant is referred to as the *Pageant of Decision*, the title I use here. See Flick, *Sesqui History*, 563–54, 570. The full title in the printed program is *The Sullivan-Clinton Campaign: A Historical Pageant of Decision, Why the Republic Westward Grew*.

2. In *Sesqui History*, 688.

3. Glassberg, *American Historical Pageantry*, 43–44, 1.

4. Glassberg, *American Historical Pageantry*, 4.

5. Glassberg, *American Historical Pageantry*, 67.

6. Glassberg, *American Historical Pageantry*, 71.

7. O'Brien, *Firsting and Lasting*.

8. Glassberg, *American Historical Pageantry*, 139.

9. Glassberg, *American Historical Pageantry*, 147.

10. Glassberg, *American Historical Pageantry*,139–40; "firsting" is from O'Brien, *Firsting and Lasting*, chapter 1.

11. Glassberg, *American Historical Pageantry*, 209.

12. Glassberg, *American Historical Pageantry*, 113.

13. Recent immigrant populations and African Americans were usually missing from these representations of the community, however, and Native Americans rarely if ever played themselves, although notable exceptions occurred in some Western pageants and pageants written and directed by Indians. Glassberg, *American Historical Pageantry*, 131; Sundstrom, "The 'Pageant of Paha Sapa,'" 10–11, 18–21.

14. Glassberg, *American Historical Pageantry*, 265.

15. A. C. Flick, "Program Suggestions."

16. "The Sullivan-Clinton Campaign in American History," 5. This is a typed manuscript that one may assume was written by state historian Alexander C. Flick. See Flick, *Sesqui History*.

17. Out of a total of $295,000 that the Regents' Sesquicentennial Executive Committee received for seven years of work, approximately $115,000 was spent on historical pageants and "hundreds of celebrations in all parts of the State." Thompson, *Observance of the 150th Anniversary*, 65.

18. "Sullivan Army to March Again in Sesqui Celebration Pageant," *Star-Gazette* (Elmira NY), February 22, 1929, 15.

19. "Sullivan's Victory to be Re-enacted in Pageant on Actual Site of Battle," *Star-Gazette* (Elmira NY), April 27, 1929, 18.

20. Flick, *Sesqui History*, 549.

21. "2,000 Persons Sought to Participate," no source, no date, in Flick, *Sesqui History*.

22. The Society of Red Men was created in Philadelphia in 1812; an "Improved Order" was created in Baltimore decades later. These white-only fraternal societies were widespread. In Elmira, three "tribes" of "Red Men" and associated "councils" of the "Daughters of Pocahontas" were meeting in the 1920s, and they continued into the 1970s, *Star-Gazette* (Elmira NY), October 29, 1921, 7; July 13, 1974, 7. For a history and analysis of the "fraternal Indian" movement, see Deloria, *Playing Indian*, 38–70.

23. "Two thousand persons."

24. "Over 1,000 at Mobilization Meeting in Preparation for Sullivan Pageant; Rehearsals will Be Begun Wednesday," *Star-Gazette* (Elmira NY), August 20, 1929, 2.

25. "Real Indian Braves Appear in Pageant," *Dunkirk (NY) Evening Observer*, June 4, 1927, 11. In this era, Native people participated in Western and Canadian pageants as well. Lakota Sioux from the Pine Ridge Reservation participated in the Pageant of Paha Sapa, which was held in Custer, South Dakota, starting in 1923. They also engaged in several Canadian pageants, including the multi-sited pageant designed to celebrate the 250th anniversary of the Hudson Bay Company held in 1920. Sundstrom, "The Pageant of Paha Sapa," 12; Norman, "A Highly Favoured People," 131.

26. Flick, *Sesqui History*, 549.

27. Brimmer, "Sesquicentennial Pageant Producers Ware and Francis," in Flick, *Sesqui History*.

28. "Five Counties are to Take Part in Great Sullivan Pageant Here," *Star-Gazette* (Elmira NY), April 26, 1929, 21. "Sullivan's Victory to be Re-Enacted in Pageant on Actual Site of Battle," *Star-Gazette* (Elmira NY), April 27, 1929, 18.

29. "Armory Rings with Shrieks as Actors Rehearse Scenes of Noted Indian Massacres," in Flick, *Sesqui History*, n.p.

30. Frank E. Brimmer, "All in Readiness Geneseo Area Sesquicentennial September 14," September 11, 1929, in Flick, *Sesqui History*, 562.

31. Frank E. Brimmer, "Geneseo Sesquicentennial," September 13, 1929, Flick, *Sesqui History*, 563.

32. Lord, *Pageant of Decision*.

33. "Pageant Text Sullivan Campaign Celebrations at Geneseo, Geneva and Elmira Closely Follows History," in Flick, *Sesqui History*, 548.

34. Flick, *Sesqui History*, 566.

35. "Arrive Early to See 2,500 Act War Epic," in Flick, *Sesqui History*.

36. "Field Hospital Workers and Red Cross Give Aid," in Flick, *Sesqui History*.

37. "Choosing Site for 'The Pageant of Decision,'" *Star-Gazette* (Elmira NY), August 22, 1929.

38. "Continental Soldier, Red Men and Others Provide Small Bits of Diversion," *Democrat and Chronicle* (Rochester NY), September 15, 1929, 10.

39. Pageant brochure, in Flick, *Sesqui History*, 569.

40. Lord, *Pageant of Decision*, 9.

41. Lord, *Pageant of Decision*, 10.

42. Graymont, "New York State," 374–75.

43. The Royal Proclamation of 1763 and the 1768 Treaty of Fort Stanwix established lines that white settlers were not to cross. In the 1768 treaty, the Iroquois Confederacy granted huge land cessions in exchange for the British government's promise to prevent white settlement on the western side of the new line. These treaty lines were regularly crossed by pioneers. Graymont, *The Iroquois*, 3, 49.

44. Williams, *Year of the Hangman*, 186.

45. Lord, *Pageant of Decision*, 11.

46. Lord, *Pageant of Decision*, 13.

47. Calloway suggests that Washington was indeed thinking ahead to the acquisition of these lands at the end of the war and cites Flick on this point. Mintz notes that nowhere in Flick's comprehensive collections is there corroborative evidence. Calloway, *The Indian World*, 259; Mintz, *Seeds of Empire*, 76.

48. Lord, *Pageant of Decision*, 15–16.

49. Lord, *Pageant of Decision*, 16.

50. This council appears to be an imaginative reconstruction of several different meetings held both prior to and during the Revolutionary War.

51. Lord, *Pageant of Decision*, 23.

52. Lord, *Pageant of Decision*, 24.

53. "Over 1,000 at Mobilization Meeting in Preparation for Sullivan Pageant; Rehearsals will Be Begun Wednesday," *Star-Gazette* (Elmira NY), August 20, 1929, 2.

54. Part of Flick's sesquicentennial ceremonies included the white settler marking of a "torture tree" with state-sponsored plaques and detailed descriptions. A detailed discus-

sion of county public history commemorations from the 1840s to 2004 can be found in Alden, ed., *The Sullivan Campaign*.

55. Lieutenant Thomas Boyd was sent to find the village of Chenussio (Geneseo) but disobeyed orders, brought more men than ordered to, and walked into an ambush. Some fourteen men were killed; Boyd and Private Michael Parker were captured alive and later killed. Soldier accounts described their awful torture; oral history accounts from Indian eyewitnesses challenge this perspective. See Williams, *Year of the Hangman*, 284; Sohso-wa (Bucktooth), a Seneca man, relayed that there was no dishonoring of bodies. In Draper, *Notes of Border History*, 108.

56. Seaver, *A Narrative of the Life of Mrs. Mary Jemison*, vii–viii.

57. Seaver, *A Narrative*, 54.

58. Lord, *Pageant of Decision*, 32.

59. Lord, *Pageant of Decision*, 33.

60. On the violation of federal Trade and Intercourse Acts in the extinguishment of Oneida title, see Hauptman, *Conspiracy of Interests*, 33; on the fraudulent nature of the treaties of 1823 and 1826 with the Seneca, 160.

61. Lord, *Pageant of Decision*, 33.

62. Lord, *Pageant of Decision*, 35.

63. Lord, *Pageant of Decision*.

64. Fischer, *A Well-Executed Failure*, 34–35.

65. Flick, "New Sources." See Mintz, *Seeds of Empire*, 76. While Flick's sources on the Sullivan Expedition are not definitive, Calloway makes a convincing argument that Washington's focus, throughout his life, was on obtaining Indian land. See *Indian World*.

66. Hauptman, *Conspiracy of Interests*, 7–8, 144–45, 150–52.

67. Hauptman finds it notable that Everett, whose career was finished after his report was submitted, went on to represent the Iroquois in a 1927 land case. See *The Iroquois and the New Deal*, 12.

68. Upton, *The Everett Commission*, 129–30.

69. Parker was born on the Cattaraugus Reservation in 1881, the son of Geneva Griswold, a missionary's daughter, and Frederick Ely Parker, a man of Seneca and English descent. He was adopted into the Seneca Bear clan at Tonawanda in 1903 (Bruchac, *Savage Kin*, 48, 55). On his early life, see Bruchac, 48–83. He had a remarkable career, publishing multiple books and serving New York as state archaeologist for two decades (1906–24). He was one of the founding members of the Society of American Indians, where he often pushed for assimilationist positions. At the time of his publication he was director of the Rochester Municipal Museum. His complicated positioning within Haudenosaunee and non-Native communities is perhaps best exemplified by the fact that he served on the Everett Commission as secretary, and the stenographer repeatedly noted that Parker regularly agreed with Everett's points, yet he refused to sign the final report. As Upton observes, he was a state employee. Upton, *The Everett Report*. On Parker's politics and ambivalent insider/outsider status, see also Colwell-Chanthaphonh, *Inheriting the Past*, and Porter, *To Be Indian*.

70. Parker, "The Indian Interpretation," 45.

71. Parker, "The Indian Interpretation," 46–47.

72. Parker, "The Indian Interpretation," 48.

73. Parker, "The Indian Interpretation," 50.

74. Parker, "The Indian Interpretation," 52.

75. Parker, "The Indian Interpretation," 53

76. Parker, "The Indian Interpretation," 53.

77. Parker, "The Indian Interpretation," 56.

78. Parker, "The Indian Interpretation," 57.

79. Parker, "The Indian Interpretation," 57.

80. O'Brien, *Firsting and Lasting*, 36.

81. According to Boyd Cothran, restoring American innocence was one of the motivations for a public history complex developed around the Modoc War. Cothran, *Remembering the Modoc War*.

82. Flick, *Sesqui History*, 550.

83. As a 1952 article in the *New York Times*, "History Tour of the Finger Lakes Area" advocates, "vacationists interested in history can see the Finger Lakes of New York by following the route of Sullivan's March." Helen Wales, "History Tour of the Finger Lakes Area," *New York Times*, July 20, 1952, x19; Cornell, "Retracing the Route."

84. H. Allen Gosnell to New York State historian, August 6, 1953. 22353–413, "Historic Area Markers," "Bronze, Sullivan-Clinton" folder, Education Department, Division of Archives and History, box 17, NYSA.

85. See for example William Tyrell to Mr. Winne, Historian, Town of Cherry Valley, October 27, 1955, "Historic Area Markers," "Bronze, Sullivan-Clinton" folder, Education Department, Division of Archives and History, box 17, NYSA.

8. A Tale of Two States

1. Helen Wales, "History Tour of the Finger Lakes Area," *New York Times*, July 20, 1952, x19; Cornell, "Retracing the Route"; Zackery Irwin, "Sullivan Made Historic Indian March through Poconos," *Pocono Record* (Stroudsburg PA), July 20, 1968, 29.

2. Charles Hunt writes about the difficulty in locating "the trail" in 1923 and calls on organizations such as the DAR and historical societies to put up more markers. "Jaunt Along Sullivan Trail from Townersville PA to Ithaca," unknown news source, August 31, 1923. CCHSC.

3. Foote, *Shadowed Ground*, 7–35.

4. Foote, *Shadowed Ground*, 8.

5. Foote, *Shadowed Ground*, 263.

6. Foote, *Shadowed Ground*, 35.

7. Foote, *Shadowed Ground*, 29.

8. The monument to the Groveland ambuscade memorializes thirteen men killed in an ambush that occurred at the end of the Sullivan Expedition in September 1779. See chap8n11.

9. Giguere, *Memorial Architecture*, 3, 103.

10. James Young makes a similar point about uncut stones.

11. The Cuylerville complex has an elaborate history and merits its own thorough treatment. Early white settlers found the remains of two men five decades after the expedition and determined that these were the remains of Thomas Boyd and Michael Parker, two men captured with an Oneida man, Honyose Thaosagwat, in an ambush that left thirteen men dead. The remains were reburied in a grand ceremony at Rochester's Mount Hope Cemetery in 1841. Descriptions of Boyd's and Parker's corpses and discussions of torture appear in several soldiers' journals, while Native eyewitnesses deny that torture occurred. Livingston County Historical Society established a monument to the Groveland ambuscade in 1901 and a wayside "shrine" next to the alleged "torture tree" in 1927. Mintz, *Seeds*

of Empire, 137–45; on this Livingston County commemorative complex over time, see Alden, *The Sullivan Campaign*; "General Sullivan Memorial Will Be Unveiled Thursday," *Wilkes-Barre (PA) Times Leader*, November 21, 1927; "Wilkes-Barre Set Like a Gem on Sullivan Trail," *Wilkes-Barre (PA) Record*, October 17, 1927, 17; "Wilkes-Barre To-day Proclaims Its Delight over Sullivan Trail Opening," *Wilkes-Barre (PA) Record*, October 17, 1927, 17.

12. Deloria, *Indians in Unexpected Places*; Hamann, "Chronological Pollution."

13. Mintz, *Seeds of Empire*, 94; Harding, *The Sullivan Road*, 14. Wallace offers a detailed discussion of Indian routes across Pennsylvania and Sullivan's troops' use of them, *Indian Paths*, 124, 157, 188, 191. By the 1760s, the route from Easton to Wyoming was "more than a bridle path" but in no way passable for the army's wagon trains. Harding, *The Sullivan Road*, 7.

14. Maoz Azaryahu, "The Power of Commemorative Street Names"; Maoz Azaryahu and Arnon Golan, "(Re)Naming the Landscape"; Carter, *The Road to Botany Bay*; Smith, *Decolonizing Methodologies*, 84.

15. "General Sullivan Trail Boosters," *Wilkes-Barre (PA) Semi-Weekly Record*, March 9, 1917, 6.

16. "Parting Shots," *Wilkes-Barre (PA) Times Leader*, September 30, 1929, 25.

17. "Parting Shots" compares at length the New York and Wilkes-Barre pageants, finding the former much smaller, lacking the colorful effects of the lighting system.

18. "Parting Shots."

19. "Sullivan Thanksgiving Service Witnessed by Large Audience," *Easton (PA) Express*, October 18, 1929, 1.

20. O'Brien, *Firsting and Lasting*, 26, 36.

21. Penn's repeated land purchases led to nearly complete dispossession of the colony's original inhabitants by the late eighteenth century. Newman, *On Records*, 130; Kenny, *Peaceable Kingdom Lost*, 15–19.

22. Venables, "A Battle of Remembrance," 152.

9. Dueling Celebrations

1. New York State ceded control of the park to Chemung County from 1991 to January 1, 2005. Office of Parks, Recreation, and Historic Preservation, "Newtown Battlefield Reservation State Park" pamphlet. State of New York, "History of the Newtown Battlefield Reservation," http://chemungvalley.org/history%20park.htm.

2. Jeff Murray, "Revolutionary War Comes Alive at Park," *Star-Gazette* (Elmira NY), August 31, 2015, 3A.

3. Mark Andrew, interview by the author, August 29, 2015, Newtown Battlefield Park.

4. Donating groups in 2015 included several branches of the Knights of Columbus, the Italian-American Veterans of Luzerne County, veterans organizations (the American Legion, Sons of the American Legion, the Korean War Veterans Association of Wyoming Valley), one chapter of the Sons of the American Revolution, four chapters of the Daughters of the American Revolution, the Children of the Revolution, Daughters of 1812, Society of Mayflower Descendants, and the Sons and Daughters of the Susquehanna Company.

5. Connerton, *How Societies Remember*, 65.

10. Wyoming's Lasting Shadow

1. Ed, interview by the author, March 5, 2017, Sugar Run PA.

2. Ida, interview by the author, August 9, 2016, Tunkhannock PA.

3. Laura, Gertrude, and Geraldine (retired schoolteachers, Wyoming County schools), interview by the author, August 11, 2016, Tunkhannock PA.

4. Lowenthal, *The Past Is a Foreign Country*, 49.

5. Lowenthal, *The Past Is a Foreign Country*, 49.

6. Henry (metal detectorist), interview by the author, May 26, 2016, Tunkhannock PA.

7. John (retired surveyor), interview by the author, Tunkhannock PA, June 23, 2015.

8. John was talking about the "Great Warrior Path" that ran from Athens to Sunbury, a trail used in times of war and peace. Sullivan's troops followed it from Wyoming to Tioga Point (see Wallace, *Indian Paths*, 72–74, 157). John was critiquing both the inappropriate use of the label "Sullivan's" for paths created by Native Americans and the underlying assumption that Native Americans were innately "warlike." On the building of the route across the Pocono Mountains, see Mintz, *Seeds of Empire*, 94–95. On remnants of the military road in the late nineteenth century, see Harding, *The Sullivan Road*.

9. It is not my place to police Native boundaries, but I should note that this organization is not recognized by the federal government or federally recognized Lenape nations.

10. Barbara, interview by the author, October 2, 2015, Towanda PA.

11. Bob (boilermaker), interview by the author, September 24, 2016, Noxen PA.

12. Connerton, *How Modernity Forgets*, 19–33.

13. Harding says that he was killed by a falling tree. *The Sullivan Road*, 10. "Plan Dedication of Hungry Hill Next Month," *Morning Call* (Allentown PA), September 4, 1943, 5.

14. "Will Preserve Monroe Shrine," *Morning Call* (Allentown PA), January 15, 1943, 30.

15. "To Preserve Hungry Hill as Shrine in Monroe," *Morning Call* (Allentown PA), February 17, 1943, 15.

16. Kietryn Zychal, "Hungry Hill Revolutionary War Monument Undergoing Restoration," *Pocono (PA) Record*, November 8, 2007.

17. Beth Brelje, "Hungry Hill: Preserved for Future Generations," *Pocono (PA) Record*, May 28, 2013.

18. "Official Program. Dedication of Granite Tablets at Memorial Park, Laurel Run Road, Bear Creek Township PA."

19. Note the use of "we" in this statement: "We do this so that we can remember, memorialize, and preserve the historic significance of Major General John Sullivan's campaign during the Revolutionary War for our posterity. We and our future generations must never forget how those troops of the American Revolutionary Army and these courageous frontier men and women settlers molded our lives more than even our own parents," taped public ceremony, June 24, 2017.

20. Kresge, public address, June 24, 2017, Bear Creek Township PA.

21. Kresge, interview by the author, July 3, 2018, Bear Creek Township PA.

11. New York's Conflicting Voices

1. Payne Horning, "Replica Columbus Ships Draw Thousands of People—and a Few Protesters—to Oswego Harbor," WRVO Public Media Here & Now, Morning Edition, July 24, 2017.

2. Hauptman, *The Iroquois Struggle*; Hauptman, *In the Shadow*, 21–48, 224–64; "Taxation Disputes, Late Twentieth Century."

3. Laurence M. Hauptman, "The Historical Background to the Present-Day Seneca Nation–Salamanca Lease Controversy," 70–71.

4. Hauptman, *The Iroquois Struggle*, 202.

5. Hauptman discusses how in a context of pending land claims, it is difficult for municipalities to secure bank loans or even federal grants. "The Historical Background," 74.

6. Minutes, "Sullivan-Clinton Expedition Bicentennial—1979," Chemung County Historical Society, November 4, 1977. SCF, CCHA.

7. General letter of June 22, 1978, from Thomas Byrne, Chemung County Historian. SCF, CCHA; Walter Long, "Sullivan-Clinton '79," unpublished memorandum, SCF.

8. Byrne, "A Bicentennial Remembrance."

9. Ed Rossman, "Sullivan-Clinton Campaign," news clipping, n.d., SCF.

10. Sessler in Chris Lavin, "Responses to the Cayuga Land Claim," 92–94.

11. NOON, Neighbor to Neighbor, 33–34. See also Bruyneel, Third Space, 205–14.

12. A good review of this era can be found in Vecsey and Starna, Iroquois Land Claims.

13. Joan O'Dell, interview by the author, June 10, 2017, Horseheads NY.

14. Ellsworth Cowles, "The Sullivan Campaign, 1978 & 1979."

15. This and all subsequent passages with Dick Cowles are from an interview by the author conducted November 11, 2016, Waverly NY.

16. Cowles, "The Sullivan Expedition," 4.

17. Cowles, "The Sullivan Expedition," 5.

18. Cowles, "The Sullivan Expedition," 5.

19. Dick Cowles, interview by the author, November 11, 2016, Waverly NY.

20. Blee and O'Brien, Monumental Mobility, 202.

21. G. Peter Jemison, interview by the author, July 12, 2017, Victor NY. All subsequent statements from Jemison are from this interview.

12. Changing the Narrative

1. Loewen, Lies Across America, 443–45.

2. Broadrose, "Memory Spaces and Contested Pasts," 241.

3. Coupal, "Vandalism on the Santa Fe Trail."

4. Osborne, "Counter-Monumentality," 163.

5. Osborne, "Counter-Monumentality," 164.

6. Osborne, "Counter-Monumentality," 164.

7. Amy, interview by the author, July 20, 2016, Tunkhannock PA. All subsequent passages from Amy are from the same interview.

8. Remsen, "Visions of Teaoga," 58.

9. Remsen, "Visions of Teaoga," 76.

10. Remsen, "Visions of Teaoga," 12.

11. Remsen, "Visions of Teaoga," 87.

12. Remsen, interview by the author, December 4, 2017.

13. Remsen, "Visions of Teaoga."

14. Remsen, "Visions of Teaoga," 174.

15. Remsen, interview by the author, December 4, 2017.

16. Remsen, interview by the author, December 4, 2017.

17. Popular Memory Group, "Popular Memory," 207.

18. NOON, Neighbor to Neighbor, 7.

19. In some sources, 1613 is identified as the year of the treaty meeting. The significance of the treaty into the present day is attested by many: see Lyons, "Indian Self-Government"; Jemison, "Sovereignty and Treaty Rights." For a thorough discussion of the origins of wam-

pum and the foundational role the Two Row wampum plays in shaping how Haudenosaunees see their relationship to Euro-Americans today, see Kelsey, *Reading the Wampum*, 2–26. The "kaswentha" or "guswenta" is described as the political philosophy and message of "mutual assistance and noninterference" (Parmenter, *Edge of the Woods*, 64). Sources that consider the tension between the documentary and oral historical records on existing "two row" or "two stripe" wampum include Becker, "Two Stripe"; and Parmenter, "The Meaning of Kaswentha." Michael Oberg notes that whether or not the Two Row belt represents what contemporary Haudenosaunees claim that it means, "there is powerful evidence that the Haudenosaunee conducted their relations with their neighbors in accord with the contemporary understandings of the principle of guswenta." Oberg, *Peacemakers*, 13. There were some eighty educational programs across New York to commemorate the Two Row Wampum Treaty's 400th anniversary, which culminated in a paddling trip down the Hudson River, from Albany to New York City, featuring a row of Native paddlers on one side and a row of non-Native allies on the other. Andy M., interview by the author, July 13, 2017, Syracuse NY.

20. NOON, *Neighbor to Neighbor*, 8.

21. NOON, *Neighbor to Neighbor*, 8.

22. Author interview of Sue Eiholzer and Gail Bundy, June 18, 2018, Liverpool NY.

23. Eiholzer and Bundy interview. All subsequent excerpts are from this taped interview.

24. Andy, interview by author, July 13, 2017, Syracuse NY.

25. "Sullivan and Clinton," Neighbors of the Onondaga Nation, www.peacecouncil.net/NOON/markers-sullivanclinton.html.

26. O'Brien, *Firsting and Lasting*.

27. Eiholzer and Bundy interview.

28. These questions are also available via the "start here" tab: www.peacecouncil.net/NOON/markers/marker-sullivanclinton.html.

29. "Sullivan and Clinton," Neighbors of the Onondaga Nation, www.peacecouncil.net/NOON/markers-sullivanclinton.html.

30. An article on the saga of this marker is in preparation by Randy A. John and Andrea Smith.

31. Connerton, *How Modernity Forgets*, 20.

32. Connerton, *How Modernity Forgets*, 11.

33. Smith and Eisenstein offer a rich literature review on displacement, place loss, and psychic harm: *Rebuilding Shattered Worlds*.

34. G. Peter Jemison, interview by author, July 12, 2017, Victor NY.

13. Haudenosaunee Consciousness

1. The forum, "Revisiting Washington's Assault on the Haudenosaunee 240 Years Later," was sponsored by Skä•nonñ–Great Law of Peace Center, Syracuse University Humanities Center, and the Indigenous Values Initiative, October 10, 2020. Also speaking that day were Alyssa Mt. Pleasant (historian and scholar of Native American & Indigenous studies, University at Buffalo) and Philip Arnold (associate professor and religion dept. chair, Syracuse University).

2. This is the subject of works in anthropology and related fields. For an excellent literature review of works on Native American views of the past that includes Native American historians and other scholars, see Nabokov, "Native Views of History."

3. Some soldiers expressed misgivings in their journals. See Jabez Campfield, in Calloway, *The Indian World*, 253.

4. An excellent meditation on the infiltration of terms from Indian wars into the military can be found in Bruyneel, "Codename Geronimo."

5. On dating the founding of the Confederacy, see George-Kanentiio, *Iroquois Culture and Commentary*, 27–28. On the origin of wampum and their politics within settler society, see Kelsey, *Reading the Wampum*, xi–xxvii.

6. Cornplanter's statement in Kent and Deardorff, "View of John Adlum on the Allegheny," 459. These actions by Sullivan's soldiers are corroborated in soldiers' journals.

7. Rossen, *Corey Village and the Cayuga World*, 2.

8. "Ogweñ•yó'da' déñ'se' Hanadagá•yas: The Cicada and George Washington," Onondaga Nation, May 14, 2018, https://www.onondaganation.org/blog/2018/ogwenyoda-dense-hanadagayas-the-cicada-and-george-washington/.

9. G. Peter Jemison, "The American Revolution and the Battle of Newtown," in NBP, 43.

10. Richard Hill, "The Indian Expedition of 1779 and Haudenosaunee Responses," in CBP, 79–80.

11. Ferdinand de Jong, "Archiving after Empire"; Swedenburg, *Memories of Revolt*; Rappaport, *Cumbe Reborn*; Smith, "Heteroglossia, 'Common Sense,' and Social Memory."

12. Cook, *Journals of the Military Expedition*.

13. Public Archaeology Facility CBP, NBP.

14. Conversation in Salamanca, August 13, 2017.

15. Vizenor coined the term "survivance" to capture the experience of survival and resistance together, how he viewed Indigenous experience. Vizenor, *Manifest Manners*, vii.

16. "George Washington to Major General John Sullivan, May 31, 1779," GWP. https://www.loc.gov/item/mgw3b.009/.

17. Other renditions of the name include Caunotaucarius and Ganondaganiou (devourer of villages). See John, *Seneca People*, 157; Congdon, *Allegany Oxbow*, 142; "George Washington to Andrew Montour, October 10, 1755," National Archives. This name was originally given to John Washington, Washington's great-grandfather.

18. "The Speech of the Cornplanter, Half-Town, and Great-Tree, Chiefs and Councillors of the Seneca Nation to the Great Councillor of the Thirteen Fires," in Abler, *Chainbreaker*, 238. See Calloway, *The Indian World*, 397–404, for additional context for these meetings.

19. This point is especially developed in Hill, *The Clay We Are Made Of*.

20. We might see this stance on my part as a kind of ethnographic "refusal," à la Simpson. I want to also point out that scholars such as Alyssa Mt. Pleasant have commenced such a project.

21. Lonetree, *Decolonizing Museums*, 5.

22. Nason, "'Our' Indians," 35.

23. Nason, "'Our' Indians," 36–37.

24. West, "A New Idea of Ourselves," 7–8.

25. Lonetree, *Decolonizing Museums*, 16.

26. Lonetree, *Decolonizing Museums*, 19.

27. Root, "New Museum."

28. Shako:wi Cultural Center, Oneida, accessed July 8, 2018, http://www.oneidaindiannation.com/shakowiculturalcenter/.

29. Ironically, the most prominent actors had been the men most closely tied to the Oneidas during the Revolutionary War. Hauptman, *Conspiracy of Interests*, 16.

30. Glatthaar and Martin, *Forgotten Allies*, 314.

31. Glatthaar and Martin, *Forgotten Allies*, 314–19.

32. Hauptman, *Conspiracy of Interests*, 56.

33. Glatthaar and Martin, *Forgotten Allies*, 319.

34. Kandyce Watson, interview by author, June 7, 2017. All other passages are from this interview.

35. Bilharz, *Oriskany*, ii.

36. After major protests by Mohawks in 1868 and Onondagas in 1971 involving boycotts of the public schools, the New York Legislature passed a bill in 1977 creating an Indian public library system. Hauptman, *Seven Generations of Iroquois Leadership*, 197–99.

37. "Ska•noñh Visitor's Guide," Onondaga Historical Association.

38. Phil Arnold, interview by the author, July 13, 2017, Liverpool NY; Phil Arnold and Sandy Bigtree, interview by the author, September 30, 2021, Liverpool NY.

39. Ryan and Stokes-Rees, "A Tale of Two Missions," 26. This article offers an excellent examination of the updating of two French Jesuit mission sites.

40. Ryan and Stokes-Rees, 28.

41. Ryan and Stokes-Rees, 28–31. The saga of the French fort park reflects the burden faced by other historic sites with irregular and inadequate funding. The Onondaga County Parks and Recreation's Living History program took it over in 1975. It was renovated in 1991 and renamed "Sainte Marie among the Iroquois," but budget constraints led the parks and recreation department to close the site. Reopened by volunteers in 2004, it was brought under the purview of the Friends of Historic Onondaga Lake, another volunteer organization. A few years later, the second-floor space of the visitor center was leased to the County Soil and Water District. Russ Tarby, "Great Law of Peace Center to Transform Ste. Marie," November 28, 2012, Onondaga Historical Association, https://www.cny-history.org/wp-content/themes/oha/press/2012-11-28-SR-GL.pdf.

42. Ryan and Stokes-Rees, "A Tale," 31.

43. Smith, "Settler Historical Consciousness," 156–57.

44. Onondaga clan mother Dorothy Webster met OHA director Gregg Tripoli at an Onondaga Nation craft fair and explained, "You have something that belongs to us," referring to human remains and sacred objects she had learned were being held at a downtown Syracuse storeroom. Since the OHA was a privately funded museum, it was not required to repatriate these items under NAGPRA. After receiving the approval of the museum board, the OHA returned the human remains to the Onondaga nation in a private ceremony, and held a public ceremony at its downtown Syracuse museum, on June 12, 2012, to mark the return of a 212-year-old wampum belt to the Onondaga Nation. Soon after, the Cayuga Museum of History and Art, of nearby Auburn, New York, followed suit by returning twenty-one sacred objects to the Onondaga Nation. Sean Kirst, "More than Objects: Sacred Artifacts Return to the Onondagas," *Post-Standard* (Syracuse NY), June 5, 2012. Sean Kirst, "A Modern Exchange of Wampum: In a Museum, Healing Wounds"; *Post-Standard* (Syracuse NY), June 12, 2012; Gale Toensing, "Return of Sacred Items Heals Onondaga Nation," *Indian Country Today*, accessed June 16, 2012, https://indiancountrytoday.com/archive/return-of-sacred-items-heals-onondaga-nation; Moses, "Onondaga Nation Thanks Cayuga Museum with Replica Wampum Belt," *Post-Standard* (Syracuse NY), December 19, 2012.

45. Phil Arnold, interview by the author, July 13, 2017, Liverpool NY; Phil Arnold and Sandy Bigtree, interview with the author, September 30, 2021, Liverpool NY. The

institutional structure poses challenges: the center is not an official tribal museum owned and operated by the Haudenosaunee, but an Onondaga County facility that is managed by the OHA, and the museum staff are OHA employees. See Ryan and Stokes-Rees, "A Tale," 32.

46. Eiholzer and Bundy interview; Ryan and Stokes-Rees, "A Tale," 28.

47. Post-Standard Editorial Board, "Great Law: Education Center Would Honor Haudenosaunee Contributions," *Post-Standard* (Syracuse NY), November 27, 2012; Michelle Breidenbach, "Old Sainte Marie Among the Iroquois to Start Switch to Ska-nonh Great Law of Peace Center," Syracuse.com, August 8, 2015, https://www.syracuse.com/news/2015/08/old_sainte_marie_among_the_iroquois_to_start_switch_to_ska-nonh_great_law_of_pea.html.

48. Post-Standard Editorial Board, "Great Law."

49. Glenn Coin, "Onondaga Historical Association to Transform County Historic Site into Haudenosaunee Museum," *Post-Standard* (Syracuse NY), November 19, 2012; OHA website, accessed June 10, 2018.

50. Michelle Breidenbach, "OHA Director Answers Reader Comments about New Ska-Noñh–Great Law of Peace Center," Syracuse.com, August 19, 2015, https://www.syracuse.com/news/2015/08/oha_director_answers_reader_comments_about_new_ska-nonh_great_law_of_peace_cente.html.

51. Breidenbach, "OHA Director."

52. Ryan and Stokes-Rees, "A Tale," 32. Phil Arnold, Jack Mano, and Betty Lyons are collaborative directors. Interview with Phil Arnold and Sandy Bigtree, Liverpool NY, September 30, 2021.

53. Ryan and Stoke-Rees, "A Tale," 32.

54. Ryan and Stoke-Rees, "A Tale," 36.

55. Hamer, "Learn about the Haudenosaunee;" Moses, "Ska-nonh Great Law of Peace Center to Open Saturday," *Post-Standard* (Syracuse NY), November 20, 2015; Rob Enslin, "University Joins in Grand Opening of Ska-honh Center Nov. 20–21," *Syracuse University News* November 18, 2015.

56. Ryan and Stoke-Rees, 35; "Skä noñh Visitor's Guide."

57. Lyons in Alex Hamer, "Learn about the Haudenosaunee."

58. Liptak, "Meet Tadodaho," 44.

59. Ska•noñh exhibit text, Liverpool NY.

60. Ska•noñh exhibit text, Liverpool NY.

61. "Ska•noñh Visitor's Guide."

62. New York State Office of Parks, Recreation and Historic Preservation, "Granary Trail at Fort Hill," Ganondagan State Historic Site, undated brochure.

63. Will Harrison, "Historic Indian Site Imperiled?" *Democrat and Chronicle* (Rochester NY), December 10, 1966, 14; "Seneca Indians' Eyes Site for U.S. Park," *Democrat and Chronicle* (Rochester NY), May 12, 1960; Charles Dorland, "A Gatherer of History," Upstate Update, August 9, 1987.

64. Rich Thomas, "Dirt Washer Bares History of Senecas," *Democrat and Chronicle* (Rochester NY), May 8, 1966, 34; George Murphy, "A Tree Grows in Gannagaro," *Democrat and Chronicle* (Rochester NY), May 21, 1967, 28; "Two Syracuse Senators Try to Kill Gannagaro Project," *Daily Messenger* (Canandaigua NY), 3.

65. Jack Jones, "Seneca Indian Park to Open Next Summer," *Democrat and Chronicle* (Rochester NY), October 17, 1986, 5.

66. G. Peter Jemison, "History and Culture Come to Life."

67. Rebecca Rafferty, "The Freedom of Perspective. At the Seneca Art & Culture Center, People Tell Their Own Stories," *Greater Rochester's Alternative Newsweekly*, 45, no. 9 (November 4–10, 2015): 28.

68. Rafferty, "The Freedom," 29.

69. Peter Jemison and Michael Galban, "Completion of a Dream: The Seneca Art & Culture Center," Rochestercitynewspaper.com, 11.

70. Ganondagan, accessed June 1, 2018, http://www.ganondagan.org.

71. Jemison and Galban, "Completion of a Dream," 11.

72. Rafferty, "The Freedom," 29.

73. The Seneca Nation was awarded direct damages from the breaking of the 1794 Canandaigua Treaty in Section 4 of the Final Settlement (Public Law 88–533, August 31, 1964). Over $12 million was deposited into an account that generates interest to be used for community members, to be used to improve the economic, social, and educational conditions of enrolled members. These funds are sometimes referred to as "Section 4 monies." See Bilharz, *The Allegany Senecas*, 71. The hard-fought struggle to use the funds for the museum and library is discussed in Hauptman, *In the Shadow of Kinzua*.

74. The Pennsylvania legislature granted three tracts of land to Seneca leader Cornplanter on February 3, 1791, to recognize his assistance in preventing war in the Ohio country. Abler, *Cornplanter*, 83.

75. Bilharz, *The Allegany Senecas*, v, xx; Hauptman, *In the Shadow of Kinzua*, xv. Seneca villages developed along the Allegheny River on both sides of the state boundaries. See Bilharz, *The Allegany Senecas*; Abler, *Cornplanter*, 83.

76. Tribal Council for the Seneca Nation, Special Session Resolution of September 5, 1984, cited in Bilharz, *The Allegany Senecas*, 1; See John, *Social Integration of an Elderly Native American*.

77. Seneca-Iroquois National Museum, accessed October 5, 2021, https://www.senecamuseum.org/.

78. Lonetree, *Decolonizing Museums*, 26.

79. Lonetree, *Decolonizing Museums*, 26, 173.

80. An excellent discussion of Haudenosaunee land-centered historical consciousness can be found in Hill, *The Clay We Are Made Of*.

14. Epilogue

1. Rifkin, *Settler Common Sense*, xvii.

2. Blackhawk, *Violence over the Land*; Ostler, *Surviving Genocide*; Estes, *Standing Rock*.

3. Anderson, *Imagined Communities*.

4. Zerubavel, *Time Maps*.

5. Denson, *Monuments to Absence*.

6. The Voortrekker monument in South Africa and its related story of Afrikaan sacrifice and martyrdom shares many parallels with the Wyoming Monument. See Grundlingh, "A Cultural Conundrum"; Weaver-Hightower, "'Before God This Was.'"

7. Conn, *History's Shadow*, 5; Deloria, *Playing Indian*, 5.

8. Timothy and Boyd, *Tourism and Trails*, 26–27.

9. Denson, *Monuments to Absence*, 8.

10. Smith, *Decolonizing Methodologies*, 84

11. Smith, *Decolonizing Methodologies*, 84.

12. Conner, "Our People Have Always Been Here," 107–12. See also Deloria, *Custer Died for Your Sins*.

13. Cameron, *Far off Metal River*, 133.

14. Connerton, *How Modernity Forgets*, 89; Smith and Eisenstein, *Rebuilding Shattered Worlds*.

15. Connerton makes a similar point regarding mass migrations in general, writing "the history of mass migration is part of the history of modern forgetting, and of forgetting places in particular." *How Modernity Forgets*, 135.

16. Henry, *Performing Place*, 42.

17. Henry, *Performing Place*, 66.

18. Henry, *Performing Place*, 31.

19. Henry, *Performing Place*, 32.

20. Carter, *The Road to Botany Bay*, 340.

21. Anderson, *The Storied Landscape*.

22. While she clearly outlines the trauma experienced by Haudenosaunee by the many removals associated with the American Revolution and the division of families, Mohawk scholar Susan Hill also notes that many Grand River families stay in touch with relatives in the original homelands. *The Clay We Are Made Of*, 270.

23. Anderson, *The Storied Landscape*.

24. Smith and Eisenstein, *Rebuilding Shattered Worlds*.

25. This indigenization drive is outlined in many sources. See O'Brien, *Firsting and Lasting*; Johnston and Lawson, "Settler Colonies."

26. Navaro-Yashin, *The Make-Believe Space*, 13.

27. Navaro-Yashin, *The Make-Believe Space*, 144.

28. Navaro-Yashin, *The Make-Believe Space*, 144.

29. Navaro-Yashin, *The Make-Believe Space*, 153.

30. Navaro-Yashin, *The Make-Believe Space*, 152.

31. Navaro-Yashin, *The Make-Believe Space*, 191.

32. Williams, *Marxism and Literature*, 116.

BIBLIOGRAPHY

Archives

BCHS. Bradford County Historical Society. Towanda PA.

CBP. Public Archaeology Facility. "Chemung Battlefield Project." Documentary Research Report and Research Design. ARPA Compliant Copy. National Park Service. Coedited by Brian Grills, Michael Jacobson, Richard Kastl, and Nina Versaggi. Report submitted to the American Battlefield Protection Program (Grant #GA-2255-09-022). Prepared by the Public Archaeology Facility, Binghamton University. Binghamton NY.

CCHO. Cayuga County Historian's Office. Auburn NY.

CCHSC. Cayuga County Historical Society Collection. Cayuga Museum of History and Art. Auburn NY.

CSPR. Correspondence of the Supervisor of Public Records and the Secretary of the Advisory Committee on the Commemoration of the Sullivan Campaign. Series B0566. New York Education Department, Division of Archives and History. NYSA.

EBP. Erl Bates Papers. #21-24-790. Division of Rare and Manuscript Collections. Cornell University. Ithaca NY.

GWP. George Washington Papers. Series 3: Varick Transcripts, 1775 to 1785. Subseries 3B: Continental and State Military Personnel, 1775 to 1783. Letterbook 9: September 9, 1779. Manuscript/Mixed Material.

HAF. "Indians, Onondaga. Individuals, Hill, Avis, David R." Folder. Onondaga Historical Association. Syracuse NY.

HASMF. Historic Area/Site Marker Files, 1927–2005. Series 22353. Records of the New York State Education Department, Division of Archives and History. NYSA.

HDF. "Indians–Onondaga Individuals, Hill, David R." Folder. Onondaga Historical Association, Syracuse NY.

HMPR. Historical Marker Program. Reports, Contracts, Correspondence, and Miscellaneous Records 1924–1945. RG13.100. Records of the Pennsylvania Historical and Museum Commission. PSA.

IHB. Bronze Plaques, 1914–1995. Bradford County–Indian Hill Battlefield, 1929. RG13.112, Carton 6, Folder 5/30. Historical Marker Files. Records of the Pennsylvania Historical and Museum Commission. PSA.

JF. Johnson Fort. Site–Syr-Sullivan and Clinton Johnson Fort.

LCHS. Luzerne County Historical Society, Wilkes-Barre PA.

LCR. Historical Markers, 1916–1968. Luzerne County Roadside, 1933–1946. RG13.112, Carton 15, Folder 14/28. Historical Marker Files. Records of the Pennsylvania Historical and Museum Commission. PSA.

LCSC. Lafayette College Special Collections. Skillman Library, Easton PA.

LHB. Bronze Plaques, 1914–1995. Bradford County–Lime Hill Battlefield, 1929. RG13.112, Carton 6, Folder 5/23. Historical Marker Files. Records of the Pennsylvania Historical and Museum Commission. PSA.

NBP. Public Archaeology Facility, "Newtown Battlefield Project." Documentary Research Report and Research Design. ARPA Compliant Copy. National Park Service. Co-edited by Brian Grills, Michael Jacobson, Richard Kastl and Nina Versaggi. Report submitted to the American Battlefield Protection Program (Grant #GA-2255-08-017). Prepared by the Public Archaeology Facility, 2010. Binghamton University. Binghamton NY.

NYSA. New York State Archives. Albany NY.

PHC. Pennsylvania Historical Commission.

PHC. Minutes. Minutes of the Pennsylvania Historical Commission. RG13.102. Records of the Pennsylvania Historical and Museum Commission. PSA.

PSA. Pennsylvania State Archives. Harrisburg PA.

SCCF. Sullivan-Clinton Centennial Folder. Subject Files, Code VF, 500–110. Chemung County Historical Society, Elmira NY.

SCEF. Sullivan Clinton Expedition Folder, Military History: Revolution. Onondaga Historical Association. Syracuse NY.

SCF. Sullivan-Clinton Folder. Cayuga County Historian Archives. Auburn NY.

SCSCF. Celebration–1929–Sullivan-Clinton Sesqui-Centennial. Folder of clippings and correspondence. Onondaga Historical Association, Syracuse NY.

SEF. Sullivan Expedition folder. BCHS.

TPDAR. Tioga Point Chapter Daughters of the American Revolution. Clippings file. Tioga Point Museum, Athens PA.

WCHS. Wyoming County Historical Society, Tunkhannock PA.

WMBMS. "Wyoming Memorial Battle and Massacre Scrapbook, 1778–1878." Prepared by F. C. Johnson. Paginated manuscript of clippings compiled from several newspapers. LCHS.

WMF. Wyoming Monument Folder. LCHS.

WPWP. W. Pierrepont White Papers. Correspondence. Oneida County History Center, Utica NY.

Published Works and Unpublished Manuscripts

Abler, Thomas S. *Cornplanter: Chief Warrior of the Allegany Senecas.* Syracuse NY: Syracuse University Press, 2007.

———, ed. *Chainbreaker: The Revolutionary War Memoirs of Governor Blacksnake as Told to Benjamin Williams.* Lincoln: University of Nebraska Press, 2006.

Alden, Amie, ed. *The Sullivan Campaign of the Revolutionary War. The Impact on Livingston County NY, 1779–2004.* Henrietta NY: Pioneer, 2006.

Allen, Thomas B. *Tories: Fighting for the King in America's First Civil War.* New York: Harper, 2010.

Alonso, Ana. "The Effects of Truth." *Journal of Historical Sociology* 1, no.1 (1988): 33–57.

Amato, Alain. *Monuments en exil.* Paris: Éditions de l'Atlanthrope, 1979.

Ames, Michael. *Cannibal Tours and Glass Boxes: The Anthropology of Museums.* Vancouver: University of British Columbia Press, 1992.

Anderson, Benedict R. *Imagined Communities: Reflections on the Origin and Spread of Nationalism.* Brooklyn: Verso, 2006.

Anderson, Chad. *The Storied Landscape of Iroquoia: History, Conquest, and Memory in the Native Northeast.* Lincoln: University of Nebraska Press, 2020.

Andrlik, Todd. "The Twenty-Five Deadliest Battles of the Revolutionary War." In *Journal of the American Revolution.* May 13, 2014. https://allthingsliberty.com/2014/05/the-25-deadliest-battles-of-the-revolutionary-war/.

Appel, John C. "Colonel Daniel Brodhead and the Lure of Detroit." *Pennsylvania History: A Journal of Mid-Atlantic Studies* 38, no. 3 (1971): 265–82.

———. "Colonel Daniel Brodhead and the Problems of Military Supply on the Western Frontier, 1779–1781." *Milestones* 4 (1978).

Asad, Talal. *Anthropology and the Colonial Encounter.* New York: Humanities Press, 1973.

Assmann, Jan. "Communicative and Cultural Memory." In *A Companion to Cultural Memory Studies,* edited by Astrid Erll and Ansgar Nünning, 109–18. Berlin: Walter de Gruyter, 2010.

———. *Moses the Egyptian: The Memory of Egypt in Western Monotheism.* Cambridge MA: Harvard University Press, 1997.

Attwood, Bain. "Denial in a Settler Society: The Australian Case." *History Workshop Journal* 84, no. 1 (October 25, 2017): 24–43.

———. *Telling the Truth about Aboriginal History.* Crows Nest, Australia: Allen & Unwin, 2005.

Autry, Robyn K. *Desegregating the Past: The Public Life of Memory in the United States and South Africa.* New York: Columbia University Press, 2017.

Azaryahu, Maoz. "The Power of Commemorative Street Names." *Environment and Planning.* 14, no. 3 (1996): 311.

Azaryahu, Maoz, and Arnon Golan. "(Re)Naming the Landscape: The Formation of the Hebrew Map of Israel 1949–1960." *Journal of Historical Geography* 27, no. 2 (2001): 178–95.

Baker, Paula. "The Gilded Age: 1860–1914." In *The Empire State: A History of New York,* edited by Milton M. Keith, 419–515. Ithaca NY: Cornell University Press, 2001.

Basso, Keith. *Wisdom Sits in Places. Landscape and Language among the Western Apache.* Albuquerque: University of New Mexico Press, 1996.

Becker, Howard. *Outsiders: Studies in the Sociology of Deviance.* New York: Free Press, 1963.

Becker, Marshall. "Native Settlements in the Forks of Delaware PA in the 18th Century: Archaeological Implications." *Pennsylvania Archaeologist* 58, no. 1 (1988): 43–60.

———. "Two Stripe ('Two Path') Wampum Belts: Different Tropes for a Single Decorative Theme." *Northeast Anthropology* 87–88 (2021): 37–71.

Berkhofer, Robert F. *The White Man's Indian: Images of the American Indian from Columbus to the Present.* New York: Knopf, 1978.

Bilharz, Joy Ann. *The Allegany Senecas and Kinzua Dam: Forced Relocation through Two Generations.* Lincoln: University of Nebraska Press, 1998.

———. *Oriskany: A Place of Great Sadness.* Boston: National Park Service, 2009.

A Biographical Record of Chemung County NY. New York: S. J. Clarke, 1902.

Blackhawk, Ned. "The Iron Cage of Erasure: American Indian Sovereignty in Jill Lepore's *These Truths.*" *American Historical Review* 125, no. 5 (December 29, 2020): 1752–63.

———. *Violence over the Land: Indians and Empires in the Early American West.* Cambridge MA: Harvard University Press, 2006.

Blee, Lisa, and Jean M. O'Brien. *Monumental Mobility: The Memory Work of Massasoit.* Chapel Hill: University of North Carolina Press, 2019.

Bloch, Maurice. *From Cognition to Ideology: In Power and Knowledge: Anthropological and Sociological Approaches.* Edinburgh: Scottish Academic Press, 1985.

———. *How We Think They Think: Anthropological Approaches to Cognition, Memory, and Literacy.* Boulder CO: Westview, 1998.

Bodnar, John. *Remaking America: Public Memory, Commemoration, and Patriotism in the Twentieth Century.* Princeton NJ: Princeton University Press, 1992.

Bokovoy, Matthew F. *The San Diego World's Fairs and Southwestern Memory, 1880–1940.* Albuquerque: University of New Mexico Press, 2005.

Boyarin, Jonathan. *Space, Time, and the Politics of Memory.* Minneapolis: University of Minnesota Press, 1995.

Bradsby, H. C., ed. *History of Luzerne County, Pennsylvania, with Biographical Selections.* Chicago: S. B. Nelson, 1893.

Bright, William. *Native American Placenames of the United States.* Norman: University of Oklahoma Press, 2004.

Broadrose, Brian. "Memory Spaces and Contested Pasts in the Haudenosaunee Homeland." In *Between Memory Sites and Memory Networks: New Archaeological and Historical Perspectives,* edited by Kerstin Hofmann, Reinhard Bernbeck, and Ulrike Sommer, 227–252. Berlin: Edition Topoi, 2017.

Bronner, Edwin B. *William Penn's "Holy Experiment": The Founding of Pennsylvania, 1681–1701.* Philadelphia: Temple University Publications, 1962.

Bronner, Simon J. *Popularizing Pennsylvania: Henry W. Shoemaker and the Progressive Uses of Folklore and History.* University Park: Pennsylvania State University Press, 1996.

Brooks, Lisa Tanya. *Our Beloved Kin: A New History of King Philip's War.* New Haven: Yale University Press, 2018.

Brow, James. "Notes on Community, Hegemony, and the Uses of the Past." *Anthropological Quarterly* 63, no. 1 (January 1990): 1–6.

Brown, James, and Rita Kohn, eds. *Long Journey Home: Oral Histories of Contemporary Delaware Indians.* Bloomington: Indiana University Press, 2008.

Bruchac, Margaret. *Savage Kin: Indigenous Informants and American Anthropologists.* Tucson: University of Arizona Press, 2018.

Bruyneel, Kevin. "Codename Geronimo: Settler Memory and the Production of American Statism." *Settler Colonial Studies* 6, no. 4 (2016): 349–64.

———. *The Third Space of Sovereignty: The Postcolonial Politics of U.S.-Indigenous Relations.* Minneapolis: University of Minnesota Press, 2007.

Bryant, Rebecca. *The Past in Pieces: Belonging in the New Cyprus.* Philadelphia: University of Pennsylvania Press, 2010.

Bryant, William Cullen, and Sydney Gay. *A Popular History of the United States: From the First Discovery of the Western Hemisphere by the Northmen to the End of the First Century of the Union of the States: Preceded by a Sketch of the Prehistoric Period and the Age of the Mound Builders.* New York: Charles Scribner's Sons, 1883.

Buss, Jim J. "'They Found and Left Her an Indian': Gender, Race, and the Whitening of Young Bear." *Frontiers: A Journal of Women Studies* 29, no. 2–3 (2008): 1–35.

Butterfield, Lyman. "History at its Headwaters." *New York History* 51, no. 2 (1970): 127–46.

Byrne, Thomas E. "A Bicentennial Remembrance of the Sullivan-Clinton Expedition 1779 in Pennsylvania and New York." New York State Bicentennial Commission, Chemung County Historical Society. S E F.

———. "Sullivan Centennial Drew 50,000 in 1879." *Chemung Historical Journal* (June 1979): 2885–890.

Calloway, Colin G. *The American Revolution in Indian Country: Crisis and Diversity in Native American Communities*. Cambridge: Cambridge University Press, 1995.

———. *The Indian World of George Washington: The First President, the First Americans, and the Birth of the Nation*. New York: Oxford University Press, 2018.

Cameron, Emilie. *Far off Metal River: Inuit Lands, Settler Stories, and the Makings of the Contemporary Arctic*. Vancouver: University of Columbia Press, 2016.

Campbell, Thomas. *Gertrude of Wyoming: A Pennsylvanian Tale. And Other Poems*. London: T. Bensley, 1809.

Campisi, Jack, and William A. Starna. "On the Road to Canandaigua: The Treaty of 1794." *American Indian Quarterly* 19, no. 4 (Fall 1995): 467–90.

Cardinia, Miguel and Inês Rodrigues. "The Mnemonic Transition: The Rise of an Anti-Anticolonial Memoryscape in Cape Verde." *Memory Studies* 14, no. 2 (2020): 380–94.

Carl, Matthew T., ed. *A Traveler's Guide to Bradford County Historical Markers and Monuments*. Towanda P A: Bradford County Historical Society, 2014.

Carter, Paul. *The Road to Botany Bay: An Exploration of Landscape and History*. New York: Alfred A. Knopf, 1987.

Casey, Edward. *Getting Back into Place. Toward a Renewed Understanding of the Place-World*. Bloomington: Indiana University Press, 1993.

Chujo, Ken. "The Daughters of the American Revolution and Its Attitude toward African Americans." *Transforming Anthropology* 13, no. 2 (October 2005): 160–64.

Colwell-Chanthaphonh, Chip. *Inheriting the Past. The Making of Arthur C. Parker and Indigenous Archaeology*. Tucson: University of Arizona Press, 2009.

———. *Massacre at Camp Grant: Forgetting and Remembering Apache History*. Tucson: University of Arizona Press, 2007.

Congdon, Charles E. *Allegany Oxbow: A History of Allegany State Park and the Allegany Reserve of the Seneca Nation*. United States: n.p., 1967.

Conn, Steven. *History's Shadow: Native Americans and Historical Consciousness in the Nineteenth Century*. Chicago: University of Chicago Press, 2004.

Conner, Roberta. "Our People Have Always Been Here." In *Lewis and Clark through Indian Eyes*, edited by Alvin M. Josephy, 85–119. New York: Knopf, 2006.

Connerton, Paul. *How Modernity Forgets*. Cambridge: Cambridge University Press, 2009.

———. *How Societies Remember*. Cambridge: Cambridge University Press, 1989.

Cook, Frederick, and New York (State) Secretary's Office. *Journals of the Military Expedition of Major General John Sullivan against the Six Nations of Indians in 1779*. Auburn N Y: Knapp, Peck & Thomson, Printers, 1887.

Coombes, Annie E. *Rethinking Settler Colonialism: History and Memory in Australia, Canada, Aotearoa New Zealand and South Africa*. Manchester: Manchester University Press, 2006.

Cooper, Frederick, and Ann Laura Stoler, eds. *Tensions of Empire: Colonial Cultures in a Bourgeois World*. Berkeley: University of California Press, 1997.

Cornell, Thomas D. "Retracing the Route of the Sullivan Expedition through Pennsylvania." *Crooked Lake Review* (Fall 1999). https://www.crookedlakereview.com/articles/101_135/113fall1999/113cornell.html.

Cothran, Boyd. *Remembering the Modoc War: Redemptive Violence and the Making of American Innocence.* Chapel Hill: The University of North Carolina Press, 2014.

Countryman, Edward. *Enjoy the Same Liberty: Black Americans and the Revolutionary Era.* Lanham MD: Rowman & Littlefield, 2012.

———. *A People in Revolution: The American Revolution and Political Society in New York, 1760–1790.* Baltimore: Johns Hopkins University Press, 1981.

Coupal, Shirley. "Vandalism on the Santa Fe Trail DAR Markers." *Wagon Tracks* 29, no. 1 (November 2014): 18.

Cowles, Ellsworth. "The Sullivan Campaign. 1978 and 1979." Typed manuscript. Susquehanna River Archaeological Center of Native Indian Studies. Waverly NY. Author's collection.

Dahl, Adam. *Empire of the People: Settler Colonialism and the Foundations of Modern Democratic Thought.* Lawrence: University Press of Kansas, 2018.

Daughters of the American Revolution, Pennsylvania. *Pennsylvania State History of The Daughters of the American Revolution,* n.d.

Davies, Edward J., II. *The Anthracite Aristocracy: Leadership and Social Change in the Hard Coal Regions of Northeastern Pennsylvania, 1800–1930.* DeKalb: Northern Illinois University Press, 1985.

Davies, Wallace Evan. *Patriotism on Parade: The Story of Veterans' and Hereditary Organizations in America, 1783–1900.* Cambridge MA: Harvard University Press, 1955.

Davis, Rochelle. *Palestinian Village Histories: Geographies of the Displaced.* Stanford CA: Stanford University Press, 2011.

de Jong, Ferdinand, "Archiving after Empire. Saint-Louis and its Sufi Counter-Memory," *Francosphères* 3, no. 1 (2014): 25–41.

Deloria, Philip Joseph. *Indians in Unexpected Places.* Lawrence: University Press of Kansas, 2004.

———. *Playing Indian.* New Haven: Yale University Press, 1998.

Deloria, Vine. *Custer Died for Your Sins: An Indian Manifesto.* New York: Macmillan Company, 1969.

DeLucia, Christine M. *Memory Lands: King Philip's War and the Place of Violence in the Northeast.* New Haven: Yale University Press, 2018.

Denson, Andrew. *Monuments to Absence.* Chapel Hill: The University of North Carolina Press, 2017.

Dippie, Brian W. *The Vanishing American: White Attitudes and U.S. Indian Policy.* Middletown CT: Wesleyan University Press, 1982.

Division of Archives and History. *The American Revolution in New York: Its Political, Social, and Economic Significance: For General Use as Part of the Program of the Executive Committee on the One Hundred and Fiftieth Anniversary of the American Revolution.* Albany NY: University of the State of New York, 1926.

———*The Sullivan-Clinton Campaign in 1779: Chronology and Selected Documents.* Albany: University of the State of New York, 1929.

Doss, Erika. *Memorial Mania: Public Feeling in America.* Chicago: University of Chicago Press, 2010.

Downes, Randolph C. *Council Fires on the Upper Ohio: A Narrative of Indian Affairs in the Upper Ohio Valley until 1795*. Pittsburgh: University of Pittsburgh Press, 1977.

Draper, Lyman Copeland, and Jare R. Cardinal (transcriptionist). *Notes of Border History: Taken on a Trip to the Western Part of Penn., & the Adjoining Parts of New York & Ohio, from Jan. 30th to March 9th, 1850: Relating to the Lives & Adventures of Western Pioneers—and the History & Warfare of the Six Nations*. Salamanca NY: RAJ, 2017.

Drummond, Richard C. S. "Original Manuscript of Richard C. S. Drummond. At Dedication of Monument at Great Gully. September 24, 1929." CCHSCF.

Dunbar-Ortiz, Roxanne. *An Indigenous Peoples' History of the United States*. Boston: Beacon Press, 2014.

Edson, Obed. "Brodhead's Expedition against the Indians of the Upper Allegheny 1779." *Magazine of American History* 3, no. 11 (1879): 649–75.

Elago, Helvi. "Colonial Monuments in a Post-Colonial Era: A Case Study of the Equestrian Monument." In *Re-Viewing Resistance in Namibian History*, edited by Jeremy Silvester, 276–91. Windhoek: University of Namibia Press, 2015.

Elkins, Caroline, and Susan Pedersen. *Settler Colonialism in the Twentieth Century: Projects, Practices, Legacies*. New York: Routledge, 2005.

Engels, Jeremy, and Greg Goodale. "'Our Battle Cry Will Be: Remember Jenny McCrea!': A Précis on the Rhetoric of Revenge." *American Quarterly* 61, no. 1 (2009): 93–112.

Epstein, Andrew Bard. "Unsettled New York: Land, Law, and Haudenosaunee Nationalism in the Early Twentieth Century." Master's thesis, University of Georgia, 2012.

Erll, Astrid, and Nünning, Ansgar. *A Companion to Cultural Memory Studies*. Berlin: De Gruyter, 2010.

Errington, Jane. "Loyalists and Loyalism in the American Revolution and Beyond." *Acadiensis* 41, no. 2 (2012): 164–73.

Estes, Nick. *Standing Rock versus the Dakota Access Pipeline, and the Long Tradition of Indigenous Resistance*. London: Verso, 2019.

Evensen, Bruce J. "'Saving the City's Reputation': Philadelphia's Struggle over Self-Identity, Sabbath-Breaking, and Boxing in America's Sesquicentennial Year." *Pennsylvania History: A Journal of Mid-Atlantic Studies* 60, no. 1 (1993): 6–34.

Fanon, Frantz, Richard Philcox, and Jean-Paul Sartre. *The Wretched of the Earth*. New York: Grove, 2004.

Feld, Steven, and Keith Basso. *Senses of Place*. Santa Fe NM: School of American Research Press, 1996.

Fenton, William N. *The Great Law and the Longhouse: A Political History of the Iroquois Confederacy*. Norman: University of Oklahoma Press, 1998.

———. "Northern Iroquoian Cultural Patterns." In *Handbook of North American Indians*. Vol. 15, *Northeast*, edited by Bruce Trigger, 296–321. Washington DC: Smithsonian, 1978.

Ferguson, T. J., and Chip Colwell. *History is in the Land: Multivocal Tribal Traditions in Arizona's San Pedro Valley*. Tucson: University of Arizona Press, 2006.

Fischer, Joseph R. "The Forgotten Campaign of the American Revolution: The Sullivan-Clinton Expedition Against the Iroquois in 1779." *Valley Forge Journal* 4, no. 4 (1989): 279–306.

———. *A Well-Executed Failure: The Sullivan Campaign against the Iroquois, July–September 1779*. Columbia: University of South Carolina Press, 1997.

Flick, Alexander C. "New Sources on the Sullivan-Clinton Campaign in 1779." *Quarterly Journal of the New York State Historical Association* 10, no. 3 (1929): 185–224.

———. "Program Suggestions for 150th Anniversary of the Revolution." *Bulletin to the Schools.* The State Department of Education, April 15, 1926.

———. *Sesqui History: General Files Relating to Observances of the 150th Anniversary of the American Revolution and Other Events* (unpublished manuscript). New York State Education Department, Division of Archives and History, NYSA. (This mostly paginated manuscript includes hundreds of clippings organized by location and the pages are stored as follows: 1–139 are in 13912–83, box 1; 140–290 are in 13912–00, box 2; and 291 and above are in 13912–00, box 1. When possible, relevant page numbers are included.)

Folts, James. "The Munsee Delawares of Chemung/Wilawana in the Revolutionary War Era." The Public Archaeology Facility, Binghamton University. April 12, 2019.

———. "The Sullivan Campaign: A Bibliography," *University of Rochester Library Bulletin* 32 (Winter 1979): 1–9.

Foote, Kenneth E. *Shadowed Ground: America's Landscapes of Violence and Tragedy.* Austin: University of Texas Press, 1997.

Fujikane, Candace, and Jonathan Okamura, eds. *Asian Settler Colonialism: From Local Governance to the Habits of Everyday Life in Hawai'i.* Honolulu: University of Hawai'i Press, 2008.

Furniss, Elizabeth. *The Burden of History: Colonialism and the Frontier Myth in a Rural Canadian Community.* Vancouver: University of British Columbia Press, 1999.

Gay, W. B. *Historical Gazetteer of Tioga County, New York, 1785–1888.* Evansville IN: Unigraphic, 1978.

George-Kanentiio, Douglas M. *Iroquois Culture & Commentary.* Santa Fe NM: Clear Light, 2000.

Giguere, Joy M. *Memorial Architecture, National Identity, and the Egyptian Revival.* Knoxville: University of Tennessee Press, 2014.

Glassberg, David. *American Historical Pageantry: The Uses of Tradition in the Early Twentieth Century.* Chapel Hill: University of North Carolina Press, 1990.

———. *Sense of History: The Place of the Past in American Life.* Amherst: University of Massachusetts Press, 2001.

Glatthaar, Joseph T., and James Kirby Martin. *Forgotten Allies: The Oneida Indians and the American Revolution.* New York: Hill and Wang, 2006.

Gordon, Scott Paul. "The Paxton Boys and the Moravians: Terror and Faith in the Pennsylvania Backcountry." *Journal of Moravian History* 14, no. 2 (October 1, 2014): 119–52.

———. "Yoked by Violence: The Paxton Boys, Representation, and a 'Humble Petition.'" *Journal of Early American History* 11, no. 2–3 (May 2021): 169–92.

Graham, Jack. "The Keystone Markers of Pennsylvania: History in Cast Iron and a Good Sign for the Future." *Pennsylvania History* 84, no. 2 (April 1, 2017): 239–48.

Graymont, Barbara. *The Iroquois in the American Revolution.* Syracuse NY: Syracuse University Press, 1972.

———. "New York State Indian Policy After the Revolution." *New York History* 57, no. 4 (1997): 438–74.

Griffis, William. "The History and Mythology of Sullivan's Expedition." *Report of the Proceedings of the Wyoming Commemorative Association on the Occasion of the 125th Anniversary of the Battle and Massacre of Wyoming.* July 3, 1903. Wilkes-Barre PA.

Grumet, Robert Steven. *Historic Contact*. Norman: University of Oklahoma Press, 1995.

——. *The Munsee Indians: A History*. Norman: University of Oklahoma Press, 2009.

Grundlingh, Albert M. "A Cultural Conundrum? Old Monuments and New Regimes: The Voortrekker Monument as Symbol of Afrikaner Power in a Postapartheid South Africa." *Radical History Review* 81, no. 1 (October 1, 2001): 95–112.

Haan, Richard. "Covenant and Consensus: Iroquois and English, 1676–1760." *Beyond the Covenant Chain: The Iroquois and Their Neighbors in Indian North America, 1600–1800*, edited by Daniel Richter and James Merrell, 42–32. Syracuse NY: Syracuse University Press, 1987.

Halbwachs, Maurice. *The Collective Memory*. New York: Harper Colophon, 1980.

Halbwachs, Maurice, and Lewis A. Coser. *On Collective Memory*. Chicago: University of Chicago Press, 1992.

Hamann, Byron Ellsworth. "Chronological Pollution. Potsherds, Mosques, and Broken Gods before and after the Conquest of Mexico." *Current Anthropology* 49, no. 5, 803–36.

Hamer, Alex. "Learn About the Haudenosaunee: Great Law of Peace Center Opens." *Indian Country Today*. https://indiancountrytoday.com/archive/learn-about-the-haudenosaunee-great-law-of-peace-center-opens-14-images.

Handler, Richard, and Eric Gable. *The New History in an Old Museum: Creating the Past at Colonial Williamsburg*. Durham: Duke University Press, 1997.

Handsman, Richard G. "Landscapes of Memory in Wampanoag Country—and the Monuments Upon Them." In *Archaeologies of Placemaking: Monuments, Memories, and Engagement in Native North America*, edited by Patricia E. Rubertone, 161–193. Walnut Creek CA: Left Coast, 2008.

Harding, Garrick M. *The Sullivan Road, A Paper Read by Garrick M. Harding before the Wyoming Valley Chapter, Daughters of the American Revolution*. Wilkes-Barre: Press of the Wilkes-Barre Record, 1900.

Harned, Miriam Kern, and Daughters of the American Revolution. *Pennsylvania State History of the Daughters of the American Revolution, 1947*. Lititz PA: Wagaman Bros., 1947.

Harper, Steven Craig. *Promised Land: Penn's Holy Experiment, the Walking Purchase, and the Dispossession of Delawares, 1600–1763*. Bethlehem PA: Lehigh University Press, 2006.

Harvey, Oscar Jewell. *A History of Wilkes-Barré, Luzerne County, Pennsylvania: From Its First Beginnings to the Present Time, Including Chapters of Newly Discovered Early Wyoming Valley History, Together with Many Biographical Sketches and Much Genealogical Material*. Wilkes-Barre PA: Raeder, 1909.

Hauptman, Laurence M. *Coming Full Circle: The Seneca Nation of Indians, 1848–1934*. Norman: University of Oklahoma Press, 2019.

——. *Conspiracy of Interests: Iroquois Dispossession and the Rise of New York State*. Syracuse NY: Syracuse University Press, 1999.

——. "Designing Woman: Minnie Kellogg, Iroquois Leader." In *Indian Lives: Essays on Nineteenth- and Twentieth-Century Native American Leaders*, 159–88. Syracuse NY: Syracuse University Press, 1993.

——. "The Historical Background to the Present-Day Seneca Nation–Salamanca Lease Controversy." In *Iroquois Land Claims*, edited by Christopher Vecsey and William A. Starna, 100–122. Syracuse NY: Syracuse University Press, 1988.

——. *In the Shadow of Kinzua: The Seneca Nation of Indians since World War II*. Syracuse NY: Syracuse University Press, 2013.

——. *The Iroquois and the New Deal*. Syracuse NY: Syracuse University Press, 1981.

———. "Iroquois Land Issues: At Odds with the 'Family of New York.'" In *Iroquois Land Claims*, edited by Christopher Vecsey and William A. Starna, 67–86. Syracuse NY: Syracuse University Press, 1988.

———. *The Iroquois Struggle for Survival: World War II to Red Power*. Syracuse NY: Syracuse University Press, 1986.

———. *An Oneida Indian in Foreign Waters: The Life of Chief Chapman Scanandoah, 1870–1953*. Syracuse NY: Syracuse University Press, 2016.

———. *Seven Generations of Iroquois Leadership: The Six Nations since 1800*. Syracuse NY: Syracuse University Press, 2008.

———. *The Tonawanda Senecas' Heroic Battle against Removal: Conservative Activist Indians*. Albany NY: Excelsior/State University of New York Press, 2011.

Henry, Rosita. *Performing Place, Practising Memories: Aboriginal Australians, Hippies, and the State*. New York: Berghahn, 2014.

Heverly, Clement Ferdinand. *History and Geography of Bradford County, Pennsylvania, 1615–1924*. Towanda PA: Bradford County Historical Society, 1926.

Hewitt, J. N. B., "Etymology of the Word Iroquois." *American Anthropologist* 1, no. 2 (April 1888): 188–89.

Hild, Matthew. *Greenbackers, Knights of Labor, and Populists: Farmer-Labor Insurgency in the Late–Nineteenth Century South*. Athens: University of Georgia Press, 2007.

Hill, Susan M. *The Clay We Are Made Of: Haudenosaunee Land Tenure on the Grand River*. Winnipeg: University of Manitoba Press, 2017.

Hixson, Walter L. *American Settler Colonialism: A History*. New York, NY: Palgrave Macmillan, 2013.

Hobsbawm, E. J., and T. O. Ranger. *The Invention of Tradition*. Cambridge: Cambridge University Press, 1983.

Hopkins, Julia. "Mach-wi-hi-lu-sing Chapter." *Daughters of the American Revolution Magazine* 46, no. 4 (April 2015): 230–31.

Hristova, Marije, Francisco Ferrándiz and Johanna Vollmeyer. "Memory Worlds: Reframing Time and the Past—An Introduction." *Memory Studies* 13, no. 5 (October 1, 2020): 777–91. https://doi.org/10.1177/1750698020944601.

Ingalsbe, Grenville M. "A Bibliography of Sullivan's Indian Exhibition." *Proceedings of the New York State Historical Association* 6 (1906): 37–70.

Ingold, Tim. *Lines: A Brief History*. London: Routledge, 2007.

Irwin-Zarecka, Iwona. *Frames of Remembrance: The Dynamics of Collective Memory*. New Brunswick NJ: Transaction, 1994.

Jacobs, Margaret D. "Parallel or Intersecting Tracks? The History of the U.S. West and Comparative Settler Colonialism." *Settler Colonial Studies* 4, no. 2 (April 3, 2014): 155–161.

———. *White Mother to a Dark Race: Settler Colonialism, Maternalism, and the Removal of Indigenous Children in The American West and Australia, 1880–1940*. Lincoln: University of Nebraska Press, 2009.

Jacoby, Karl. *Shadows at Dawn: A Borderlands Massacre and the Violence of History*. New York: Penguin, 2008.

Jemison, G. Peter. "History and Culture Come to Life. The Seneca Art and Culture Center at Ganondagan." *New York State Conservationist*, October 2016, 14–16.

———. "Sovereignty and Treaty Rights—We Remember." In *Treaty of Canandaigua 1794: 200 Years of Treaty Relations between the Iroquois Confederacy and the United States*, edited by G. Peter Jemison and Anna M. Schein, 148–61. Santa Fe NM: Clear Light, 2000.

Jemison, G. Peter, and Anna M. Schein, eds. *Treaty of Canandaigua 1794: 200 Years of Treaty Relations between the Iroquois Confederacy and the United States.* Santa Fe NM: Clear Light, 2000.

Jenkins, John. "Journal of Lieut. John Jenkins." In *Journals of the Military Expedition of Major General John Sullivan against the Six Nations of Indians in 1779,* edited by Frederick Cook, 168–77. Auburn NY: Knapp, Peck & Thomson, 1887.

Jennings, Francis. *The Ambiguous Iroquois Empire: The Covenant Chain Confederation of Indian Tribes with English Colonies from Its Beginnings to the Lancaster Treaty of 1744.* New York: Norton, 1984.

———. "The Bicentennial, A Report and an Invitation," *Pennsylvania History: A Journal of Mid-Atlantic Studies* 39, no. 3 (1972): 298–300.

John, Randy A. *Seneca People: Places and Names.* Salamanca NY: RAJ, 2017.

———. *Social Integration of an Elderly Native American Population.* 2nd ed. Allegany Territory, Seneca Nation: RAJ, 2013.

———. *Who is Walter Kennedy?* Allegany Territory, Seneca Nation: RAJ, 2019.

Johnston, Anna, and Alan Lawson. "Settler Colonies." In *A Companion to Postcolonial Studies,* edited by Henry Schwartz and Sangeeta Ray, 360–76. Oxford: Blackwell, 2000.

Jones, Dorothy V. *License for Empire: Colonialism by Treaty in Early America.* Chicago IL: University of Chicago Press, 1982.

Jones, Jeffrey Owen, and Peter Meyer. *The Pledge: A History of the Pledge of Allegiance.* New York: St. Martin's, 2010.

Jordan, Kurt A. *The Seneca Restoration, 1715–1754: An Iroquois Local Political Economy.* Gainesville: University Press of Florida, 2008.

Kadman, Noga, Oren Yiftachel, and Dimi Reider. *Erased from Space and Consciousness: Israel and the Depopulated Palestinian Villages of 1948.* Bloomington: Indiana University Press, 2015.

Kammen, Michael G. *A Season of Youth: The American Revolution and the Historical Imagination.* New York: Knopf, 1978.

———. *Mystic Chords of Memory: The Transformation of Tradition in American Culture.* New York: Knopf, 1991.

Kelman, Ari. *A Misplaced Massacre: Struggling over the Memory of Sand Creek.* Cambridge: Harvard University Press, 2013.

Kelsey, Penelope Myrtle. *Reading the Wampum: Essays on Hodinöhsö:ni' Visual Code and Epistemological Recovery.* Syracuse NY: Syracuse University Press, 2014.

Kenny, Kevin. *Peaceable Kingdom Lost: The Paxton Boys and the Destruction of William Penn's Holy Experiment.* New York: Oxford University Press, 2009.

Kent, Donald H., and Merle H. Deardorff. "John Adlum on the Allegheny: Memoirs for the Year 1794: Part 2." *Pennsylvania Magazine of History and Biography* 84, no. 4 (1960): 435–80.

Koehler, Rhiannon. "Hostile Nations: Quantifying the Destruction of the Sullivan-Clinton Genocide of 1779." *American Indian Quarterly* 42, no. 4 (October 1, 2018): 427–53.

Kosasa, Karen. "Sites of Erasure. The Representation of Settler Culture in Hawai'i." In *Asian Settler Colonialism: From Local Governance to the Habits of Everyday Life in Hawai'i,* edited by Candace Fujikane and Jonathan Y. Okamura, 195–208. Honolulu: University of Hawai'i Press, 2008.

Koselleck, Reinhart. *Futures Past: On the Semantics of Historical Time.* New York: Columbia University Press, 2004.

Kugelmass, Jack, and Jonathan Boyarin, eds. *From a Ruined Garden: The Memorial Books of Polish Jewry*. Bloomington: Indiana University Press, 1998.

Lamar, Clarinda Pendleton. *A History of the National Society of the Colonial Dames of America, from 1891 to 1933*. Atlanta: Walter W. Brown, 1934.

Laubach, Amber. "Queen Esther Montour of the Munsee Delawares: An Ethnohistoric and Archaeological History of Esther Montour and Queen Esther's Town Preserve." Master's thesis, Binghamton University, 2018.

Lavin, Chris. "Responses to the Cayuga Land Claim." In *Iroquois Land Claims*, edited by Christopher Vecsey and William A. Starna, 87–100. Syracuse NY: Syracuse University Press, 1988.

Lévi-Strauss, Claude. *The Savage Mind*. Chicago: University of Chicago Press, 1966.

Levin, Amy K. *Defining Memory: Local Museums and the Construction of History in America's Changing Communities*. Lanham MD: AltaMira, 2007.

Liptak, Matthew. "Meet Tadodaho Sid Hill," *55 Plus*, October-November, 2015, 43–44.

Lockwood, Mary S., and Susan Rivière Hetzel, eds. *Lineage Book of the Charter Members of the National Society of the Daughters of the American Revolution*. Harrisburg PA: Telegraph, 1908.

Loewen, James W. *Lies across America: What Our Historic Sites Get Wrong*. New York: New York University Press, 1999.

Lonetree, Amy. *Decolonizing Museums: Representing Native America in National and Tribal Museums*. Chapel Hill: University of North Carolina Press, 2012.

Lord, George V. C. *The Sullivan-Clinton Campaign. A Historical Pageant of Decision. Why the Republic Westward Grew* (script of the play). In *One Hundred Fiftieth Anniversary of the Sullivan-Clinton Campaign. Historical Programs and Dedication of Markers along Route of March*. Albany: University of the State of New York, 1929.

Lowenthal, David. *The Past Is a Foreign Country*. Cambridge: Cambridge University Press, 1985.

Luzerne County Historical Society. *Warrior Road: The Story of Sullivan's March through Pennsylvania before the Invasion of the Iroquois Homelands*. Audio CD set. Wilkes Barre PA: Luzerne County Convention and Visitor's Bureau, 2006.

Lyons, Oren. "Indian Self-Government in the Haudenosaunee Constitution." *Nordic Journal of International Law* 55, no. 1–2 (January 1, 1986): 117–21.

Lyons, Scott Richard. *X-marks: Native Signatures of Assent*. Minneapolis: University of Minnesota Press, 2010.

Mancall, Peter C. *Valley of Opportunity: Economic Culture along the Upper Susquehanna, 1700–1800*. Ithaca NY: Cornell University Press, 1991.

March, Francis A. "Biographical Note." In *Addresses Delivered at a Celebration in Honor of Prof. Francis A. March at Lafayette College, October 24, 1895*. Easton: Lafayette Press.

Marsh, Dawn G. *A Lenape among the Quakers: The Life of Hannah Freeman*. Lincoln: University of Nebraska Press, 2014.

McAdams, Donald R. "The Sullivan Expedition, Success or Failure." *New York Historical Society Quarterly* 54, no. 1 (1970): 53–81.

McCarthy, Theresa. *In Divided Unity: Haudenosaunee Reclamation at Grand River*. Tucson: University of Arizona Press, 2016.

McDonnell, Michael A., Clare Corbould, Frances M. Clarke, and W. Fitzhugh Brundage. *Remembering the Revolution: Memory, History, and Nation Making from Independence to the Civil War*. Amherst: University of Massachusetts Press, 2013.

McDonnell, Michael A. "War and Nationhood. Founding Myths and Historical Realities." In *Remembering the Revolution: Memory, History, and Nation Making from Independence to the Civil War*, edited by Michael A. McDonnell, Clare Corbould, Frances M. Clarke, and W. Fitzhugh Brundage, 19–40. Amherst: University of Massachusetts Press, 2013.

Meginness, John Franklin. *Biography of Frances Slocum, the Lost Sister of Wyoming.* New York: Arno, 1974.

Meier, Kathryn Shively. "'Devoted to Hardships, Danger, and Devastation': The Landscape of Indian and White Violence in Wyoming Valley, Pennsylvania, 1753–1800." In *Blood in the Hills, A History of Violence in Appalachia*, edited by Bruce E. Stewart, 53–79. Lexington: University Press of Kentucky, 2012.

Memmi, Albert. *The Colonizer and the Colonized.* Translated by Howard Greenfield. New York: Orion, 1965.

Mercur, Mary Ward. "The George Clymer Chapter." *American Monthly Magazine* 34, no. 3 (March 1909): 299–301.

Merrell, James Hart. *Into the American Woods: Negotiators on the Pennsylvania Frontier.* New York: Norton, 1999.

Michalski, Sergiusz. *Public Monuments: Art in Political Bondage, 1870–1997.* London: Reaktion, 1998.

Minderhout, David J. *Native Americans in the Susquehanna River Valley, Past and Present.* Lewisburg PA: Bucknell University Press, 2013.

Miner, Charles. *History of Wyoming, in a Series of Letters from Charles Miner to His Son William Penn Miner.* Philadelphia: J. Crissy, 1845.

Mintz, Max M. *Seeds of Empire: The American Revolutionary Conquest of the Iroquois.* New York: New York University Press, 1999.

Morgan, Francesca Constance. "'Home and Country': Women, Nation, and the Daughters of the American Revolution, 1890–1939." PhD diss., Columbia University, 1998.

———. *Women and Patriotism in Jim Crow America.* Chapel Hill: University of North Carolina Press, 2005.

Morgan, Lewis Henry. *League of the Iroquois.* New York: Corinth, 1851.

Moses, A. Dirk, ed. *Genocide and Settler Society: Frontier Violence and Stolen Indigenous Children in Australian History.* New York: Berghahn, 2005.

Moyer, Paul Benjamin. *Wild Yankees: The Struggle for Independence along Pennsylvania's Revolutionary Frontier.* Ithaca NY: Cornell University Press, 2007.

Mt. Pleasant, Alyssa. *After the Whirlwind: Maintaining a Haudenosaunee Place at Buffalo Creek, 1780–1825.* PhD diss., Cornell University, 2007.

Mt. Pleasant, Alyssa, Caroline Wigginton, and Kelly Wisecup. "Materials and Methods in Native American and Indigenous Studies: Completing the Turn." *William & Mary Quarterly* 75, no. 2 (2018): 207–236.

Munn, Nancy D. "The Cultural Anthropology of Time: A Critical Essay." *Annual Review of Anthropology* 21 (January 1, 1992): 93–123.

Murray, Louise Welles. *A History of Old Tioga Point and Early Athens, Pennsylvania.* Athens PA, 1908.

———. "A Memorial of Charlotte Marshall Holbrooke Maurice, Regent and Founder of Tioga Chapter, DAR, Athens PA," n.d. Towanda PA: Bradford County Historical Society.

Nabokov, Peter. "Native Views of History." In *The Cambridge History of the Native Peoples of the Americas.* Vol 1, *North America*, part 1, edited by Bruce Trigger and Wilcomb Washburn, 1–60. Cambridge: Cambridge University Press, 1996.

Nason, James. "'Our' Indians: The Unidimensional Indian in the Disembodied Local Past." *The Changing Presentation of the American Indian: Museums and Native Cultures*. Washington DC: National Museum of the American Indian, 2000.

National Museum of the American Indian (U.S.), ed. *The Changing Presentation of the American Indian: Museums and Native Cultures*. Seattle: University of Washington Press, 2000.

National Society of the Daughters of the American Revolution. "George Taylor Chapter," *American Monthly Magazine* 19, no. 4 (October 1901), 426.

Navaro-Yashin, Yael. *The Make-Believe Space: Affective Geography in a Postwar Polity*. Durham NC: Duke University Press, 2012.

Ndletyana, Mcebisi. "Changing Place Names in Post-Apartheid South Africa: Accounting for the Unevenness." *Social Dynamics* 38, no. 1 (March 2012): 87–103.

Newman, Andrew. *On Records: Delaware Indians, Colonists, and the Media of History and Memory*. Lincoln: University of Nebraska Press, 2012.

———. *Allegories of Encounter. Colonial Literacy and Indian Captivities*. Chapel Hill: University of North Carolina Press, 2019.

New York State Historical Association. *Proceedings of the New York State Historical Association with the Quarterly Journal: 2nd–21st Annual Meeting with a List of New Members*. Albany: New York State Historical Association, 1901.

Nora, Pierre. "Between Memory and History: Les Lieux de Mémoire." *Representations* 26 (July 24, 1989).

———. *Les Lieux de Mémoire*. 7 vols. Paris: Gallimard, 1984–1992.

Neighbors of the Onondaga Nation (NOON). *Neighbor to Neighbor Nation to Nation, Readings about the Relationship of the Onondaga Nation with Central New York, USA*. Rev. ed. Syracuse NY: NOON Peace Council, 2014.

Norman, Alison. "'A Highly Favoured People': The Planter Narrative and the 1928 Grand Historic Pageant of Kentville, Nova Scotia." *Acadiensis* 38, no. 2 (2009): 116–40.

Norton, A. Tiffany. *History of Sullivan's Campaign against the Iroquois*. Lima NY, 1879.

Novick, Peter. *That Noble Dream: The "Objectivity Question" and the American Historical Profession*. Cambridge: Cambridge University Press, 1988.

O'Brien, Jean M. *Firsting and Lasting: Writing Indians out of Existence in New England*. Minneapolis: University of Minnesota Press, 2010.

Oberg, Michael Leroy. *Peacemakers: The Iroquois, the United States, and the Treaty of Canandaigua, 1794*. Oxford: Oxford University Press, 2016.

Ohnuki-Tierney, Emiko. *Cultures through Time: Anthropological Approaches*. Stanford CA: Stanford University Press, 1990.

Osborne, James F. "Counter-Monumentality and the Vulnerability of Memory." *Journal of Social Archaeology* 17, no. 2 (2017): 163–87.

Ostler, Jeffrey. *Surviving Genocide: Native Nations and the United States from the American Revolution to Bleeding Kansas*. New Haven CT: Yale University Press, 2019.

Ousterhout, Anne M. "Frontier Vengeance: Connecticut Yankees vs. Pennamites in the Wyoming Valley." *Pennsylvania History: A Journal of Mid-Atlantic Studies* 62, no. 3 (1995): 330–63.

———. *A State Divided: Opposition in Pennsylvania to the American Revolution*. New York: Greenwood Press, 1987.

Palmié, Stephan, and Charles Stewart. "Introduction: For an Anthropology of History." *HAU: Journal of Ethnographic Theory* 6, no. 1 (July 1, 2016): 207.

Parker, Arthur C. "The Indian Interpretation of the Sullivan-Clinton Campaign." Publication Fund Series. Rochester Historical Society. Vol. 8. 45–59.

Parkinson, Robert G. *The Common Cause: Creating Race and Nation in the American Revolution*. Chapel Hill: University of North Carolina Press, 2016.

Parmenter, Jon. *The Edge of the Woods: Iroquoia, 1534–1701*. East Lansing: Michigan State University Press, 2010.

———. "The Meaning of Kaswentha and the Two Row Wampum Belt in Haudenosaunee (Iroquois) History: Can Indigenous Oral Tradition Be Reconciled with the Documentary Record?" *Journal of Early American History* 3, no. 1 (January 2013): 82–109.

Paxton, James. "Remembering and Forgetting: War, Memory, and Identity in the Post-Revolutionary Mohawk Valley." In *Remembering the Revolution: Memory, History, and Nation Making from Independence to the Civil War*, edited by Michael A. McDonnell, Clare Corbould, Frances M. Clarke, and W. Fitzhugh Brundage, 179–97. Amherst: University of Massachusetts Press, 2013.

Pearce, Roy Harvey. *Savagism and Civilization: A Study of the Indian and the American Mind*. Berkeley: University of California Press, 1988.

Peirce, H. B. Hurd, and D. Hamilton. *History of Tioga, Chemung, Tompkins, and Schuyler Counties, New York*. Philadelphia: Everts & Ensign, 1879.

Pencak, William, and Daniel K. Richter. *Friends and Enemies in Penn's Woods: Indians, Colonists, and the Racial Construction of Pennsylvania*. University Park PA: Pennsylvania State University Press, 2004.

Pennsylvania Historical Commission, ed. *First Report of the Historical Commission of Pennsylvania*. Lancaster PA: New Era, 1915.

———. *Second Report of the Pennsylvania Historical Commission*. n.p. 1915.

———. *Fifth Report of the Pennsylvania Historical Commission*. Pennsylvania Historical Commission, Commonwealth of Pennsylvania, 1931.

Pennsylvania Historical Preservation Office. "Society at 90, Celebrating the Society for Pennsylvania Archaeology's 90th Year with a Look Back at our Beginnings." https://pahistoricpreservation.com/the-society-90-spas-past/.

Perkins, George A. *Early Times on the Susquehanna*. Binghamton NY: Herald, 1906.

Pessard, Gustave. *Statuomanie Parisienne: Etude critique sur l'abus des statues*. Paris: H. Daragon.

Petrillo, F. Charles. *Albert Lewis, the Bear Creek Lumber and Ice King: The Bear Creek Ice Company*. Kearney NE: Morris, 1998.

Phelps, Martha Bennett. *Frances Slocum the Lost Sister of Wyoming*. Variation: History of Women. Reel 917, No. 7674. Self-published, 1916.

Phelps, Mrs. John Case, and Horace Edwin Hayden. *An Address: Delivered on the Occasion of the Erection of a Monument at Laurel Run, Luzerne County, Pennsylvania, September 12, 1896, to Mark the Spot Where Capt. Joseph Davis and Lt. William Jones of the Pennsylvania Line Were Slain by the Indians, April 23, 1779; with a Sketch of These Two Officers by Rev. Horace E. Hayden*. Wyoming Historical and Geological Society, 1897.

Popular Memory Group. "Popular Memory: Theory, Politics, Method." In *Making Histories: Studies in History-writing and Politics*, edited by Richard Johnson, 205–252. Birmingham, UK: Centre for Contemporary Cultural Studies, 1982.

Porter, Joy. *To Be Indian. The Life of Iroquois-Seneca Arthur Caswell Parker*. Norman: University of Oklahoma Press, 2001.

Powless, Irving, Anna M. Schein, and G. Peter Jemison, eds. *Treaty of Canandaigua 1794*. Santa Fe NM: Clear Light, 2000.

Preston, David L. *The Texture of Contact: European and Indian Settler Communities on the Frontiers of Iroquoia, 1667–1783*. Lincoln: University of Nebraska Press, 2009.

Prochaska, David. *Making Algeria French: Colonialism in Bône, 1870–1920*. Cambridge: Cambridge University Press, 1990.

Purcell, Sarah J. "Commemoration, Public Art, and the Changing Meaning of the Bunker Hill Monument." *Public Historian* 25, no. 2 (May 1, 2003): 55–71.

Radding, Lisa, and John Western. "What's in a Name? Linguistics, Geography, and Toponyms." *Geographical Review* 100, no. 3 (July 2010): 394–412.

Rana, Aziz. *The Two Faces of American Freedom*. Cambridge MA: Harvard University Press, 2010.

Raphael, Ray. *Founding Myths: Stories That Hide Our Patriotic Past*. New York: New Press, 2004.

Rappaport, Joanne. *Cumbe Reborn: An Andean Ethnography of History*. Chicago: University of Chicago Press, 1994.

Remsen, Jim. *Visions of Teaoga*. Mechanicsburg PA: Sunbury, 2014.

Richter, Daniel K. *Facing East from Indian Country: A Native History of Early America*. Cambridge MA: Harvard University Press, 2001.

———. *The Ordeal of the Longhouse: The Peoples of the Iroquois League in the Era of European Colonization*. Chapel Hill: University of North Carolina Press, 1992.

Richter, Daniel K., and James H. Merrell. "Introduction." In *Beyond the Covenant Chain, The Iroquois and Their Neighbors in Indian North America, 1600–1800*, edited by Daniel K. Richter and James H. Merrell, 5–8. Syracuse NY: Syracuse University Press, 1987.

Rickard, Clinton, and Barbara Graymont. *Fighting Tuscarora: The Autobiography of Chief Clinton Rickard*. Syracuse NY: Syracuse University Press, 1973.

Ricoeur, Paul. *Memory, History, Forgetting*. Chicago: University of Chicago Press, 2004.

Riffe, Jed. *Who Owns the Past?* Videorecording. Berkeley CA: Berkeley Media, 2002.

Rifkin, Mark. *Beyond Settler Time: Temporal Sovereignty and Indigenous Self-Determination*. Durham: Duke University Press, 2017.

———. *Settler Common Sense: Queerness and Everyday Colonialism in the American Renaissance*. Minneapolis: University of Minnesota Press, 2014.

Robinson, John K., and Karen Galle. "A Century of Marking History: 100 Years of the PA Historical Marker Program." *Pennsylvania Heritage* 40, no. 4, Fall 2014.

Root, Leanne. "New Museum of the American Revolution Shines Light on Oneida Indian Nation Contributions." *Indian Country Today*, September 13, 2018.

Rose, Deborah Bird. "New World Poetics of Place: Along the Oregon Trail and in the National Museum of Australia." In *Rethinking Settler Colonialism: History and Memory in Australia, Canada, Aotearoa New Zealand and South Africa*, edited by Annie E. Coombes, 228–44. Manchester: Manchester University Press, 2006.

Rosen, Deborah A. *American Indians and State Law: Sovereignty, Race, and Citizenship, 1790–1880*. Lincoln: University of Nebraska Press, 2007.

Rosenzweig, Roy, and David P. Thelens, eds. *The Presence of the Past: Popular Uses of History in American Life*. New York: Columbia University Press, 1998.

Rossen, Jack, ed. *Corey Village and the Cayuga World: Implications from Archaeology and Beyond*. Syracuse NY: Syracuse University Press, 2015.

Rüsen, Jörn. *Western Historical Thinking: An Intercultural Debate*. New York: Berghahn, 2002.

Russell, Lynette. *Colonial Frontiers: Indigenous-European Encounters in Settler Societies*. Manchester: Manchester University Press, 2001.

Ryan, Beth. *Crowding the Banks: The Historical Archaeology of Ohagi and the Post-Revolutionary Haudenosaunee Confederacy, ca. 1780–1826*. Ann Arbor MI: ProQuest Information and Learning, 2017.

Ryan, Debora, and Emily Stokes-Rees. "A Tale of Two Missions: Common Pasts/Divergent Futures at Transnational Historic Sites." *Public Historian* 39, no. 3 (2017): 10–39.

Sahlins, Marshall. *Islands of History*. Chicago: University of Chicago Press, 1985.

Said, Edward W. *Culture and Imperialism*. New York: Knopf, 1993.

Samuel, Raphael. *Theatres of Memory*. London: Verso, 1994.

Schlereth, Thomas J. *Cultural History and Material Culture: Everyday Life, Landscapes, Museums*. Ann Arbor MI: UMI Research Press, 1990.

Schutt, Amy C. *Peoples of the River Valleys: The Odyssey of the Delaware Indians*. Philadelphia: University of Pennsylvania Press, 2007.

Seaver, James E. *Deh-He-Wa-Mis: A Narrative of the Life of Mrs. Mary Jemison*. Ann Arbor MI: Allegany, 1967.

Seed, Patricia. *Ceremonies of Possession in Europe's Conquest of the New World, 1492–1640*. Cambridge: Cambridge University Press, 1995.

Segesten, Anamaria Dutceac, and Jenny Wüstenberg. "Memory Studies: The State of an Emergent Field." *Memory Studies* 10, no. 4 (October 2017): 474–89.

Seixas, Peter. *Theorizing Historical Consciousness*. Toronto: University of Toronto Press, 2006.

Shannon, Timothy J., and New York State Historical Association. *Indians and Colonists at the Crossroads of Empire: The Albany Congress of 1754*. Ithaca NY: Cornell University Press, 2002.

Shryock, Andrew. *Nationalism and the Genealogical Imagination. Oral History, and Textual Authority in Tribal Jordan*. Berkeley: University of California Press, 1987.

Silver, Peter Rhoads. *Our Savage Neighbors: How Indian War Transformed Early America*. New York: W. W. Norton, 2008.

Simpson, Audra. *Mohawk Interruptus: Political Life across the Borders of Settler States*. Durham NC: Duke University Press, 2014.

Sleeper-Smith, Susan, Juliana Barr, Jean M. O'Brien, Nancy Shoemaker, and Scott Manning Stevens, eds. *Why You Can't Teach United States History without American Indians*. Chapel Hill: University of North Carolina Press, 2015.

Slocum, Charles Elihu. *A Short History of the Slocums, Slocumbs, and Slocombs of America*. Syracuse NY: C. E. Slocum, Truair, Smith & Bruce, 1882.

Slotkin, Richard. *The Fatal Environment: The Myth of the Frontier in the Age of Industrialization, 1800–1890*. New York: Atheneum, 1985.

Smith, Andrea Lynn. *Colonial Memory and Postcolonial Europe: Maltese Settlers in Algeria and France*. Bloomington: Indiana University Press, 2006.

———. "Heteroglossia, 'Common Sense,' and Social Memory." *American Ethnologist* 31, no. 2 (2004): 251–69.

———. "Mormon Forestdale." *Journal of the Southwest* 47, no. 2 (July 1, 2005): 165–208.

———. "Place Replaced: Colonial Nostalgia and Pied-Noir Pilgrimages to Malta." *Cultural Anthropology* 18, no. 3 (August 1, 2003): 329–64.

———. "Settler Historical Consciousness in the Local History Museum." *Museum Anthropology* 34, no. 2 (September 1, 2011): 156–72.

———. "Settler Sites of Memory and the Work of Mourning." *French Politics, Culture and Society* 31, no. 3 (December 22, 2013): 65–92.

Smith, Andrea Lynn, and Anna Eisenstein. *Rebuilding Shattered Worlds: Creating Community by Voicing the Past.* Lincoln: University of Nebraska Press, 2016.

Smith, Linda Tuhiwai. *Decolonizing Methodologies: Research and Indigenous Peoples.* London: Zed Books; and Dunedin, New Zealand: University of Otago Press, 1999.

Soderlund, Jean R. *Lenape Country: Delaware Valley Society before William Penn.* Philadelphia: University of Pennsylvania Press, 2015.

Speck, Frank G., Witapanóxwe, and Pennsylvania Historical Commission. *A Study of the Delaware Indian Big House Ceremony, in Native Text Dictated by Witapanóxwe.* Harrisburg: Pennsylvania Historical Commission, 1931.

Stasiulis, Daiva K., and Nira Yuval-Davis. *Unsettling Settler Societies: Articulations of Gender, Race, Ethnicity, and Class.* Thousand Oaks CA: Sage, 1995.

Stevens, Scott Manning. "Tomahawk: Materiality and Depictions of the Haudenosaunee." *Early American Literature* 53, no. 2 (2018): 475–511.

Stevens, S. K. "Operation Heritage—A Glance Backward and a Look Forward." *Pennsylvania History: A Journal of Mid-Atlantic Studies* 33, no. 1 (1966): 1–12.

———. "The Pennsylvania Historical and Museum Commission." *History News,* 20, no. 7 (1965): 146–48.

Stewart, Charles. "Historicity and Anthropology." *Annual Review of Anthropology* 45 (October 2, 2016): 79–94.

Stoler, Ann Laura. *Imperial Debris: On Ruins and Ruination.* Durham NC: Duke University Press, 2013.

Stoler, Ann Laura, Carole McGranahan, and Peter C. Perdue. *Imperial Formations.* Santa Fe NM: School for Advanced Research Press, 2007.

Stone, Rufus B. "Brodhead's Raid on the Senecas." *Western Pennsylvania Historical Magazine* 7, no. 2 (1924): 88–101.

———. "Sinnontouan, or Seneca Land, in the Revolution." *Pennsylvania Magazine of History and Biography* 48, no. 3 (1924): 201–26.

Stone, William L. *Life of Joseph Brant: (Thayendanegea) Including the Border Wars of the American Revolution, and Sketches of the Indian Campaigns of Generals Harmar, St. Clair, and Wayne, and Other Matters Connected with the Indian Relations of the United States and Great Britain, from the Peace of 1783 to the Indian Peace of 1795.* New York: Kraus Reprint, 1838.

Stone, William L. *The Poetry and History of Wyoming: Containing Campbelle's Gertrude, and the History of Wyoming, from Its Discovery to the Beginning of the Present Century.* New York: M. H. Newman, 1844.

Strange, Carolyn. "The Battlefields of Personal and Public Memory: Commemorating the Battle of Saratoga (1777) in the Late Nineteenth Century." *Journal of the Gilded Age and Progressive Era* 14, no. 2 (April 2015): 194–221.

———. "Sisterhood of Blood: The Will to Descend and the Formation of the Daughters of the American Revolution." *Journal of Women's History* 26, no. 3 (2014): 105–28.

Strong, Pauline Turner. *American Indians and the American Imaginary: Cultural Representation across the Centuries.* Boulder CO: Paradigm, 2013.

———. *Captive Selves, Captivating Others: The Politics and Poetics of Colonial American Captivity Narratives.* Boulder CO: Westview, 1999.

Sundstrom, Linea. "The 'Pageant of Paha Sapa': An Origin Myth of White Settlement in the American West." *Great Plains Quarterly* 28, no. 1 (2008): 3–26.

Swedenburg, Ted. *Memories of Revolt: The 1936–39 Rebellion and the Palestinian National Past.* Minneapolis: University of Minnesota Press, 1995.

Syracuse Peace Council. Sullivan marker website. www.peacecouncil.net/NOON/markers/marker-sullivanclinton.html.

Tantaquidgeon, Gladys, and Pennsylvania Historical Commission. *A Study of Delaware Indian Medicine Practice and Folk Beliefs.* Harrisburg: Pennsylvania Historical Commission, 1942.

"Taxation Disputes, Late Twentieth Century." In *Encyclopedia of the Haudenosaunee (Iroquois Confederacy)*, edited by Bruce E. Johansen, and Barbara Alice Mann, 301–4. Westport CT: Greenwood, 2000.

Taylor, Alan. *American Revolutions: A Continental History, 1750–1804.* New York: W. W. Norton & Company, 2016.

———. *The Divided Ground: Indians, Settlers, and the Northern Borderland of the American Revolution.* New York: Alfred A. Knopf, 2006.

Taylor, Robert, ed. *The Susquehannah Company Papers.* Vol. 7, 1776–1784. Wilkes-Barre PA: Wyoming Historical and Geological Society, 1969.

Tharp, William. "Savage and Bloody Footsteps through the Valley: The Wyoming Massacre in the American Imagination." Master's thesis, Virginia Commonwealth University, 2021.

Thompson, William Leland. "The Observance of the 150th Anniversary of the American Revolution in New York." *New York History* 15, no. 1 (1934): 59–65.

Timothy, Dallen J., and Stephen W. Boyd. *Tourism and Trails. Cultural, Ecological, and Management Issues.* Bristol: Channel View, 2015.

Tiro, Karim M. *The People of the Standing Stone: The Oneida Nation from the Revolution through the Era of Removal.* Amherst: University of Massachusetts Press, 2011.

Toensing, Gale. "Return of Sacred Items Heals Onondaga Nation." *Indian Country Today.* Accessed June 16, 2012. http://indiancountrytodaymedianetwork.com/2012/06/15/return-of-sacred-.

Tonkin, Elizabeth. *Narrating Our Pasts: The Social Construction of Oral History.* Cambridge: Cambridge University Press, 1992.

Towner, Ausburn. *Our County and Its People: A History of the Valley and County of Chemung, from the Closing Years of the Eighteenth Century.* Syracuse NY: D. Mason, 1892.

Trachtenberg, Alan. *Shades of Hiawatha: Staging Indians, Making Americans: 1880–1930.* New York: Hill and Wang, 2004.

Trouillot, Michel-Rolph. *Silencing the Past: Power and the Production of History.* Boston: Beacon, 1995.

Truesdell, Barbara. "God, Home, and Country: Folklore, Patriotism, and the Politics of Culture in the Daughters of the American Revolution." Dissertation, Indiana University, 1996.

Upton, Dell. "Why do Contemporary Monuments Talk So Much." In *Commemoration in America: Essays on Monuments, Memorialization, and Memory*, edited by David Walter Gobel and Daves Rossell, 11–35. Charlottesville: University of Virginia Press, 2013.

Upton, Helen M. *The Everett Report in Historical Perspective: The Indians of New York.* Albany: New York State American Revolution Bicentennial Commission, 1980.

Urquhart, George. "Masonic Celebration. The Hundredth Anniversary of the Founding of Lodge No. 61." *Historical Record* 5, no. 2: 55–59, 67–73. Wilkes-Barre PA: Press of the Wilkes-Barre Record, 1895.

Vecsey, Christopher. "The Story and Structure of the Iroquois Confederacy," *Journal of the American Academy of Religion* 54 (1986): 79–106.

Vecsey, Christopher, and William A. Starna, eds. *Iroquois Land Claims*. Syracuse NY: Syracuse University Press, 1988.

Venables, Brant. "A Battle of Remembrance: Memorialization and Heritage at the Newtown Battlefield, New York." *Northeast Historical Archaeology* 41 (January 2012): 144–65.

Venables, Robert W. "The Historical Context of Chemung," 2011, in CBP.

———. *The Six Nations of New York: The 1892 United States Extra Census Bulletin*. Ithaca NY: Cornell University Press, 1995.

Veracini, Lorenzo. "Settler Collective, Founding Violence and Disavowal: The Settler Colonial Situation." *Journal of Intercultural Studies* 29, no. 4 (2008): 363–79.

———. *Settler Colonialism: A Theoretical Overview*. Houndmills: Palgrave Macmillan, 2010.

———. *The Settler Colonial Present*. Houndmills: Palgrave Macmillan, 2015.

"Visions of Teaoga," Jim Remsen. https://www.jimremsen.com/bio.htm.

Vizenor, Gerald. *Manifest Manners: Narratives of Postindian Survivance*. Lincoln: University of Nebraska Press, 1999.

Wallace, Anthony F. C. *King of the Delawares: Teedyuscung, 1700–1763*. Philadelphia: University of Pennsylvania Press, 1949.

Wallace, Anthony F. C. *The Death and Rebirth of the Seneca*. New York: Knopf, 1970.

Wallace, Paul A. W. *Indian Paths of Pennsylvania*. Harrisburg PA: Pennsylvania Historical Commission, 1971.

Weaver-Hightower, Rebecca. "'Before God This Was Their Country:' History and Guilt in Stuart Cloete's 'Turning Wheels' and the Voortrekker Monument." *English in Africa* 40, no. 2 (2013): 101.

Weslager, C. A. *The Delaware Indians: A History*. New Brunswick NJ: Rutgers University Press, 1972.

West, W. Richard, Jr. "A New Idea of Ourselves: The Changing Presentation of the American Indian." *The Changing Presentation of the American Indian: Museums and Native Cultures*. Washington DC: National Museum of the American Indian, 2000.

White, Geoffrey M. *Memorializing Pearl Harbor: Unfinished Histories and the Work of Remembrance*. Durham NC: Duke University Press, 2016.

White, Hayden. "Historical Pluralism." *Critical Inquiry* 12, no. 3 (1986): 480–93.

Wilcox, William Alonzo. "The Story of Wyoming: An Oft-told Tale Retold." In *Proceedings of the Wyoming Commemorative Association. On the 151st Anniversary of the Battle and Massacre of Wyoming, July 3rd, 1929*. Wilkes Barre PA: WCA.

Wildcat, Matthew. "Fearing Social and Cultural Death: Genocide and Elimination in Settler Colonial Canada—An Indigenous Perspective." *Journal of Genocide Research* 17, no. 4 (2015): 391–409.

Williams, Glenn F. *Year of the Hangman: George Washington's Campaign against the Iroquois*. Yardley PA: Westholme, 2005.

Williams, Raymond. *Marxism and Literature*. Oxford: Oxford University Press, 1977.

Winter, Jay. "Sites of Memory and the Shadow of War," In *A Companion to Cultural Memory Studies*, edited by Astrid Erll and Ansgar Nünning, 61–74. Berlin: De Gruyter, 2010.

Wolfe, Patrick. *Settler Colonialism and the Transformation of Anthropology: The Politics and Poetics of an Ethnographic Event.* London: Cassell, 1988.

———. "Structure and Event: Settler Colonialism, Time, and the Question of Genocide." In *Empire, Colony, Genocide: Conquest, Occupation, and Subaltern Resistance in World History,* edited by A. Dirk Moses, 102–32. New York: Berghahn, 2008.

Wood, Karenne. "Prisoners of History: Pocahontas, Mary Jemison, and the Poetics of an American Myth." *Studies in American Indian Literatures* 28, no. 1 (May 14, 2016): 73–82.

Wyoming Commemorative Association, *Reports of the Proceedings of the Wyoming Commemorative Association on the Occasion of the 125th Anniversary of the Battle and Massacre of Wyoming.* July 3, 1903. Wilkes-Barre PA.

Young, James Edward. *The Stages of Memory: Reflections on Memorial Art, Loss, and the Spaces Between.* Amherst: University of Massachusetts Press, 2016.

Zerubavel, Eviatar. *The Elephant in the Room: Silence and Denial in Everyday Life.* Electronic resource. Oxford: Oxford University Press, 2006.

———. *Social Mindscapes: An Invitation to Cognitive Sociology.* Cambridge MA: Harvard University Press, 1997.

———. *Time Maps: Collective Memory and the Social Shape of the Past.* Chicago: University of Chicago Press, 2003.

INDEX

Page numbers in italics indicate illustrations.

Abbott, W. P., 356n116

activism: commemorative markers as potential focal points for, 3. *See also* iconoclasm and monument revisionism

activism, Native American: anti-Columbus, 251; contemporary use of treaties, 161; educational curriculum and, 309–10; of Laura (Minnie) Kellogg, 164, 370n19; muted Sullivan bicentennial and, 253; New York, 226; post–World War II issues, 252; public school, 383n36; Sullivan-Clinton events in New York as reaction to, 181; of Suzan Shown Harjo, 3. *See also* land claims and land rights

activism, non-Native: anti-Haudenosaunee backlash, 251, 254; fictional counter-narratives, 273–78, 290; NOON, 278–86, *285*, 289–90, 339. *See also* interventions

Adlum, John, 15

African Americans: at Battle of Newport, 258–59; Black Lives Matter movement, 271; British efforts to enlist, 56–57; Diven's resolution to enlist, in Civil War, 122; Newtown Centennial and abolitionists, 122–23; "pageant craze" and, 374n13; slavery and abolitionism, 3, 122–23, 259; Sullivan's Black valet, 259

Akwesasne Cultural Center, 327. *See also* Mohawk Nation

Albany Congress (1754), 71, 374n14

Albany Plan of Union (1754), 285

Algeria, French in, 7–8

Allegany Oxbow (Congdon), 180

Allegany State Park Commission, 177

Allegany Territory, Seneca Nation of Indians, xx, 20, 41, 167, 168, 171, 173–77, 180, 286, 302, 324–26, *325*, *328*, 340, 341

Allen, Ethan, 59, 101

Allen, George (Gabriel), 237

Allen, Richard, 253

American Humane Association, 165

American Legion, 107, 112, 178, 179, 378n4

American Revolution. *See* Revolutionary War

The American Revolution in New York (Calloway), 144, 145

American Scenic and Historic Preservation Society, 148

Ames, DeHart H., 177, 178

Anderson, Benedict, 34, 332

Andrew, Mark, 218–20, 255

Anglo-supremacy, 72–73, 89. *See also* Daughters of the American Revolution; white supremacy

anniversaries, 204; bicentennial of Sullivan Expedition, 206, 253, 258; sestercentennial of Sullivan Expedition, 262, 340n12; Two Row Wampum Treaty, 381n19.

anthropology of history, 24

anti-immigration sentiment, 357n26

"anti-Indian sublime," 56–57, 64, 66, 223

Apaches, and General Crook's Trail, 272

Arnold, Philip, 312, 381n1

Arnot, Stephen, 365n32

Asa Stevens chapter of DAR, Standing Stone PA, 84, 86

Assmann, Jan, 350n136

Athens/Sayre (formerly Tioga) NY: Clinton and Sullivan units meeting at, 12, 106, 107; commemorative marker at, 19, 47, 84, 87–89, *88*, 105, 106–7, *108*, 147, 233, 361–62n41; cosponsoring of marker, 106; and DAR, 84, 86–88, 105, 106, 147, 359n68, 361–62n41, 362n48; industrialization and interest in historical commemoration in, 73; Remsen's *Visions of Teaoga*, 275–76, 278; Yankee influence in, 87, 102–3, 107

409

Clinton, DeWitt, 14, 127, 130, 132

Clinton, George, 146, 194

Clinton, James: on Newtown Centennial monument, 139; in *Pageant of Decision*, 194; Sullivan-Clinton campaign renaming,146–49, 150, 208, 226; troop movements lead by, 12, 13, 106, 107

coal: "anthracite aristocracy," 60; class conflict and, 83, 95; exploitation in Wyoming Valley, 60, 70, 76, 83, 105, 111; immigration and, 60; as monument, 206; as source of Shoemaker's wealth, 97; "Yankee Notables" and, 60

collective memory, 25–26, 30, 204

Colonial Dames of America, 70–72, 80–82, 87, 90, 229, 356–57n7

colonialism. *See* settler-colonialism

Columbus, Christopher, 29, 251, 299

"The Commanders" (McMaster), 367n86

commemorative markers: decentralized development of, 203–11, 271; historiography and theorization of, 29–31; military routes dominating NHTS, 334; Native American perspectives on, 264–68, 283–84, 289–90, 306, 335; NOON approach to, 278–86, 285, 289–90, 339; purpose of, 3; shift over time from memorial to locus, 286–89, 335–38; as sites of memory, 29, 327, 349n108; state involvement in, 29–30, 72–73, 113, 271; as valorizing projects, 7, 29. *See also* Sullivan commemorative complex

commemorative practice: 33, 34, 90–91, 181, 209–10, 223–25, 248, 334–35; rhetoric of reenactment, 33, 85, 90, 224

The Common Cause (Parkinson), 56

communities of memory, 25, 26

Conestoga massacre, 52, 353n35

Confederate monuments and flags, 3, 29, 30, 239, 241, 271, 272. *See also* Civil War

Confirming Act, 59

Congdon, Charles E., 180–81

Conn, Steven, 348n98

Connecticut-Pennsylvania intra-settler war. *See* Yankee-Pennamite War

Conner, Roberta, 335

Connerton, Paul, 33, 34, 85, 288, 335, 386n15

Conoys, 49

contemporary approaches to Sullivan story, 215–27, 286–90; commercial implications of, 216, 217; communities created by, 224–25; memorials becoming loci, 286–89, 335–38; nuanced views, 219, 225, 227, 235–39, 257–62; partic-

ipation of descendants, 222, 224, 246, 257; "playing Indian," *188, 196,* 215, 216–17, 218–20, 225–27; portrayals of Native Americans, 215, 216–17, 218–20, *219,* 225–27; replacement narratives, 227, 256; research methodology, 16–22; 215, 227; ritual components of, 223–26; varieties of modern engagement, 20–22, 31. *See also* interventions; Native American perspectives; New York, contemporary views of Sullivan Expedition in; Pennsylvania, contemporary views of Sullivan Expedition in

Continental Congress: Connecticut-Pennsylvania war and, 48, 52, 58; in pageantry, 187, 192, 193, 197; Sullivan Expedition and 11, 128, 130–132, 146, 260

Cook, David, 172

Coon, Mrs. Bolton, 110

corn and other foodstuffs: burial of food supplies, 200, 319; Chemung Valley, 121; growing, 49, 121, 139; hiding corn and seeds, 174, 295; sacred to Haudenosaunee, 200, 296; three sisters, 10, 49, 199, 294, 296. *See also* destruction of foodstuffs

Cornell Indian Board, 166–69, *167,* 175, 370n28

Corning Leader, 258, 259

Cornplanter (Keyenthwahkeh) (Seneca), 15, 54, 160, 174, 296, 300, 385n74

Cothran, Boyd, 377n81

"counter-memory," 297–98

counter-monumentality, 272

counter-narratives: fictional, 273–78, 290; to replacement narratives, 277. *See also* interventions

Covenant Chain alliance, 10

Cowles, Dick, 257–62

Cowles, Ellsworth, 257–62

Craft, David, 99, 119

Crellin, Lizzie, 358n57

Crook's Trail, 272

Crouse, Edison, 177, 370n28

Crouse, Jerome, 177, 370n28

Crouse, Jonas, 177

Crouse, Sylvester C., 176–77, 370n28

Culture and Imperialism (Said), 23

Custer, George Armstrong, 65

Cuylerville NY, "torture tree" in, 206, 375n54, 377–78n11

Cyprus and Turkish-Cypriots, 338–39

Daily Times, 64

Dana, Anderson, 86

Daughters of 1812, 369n51, 378n4

Daughters of Pocahontas, 188, 374n22
Daughters of the American Revolution (DAR):
Americanization and, 34; Anglo-supremacy
and, 72–73, 89; composition of, 73; contemporary chapter activities and viewpoints, 222,
230, 235–36, 255, 256, 378n4; as hereditary
society, 71, 184; inauguration rituals used by,
205, 209, 244; instructing patriotism and, 73,
205; membership rules, 71; in New York, 117,
364n3, 369n51; origins of, 71, 80; pageantry
movement in, 184; PHC monuments and, 95,
101, 105–7, 111, 361–62n41, 362n48; public
history and, 72; women's involvement in Sullivan commemorations and, 1, 20, 47, 69–76,
80, 84–91, 356n6, 357n26, 359n67. *See also
specific chapter names and locations*
Davies, Wallace Evan, 71, 357n26
Davis, Capt., 76, 78, 91
Davis, Edward, 86
Davis, Nathan, 129
Dean's Cove memorial, *19*
Decker, George, 372n52
declension narrative (Iroquois), 14, 136, 137–38,
238, 317, 321, 340, 346n52
Decolonizing Museums (Lonetree), 302, 327
Dehowäda:dih, 296
Delaware Indians. *See* Lenape/Delaware Nation
Delaware River watershed, 9, 49, 52
de la Warr, Thomas West, Baron, 344n21
Deloria, Philip, 334, 356n127
DeLucia, Christine, 38, 351n155
democratization of historical commemoration, 141
Denison, Nathan, 54, 98
Denonville, Marquis de, 318–19, 322
Denson, Andrew, 333–34
descendants; of the Connecticut-Pennsylvania
intra-settler war, 70, 74, 76–77, 80, 83, 84,
85–89, 90, 101–4, 107, 110, 362n48; at contemporary commemorations, 222, 224, 246,
257; Newtown Centennial, 124, 138; in New
York's Sullivan-Clinton Campaign, 149, *179*;
PHC monuments, 101–4, 107, 110, 362n48;
women, 70, 74, 76–77, 80, 83, 84, 85–89,
90, 107; of Wyoming and Sullivan participants, 209
Deskaheh (General, Levi), 317
destruction of foodstuffs: by Brodhead, 174;
definition of genocide and, 344n13; by Denonville, 319; Parker on Native American view
of, 200; reenactments of, 147, 186, 189–90,

194, 195, 198; in Revolutionary War, 14; by
Sullivan campaign, 2, 4, 13, 37, 129, 151, 154,
156, 200, 219, 294–95, 296–97, 344n13; in
Washington's orders, 4, 12, 131; in Yankee-
Pennamite War, 58
Dial Rock chapter of DAR, West Pittson PA, 70,
84, 85, 360n86
dispossession: Doctrine of Discovery, 317. *See
also* treaties; treaties, fraudulent
dispossession, New York: Cayuga, 161, 162;
Haudenosaunee lands, 161–62, 168, 183, 198–
99, 372n53; highway and thruway construction, 41, 252; Kinzua Dam flooding, 41, 226,
252, 263, 324, 325–26; Mohawk, 162; Niagara power plant, 252; Oneida, 161, 162, 304;
Onondaga, 161; Saint Lawrence seaway construction, 41, 252; Seneca, 161, 162, 173, 198;
Tuscarora, 252
dispossession, Pennsylvania: by land sales, 51,
161; Quaker, 9, 210; Walking Purchase and,
9, 345n23, 352n17
Diven, Alexander S., 120, 122–23
Doctrine of Discovery, 317
Dodge, Jonathan, 359n74
Dodge, Oliver, 359n74
Dorrance, Anne, 104
Dorrance, Frances, 104–6, 180
Dorrance, George, 104
Draper, Lyman C., 174–75, 180
Drummond, Richard C. S., 169, 170–71, 172,
181, 206, 368n28, 371n40
Dutcher, Fred, 152
Dutch in America, 10, 51, 279, 299, 304, 317

Eastern Delaware Nation, Inc., 240, 379n9
Easton PA: commemorative markers at, 1–2,
2, 16, 37, 47, 48, 68, 69, 71–72, 84, 107–10,
347n62; George Taylor chapter of DAR in, 1,
2, 68, 69, 71, 72, 84, 357n12; historical commemoration in, 73; Lafayette College, 16, 47,
72, 107; in *Pageant of Decision*, 194; sesquicentennial commemoration at, 209; troop
movements through, 1–2, *2*
economy: class conflict and, 83, 95; collapse of
1873, 123; industrialization, social change,
and interest in historical commemoration,
60, 70, 73–74, 90, 336; railroads and other
big business growth, 123. *See also* coal
Edwards, Jake (Haiwhagai'i) (Onondaga),
293–301
Eghohowin (Munsee), 55, 276
Eisenstein, Anna, 337

Elliot, Henry, 359n74
Elliott, A. C., 179
Elliott, Joseph, 86, 100, 354n58, 359n74, 362n48
Elmer, Sarah Perkins, 360nn82–83
Elmira College, 123, 187
Elmira Daily Advertiser, 118–22, 124
Elmira Junior League, 187
Elmira NY: DAR chapter of, 360n81; Newtown Centennial and, 118, 122–27, 137; *Pageant of Decision* performed at, 183, 186, *187*, 188, *188*–91, *191*; reenactment of Battle of Newtown in, 215–21, *217–19*, 224, 225, *225*, 226; Sullivan-Clinton Campaign memorial, 5
emplacement theory, 288
Engels, Jeremy, 68
English in America. *See* British
Enoch Brown Association, 96
Esther Montour. *See specific entries at* "Queen Esther"
eugenics laws, 240
Evans, Israel, 209
Everett, Edward A., 162–64, *163*, 167, 199, 251, 370n14, 376n69

Fadden, Ray (Tehanetorens), 327
Fairman, Charles, 119–20, 121, 124
Fanon, Franz, 7
Farley, Henry, 112
Fatigue Camp marker, 244
federal government. *See* governments, state and federal
Fenton, William N., 346n52
Fess, Leroy, 168
Finger Lakes Association, 148
"firsting," 28, 91, 184, 313, 338
Firsting and Lasting (O'Brien), 28, 201, 210
Fischer, Joseph R., 13
Fishcarrier, Robert, 172
Fisher, John S., 98
Fisher, J. Sheldon, 319
Fitch, John, 95
Five Nations. *See* Haudenosaunee nations
Flick, Alexander C.: framing of Sullivan story by, 146–47, 198, 201, 256; and Haudenosaunee, 164, 166, 169, 171, 173, 175–80, 264; *Pageant of Decision* and, 183, 185–86, 189, 197, 198, 199, 207–8, 375n43; Pennsylvania monuments and, 106; publicity efforts of, 204; renaming as "Sullivan-Clinton," 146–47, 226; republishing writings of, 253; Sullivan-Clinton Campaign memorial program, 144,

145–49, 151, 153, 157, 211, 226, 376n65; "torture tree" set up by, 375n54
foodstuffs. *See* corn and other foodstuffs; destruction of foodstuffs
Foote, Kenneth, 203–4
Forbidden Path, 206–7
Fort Augusta, 98, 106, 363n60
Fort Johnson, 152, 154, 156
Fort McCord Memorial, 96
Fort Muncy, 98, 99
Fort Niagara, 12, 13, 53, 54, 130, 147, 151, 174, 176, 259
Fort Pitt, 12, 13–14, 173, 176, 372n60a
Fort Schuyler, 149, 151
Fort Stanwix. *See* Treaty of Fort Stanwix
Fort Sullivan, 88
Forty Fort, 54, 64
Francis, William J., 188–89
Francis, William J., Jr., 189
Franklin, Benjamin, 30, 285
Franklin, John, 59–60, 101–3, 355n92, 361n35, 362n48, 362n51
Franklin, Roswell, and family, 100
Freemasons, 76, 124, 187
French and Indian War, 157, 322, 345n31. *See also* Seven Years' War
French Fort park. *See* Sainte Marie de Gannentaha site
French in Algeria, 7–8
French in America: Haudenosaunee and, 10, 263, 265–66, 318–19, 322, 324, 327; "Iroquois," etymology of, xix, 345n24; Native Americans allied with, 56; and Onondaga Lake, 312, 314; reenactors portraying, 220; Seneca villages attacked by, 265–66, 318–19, 322, 324, 327; Sherman on, 134
Fryer, George, 151–52, 157, 313–14
Fun, Charles (Cayuga), 172

Ganesworth, Gladys, 370n28
Ganesworth, Ray, 370n28
Ganondagan (Seneca Art & Culture Center), 302, 303, 318–24, *319*
Ganondagan State Historic Site, 318–19
Ganonhanyonh, Ganǫ́nyǫ́k. See Thanksgiving Address
Gansevoort, Peter, 154, 156, 157
Gates, Horatio, 130, 131
Gay, Sydney, 372n59
Gayaneñha' go:nah. See The Great Law of Peace
Gaylord, Justus, Jr., 86
Gaylord, Katherine, 74

Indian Rights Association, 372n52
Indians. *See* Native Americans
"Indian shade," 236
Indian Silver Cornet Band of Cattaraugus, 138
Indian Trade and Intercourse Acts, 161, 253, 376n60
Indian Wars, 133–35, 272
Indigenous peoples. *See* Native Americans
industrialization, 60, 70, 73–74, 336
interventions, 271–86, 339; counter-monumentality, 272; fictional counter-narratives, 273–78, 290; Haudenosaunee confederacy, 283–86, *285*; non-Native involvement in, 269, 271–73; NOON, 278–86, *285*, 289–90, 339; and removal and replacement of monuments, 271–72, 283–86, *285*, *287*, 289–90. *See also* Native American perspectives
Iroquois. *See* Haudenosaunee

Jack, Havemeyer, 370n28
Jacques, Frieda (Onondaga), 315
James, George Wharton, 166
James Deere v. St. Lawrence River Power, 251, 370n20. *See also* Everett Commission; land claims
Jameson, John, 65
Jamestown Evening Journal, 172
Jefferson, Thomas, 335
Jemison, G. Peter (Seneca), 264, 265–68, 289, 296, 319–24
Jemison, Mary, 195, *196*, 198–99
Jenkins, John, Jr., 62, 74, 78, 79, 356n116, 358n43, 360n86
Jenkins, Steuben, 62, 135–36, 356n116, 360n86
Jenkins Fort PA, 54, 70, 360n86
Jesuits, 170, 265, 312, 317, 322, 327
Jimerson, Ray, 177
John, Adelbert, 370n28
John, Alexander, *163*
John, Frank, 370n28
John, Randy A. (Nëhdöwes) (Seneca), xix, 264, 290
Johnny-John, Richard (Gwë:de') (Seneca), 326
Johnson, Sir William, 11, 154, 156, 200
Jonathan, James, 370n28
Jones, James, 370n28
Jones, Lt., 76, 78, 91
Jordan, Kurt A., 346n45

Kammen, Michael G., 3, 30, 113, 360n10
Kanadesaga NY, 129

Kanyen'kehaka. *See* Mohawk Nation
Keeler, 111
Keeler, Elisha, 359n74
Keeler, John, 359n74
Kellogg, Laura (Minnie) Cornelius (Oneida), 164, 370n19
Kennedy, Mr. and Mrs. Ulysses, 370n28
Kennedy, Mrs. Walter, 370n28
Kennedy, Walter "Boots," 167–68, 175–77, 370–71nn28–29
Kenney, Adelaide, 101
Kent, Mr. (PHMC director), 112–13
Kerney, Karen, 284
Keyenthwahkeh (Cornplanter) (Seneca), 15, 54, 160, 174, 296, 300, 385n74
Khrin, 265
Killian, Stephen, 246
King George's War, 345n31
King Philip (Metacom), 36
King Philip's War, 36, 38
Kinney, Thomas, 87
Kinzua Dam flooding, 41, 226, 252, 263, 324, 325–26
Kirkland, Lehigh G., 178–79
Kittanning Indian Town marker, 98
Knickerbocker Press, The, 162
Kosasa, Karen, 24
Kresge, Willard, 244, 246–48
Kryn (Togouiroui) (Mohawk), 265–66
Kunz, George F., 148

laches, 254, 263
Ladies' Wyoming Monumental Association. *See* Wyoming Monument Association (WMA)
Lafayette, Marquis de, 95
Lafayette College, 16, 47, 72, 107
land, boundaries: after Revolutionary War, 67; Royal Proclamation of 1763 and, 11, 352n20, 375n43; settler defiance of boundary laws, 50, 192; Susquehannah Company and Pennsylvania boundaries, 53; Treaty of Fort Stanwix and, 11, 50, 304, 352n21, 375n43
land back proposal, 269
land claims and land rights: Cayuga, 171; contemporary court cases, Cayuga, Oneida, Onondaga, 251–54; federal vs. state authority over, 41, 161, 162, 164, 173; and the Revolutionary War, 324; settler-colonialism as, 332–35, 338; Six Nations land-claims movement, 162–66, *163*, 167, 172, 181, 199, 251, 370n22; U.S. Supreme Court and, 253, 254, 263, 370n17, 370n22

propriately framed as, 297–98; Indigenous memory, 296–99, 314–17, 336, 347–48n86; individual vs. collective, 25; national memory, 26; performance and, 31–34, 85, 181, 208–9; popular memory, 25, 26; public memory, 70, 141, 227, 276, 286, 350n128; social memory, 25. *See also* historiography; narrative; oral vs. written history; sites of memory

memory entrepreneurs: concept of, 31–32, 350n126; construction of narrative by, 31–38, 39, 297, 350n128; contemporary Sullivan Expedition commemorations and, 215, 233, 242; decentralized development of Sullivan commemorative complex and, 204–7, 209–10; PHC monuments and, 104; women as, 70, 72, 89, 350n128

Memory Lands (DeLucia), 38, 351n155

memoryscapes, settler-colonial and Native, 38–42

memory studies, 25–27

Metacom, *See* King Philip

Metahistory (White), 35

methodology: author's, 16–22; 215, 227; decolonizing, 40; longitudinal memory studies, 31, 350n125

Michalski, Sergiusz, 349n111

microhistorical approach, 32

Miner, Charles, 80, 84, 102, 354n72

Mintz, Max M., 346n47, 375n43

missionaries and missionizing, 170, 242, 312, 314

mnemonic decapitation, 35, 36, 332, 334

mnemonic myopia, 41, 338

mnemonic socialization, 25, 332

mnemonic synchronization, 33

modern perspectives. *See specific entries at* contemporary

Mohawk Interruptus (Simpson), 23

Mohawk Nation (Kanyen'kehaka): active presence of federally recognized nation in NY, 226; at Akwesasne/St. Regis, 226, 327; Battle of Oriskany, 11; and Great Gully (Cayuga Castle), 171; historic and current territory, 10; land-claims movement and Everett Commission, 164; Revolutionary War and, 118, 346; seizure of Native lands, 162; settler commemoration of Kryn, 265–66; settler encroachment on, 345n35; Sullivan Expedition troop movements against, 15, 130; terminology issues, xix. *See also* Joseph Brant

Mohawk Valley Historical Association, 165

Mohawk Valley Historical Society, 142

Montour, Esther. *See entries at* "Queen Esther"

monuments. *See* commemorative markers; sites of memory; Sullivan commemorative complex; *specific markers*

Monuments to Absence (Denton), 333–34

Moravians, 170

Morgan, Francesca, 72, 90

Morgan, Lewis Henry, 14, 127, 346n52

Morris, Gouverneur, 193

Morris, Robert, 372n53

Moses, Dorothy, 370n28

Mount Morris Post, 190

Moyer, Paul, 58, 59

Mt. Pleasant, Alyssa, 14, 161, 381n1, 382n20

Mullen, Bill, 243–44

Munsees, xix, 49, 55, 98, 101, 276, 344–45nn21–23, 364n4. *See also* Lenape/Delaware Nation

Murray, Elsie, 112

Murray, Louise Welles, 58, 102–3, 106, 107, 112, 257, 359n68

Murray, Nicholas, 61, 355n100

museums and museology, 301–3, 327–28. *See also specific museums and cultural centers*

Myers, Albert Cook, 362n45

myth and story, use of, 34n136

names and naming: of commemorative events, 62–63, 64; discoverer's rights and, 335; renaming, as settler-colonial practice, 207, 334, 336, 338; road naming practices, 207; settler-colonial naming practices, 19, 62–63, 207, 335, 336, 338; state of Wyoming named for Battle of Wyoming, 2, 66, 256n126; Sullivan Expedition renamed Sullivan-Clinton campaign in New York, 146–49, 150, 208, 226; "Sullivan trail(s)" and Sullivan Road(s), xx, 16, 21, 206–7, 208, 237–38, 377n2, 378n13, 379n8; of wars and battles, 36, 37, 64, 295

Nanticokes, 49, 101

narrative, 24–27; captivity narratives, 55–56, 65, 96, 195; "containment," 36–37, 210, 340; emplotment, 35, 350n143; lumping and splitting, xx, 32, 35, 135; memory entrepreneurs constructing, 31–38, 39, 297, 350n128; mnemonic decapitation, 35, 36, 332, 334; periodization and, 36; silencing in, 35, 36, 37; vanishing Indian trope, 14, 98, 136, 137–38, 238, 321, 333, 346n52, 349n105; war stories and, 34–38. *See also* counter-narratives; interventions; names and naming; replacement narrative

Nason, James, 301–2
national memory, 26
National Museum of the American Indian, 302
National Museum of the American Revolution, 303
Native American cultural centers: Akwesasne Cultural Center (Mohawk), 327; Ganondagan (Seneca Art & Culture Center), 302, 303, 318–24, *319*; Onöhsagwë:de' Cultural Center, 302, 303, 324–29, *328*; Shako:wi Cultural Center (Oneida), 302, 303–6; SINM (Seneca-Iroquois National Museum), 262, 264, 290, 303, 325; Skä·noñh–Great Law of Peace Center, 20, 293, 302, 303, 311–18, *312*, *313*, 383–84n45
Native American Graves Protection & Repatriation Act (NAGPRA), 302, 383n44
Native American perspectives, 293–329; of contemporary Indigenous New Yorkers, 262–68; of contemporary Indigenous Pennsylvanians, 239–42; "counter-memory," inappropriately framed as, 297–98; educational efforts aimed at non-Natives, 309–11, 317–18; ethnographic approach to, 301, 382n20; on historical marking and removal of markers, 264–67, 280, 290, 306, 335; historical temporalities of, 263, 294, 296–97, 303, 316–17, 347–48n86; on military terminology of Sullivan story, 295–96; museums and museology, 301–3, 327–28; nineteenth to early twentieth centuries, 4, 14–15, 37, 38, 40–42; on offensiveness of Sullivan markers, 238–39, 240, 242, 264, 266–67, 271, 289; on replacement narrative, 323–24; on Revolutionary War, 302–3, 323–24; on settler-colonialism, 298–301, *340*, 340–41, *341*; Sullivan story as false reporting of true genocide, 293–301; unofficial defacements, 272. *See also* activism, Native American; Native American cultural centers
Native Americans: and anti-Indian backlash in contemporary New York, 251, 254; "anti-Indian sublime," 56–57, 64, 66, 223; and the Battle of Wyoming, 54–55; boarding schools for, 306–7, 317, 318; and "bootleg" monuments, 95; British relationships with, 10–11, 49, 56, 192, 200, 345n36; burial grounds and, 168, 169, 172, 306, 314, 371n41, 383n44; citizenship rights of, 132, 164, 181; contemporary non-Native New Yorkers on, 259–62; contemporary non-Native Pennsylvanians on, 235–36, 237; contemporary Sullivan Expedition commemorations' portrayal of, 215, 216–17,

218–20, *219*, 225–27; and declension narrative (Iroquois), 14, 136, 137–38, 238, 317, 321, 340, 346n52; federally recognized nations in New York vs. Pennsylvania, 226–27, 239; Indian Wars (19th century), 133–35, 272; memoryscapes of, 38–42; missionizing of, 170, 242, 312, 314; Newtown Centennial and, 127, 128–35, 137–38; *Pageant of Decision*'s portrayal of, 192–96, *196*, 198; "pageantry craze" and, 184–85, 374n13, 374n25; PHC monuments and, 97–98, 99, 100–101, *102*, 104, 107, 109, 112–13, 114; purchase of lands from, 352n15; Revolutionary War and, 8–11, *10*; as "Romans of the Western World," 127, 132; Sullivan Expedition's use of Indian trails, 21, 206–7, 378n13; terminology issues, xix–xx, 237; traditional portrayals as, 206; vanishing trope, 333, 349n105. *See also* replacement narrative; savagist trope; *specific peoples*
nativism, 357n26
Navaro-Yashin, Yael, 338
Nëhdöwes (Randy A. John) (Seneca), xix, 264, 290
Neighbors of the Onondaga Nation (NOON), 278–86, *285*, 289–90, 339
Neighbor to Neighbor Nation to Nation, 279
Neilson, Harvey, 247
Nelson, Peter: and Haudenosaunee, 166–69, 173, 175, 177–80; *Pageant of Decision* and, 183, 189; and the Sullivan-Clinton Campaign program, 144, 148, 149, 152–54, 157
New Arrow (Seneca), 15
New England: New York's reaction to Plymouth landing commemoration in, 142; PHC's reaction to cultural hegemony of, 95; replacement narrative in, 210, 333; Vermont independence movement, 353n33. *See also* Connecticut-Pennsylvania intra-settler war; Massachusetts
New England Women, 369n51
Newport, Battle of. *See* Battle of Newport
Newtown, Battle of. *See* Battle of Newtown
Newtown Battlefield State Park, 216, 220, 264, 265
Newtown Centennial, 117–39; ambivalence expressed by speakers at, 128–32, 136, 137–38, 147; attendance and events, 125–27; descendants of participants, as commemorators, 124, 138; organizing committee, 119–25, 204; original monument and plaque, 120–21, 123–24, *126*, 138–39, 147, 205, 216; political context of, 122–23; publicity efforts of, 118–22, 204;

replacement monument and plaque, 211, 216; "Romans of the Western World," Native Americans described as, 127, 132; savagist trope, 129, 132–35; Sherman's address at, 127, 133–35, 136, 137, 147; and the Sullivan story as replacement narrative, 117–18, 122, 135–36; William Fiske Warner's original proposal for, 118–19; Wyoming and, 118–19, 128, 131, 207

New York, 38, 225–27; active presence of federally recognized Indian nations in, 226–27, 251–54, 269; commemorative markers in, 47, 148–49; framing of Sullivan story as replacement narrative, 38, 117–18, 122, 160–62, 164–66, 181–82, 183, 185, 197–99, 201–2, 210–11, 322–23; patriotic and historical societies in, 142, 148, 151–53, 157, 173, 186–87; Pennsylvania compared, 204–11; roadside signs, posting of, 202, 251, 252; sesquicentennial of Sullivan Expedition 104, 106, 117, 138, 141, 145–49, 205–6; state Revolutionary War commemorative program, 141–45; seizure of Native lands, 161–62; Sullivan-Clinton renaming and, 146–49, 150, 208, 226; Supreme Court of, 122; Van Shaick expedition and, 12, 15, 149–57, 155, 295, 303, 313, 371n36; Vermont independence movement, 353n33. *See also* Haudenosaunee and New York Sullivan-Clinton commemorations; Newtown Centennial; *Pageant of Decision; specific locations*

New York, contemporary views of Sullivan Expedition in, 251–69; anti-Indian backlash, 251, 254; apathy about markers and memorials, 255, 263, 269; history enthusiasts, 255–57; Indigenous New Yorkers, 262–68; Native presence in state and, 251–54, 269; non-Native view of Native Americans, 259–62; nuanced responses to, 257–62, 269; reenactment of Battle of Newtown in Elmira, 215–21, 217–19, 224, 225, 225, 226; replacement narrative, use of, 256

New York Historical Society, 127
New York History, 16
New York Humane Association (NYHA), 165–66
New-York Journal, 55
New York State Historical Association (NYSHA), 142–43, 165
New York State Museum, 168
"noble savage" construct, 38, 197, 351n52
NOON. *See* Neighbors of the Onondaga Nation (NOON)

Nora, Pierre, 349n108
Northampton Genealogical and Historical Society (NGHS), 209
nuanced responses to Sullivan Expedition: at contemporary events, 219, 225, 227, 235–39, 257–62, 269; from contemporary Native Americans, 239–42, 262–68; critique of Sullivan's tactics, 109; neutral language, 106, 107, 112–13, 114; Newtown Centennial addresses, 128–32, 136, 137–38, 147; New York state program and, 147, 151–52, 154, 368n28; Parker's "The Indian Interpretation of the Sullivan-Clinton Campaign," 199–201; "Queen Esther's Rock" marker, 112–13; Van Schaick expedition and memorial, 151–52, 154, 157, 371n26; varieties of modern engagement with commemorative complex, 20–22, 31. *See also* Haudenosaunee and New York Sullivan-Clinton commemorations

O'Bail, Charles (Seneca), 174
obelisk memorials, 62, 63, 126, 138, 205, 216, 224, 355n103
Oberg, Michael, 381n19
O'Brien, Jean, 28, 68, 201, 210, 281, 349n105
O'Dell, Joan, 255–56
Ogden, Amos, 353n36
Ogden, Nathan, 353n36
OHA. *See* Onondaga Historical Association (OHA)
Ohnuki-Tierney, Emiko, 348n93
Old Smoke (Sayenqueraghta) (Seneca), 54, 118
Olean *Times Herald*, 178
Oneida Nation (Onyota'a:ka): active presence of federally recognized nation in NY, 226; Battle of Oriskany, 11, 304–05, 308; communities outside of New York, 304, 308–9; historic and current territory, 10; land-claims movement and, 162, 164, 253, 254, 369n13; Native lands, seizure of, 161, 162, 304, 376n60; in Revolutionary War, 303, 304; settler encroachment on, 303, 345n35; and Sullivan Expedition, 15, 130, 303, 377n11; terminology issues, xix; Van Schaick raid on Onondaga and, 149–51
Oneida Cultural Center 302, 303–11
Oneida language, 308
Onöhsagwë:de' Cultural Center, 302, 303, 324–29, 328. *See also* Seneca-Iroquois National Museum
Onondaga Historical Association (OHA), 151–53, 312–15, 369n51, 383–84nn44–45
Onondaga Lake Park marker, 283–86, 285

women and Sullivan commemorations; *specific locations*

Pennsylvania, contemporary views of Sullivan Expedition in, 229–49; apathy about markers and memorials, 229–32, 248, 263; DAR chapters and, 235–36; history enthusiasts, 232–35, 248–49; "Indigenous" Pennsylvanians, 239–42, 248; Native Americans, non-Native view of, 235–36, 237–39; nuanced responses, 235–39; repair and maintenance of monuments, 239–40, 242–48; Wyoming, PA commemoration of Battle of Wyoming, 215, 221–23, *223*, 224, 225, 226; Wyoming as framework for, 246, 247, 248–49

Pennsylvania Historical and Museum Commission (PHMC), reestablishment of PHC as, 111, 114, 363n73

Pennsylvania Historical Commission (PHC): establishment of, 93–96, 360n3; funding issues, 94, 96, 110; New England and Virginia's cultural hegemony, reaction to, 95; PHMC (Pennsylvania Historical and Museum Commission), reestablishment as, 111, 114, 363n73

Pennsylvania Historical Commission (PHC) monuments, 91, 93–114; automobile tourism and, 105, 110–11; "bootleg" monuments and, 93–94, 95, 104, 109; Connecticut descendants and, 101–4, 107, 110, 362n48; contemporary state of, 229, *230*; damaged and stolen plaques, 110, 111, 112; Hungry Hill marker, 243; "Indian Hill" and "Lime Hill" sites, 97–104, *102*, *103*, 109, 111, 362n48; marker-series set up by, 105, 362n56; marker unveilings compared, *105*, 106–10, *108*, 363n69; Native Americans and, 97–98, 99, 100–101, *102*, 104, 107, 109, 112–13, 114; neutral language and, 106, 107, 112–13, 114; patriotic and historical societies and, 84, 94, 96, 106, 111, 113–14, 361–62n41; "Queen Esther's rock" marker, 112–13, 114; roadside signs and, 110–13, 229, *230*; savagist trope and, 106, 107, 109–10, 112–13; sesquicentennial of Sullivan Expedition, 1929 marker program established for, 93, 104–6, 205–6; surveys of markers by, 94–95, 110, 360n1; uniformity and, 96; Wyoming commemorations and, 97–104, 107, 109–10

periodization, 340

periodization and periodicity: and Haudenosaunee accounts, 296–98, 301, 314–17, 322–24, 329; in Haudenosaunee Sullivan story, 38, 41, 199, 301, 340; lumping and splitting, 32,

35; mnemonic decapitation, 35, 36, 332, 334; in settler Sullivan story ("periodization play") 36–38, 209–211; silencing and, 27–28, 35; in war stories ("containment"), 35, 41, 199

Perkins, Edward H., 360nn82–83

Perkins, George, 360n83

Perkins family, 89, 360nn82–83

PHC. *See* Pennsylvania Historical Commission (PHC)

Phelps, Anna, 69

Phelps, Francis A., 78, 358n48

Phelps, John Case, 76–77

Phelps, Martha Bennett, 69–70, 73, 76–80, 82, 83, 84, 89, 110, 229, 358nn47–48

Phelps, William G., 358n48

Phelps, Ziba Bennett, 358n48

Philadelphia Centennial Exposition, 123

Philadelphia sesquicentennial, 141, 367n15

PHMC. *See* Pennsylvania Historical and Museum Commission (PHMC)

Pickering, Daniel, 119, 120–21, 123

Pickering, Timothy: kidnapping, 60, 355n90; at treaty meetings, 277, 323. *See also* Treaty of Canandaigua

Pickering Treaty. *See* Treaty of Canandaigua

Pierce, Mrs. Joshua, 370n28

Pierce, Ruth, 370n28

Pinchot, Gifford, 97

place-loss: settler-colonialism and, 336–9; trauma of, 336, 337. *See also* dispossession

placemaking: memoryscape and, 38; Native vs. settler-colonial, 38–39; Native view of settler-colonial; 264; patriotic, 89–92; settler-colonial, 39, 334, 336

place-names. *See* names and naming

place-naming practices and settler-colonialism, 207, 336, 338

Playing Indian (Deloria), 334

"playing Indian" examples, *188*, *196*, 215, 216–17, 218–20, 225–27

Plymouth landing, 142

Pomeroy Foundation, 262, 340n12

Poodry, Aaron, 370n28

Poodry, Irene, 370n28

Poodry, Rose, 370n28

Poor, Enoch, 139, 147, 364n5

popular memory and Popular Memory Group, 25, 26

positionality, of author, 7, 301, 362

postage stamp commemorating Sullivan Expedition, 141

Wyandot, 13–14

Wyndcliffe, 69

Wyoming, modern commemoration of: Dick Cowles on, 257–58; Sullivan story still overshadowed by, 114; Wyoming framework for contemporary Sullivan Expedition commemorations, 246, 247, 248–49; Wyoming, PA commemoration, 215, 221–23, 223, 224, 225, 226, 289

Wyoming (modern town) PA, request for marker for "Queen Esther Rock" from, 112–13

Wyoming (Native village) PA: in Fort Stanwix Treaty, 50; settlement of, 9

Wyoming (state) , 2, 66, 256n126

Wyoming Centennial Association/Wyoming Commemorative Association (WCA), 66, 104, 222, 356n122

Wyoming County Historical Society (WCHS), 233, 238

Wyoming Geological and Genealogical Society, 104

Wyoming Monument: establishment of, 61–62, 63; obelisk form, 62, 63, 205, 355n103; popularity of modern ceremony at, 114; Voortrekker monument, South Africa, compared, 385n6

Wyoming Monument Association (WMA; formerly Ladies' Wyoming Monumental Association), 61–62, 222, 355n102

Wyoming Valley chapter of DAR, 69, 75, 110, 360n86

Yankee-Pennamite War (Connecticut-Pennsylvania intra-settler war): Battle of Wyoming and, 55–58; cultural differences and, 51; descendants of Yankee participants as commemorators, 70, 74, 76–77, 80, 83, 84, 85–89, 90, 101–4, 107, 110, 362n48; origins and prosecution of, 48–53, 53; post-Wyoming continuation of, 58–60, 355n91; Revolutionary War and, 51–53, 57–58; and the Vermont independence movement, 353n33; "Wyoming Massacre" commemorations, 61, 64, 67; and Yankee cultural identity, 61, 66, 226; "Yankee"/"Pennamite" descriptors, 53. See also destruction of foodstuffs; "Wild Yankees"

"Yankees": as descriptor, 50, 57; identity as, 53, 60–63, 80, 84, 85, 91, 102–3, 226; "Patriot," equated with, 53; "Yankee notables," 60, 85–86, 104. See also "Wild Yankees"

Yorktown, Battle of (1781), 13

Zerubavel, Eviatar, 35, 66

CPSIA information can be obtained
at www.ICGtesting.com
Printed in the USA
LVHW041635130623
749648LV00003B/18